CURRICULUM, PLANS, AND PROCESSES IN INSTRUCTIONAL DESIGN

International Perspectives

CURRICULUM, PLANS, AND PROCESSES IN INSTRUCTIONAL DESIGN

International Perspectives

Edited by

Norbert M. Seel
Albert-Ludwigs University of Freiburg, Germany

Sanne Dijkstra
University of Twente, The Netherlands

 LAWRENCE ERLBAUM ASSOCIATES, PUBLISHERS
2004   Mahwah, New Jersey   London

Lawrence Erlbaum Associates, Inc., Publishers
10 Industrial Avenue
Mahwah, New Jersey 07430

Cover design by Kathryn Houghtaling Lacey

Library of Congress Cataloging-in-Publication Data

Curriculum, Plans, and Processes in Instructional Design: International Perspectives,
  edited by Norbert M. Seel and Sanne Dijkstra.
    p. cm.
  Includes bibliographical references and index.
  ISBN: 0-8058-4465-1 (cloth: alk. paper)—ISBN 0-8058-4466-X (pbk. : alk. paper)

Copyright information for this volume can be obtained by contacting the Library of Congress.

Contents

Preface

People who have enjoyed regular education often remember how the way that teachers modeled their instruction helped their understanding and learning. Because education is of such importance, the scientific study of the design of instruction has received considerable funding and yielded many interesting and sometimes controversial results.

Different labels are used to denote the field. The label *teaching methods* is mainly used in the English-speaking part of the world, whereas the label *didactics* is dominant in the European countries. In the last 50 years, the label *instructional design* (ID) became established almost all over the world. This label is used to cover a range of activities, which are usually summarized into (a) needs assessment for determining which knowledge and skills the students should acquire, (b) the design of the instructional program, (c) the development of learning materials and delivery systems as well as the construction of learning tasks (texts and other materials), (d) the implementation of the program, and (e) the evaluation of the outcomes of learning. Several authors have detailed the range of activities and many "instructional design models" have been published. Though the models have been and are used intensely, especially for designing instruction for training of personnel in business and industry, they are often criticized.

The criticism is directed at various separate shortcomings of the design models. First, the models are so general that a genuine instructional or learning technology that is clearly related to cognition and learning is lacking. There is no clear integration of instruction with the student's individual problem-solving and learning processes. All the findings of research on cognition are poorly used in detailing instruction, which often leads to the criticism that the models are used only for the presentation of information. Second, though the models refer to parts of curriculum design, there is no clear integration between curriculum and instructional design. Finally, in all instructional design models, statements are made that media selection is part of the design decisions and that the way to "deliver" the materials should be clear at the beginning of the development activities. The problem, however, is that the qualities of the representation of the reality about which the conceptions and methods should be acquired determine what will be understood and learned. Moreover, understanding of the conceptions is related to the methods that are used to get the relevant information from the reality, and simulation of these activities determines how to represent and manipulate the world involved. Thus, the selection of a medium is related to the activities needed for understanding and learning, and the instructional design models are not detailed enough for this. Finally, most models of ID can be characterized by a substantial lack of integration of curriculum development, with its emphasis on the contents to be taught and the objectives to be reached in the course of an educational program that span time and space beyond the design of a specific learning environment.

From our point of view, ID and curriculum development are two sides of the same coin. Simply said, whereas curriculum development is mainly concerned with the question "what and why to teach?" most models of ID are centrally concerned with the question of "how to teach?" However, when we take into consideration both fields of educational planning, ID and curriculum development, we can conclude that they are separated from each other by different issues, vocabulary, and literature.

A central objective of this volume is to reconcile the disintegration of ID and curriculum development. More specifically, the content of this volume addresses these aforementioned issues in three separate parts. The chapters show how scholars in the field who have thoroughly studied both cognition and learning, and who used their results in designing innovative instructional materials, were able to solve the various categories of criticisms.

In Part I, new theoretical and innovative approaches of ID are described and discussed that integrate, to a large extent, curriculum development and information and communication technologies (ICT) in comprehensive models of instructional planning.

In Part II, the focus of the content is on curriculum development and its impact on models of ID. Not only theoretical considerations are presented, but also examples of the realization of integrated and comprehensive planning in various fields of education.

In Part III, the various chapters focus on the challenges of ICT for instructional planning and curriculum development. Again, a main concern of these authors consists in contributing to more integrated and holistic perspectives on learning, instruction, curriculum, and technology.

We are convinced that those students who use the innovative materials will later remember how the instruction helped their understanding and learning.

—Norbert M. Seel
Sanne Dijkstra

SPECIAL NOTE

In 1997, Dijkstra, Schott, Seel, and Tennyson edited two volumes on *Instructional Design: International Perspectives*, also published by Lawrence Erlbaum Associates. This volume, which can be seen as a third one, continues to present international perspectives on a broader scope, including curriculum, instructional design, and information and communication technology.

About the Editors

Norbert M. Seel is Professor of Research on Learning and Instructional Design in the Faculty of Economics and Behavioral Sciences at the Albert-Ludwigs-University of Freiburg, Germany. He is chair and head of the Department of Educational Science. His research interests include model-based learning and thinking, inductive reasoning and complex problem solving, the investigation of exploratory learning within technology-enhanced environments, and processes of decision making in instructional design. Dr. Seel has published 16 books, among them the textbook *Psychology of Learning*, as well as more than 100 refereed journal articles and book chapters in the areas of cognitive psychology, learning research, and instruction. He is the European Editor of the journal *Technology, Instruction, Cognition, and Learning*.

Sanne Dijkstra is Professor of Instructional Technology in the Faculty of Educational Science and Technology at the University of Twente, The Netherlands. His areas of interest include industrial and educational psychology. Many of his research publications are on instructional design and the effectiveness and efficiency of the models used. He has a strong interest in the acquisition of knowledge and skills by solving problems.

Introduction: Instructional Design and Curriculum Development

Norbert M. Seel
Albert-Ludwigs-University of Freiburg, Germany

Sanne Dijkstra
University of Twente, The Netherlands

Looking at the year 2000, Gustafson, Tillman, and Childs (1992) suggested that "we shall eventually find ourselves on the path toward a theory of instructional design" (p. 456) if instructional design (ID) is able to expand its intellectual basis in the not-too-distant future. In the year 2000, the suggestion was made (Gordon & Zemke, 2000) that ID in its current form is as good as dead because its foundation is not suitable for facing new societal and technological demands. Gordon and Zemke argued that education and training should accommodate a diverse, widely distributed set of students who need to learn and transfer complex cognitive skills to an increasingly varied set of real-world contexts and settings. When we take these pessimistic positions into consideration, the question arises as to what went wrong in an applied field of science that has contributed substantially to education and training. What happened—or what did not happen—within the field of ID in the last half of the previous century?

DIDACTICS AND ID

Constructing a theory (that serves both explanation and discovery) is a slow process that more often proceeds step-by-step by accretion and tuning than by sudden decisive changes and shifts of paradigms. Sometimes it takes centuries before a paradigm is rejected (cf. Kuhn, 1970). Accordingly, we can think of the history of education and its disciplines as a continuous process

1

of evolution, in which only theories that are theoretically sound and can be effectively situated in educational practice can survive. When we consider the history of educational science and, in particular, of didactics (defined here as the science of teaching and learning), we can see several movements over the centuries, and especially in the 20th century.

Actually, we can find in the work of Comenius (1592–1670) the first curriculum of modern history, and Herbart (1776–1841) developed the first outline of culture-related didactics. Inspired by Herbart, Ziller (1817–1882) and Rein (1847–1929) made important contributions to the development of a theory of formal steps of instruction. At the beginning of the 20th century, two broad educational movements emerged: the *reform pedagogy* and the approach of *experimental education and didactics*. Whereas the reform pedagogy movement—associated with Dewey, Washburne, Kerschensteiner, Otto, Montessori, Steiner, Petersen, Makarenko, Freinet, and many others (for an overview, see Scheuerl, 1979)—had a strong influence on educational practice, the approach of experimental education (as developed by Meumann [1862–1915] and Lay [1862–1926]) obviously did not survive the evolutionary process. Nevertheless, there still exists a *Journal of Experimental Education* and other journals in which an empirical approach to education is the guiding principle. We cannot do justice here to the influence of reform pedagogy on didactics and educational practice but today we can still find instructional approaches that are inspired by reform pedagogy. This even holds true with regard to several chapters in this volume (Kafai & Ching, chap. 5; Kolodner et al., chap. 4) and we can also currently find attempts to combine multimedia learning environments with reform pedagogy (cf. Bronkhorst, 2000).

Over the centuries—from Herbart until today—many different approaches of didactics have emerged. Kron (1994) amazingly distinguished between 30 different didactics. This state of the art has been criticized by several authors, such as Blankertz (1971), Kron (1994), and Nicklis (1989), who have pointed out that the dozens of different conceptions of didactics do not specify the field of interest in a unique and comprehensive manner but rather center around scientific desiderata. Therefore, these and other authors classify the huge number of didactics into several main categories that are oriented toward the concepts Bildung, learning, and interaction. In consequence, it has become commonplace to distinguish between (a) didactics as a culture-related education (in the sense of the German word *Bildung*; Weniger, 1956), (b) didactics as the theory of teaching and learning in general (Dolch, 1965), and (c) didactics as a theory of instruction with an emphasis on interactions and curriculum development (Heimann, 1962; Schulz, 1980). From our point of view, these different didactics are characterized by the dichotomy of Bildung and learning. On the one hand, a culture-related education emphasizes the individual's constructive interactions with culture in the attempt to understand its sense and meaning. To illustrate this we can refer to Dolch's (1959) *Syllabus of the Occident* as well as to the work of Willmann (1967) and Weniger (1956). On the other hand, didactics is related to learning and teaching for which specific situations are constructed. The contents of learning are determined through the well-grounded selection and sequence of cultural contents, for example, in the form of a curriculum or syllabus, whereas the intent of learning is related to different personality traits of the subjects, for example, at the cognitive, affective, social, and behavioral levels. Both broad categories of didactics accentuate different aspects, and, in consequence, they are not homogeneous. For example, the second category includes various approaches of cybernetic didactics as well as the psychological didactics of Aebli (1963), Ausubel and Robinson (1969), and Bruner (1966), who were influenced by Piaget.

We can summarize the field of didactics as follows: In a literal sense, *didactics* (διδασκειν) means teaching and instructing, but also learning and being taught. Consequently, both the concepts of "didactics as a theory of teaching and learning" (in the sense of Dolch, 1965) and of "didactics as a theory of the contents of Bildung" correspond best with the mission of this volume. However, this leads immediately to the question of the status of ID.

Indeed, up to now we have focused on the evolution of didactics, and, therefore, the question may arise as to the evolutionary development of ID. Historically seen, ID emerged in the early 1960s. Most scholars agree that ID has its roots both in the psychology of learning and in cybernetics and system theory. As a consequence, we can find a lot of interesting correspondences between models of ID and learning-oriented didactics. For example, the approaches of Branson (Branson & Grow, 1987) and König and Riedel (1973) share their foundations in system theory, whereas Kaufman's needs-assessment approach, especially his idea of mega-planning, corresponds to a large extent with culture-related didactics (cf. Kaufman, Herman, & Watters, 1996).

However, ID is more than a combination of various didactic approaches. Beyond some correspondences with didactics, ID is mainly characterized by a strong relatedness to information and communication technologies, especially computer technology. The connections between ID and information and communications technology (ICT) are so strong that today several scholars, such as Merrill (1993, 2001), Goodyear (1994), Scandura (1995, 2003), and Spector and Ohrazda (2003), consider ID to be an engineering discipline. Consequently, they consider the development of instructional systems and support tools for instructional designers and developers as somewhat similar to software engineering systems and support tools for software engineers.

FOUNDATIONS OF ID

The development of a theoretical basis for the design of instruction has three major sources. The idea that the results of research on learning are useful for the design of instruction came first (Dijkstra & van Merriënboer, 1997). This idea has been with us for at least two millennia and has received attention from scholars and researchers in the domains of education and psychology for at least the two previous centuries. The increasing demands for training and efficient instruction during and after World War II led, in the 1950s, to an "engineering" approach to education. For this develop-ment, the labels *educational technology* and *instructional systems design* (ISD) came into use.

The Early Years of ID

For a period of 20 years, programmed instruction was seen as a representa-tive of this educational technology (cf. DeCecco, 1964). At the same time, Glaser (1964) developed a general model that showed essential parts of an educative process and their interrelationships in a sequence. As a central part of this model, Glaser introduced the technical term *instructional system*, consisting of five components: (a) the "system objectives" or instructional goals, (b) the "system input" or entering behavior, (c) the "system opera-tor" or instructional procedures, (d) the "output monitor" or the perform-ance assessment, and (e) the research and development logistics. Glaser's technical description of the students' "terminal behavior" and the "proce-dures of instructional technology" met the theory of learning and the ex-perimental findings of the psychology of learning that were known in those years, thus making clear that learning and instruction are two sides of the same coin. The third source for the theoretical foundation has its origin in the applied sciences or technology. In the 1950s and 1960s these were the teaching machine, the television, and the language laboratory. For each technical development the prediction was made that education should ben-efit from it in two ways: The developments could free the teacher from rou-tine work, and the students would learn better. The developments, some-times labeled pragmatic and used to predict an industrial revolution in education and the automation of instruction, led to doubts about the possi-ble benefits and stimulated what became labeled *research on media*. In the 1960s the computer was introduced into education. A tentative start with minicomputers already made fully clear the importance of this equipment for the study of learning and instruction. By the end of the 1970s the inven-tion of the microcomputer was of tremendous importance for ID and for education in general. We describe later developments in the introduction to Part III of this volume, which is devoted to instructional technology and media.

The findings and givens that result from these three sources for the design of instruction can hardly be treated in isolation. Many authors integrate the findings or at least try to integrate them in prescriptions for how to design instruction, though there are differences in what is emphasized. A few highlights from the last half-century are briefly sketched, taking into account the findings and givens of the three sources.

Most instructional theorists agree that ID can be traced to roots in behaviorism and related learning theories (Rowland, 1993; Skinner, 1954). The use of the model of instrumental conditioning to describe and interpret all learning, the use of five rules for the programming of instruction based on that model, and the development of a teaching machine were soon abandoned. The application of the rules led to a splitting up of the subject matter into a huge number of instructional frames that were even able to prevent the integration of the concepts and methods involved. The teaching machines were not able to adapt the instruction to the students' learning flexibly. Moreover it was shown experimentally that the interpretation of all learning from one model led to false predictions (e.g., Breland & Breland, 1961). Categories of learning (Melton, 1964), conditions of learning (Gagné, 1965), and the East–West synthesis of learned behavior and cognition by the emigrated Russian psychologist Razran (1971) replaced the use of only one model for learning. Nevertheless, Skinner clearly showed the integration of the psychology of learning, instructional technology, and the use of technical equipment.

The rejection of the use of one model for the description of learning and the interpretation of the change of behavior from the effects of the environment on that behavior led to both an extension of the categories of learning and a different interpretation of learning: the cognitive shift. A need for a change of theory was felt to interpret how human beings solve categorization problems (Bruner, Goodnow, & Austin, 1956). This change influenced the ideas about the design of instruction. Bruner (1966) wrote about the features a theory of instruction should meet. Gagné (1962) wrote an article on the acquisition of knowledge in which he paid attention to "productive learning," a label he borrowed from earlier work of Katona (1940). In the same article he summarized the work he and his colleagues had done on task analysis of complex domains resulting in "learning hierarchies." In particular, Gagné's (1965) seminal work on the conditions of human learning is often considered a fundamental basis of ID (cf. Dick, 1991; Richey, 2000). This basis was used to develop the principles of ID (Gagné & Briggs, 1974).

The Current Status of ID

In the past half-century, several colleagues have tried to adapt the learning environment and instruction to the supposed learning process in the best possible way. From both a pragmatic and scientific point of view, the defining characteristic of ID is that it makes explicit the substantive assumptions an instructional designer or a teacher uses to develop instructional materials and learning tasks. These assumptions describe the knowledge structures and cognitive processes a learner in a particular instructional setting would use, how they develop in dependence on learning, and how more competent learners differ from less competent learners. These substantive assumptions are embodied in psychological theories of human learning and thinking. From this point, a strong demand for a change of the theoretical foundations of ID resulted as a consequence of a paradigm shift in psychology in the 1960s—the "cognitive revolution" (Bruner, 1990). As a consequence of this paradigm shift, new theories of learning and teaching emerged (cf. Glaser & Bassok, 1989), often combined with a new understanding of instructional design that can be briefly characterized by attempts to determine research-based principles for the design of learning environments. Besides the approaches of "anchored instruction" and "model-centered learning and instruction" as described by Pellegrino (chap. 1) and Seel (chap. 2) respectively, in this volume, we can refer to, among others, Anderson's (1990) LISP Tutor approach; Scardamalia, Bereiter, and Lamon's (1994) CSILE Project; and Schank's "goal-based scenarios" (Schank, Fano, Bell, & Jona, 1993/1994).

Moreover, instructional designers who often worked in corporate training further described and detailed the systems approach. They organized themselves in the Association for Educational Communication and Technology. In the publications of this association, the field of instructional technology was described in detail. The development of many concepts such as ISD and its domains (design, development, utilization, management, and evaluation) was shown and described (Seels & Richey, 1994).

During the last decades of the previous century, most instructional theorists and technologists agreed on the point that ID could be considered both a discipline and a technology for instructional planning. As a science, ID aimed at detailed and theoretically well-founded specifications for the development, implementation, evaluation, and maintenance of effective learning situations (cf. Dick & Reiser, 1989; Richey, 1986). From a technological point of view, ID was mainly concerned with creating concrete instructional materials and environments in which students could learn effectively. Thus, ID is considered a science of planning whose scope ranges from the prognosis of global developments to the binding determination of instructional activities. The term *planning* here denotes both a process (i.e., the preparation and development of a plan) and a result (i.e., a particular plan). Accordingly, conventional models of ID usually entailed all steps of planning—starting with needs assessment and the construction and sequencing of learning tasks, and leading to the formative evaluation of the effectiveness of instructional materials. In sum, for decades ID has been recognized generally as a discipline that aims at the integration of different educational activities, involving a theoretically sound design, implementation, and evaluation of effective learning environments. Is something wrong with this conception of ID? The answer is no, but for instruction, which we describe as any activity that fosters learning, the "technology" should not be isolated from its essential domain, which is learning. In discussing the relationship between science and technology, Seels and Richey (1994) made the following statement: "Instructional technology is often defined as the application of principles of science in order to solve learning problems, a point of view based upon the assumption that science and technology are inseparable. This has proved to be a myth. Science and technology are related, but separable" (p. 6). The definition of the field they described reads: "Instructional technology is the theory and practice of design, development, utilization, management and evaluation of processes and resources for learning" (p. 9). Design, development, and the other components of the definition are the domains in the field that contribute to the theory and practice that is the basis of the profession. The problem with this description is the possibility of separating the technology from the domain of learning. In our view this is not possible. All instructional designs and all developed material require that the laws of learning be adequately applied and met. To make this statement clear, the conceptions of technology and design are analyzed.

A technology is the whole of the science (theory and research methods) that is valid for a domain and of the rules for solving a design problem in that domain in order to realize a public or individual goal. For example, chemical technology comprises the theory and research methods that are valid for the molecules of substances (their structure and their change) and the rules for constructing devices and installations for the production of substances and objects that can be used for a public or individual goal. Examples are the design (and development) of refineries for the production of gas for transport and heating, and the design (and development) of kilns to heat clay and produce earthenware. (Also see the introduction to Part I of this volume.) Though the use of the label *technology* often emphasizes the treatment of the domain, the knowledge of a domain and its processes of change are included in the connotation of the label. The treatment cannot be separated from the knowledge. The use of labels such as *chemical technology* and *biotechnology* clearly illustrate this.

The defining feature of a design problem is that the solution to such a problem is the sketch of a new object that can be used to fulfill a public or individual human need or motive. The defining feature of a development problem is that the sketched object is made or produced, either as an individual object or in mass production—in the aforementioned framework of chemical technology, for example, the design of a device to refine crude oil or the design of a cup and saucer for drinking tea. The device is part of the technology, and the cup and saucer are the result of the technology. They are designed and developed to fulfill a human need. All objects designed and developed by human beings have a certain life cycle. We distinguish four phases in this life cycle: (a) design, (b) development, (c) use and maintenance, and (d) discarding. The design of a new object is a creative process in which the imagination and originality of the designer are crucial. Though for all domains the design rules are well known and scientifically founded, the design of a new object is more or less an art. If the sketch of a new object is ready, a decision will be made as to whether the new object will be developed. The decision depends on various conditions, such as the program of requirements the principal has made or the results of market research. If the sketch meets the program of requirements or if the results of market research show that the object will be sold, the decision to develop the object will be positive.

The objects to be designed, realized, and used should meet four different sets of conditions and criteria: (a) principles and rules of a "good" design, which means that pertinent laws and principles of the domain and the regularities of its change are adequately applied; (b) functional requirements—designs should be functional and objects should fulfill human needs; (c) aesthetic concerns—the artistic value of a design should satisfy the tastes and preferences of a group of people that often will vary over time; and (d) financial constraints—the financial means that are available should be used efficiently (Dijkstra, 2000).

The solution to an instructional design problem is the design of a communication between an expert and a learner and an environment that supports that communication. The purpose of the communication is for the learner to develop knowledge and skills. The communication can take on many forms, such as providing information, asking questions, and giving problems to solve and tasks for training a skill. It can be anticipated in textbooks and electronic learning devices. The designed communications are the means for the "treatment" of the domain and the processes of its change, that is, for the "treatment" of cognition and learning. Although the label *learning technology* might have been more adequate, the label *instructional technology* was adopted as the standard term because the presentation part of the communication by the expert and the supply of conceptions about the structure and change of the reality that are the content of the subjects of the curriculum has been so clearly present in education.

Instructional design is part of a technology, the steps of which should meet the structure of cognition and the processes of knowledge development and learning. Some confusion is possible due to the use of the label *instructional systems design*. This is a "soft" technology or general heuristic for controlling a process of education and training. The use of the heuristics of instructional (systems) design—including the phases ("steps") (a) assessment, (b) design, (c) development, (d) implementation, and (e) evaluation—is too general. It covers parts of the life cycle of an object (e.g., design and development) and parts of the results of its use (e.g., evaluation of what is learned). It does not include detailed rules about how to activate the domain of cognition and how to support the change in knowledge and skills. A general heuristic of instructional design will be helpful in regulating a process of education and training. But the theories for the assessment of needs for the design of a curriculum and for the implementation of it are different from those of cognition, of the development of knowledge, and of learning. In addition, the theory and models of evaluation are different from those of curriculum and instruction. Curriculum, instruction, and evaluation should nevertheless be aligned (see Pellegrino, chap. 1, this volume), and the theories should meet this requirement as well.

The aforementioned pessimistic positions may be caused by too narrow a focus on design models without a clear relation to the domain of cognition and learning. Moreover, the complexity of both the representations of (the objects of) a domain and the conceptions about it may cause difficulty in making this relation to cognition and learning. How this can be done successfully is shown in the following chapters.

We see no reason to take on pessimistic positions about the future of instructional technology. Both the knowledge of the domain, which is cognition and learning, and the rules for solving ID problems have increased and changed (cf. Seel, 2003). In the past half-century, the field has witnessed many new developments. Sometimes "pragmatic" arguments for a change in instructional design were used, for example, to predict an industrial revolution in education with the use of teaching machines. Sometimes a shift in the theoretical conceptions of psychology led to new developments, for example, the cognitive shift. Sometimes the rediscovery of an epistemological point of view emphasized the possible relevance for instructional design (Seel, 2001), for example, the rediscovery of constructivism. And above all, the development of information and communication technology had a tremendous influence on the design of instruction, for representing and manipulating the objects and its conceptions, for consulting the electronic library, and for coaching students in the complexity of tasks to be performed (cf. Dijkstra, Seel, Schott, & Tennyson, 1997).

MAJOR TRENDS IN THE DEVELOPMENT
OF INSTRUCTIONAL DESIGN

Several paradigm shifts in psychology as well as new societal and technological demands have challenged ID as both a discipline and a technology in
the past two decades. As a result, we can observe a substantial uncertainty in
the field of ID with regard to its epistemological, psychological, and technological foundations. In this time period ID has continued to evolve, assimilating and advancing theories from psychology, systems theory, and communication technologies. Recent additions have been influenced by
constructivism, situated cognition, e-learning approaches to distance education, and information theory. Ritchie and Earnest (1999) pointed out
that "with each iteration, we enhance our understanding of how to impact
the performance of individuals and organizations" (p. 35). Accordingly, the
paradigm shift toward cognitive psychology occurring in the 1960s resulted
in the development and adaptation of corresponding theories of cognitive
learning (cf. Tennyson & Elmore, 1997).

Taking the long-term developments of ID into consideration, we can
state several main lines of argumentation in the 1990s that are concerned
with the missions and visions of ID:

First, there was a continuation of the search for a comprehensive theory of
ID in order to make ID viable again (cf. Tennyson, Schott, Seel, & Dijkstra,
1997). In accordance with this, van Merriënboer, Seel, and Kirschner (2002),
for example, referred to the theory of mental models in order to search for
this new foundation of ID by broadening its perspective on learning so that it
could deal effectively with today's technological demands.

Second, there was, especially in the United States, a heated debate about
the meta-theoretical status of knowledge and its development and the sup-
posedly "false" foundation of ID, culminating in the "objectivism–constructivism controversy" of the early 1990s (see, e.g., Dinter & Seel, 1993;
Jonassen, 1991; Merrill, 1992). Today, we can say that most theorists in the
field of ID accept the constructivist epistemology for the status and development of knowledge. Accordingly, today we can find several approaches that
focus on the design of learning environments that aim at learning in a
constructivist sense, namely, as a process of knowledge construction.

Third, we can find in the literature of the 1990s a strong association of
ID with artistic activities (e.g., Rowland, 1993). Clearly, this view stands in
sharp contrast to the traditional view of ID as a deterministic and rational
process that regulates the designer's actions. However, several investigations (Kerr, 1983; Rowland, 1992) indicate that even ID experts regularly
do not apply the "scientific principles" of ID for instructional planning but
rather follow more or less stereotyped expectations and routines when they

design instruction. As a consequence, ID is no longer considered "as a deterministic, essentially rational and logical process, a set of procedures to be followed" but rather "as a creative process, based on intuition as well as rationality" (Rowland, 1993, p. 79). From our point of view, this argumentation corresponds with Skinner's (1954) differentiation between "the science of learning" and "the art of teaching." The designs of instruction should meet the "laws" of cognition and learning, but no two designs of instruction are equivalent to one another.

To summarize these trends of ID in the 1990s we can state in accordance with van Merriënboer et al. (2002) that theories and models of ID come in different types and concern different worlds. In these different worlds, ideas about "how to help people learn better" lead to different answers to the two basic questions of ID: "what to teach" and "how to teach it."

The question of "how to teach" has been at the core of ID and ISD since their very beginnings, but the issue of "what to teach" lacks substantial interest for most theorists of ID. It seems that this question is a major concern of curriculum development but not of ID, which primarily refers to the methods of teaching the contents and objectives specified by a curriculum in a given subject area, such as law, economics, mathematics, or science. Actually, an analysis of the literature indicates that ID and curriculum development do not have much in common. One reason might be that curricular components are often considered in ID to be an integral part of task analysis, resulting in a restriction on the construction of learning tasks. More far-reaching content-related considerations and decisions—such as are known in the tradition of curriculum development—are widely neglected and considered a central part of needs assessment (see, e.g., Kaufman et al., 1996). Another reason for the dissolution of ID and curriculum development is situated in the limitation of theories and models of curriculum development for the foundation of educational objectives and goals. That is to say that the planning of instruction beyond decisions with regard to educational objectives does not fall within the range of curriculum development. As a consequence, ID and curriculum development are not closely interrelated, although both disciplines are concerned with the same subjects, insofar as ID focuses on the psychology-based construction of explicit prescriptions for the design of learning environments and curriculum development is concerned with the determination of the objectives of learning and instruction. Therefore, both disciplines are characterized by separate literatures, knowledge bases, and lines of argumentation.

This disintegration of curriculum development and ID and the needed reintegration was one source of motivation for editing this volume. However, its history also indicates another source, which is described briefly in the following section.

THE "HISTORY" OF THIS VOLUME

With its roots in behaviorism, which dominated psychology 50 years ago, ID was initially an American affair, whereas in Europe (and especially in Germany) approaches of a "general didactics" with roots in hermeneutics were predominant. Today, ID is an international affair and accordingly instructional researchers and educational psychologists and technologists concern themselves with ID and ISD worldwide. This can be illustrated by the increasing number of international publications (books and journals) concerning issues of ID and various conferences on both sides of the Atlantic.

Especially in the 1990s, several books and special issues of journals were published that demonstrate the internationality of ID as a discipline. For example, the books edited by Tennyson et al. (1997) and Dijkstra et al. (1997) can be considered indicative of this trend. Another indicator is the numerous international conferences and workshops organized—again especially in the 1990s—in North America as well as in Europe. For example, in 1991 Dijkstra and colleagues organized in Twente, The Netherlands, a NATO workshop on issues concerning the instructional design of computer-based learning environments (Dijkstra, Krammer, & van Merriënboer, 1992). Two years later, Tennyson organized another NATO workshop on "automated instructional design" in Grimstad, Norway (Tennyson, 1994). Some years later, in 1999, Dijkstra again organized a workshop on the "epistemological and psychological foundations of ID" (cf. Dijkstra, 2001), which was a starting point for two subsequent conferences: One was organized in 1999 by Spector in Bergen, Norway (see Spector & Anderson, 2000), the other one in 2001 by Seel and colleagues in Freiburg, Germany.

This book is the major product of the Freiburg conference in 2001. Whereas the focus of the Bergen conference was on integrated and holistic perspectives on learning, instruction, and technology, the Freiburg conference was concerned with the following three topics: (a) the progression of new theoretical approaches of ID developed in the 1990s; (b) the integration of curriculum, instruction, and assessment; and (c) ID in the face of new technological demands. Actually, the main objective of the conference was to discuss and explore the current state of research regarding two basically co-existing fields of ID: curriculum and technology. More specifically, during the conference it was examined from different angles how ID can respond to the challenges of learning through curriculum and technology.

THE CONTENTS OF THIS VOLUME

In accordance with the topics of the Freiburg conference, this volume is divided into three parts that represent the field of tension of instructional design—from approaches situated in the research of learning to ID defined as an engineering discipline.

The various chapters of Part I of this volume are concerned with new theoretical foundations of ID as well as with novel approaches that evolved in the 1990s as the result of new theoretical and meta-theoretical considerations based on the constructivist and constructionist paradigm of learning in instructional settings. These approaches correspond with Mayer's (2003) approach of looking for (a) research-based principles for the design of learning environments and (b) the extent to which these principles can be applied to different realizations of learning environments.

The chapters of Part II are concerned with general and specific relations between curriculum development and ID. We consider curriculum development to be an added value to the field of ID, and we hope that the contents of these chapters may contribute to bridging the current gap between ID and curriculum development.

The chapters of Part III of this volume focus on educational technology and media, which in many respects provided the initial foundation of ID. The central idea of this part is to highlight ID as an engineering discipline whose phases may be regarded as collections of related tasks that correspond roughly with the ADDIE (Analysis, Design, Development, Implementation, and Evaluation) generic instructional development model.

ACKNOWLEDGMENTS

We gratefully acknowledge financial support for this research from a generous grant provided by the German Research Association (Deutsche Forschungsgemeinschaft) with Grant No. 4850-30-01, as well as financial support from the Minister of Science and Arts of Baden-Wuerttemberg.

REFERENCES

Aebli, H. (1963). *Psychologische Didaktik—Didaktische Auswertung der Psychologie J. Piagets* [Psychological didactics]. Stuttgart, Germany: Klett.

Anderson, J. R. (1990). Analysis of student performance with the LISP Tutor. In N. Frederiksen, R. Glaser, A. Lesgold, & M. G. Shafto (Eds.), *Diagnostic monitoring of skill and knowledge acquisition* (pp. 27–50). Hillsdale, NJ: Lawrence Erlbaum Associates.

Ausubel, D. P., & Robinson, F. G. (1969). *School learning: An introduction to educational psychology.* New York: Holt.

Blankertz, H. (1971). *Theorien und Modelle der Didaktik* [Theories and models of didactics]. Munich, Germany: Juventa.

Branson, R. K., & Grow, G. (1987). Instructional systems development. In R. M. Gagné (Ed.), *Instructional technology: foundations.* Hillsdale, NJ: Lawrence Erlbaum Associates.

Breland, K., & Breland, M. (1961). The misbehavior of organisms. *American Psychologist, 16,* 681–684.

Bronkhorst, J. (2000). *Multimedia learning environments and reform pedagogy.* Available online at: http://www.ped.kun.nl

Bruner, J. S. (1966). *Toward a theory of instruction.* Cambridge, MA: Harvard University Press.

Bruner, J. S. (1990). *Acts of meaning.* Cambridge, MA: Harvard University Press.

Bruner, J. S., Goodnow, J. J., & Austin, G. A. (1956). *A study of thinking.* New York: Wiley.

DeCecco, J. P. (1964). *Educational technology.* New York: Holt, Rinehart & Winston.

Dick, W. (1991). An instructional designer's view of constructivism. *Educational Technology, 31*(5), 41–44.

Dick, W., & Reiser, R. A. (1989). *Planning effective instruction.* Englewood Cliffs, NJ: Prentice-Hall.

Dijkstra, S. (2000). Epistemology, psychology of learning and instructional design. In M. Spector & T. Anderson (Eds.), *Holistic and integrative perspectives on learning, instructional design and technology* (pp. 213–232). Dordrecht, The Netherlands: Kluwer.

Dijkstra, S. (2001). The design space for solving instructional-design problems. *Instructional Science, 29*(4), 275–290.

Dijkstra, S., Krammer, H. P. M., & van Merriënboer, J. J. G. (Eds.). (1992). *Instructional models in computer-based learning environments.* Berlin: Springer.

Dijkstra, S., Seel, N. M., Schott, F., & Tennyson, R. D. (Eds.). (1997). *Instructional design: International perspectives: Vol. 2. Solving of instructional design problems.* Mahwah, NJ: Lawrence Erlbaum Associates.

Dijkstra, S., & van Merriënboer, J. J. G. (1997). Plans, procedures, and theories to solve instructional design problems. In S. Dijkstra, N. M. Seel, F. Schott, & R. D. Tennyson (Eds.), *Instructional design: International perspectives: Vol. 2. Solving of instructional design problems* (pp. 23–43). Mahwah, NJ: Lawrence Erlbaum Associates.

Dinter, F. R., & Seel, N. M. (1993). What does it mean to be a constructivist in I.D.? An epistemological reconsideration. In J. Lowyck & J. Elen (Eds.), *Modelling I.D.-research* (pp. 49–66). Leuven, Belgium: Proceedings of the First Workshop of the SIG on Instructional Design of EARLI.

Dolch, J. (1959). *Lehrplan des Abendlandes* [Syllabus of the occident]. Ratingen, Germany: Henn.

Dolch, J. (1965). *Grundbegriffe der pädagogischen Fachsprache* [Basic concepts of the pedagogical vocabulary] (6th ed.). Munich, Germany: Ehrenwirth.

Gagné, R. M. (1962). The acquisition of knowledge. *Psychological Review, 69,* 355–365.

Gagné, R. M. (1965). *The conditions of learning.* New York: Holt, Rinehart & Winston.

Gagné, R. M., & Briggs, L. J. (1974). *Principles of instructional design.* New York: Holt, Rinehart & Winston.

Glaser, R. (1964). Components of the instructional process. In J. P. DeCecco (Ed.), *Educational technology* (pp. 68–76). New York: Holt, Rinehart & Winston.

Glaser, R., & Bassok, M. (1989). Learning theory and the study of instruction. *Annual Review of Psychology, 40,* 631–666.

Goodyear, P. (1994). Foundations for courseware engineering. In R. D. Tennyson (Ed.), *Automating instructional design, development, and delivery* (pp. 7–28). Berlin: Springer-Verlag.

Gordon, I., & Zemke, R. (2000). The attack on ISD: Have we got instructional design all wrong? *Training Magazine, 37,* 43–53.

Gustafson, K. L., Tillman, M. H., & Childs, J. W. (1992). The future of instructional design. In L. J. Briggs, K. L. Gustafson, & M. H. Tillman (Eds.), *Instructional design: Principles and applications* (pp. 451–467). Englewood Cliffs, NJ: Educational Technology.

Heimann, P. (1962). Didaktik als Theorie und Lehre [Didactics as theory and practice]. In D. C. Kochan (Ed.), *Allgemeine Didaktik, Fachdidaktik, Fachwissenschaft* (pp. 110–142). Darmstadt, Germany: Wissenschaftliche Buchgesellschaft.

Jonassen, D. H. (1991). Objectivism versus constructivism: Do we need a new philosophical paradigm? *Educational Technology Research and Development, 39*(3), 5–14.

Katona, G. (1940). *Organizing and memorizing*. New York: Columbia University Press.

Kaufman, R., Herman, J., & Watters, K. (1996). *Educational planning: Strategic, tactical, operational*. Lancaster, PA: Technomic.

Kerr, S. T. (1983). Inside the black box: Making design decisions for instruction. *British Journal of Educational Technology, 14*(1), 45–58.

König, E., & Riedel, H. (1973). *Systemtheoretische Didaktik* [System-theoretical didactics]. Weinheim, Germany: Beltz.

Kron, F. W. (1994). *Grundwissen Didaktik* [Basic knowledge didactics] (2nd ed.). Munich, Germany: Reinhardt.

Kuhn, T. A. (1970). *The structure of scientific revolutions* (2nd ed.). Chicago: University of Chicago Press.

Mayer, R. E. (2003). The promise of multimedia learning: Using the same instructional design methods across different media. *Learning and Instruction, 13*(2), 125–139.

Melton, A. W. (1964). *Categories of human learning*. New York: Academic Press.

Merrill, M. D. (1992). Constructivism and instructional design. In T. Duffy & D. Jonassen (Eds.), *Constructivism and the technology of instruction: A conversation*. Hillsdale, NJ: Lawrence Erlbaum Associates.

Merrill, M. D. (1993). An integrated model for automating instructional design and delivery. In J. M. Spector, M. C. Polson, & D. J. Muraida (Eds.), *Automating instructional design: Concepts and issues* (pp. 147–190). Englewood Cliffs, NJ: Educational Technology.

Merrill, M. D. (2001). First principles of instruction. *Journal of Structural Learning and Intelligent Systems, 14*(4), 459–466.

Nicklis, W. (1989). Unterricht [Instruction]. In Görres-Gesellschaft (Ed.), *Staatslexikon. Recht, Wirtschaft, Gesellschaft* (7th ed., Vol. 5, pp. 557–564). Freiburg, Germany: Herder.

Razran, G. (1971). *Mind in evolution: An East–West synthesis of learned behavior and cognition*. Boston: Houghton Mifflin.

Richey, R. (1986). *The theoretical and conceptual basis of instructional design*. New York: Nichols.

Richey, R. C. (Ed.). (2000). *The legacy of Robert M. Gagné*. Syracuse, NY: ERIC Clearinghouse on Information & Technology, Syracuse University.

Ritchie, D., & Earnest, J. (1999). The future of instructional design: Results of a delphi study. *Educational Technology, 39*(6), 35–42.

Rowland, G. (1992). What do instructional designers actually do? An initial investigation of expert practice. *Performance Improvement Quarterly, 5*(2), 65–86.

Rowland, G. (1993). Designing and instructional design. *Educational Technology: Research and Development, 41*(1), 79–91.

Scandura, J. M. (1995). Theoretical foundations of instruction: Past, present and future. *Journal of Structural Learning and Intelligent Systems, 12*(3), 231–342.

Scandura, J. M. (2003). Domain specific structural analysis for intelligent tutoring systems: Automatable representation of declarative, procedural and model-based knowledge with relationships to software engineering. *Technology, Instruction, Cognition and Learning, 1*(1), 7–57.

Scardamalia, M., Bereiter, C., & Lamon, M. (1994). The CSILE project: Trying to bring the classroom into world 3. In K. McGilly (Ed.), *Classroom lessons: Integrating cognitive theory and classroom practice* (pp. 201–228). Cambridge, MA: MIT Press.

Schank, R. C., Fano, A., Bell, B., & Jona, M. (1993/1994). The design of goal-based scenarios. *Journal of the Learning Sciences, 3*(4), 305–345.

Scheuerl, H. (Ed.). (1979). *Klassiker der Pädagogik* [Classical authors of pedagogy] (2 Vols.). Munich, Germany: Beck.

Schulz, W. (1980). *Unterrichtsplanung* [Planning of instruction]. Munich, Germany: Urban & Schwarzenberg.

Seel, N. M. (2001). Epistemology, situated cognition, and mental models: "Like a bridge over troubled water." *Instructional Science, 29*(4–5), 403–428.

Seel, N. M. (2003). *Psychologie des Lernens* [Psychology of learning] (2nd ed.). Munich, Germany: Reinhardt.

Seels, B. B., & Richey, R. C. (1994). *Instructional technology: The definition and domains of the field.* Washington, DC: Association for Educational Communications and Technology.

Skinner, B. F. (1954). The science of learning and the art of teaching. *Harvard Educational Review, 24*(2), 86–97.

Spector, J. M., & Anderson, T. M. (Eds.) (2000). *Integrated and holistic perspectives on learning, instruction and technology: Understanding complexity.* Dordrecht, The Netherlands: Kluwer.

Spector, J. M., & Ohrazda, C. (2003). Automating instructional design: Approaches and limitations. In D. H. Jonassen (Ed.), *Handbook of research in educational communications and technology* (2nd ed., pp. 685–699). Bloomington, IN: Association for Educational Communications and Technology.

Tennyson, R. D. (Ed.). (1994). *Automating instructional design: Computer-based development and delivery tools.* Berlin: Springer.

Tennyson, R. D., & Elmore, R. L. (1997). Learning theory foundations for instructional design. In R. D. Tennyson, F. Schott, N. M. Seel, & S. Dijkstra (Eds.), *Instructional design: International perspectives: Vol. 1. Theory, research, and models* (pp. 55–78). Mahwah, NJ: Lawrence Erlbaum Associates.

Tennyson, R. D., Schott, F., Seel, N. M., & Dijkstra, S. (Eds.). (1997). *Instructional design: International perspectives: Vol. 1. Theory, research, and models.* Mahwah, NJ: Lawrence Erlbaum Associates.

van Merriënboer, J. J. G., Seel, N. M., & Kirschner, P. A. (2002). Mental models as a new foundation for instructional design. *Educational Technology, 42*(2), 60–66.

Weniger, E. (1956). *Didaktik als Bildungslehre. Teil 1: Theorie der Bildungsinhalte und des Lehrplans* [Didactics as theory of education. Part 1: Theory of educational contents and curriculum] (2nd ed.). Weinheim, Germany: Beltz.

Willmann, O. (1967). *Didaktik als Bildungslehre nach ihren Beziehungen zur Sozialforschung und zur Geschichte der Bildung* [Didactics as theory of education in a relation to social research and the history of education] (7th ed.). Freiburg, Germany: Herder.

Part I

THEORETICAL FOUNDATIONS OF LEARNING AND INSTRUCTION AND INNOVATIONS OF INSTRUCTIONAL DESIGN AND TECHNOLOGY

Sanne Dijkstra
University of Twente, The Netherlands

The content of all the chapters in this part of the volume is concerned with the relation between epistemology and the psychology of learning on the one hand and the design of instruction and use of media on the other. Before I outline the highlights of the content, a framework to discuss the content is proposed.

Technology. A technology is the whole of the science (theory and research methods) that is valid for a domain and of the rules for solving a design problem in that domain in order to realize a public or individual goal. For example, chemical technology comprises the theory and research methods that are valid for the molecules of substances (their structure and their change) and the rules to construct devices and installations for producing substances that will be used for a public or individual goal, such as refineries for producing gas for transport and heating. The development and application of these rules is often labeled *engineering*.

Instructional Technology. For the description of instructional technology, first a demarcation of the domain should be given. Quite often the label *learning* is used, but this label does not adequately cover the domain. Actually the domain is the whole (human) organism, both the mind (psyche) and the body together with their physiological and neurological relationships, insofar as the description of its structures and the theory of its changes are relevant for the acquisition of knowledge and skills. The domain comprises many subdomains, such as personality and cognition as well as the neurological and muscular systems, the actions of which are used to infer the existence of these subdomains. The acquisition of knowledge and skills is described as processes of change in these domains for which labels such as insight, thinking, and learning are used. The course and the results of these processes can be inferred from the organism's actions. I presuppose that the personality directs and controls cognition and learning. Personality features and functions, such as intelligence and motivation, strongly influence (meta)cognition and learning. How do we solve design problems in this quite complex domain, and for which goals? The solution to these problems is the design of a special kind of communication between a student or group of students and an expert in a domain, the purpose of which is to initialize and promote the acquisition of knowledge and skills. This is the enrichment of cognitive constructs and of actions to do in given circumstances. As with all technologies, the general goal has a public and an individual component. A possible ultimate public goal is to maintain and strengthen the group or organization and make it competent to adapt to changing global circumstances (Dijkstra & van Merriënboer, 1997). For students in elementary, secondary, and tertiary education, individual goals will receive priority, such as to understand a concept and how and why this was developed, or to prepare themselves for a profession and career.

Instructional Design.   Though human beings are able to develop knowledge and skills without the help of an expert, they usually need help. Because of the enormous amount of information and methods, learning environments and instruction are needed to help the students to structure and understand the information and practice the methods. Instruction is the communication between a student and a teacher (expert), and the rules for how to design and develop this communication are labeled *instructional design*. It comprises verbal and written communication between students and experts and takes on special forms such as the presentation of information and illustrations. It further comprises the formulation of questions (problems) that the students should solve to develop knowledge and tasks they should execute, individually and in teams, to practice a skill. All this is realized in a special setting, labeled a *learning environment*, in which the many and sometimes strongly different tasks are assigned to the participants. The content of the communication involves a domain of the arts and sciences or a part of it (object), the conceptions about this, and the representation of both the object and the conceptions in pictures, icons, and symbols (including language).

Instructional designers are always confronted with a few problems that are difficult to solve. They have to classify a constantly increasing body of information and methods into categories that the students can and should cognize and integrate. Moreover, they have to design the learning environment and instruction in such a way that for the students the relationship between the depictions and conceptions on the one hand and the "genuine" reality on the other hand will be understood.

General and Specific Design Rules.   Some instructional design rules are specific and detailed and lead to learning materials, the content and structure of which are easily recognizable, for example, the designs for learning to read. Others are more general and declared valid for several categories of information and methods. Different general models of instructional designs were proposed, all of which were criticized and sooner or later abandoned. Why? Partly because of the development of new theories of cognition and cognitive processes, especially of thinking and learning, and partly because the results of the use of a particular design or categories of designs were criticized. It is well known that for some students the goals of education are not achieved. Irrespective of the real cause in an individual case, there always has been the assumption that the quality of education and in particular the quality of instruction has to do with these failures and therefore "education has to be improved." If a new design model or part of it or a new learning environment is proposed it has to be shown that the change of an instructional design will lead to "better" results. In order to show a better result during the past half-century many research projects to study the effects of instructional designs have been done which quite often are characterized by a kind of dichotomy. A few examples are: computer-assisted instruction versus "traditional" classroom instruction, cognitivist versus behaviorist instruction, constructivist versus objectivist instruction, designs that foster "active" learning versus designs that lead to "passive" learning, problem-based instruction versus information presentation, and situated (realistic) instruction versus "abstract" instruction. Always the designs of the first category of the dichotomies are supposed to yield better results than the designs of the second category. The way in which the research is done seldom leads to clear, generalizable results. The general outcome that 50% of the studies provide positive evidence for the assumedly more effective design and 50% do not continues the uncertainties about effective designs. The dichotomies cannot adequately cover the whole instructional designs. Many variables influence the communication. One feature of a subdomain of psychology, or one feature of a (representation on) a medium, or an epistemological point of view may be useful to label a design but cannot cover all the components of the instructional design. Moreover, it is impossible to adequately describe all instructional designs by only one label. More precision is needed (a) based on the circumstance in which the design is useful, (b) in describing the features of the content (subject matter) for which the design is effective, and (c) in formulating the principles for the use of information technologies. If instructional technology is to become an "adult" science of design, such as chemical and maritime technology are, then the evaluation of whole designs in long-term research and development projects is needed (Dijkstra, 2001). The following chapters show the value of different instructional designs and how to integrate them.

THE CONTENT OF PART I

In this part of the volume, the dichotomies for categorizing instructional designs are hardly used. Instead the authors thoroughly describe and discuss the relation between the domains of psychology and epistemology on the one hand and the different categories of instructional designs on the other. About 25 years ago, Glaser, Pellegrino, and Lesgold (1977) concluded, "Cognitive psychology's findings and techniques have not significantly influenced teaching practices" (p. 495). Now in a scholarly chapter on complex learning environments, based on nearly a hundred articles and chapters by several other scholars in the domain, Pellegrino (chap. 1) shows how in the past 25 years cognitive psychology, instructional design, and information technology influenced each other and developed into an "adult" instructional-design science. Pellegrino first considers the linkages among curriculum, instruction, and assessment and how and why these linkages should be aligned by a central theory about the nature of learning and knowing. He then discusses the results of studies on learning and teaching that revealed three important principles about how people learn. These principles are (a) the influence of existing knowledge structures and schemas, both positive and negative, for the acquisition of new knowledge; (b) the way expertise should be developed; and (c) the monitoring of learning by metacognitive control. Based on these principles that are important for how people learn, Pellegrino brings order to the "chaos" of instructional choices and reassesses choices that are often considered poor ways of teaching. Of course, the principles of how people learn have implications for curriculum, instruction, and assessment and thus for the design of learning environments. Effective learning environments are knowledge centered, learner centered, assessment centered, and community centered. These points of departure are worked out in clear design principles and illustrated with many examples in which the use of media is integrated. This chapter will be a must for all instructional designers.

Seel's chapter (chap. 2) elaborates model-centered learning and describes the appropriate learning environments. Model-centered learning "gives primacy to students' construction of knowledge through an inquiry process of experimentation, simulation, and analysis" (p. 51). Seel provides the reader a clear and helpful description of the main concepts of model-centered learning. Among these are the description of concepts such as mental model, schema, and conceptual model. These concepts and others are used to clarify how model-building activities are influenced through instruction and what is the meaning of general paradigms of instruction. Among these are self-organized discovery learning and exploratory learning, externally guided discovery learning and learning oriented toward an expert's behavior. Seel shows the reader a diagram in which model- centered teaching and learning are integrated. He then discusses the research on instruction for model-centered learning and while doing this he clearly shows the use of teaching methods to build effective learning environments. Modeling, coaching, and scaffolding support receptive meaningful learning. Articulation and reflection are part of metacognitive control. And exploration of new tasks stimulates transfer of knowledge. A special issue that is addressed in this chapter is the assessment of the existence and growth of mental models. Interesting examples of how to do this are provided. Seel finally elaborates the instructional design of model-centered learning environments. The categories he proposes are embedded in a thorough analysis of recent literature.

Jonassen, Marra, and Palmer (chap. 3) first mention a number of special instructional designs that are prototypical examples for "constructive learning." They provide the reader with short descriptions of "rich environments for active learning," "open-ended learning environments," "goal-based scenarios," and "constructivist learning environments." Do these special designs achieve the desired goals? Only partly. One of the supposed causes for this is students' familiar script for school-based learning that is developed after years of practice. Such a script includes listening to lectures, predicting what ideas will be examined on the test, and so on, and is strongly different from the approach in constructivist learning environments. A second cause may be the decrease in motivation when students' actions in constructivist learning environments do not quickly lead to "correct" answers. And an "important causal factor is the students' levels of epistemological development relative to the levels of epistemological development required by constructivist learning environments" (p. 78). The chapter then provides the reader with most important information about students' epistemic beliefs. A person's epistemological development shows transitions from one stage to another in which the person's beliefs about epistemological categories such as knowledge and truth change. The level of epistemic belief is most important for the use of constructivist learning environments. The authors propose a "two-way" relation between levels of epistemic beliefs and instruction. They write: "Instructional interventions can have an impact on students' epistemic beliefs and the students' epistemic beliefs can affect the success of certain kinds of instruction" (p. 81). For both ways the authors first summarize the small amount of available research literature. They propose that to function successfully in constructivist learning environments, the students should have reached the level of contextual relativism, which means that "most knowledge is contextual and can be judged qualitatively" (p. 79). The students' learning shows beginning metacognitive control. They should, among other requirements, be able to justify their conclusions and beliefs through argumentation. Seven epistemological requirements should be met, which are proposed as entailments and worked out in epistemic orientations required by the learner. Jonassen, Marra, and Palmer finally propose to help learners in reaching the required level of epistemic belief by scaffolding the performance that is required in the constructivist learning environment. This "provides temporary frameworks to support learning and student performance beyond their capacities" (p. 84) and represents "some manipulation by the teacher of the learning system of the task itself" (p. 84). Examples are adjusting the difficulty of the task, providing tools to engage and support task performance, and performing a task or parts of it for the learner. Based on the seven entailments, the authors finally propose detailed means of scaffolding. Among these are well-known instructional designs such as questioning information sources and concept mapping. The authors conclude that the successful use of a constructivist learning environment is dependent on the level of epistemic beliefs and that the development of these beliefs can be scaffolded.

The last two chapters in this part of the volume both report on studies of learning science "by design." Kolodner and her colleagues (chap. 4) used the ideas of case-based reasoning and problem-based learning in a long-term project on learning physics by design. What does this kind of learning mean? It is a form of project-based inquiry. In the authors' own words: "In project-based inquiry students investigate scientific content and learn science skills and practices in the context of attempting to address challenges in the world around them" (p. 93). Students learn to investigate as scientists would. This means that the students make observations, select the most productive ideas (in small groups), design and run experiments, read and produce written texts, make presentations about results, and so on. If the challenges to design are complex, students feel that they can be more successful if they share findings and experiences with each other. Learning by designing and running experiments has a cycle of activities. The authors elaborate on this cycle by describing their experiences with a project for middle school students labeled "Vehicles in Motion." The students participate in small groups and can experiment with the propulsion system of a balloon-powered car from which they can learn about effects of the forces involved. It is a challenging and creative instructional design. The cycle starts with activities in small groups to understand the challenge and then report the ideas and issues to know more about in a whole-class discussion. The teacher helps to select "those issues that will be important for investigation." The groups of students each take responsibility for investigating one of the questions. Students are requested to come up with their own ideas and make a design diary. After this activity they discuss their proposals and design an experiment that takes "the best of each." The students collect the data and make a presentation. The teacher helps the students with poor understanding to state their explanations scientifically, illustrates these with a set of demos, readings, or a short lecture. The approach has different novel features. A few of these include (a) iteration that provides the students chances to address the challenge and (b) ritualizing classroom activities that may lead to the development of new scripts. The authors theorize that the students' design activity will foster deep understanding of the science concepts that make up the content of the learning material. The evaluation data are promising but not fully convincing, the authors conclude. Nevertheless, the instructional design is both challenging and promising.

Comparable work on learning science by design is described in the final chapter of this part of the volume. Kafai and Ching (chap. 5) ran a project in which a group of fourth and fifth graders designed and implemented instructional software about neuroscience to teach younger students in their school. The project is an example of apprenticeship learning in a school setting. The authors distinguish users (third-grade students), newcomers (fourth graders who designed software for the users), and oldtimers (fifth graders who had been newcomers themselves and could apprentice newcomers). The authors examine "how students enter a community of instructional design as both learners and designers, how they collaborate with others in that community and how they reflect on and evaluate their design skills and products" (p. 117). The results of the study show that newcomers and oldtimers "inside the classroom, within the context of learning through design, do not stay constant in their respective roles or their relationship with various tools or artifacts in the environment" (p. 126). Many changes in tasks in a dynamic system can be observed. These results are comparable with other studies of apprenticeships outside the walls of schools.

In sum, the instructional designs discussed in this part of the volume all show new perspectives. They integrate epistemology and psychology with solving design problems and thus contribute to the further development of instructional technology.

REFERENCES

Dijkstra, S. (2001). The design space for solving instructional-design problems. *Instructional Science, 29*(4), 275–290.

Dijkstra, S., & van Merriënboer, J. J. G. (1997). Plans, procedures, and theories to solve instructional design problems. In S. Dijkstra, N. Seel, F. Schott, & R. D. Tennyson (Eds.), *Instructional design: International perspectives* (Vol. 2, pp. 23–44). Mahwah, NJ: Lawrence Erlbaum Associates.

Glaser, R., Pellegrino, J. W., & Lesgold, A. M. (1977). Some directions for a cognitive psychology of instruction. In A. M. Lesgold, J. W. Pellegrino, S. D. Fokkema, & R. Glaser (Eds.), *Cognitive psychology and instruction* (pp. 495–517). New York: Plenum.

Chapter 1

Complex Learning Environments: Connecting Learning Theory, Instructional Design, and Technology

James W. Pellegrino
University of Illinois at Chicago

The past three decades have produced an extraordinary outpouring of scientific work on the processes of thinking and learning and on the development of competence. Much of this work has important implications for the design of learning environments *and* for the nature of instructional practices that maximize individual and group learning. Simultaneously, information technologies have advanced rapidly. They now render it possible to design much more complex, sophisticated, and potentially more powerful learning and instructional environments. Although much is now possible given theoretical, empirical, and technological advances, many questions remain to be answered. What principles do we need to consider in connecting together learning theory, instructional practice, and information technologies? How can we do so in effective and powerful ways?

In this chapter consideration is given to how contemporary learning theory can be connected to instructional practice to build better learning environments. A special concern is how we can capitalize on some of the many capacities and potentials of information technologies. This chapter begins by considering general linkages among curriculum, instruction, and assessment. With that as a context it moves to a consideration of some of the principal findings from research on learning that have clear implications for instructional practice. This brings us back to a consideration of the implications of knowledge about how people learn for some general issues of curriculum, instruction, and assessment, which is then followed by a more detailed discussion of important principles for the design of powerful learning and instructional environments. In discussing those principles, mention is made of ways in which technology can support their realization.

THE CURRICULUM–INSTRUCTION–ASSESSMENT TRIAD

Whether recognized or not, three things are central to the educational enterprise: curriculum, instruction, and assessment. The three elements of this triad are linked, although the nature of their linkages and reciprocal influence is often less explicit than it should be. Furthermore, the separate pairs of connections are often inconsistent, which can lead to an overall incoherence in educational systems.

Curriculum consists of the knowledge and skills in subject matter areas that teachers teach and students are supposed to learn. The curriculum generally consists of a scope or breadth of content in a given subject area and a sequence for learning. Standards, such as those developed in mathematics and science (National Council of Teachers of Mathematics [NCTM], 2000; National Research Council, 1996), typically outline the goals of learning, whereas curriculum sets forth the more specific means to be used to achieve those ends. *Instruction* refers to methods of teaching and the learning activities used to help students master the content and objectives specified by a curriculum and attain the standards that have been prescribed. Instruction encompasses the activities of both teachers and students. It can be carried out by a variety of methods, sequences of activities, and topic orders. *Assessment* is the means used to measure the outcomes of education and the achievement of students with regard to important knowledge and competencies. Assessment may include both formal methods, such as large-scale state assessments, or less formal classroom-based procedures, such as quizzes, class projects, and teacher questioning.

A precept of educational practice is the need for alignment among curriculum, instruction, and assessment (e.g., NCTM, 2000). Alignment, in this sense, means that the three functions are directed toward the same ends and reinforce each other rather than working at cross-purposes. Ideally, an assessment should measure what students are actually being taught, and what is actually being taught should parallel the curriculum one wants students to master. If any of the functions are not well synchronized, it will disrupt the balance and skew the educational process. Assessment results will be misleading, or instruction will be ineffective. Alignment is often difficult to achieve, however. Often what is lacking is a central theory about the nature of learning and knowing which guides the process and around which the three functions can be coordinated.

Decisions about curriculum, instruction, and assessment are further complicated by actions taken at different levels of the educational system, including the classroom, the school or district, and the state or nation. Each of these levels has different needs, and each uses assessment data in varied ways for somewhat different purposes. Each also plays a role in making decisions and setting policies for curriculum, instruction, and assessment, although the locus of power shifts depending on the type of decision involved. Some of these actions emanate from the top down, whereas others arise from the bottom up. Nations or states generally exert considerable influence over curriculum; classroom teachers have more latitude in instruction. Nations or states tend to determine policies on assessment for program evaluation; teachers have greater control over assessment for learning. This situation means that adjustments must continually be made among curriculum, instruction, and assessment not only horizontally, within the same level (such as within school districts), but also vertically across levels. For example, a change in national or state curriculum policy will require adjustments in assessment and instruction at all levels.

Most current approaches to curriculum, instruction, and assessment are based on theories and models that have not kept pace with contemporary knowledge of how people learn (Pellegrino, Chudowsky, & Glaser, 2001; Shepard, 2000). They have been designed on the basis of implicit and highly limited conceptions of learning. Those conceptions tend to be fragmented, outdated, and poorly delineated for domains of subject matter knowledge. Alignment among curriculum, instruction, and assessment could be better achieved if all three were derived from a scientifically credible and shared knowledge base about cognition and learning in the subject matter domains.[1] The model of learning would provide the central bonding principle, serving as a nucleus around which the three functions would revolve. Without such a central core, and under pressure to prepare students for high-stakes external accountability tests, teachers may feel compelled to move back and forth between instruction and external assessment and teach directly to the items on a high-stakes test. This approach can result in an undesirable narrowing of the curriculum and a limiting of learning outcomes. Such problems can be ameliorated if, instead, decisions

---

[1]There are, of course, serious issues about what defines a subject matter domain, including its features, depth, breadth, and so on, as well as what defines a model of learning and knowing in that domain. Typically, subject matter domains are recognizable bodies of knowledge that are the focus of instruction for some significant length of time. A broad subject matter domain like physics must really be understood in terms of the subdomains that define the discipline. For some subdomains such as forces and motion we may have a substantial knowledge base to draw from about issues of learning and knowing, whereas for others like relativity theory, the empirical knowledge base may be impoverished.

about both instruction and assessment are guided by a model of learning in the domain that represents the best available scientific understanding of how people learn. This brings us to a consideration of what we actually know about the nature of learning and knowing.

IMPORTANT PRINCIPLES ABOUT LEARNING AND TEACHING

Two recent National Academy of Sciences reports on "How People Learn" (Bransford, Brown, & Cocking, 1999; Donovan, Bransford, & Pellegrino, 1999) provide a broad overview of research on learners and learning and on teachers and teaching. Although there are many important findings that bear on issues of learning and instruction, three of the findings described in those reports are highlighted in this chapter. Each has a solid research base to support it, has strong implications for how we teach, and helps us think about ways in which technology assists in the design and delivery of effective learning environments.

The first important principle about how people learn is that students come to the instructional setting with existing knowledge structures and schemas that include preconceptions about how the world works. If their initial understanding is not engaged, they may fail to grasp the new concepts, procedures, and information that are taught, or they may learn them for purposes of an exercise or test but revert to their preconceptions outside the learning or occupational setting. Those initial understandings can have a powerful effect on the integration of new concepts and information. Sometimes those understandings are accurate, providing a foundation for building new knowledge. But sometimes they are inaccurate. In science, students often have misconceptions of physical properties that cannot be easily observed (Carey & Gelman, 1991). In humanities, their preconceptions often include stereotypes or simplifications, as when history is understood as a struggle between "good guys" and "bad guys" (Gardner, 1991).

Drawing out and working with existing understandings is important for learners of all ages. Numerous research studies demonstrate the persistence of preexisting understandings even after a new model has been taught that contradicts the naive understanding (Vosniadou & Brewer, 1989). For example, students at a variety of ages persist in their beliefs that seasons are caused by the earth's distance from the sun rather than by the tilt of the earth (Harvard–Smithsonian Center for Astrophysics, 1987). They believe that an object that has been tossed in the air has both the force of gravity and the force of the hand that tossed it acting on it, despite training to the contrary (Clement, 1982). For the scientific understanding to replace the naive understanding, students must reveal the latter and have the opportunity to see where it falls short.

The second important principle about how people learn is that to develop competence in an area of inquiry, students must (a) have a deep foundation of factual and procedural knowledge; (b) understand facts, procedures, and ideas in the context of a conceptual framework; and (c) organize knowledge in ways that facilitate retrieval and application. This principle emerges from research that compares the performance of experts and novices, and from research on learning and transfer. Experts, regardless of the field, always draw on a richly structured information base. They are not just "good thinkers" or "smart people." The ability to plan a task, to notice patterns, to generate reasonable arguments and explanations, and to draw analogies to other problems are all more closely intertwined with factual and procedural knowledge than was once believed.

However, knowledge of a large set of disconnected facts or procedures is not sufficient. To develop competence in an area of inquiry, students must have opportunities to learn with understanding. Key to expertise is a deep understanding of the domain in which they are working that transforms factual and procedural information into "usable knowledge." A pronounced difference between experts and novices is that experts' command of concepts and procedures shapes their understanding of new information. It allows them to see patterns, relationships, or discrepancies that are not apparent to novices. They do not necessarily have better overall memories than other people. But their conceptual understanding allows them to extract a level of meaning from information that is not apparent to novices, and this helps them select, remember, and apply relevant information. Experts are also able to fluently access relevant knowledge because their understanding of subject matter allows them to quickly identify what is relevant. Hence, their working memory and attentional capacity is not overtaxed by complex events.

A key finding in the learning and transfer literature is that organizing information into a conceptual framework allows for greater "transfer." It allows the student to apply what was learned in new situations and to learn related information more quickly (Holyoak, 1984; Novick & Holyoak, 1991). The student who has learned geographical information for the Americas in a conceptual framework approaches the task of learning the geography of another part of the globe with questions, ideas, and expectations that help guide acquisition of the new information. Understanding the geographical importance of the Mississippi River sets the stage for the student's understanding of the geographical importance of the Rhine. And as concepts are reinforced, the student will transfer learning beyond the classroom, observing and inquiring about the geographic features of a visited city that help explain its location and size.

A third critical idea about how people learn is that a "metacognitive" approach to instruction can help students learn to take control of their own learning by defining learning goals and monitoring their progress in achieving them. In research with experts who were asked to verbalize their thinking as they worked, it has been revealed that they monitor their own understanding carefully. They make note of when additional information is required for understanding, whether new information is consistent with what they already know, and what analogies can be drawn that would advance their understanding. These metacognitive monitoring activities are an important component of what is called *adaptive expertise* (Hatano, 1990).

Because metacognition often takes the form of an internal conversation, it can easily be assumed that individuals will develop the internal dialogue on their own. Yet many of the strategies we use for thinking reflect cultural norms and methods of inquiry in a given domain of knowledge or work (Brice-Heath, 1981, 1983; Hutchins, 1995; Suina & Smolkin, 1994). Research has demonstrated that individuals can be taught these strategies, including the ability to predict outcomes, explain to oneself in order to improve understanding, and note failures to comprehend. They can learn to activate background knowledge, plan ahead, and apportion time and memory. However, the teaching of metacognitive activities must be incorporated into the subject matter and occupational skills that students are learning. These strategies are not generic across situations, and attempts to teach them as generic can lead to failure to transfer. Teaching metacognitive strategies in context has been shown to improve understanding and problem solving in physics (White & Frederiksen, 1998) and to facilitate heuristic methods for mathematical problem solving (Schoenfeld, 1983, 1984, 1991). And metacognitive practices have been shown to increase the degree to which students transfer to new settings and events (Palincsar & Brown, 1984; Scardamalia, Bereiter, & Steinbach, 1984; Schoenfeld, 1983, 1984, 1991).

The three core learning principles briefly described, simple though they may seem, have profound implications for teaching and for the potential of technology to assist in that process. First, teachers must draw out and work with the preexisting understandings that their students bring with them. The teacher must actively inquire into students' thinking, creating classroom tasks and conditions under which student thinking can be revealed. Students' initial conceptions then provide the foundation on which the more formal understanding of the instructional content is built. The roles for assessment must be expanded beyond the traditional concept of "testing." The use of frequent formative assessment helps make students' thinking visible to themselves, their peers, and their teacher. This provides feedback that can guide modification and refinement in thinking. Given goals of learning with understanding, assessments must tap understanding rather than the mere ability to repeat facts or perform isolated skills.

Second, teachers must teach some subject matter in depth, providing many examples in which the same concept is at work and providing a firm foundation of factual and procedural knowledge. This requires that superficial coverage of all topics in a subject area must be replaced with in-depth coverage of fewer topics that allows key concepts and methods in that domain to be understood. The goal of coverage need not be abandoned entirely, of course. But there must be a sufficient number of cases of in-depth study to allow students to grasp the defining concepts in specific domains or areas of occupational skill.

Third, the teaching of metacognitive skills should be integrated into the curriculum in a variety of content areas. Because metacognition often takes the form of an internal dialogue, many students may be unaware of its importance unless the processes are explicitly emphasized by teachers. An emphasis on metacognition needs to accompany instruction in multiple areas of study because the type of monitoring required will vary. Integration of metacognitive instruction with discipline-based learning can enhance student achievement and develop in students the ability to learn independently.

IMPLICATIONS FOR CURRICULUM, INSTRUCTION, AND ASSESSMENT

There are multiple benefits of focusing on issues of how people learn with regard to matters of curriculum, instruction, and assessment. At the level of curriculum, knowledge of how people learn will help teachers and the educational system move beyond either–or dichotomies regarding the curriculum that have plagued the field of education. One such issue is whether the curriculum should emphasize "the basics" or teach thinking and problem-solving skills. Both are necessary. Students' abilities to acquire organized sets of facts and skills are actually enhanced when they are connected to meaningful problem-solving activities, and when students are helped to understand why, when, and how those facts and skills are relevant. And attempts to teach thinking skills without a strong base of factual knowledge do not promote problem-solving ability or support transfer to new situations.

Focusing on how people learn also helps bring order to a seeming chaos of instructional choices. Consider the many possible teaching strategies that are debated in education circles and the media. They include lecture-based teaching, text-based teaching, inquiry-based teaching, technology-enhanced teaching, teaching organized around individuals versus cooperative groups, and so forth. Are some of these teaching techniques better than others? Is lecturing a poor way to teach, as many seem to claim? Is cooperative learning good? Does technology-enhanced teaching help achievement or hurt it?

Research and theory on *how people learn* suggests that these are the wrong questions. Asking which teaching technique is best is analogous to asking which tool is best—a hammer, a screwdriver, a plane, or pliers. In teaching, as in carpentry, the selection of tools depends on the task at hand and the materials one is working with. Books and lectures *can* be wonderfully efficient modes of transmitting new information for learning. They can excite the imagination, and hone students' critical faculties. But one would choose other kinds of activities to elicit from students their preconceptions and level of understanding, or to help them see the power of using metacognitive strategies to monitor their learning. Hands-on activities and experiments can be a powerful way to ground emergent knowledge, but they do not alone evoke the underlying conceptual understandings that aid generalization. There is no universal best teaching practice.

If, instead, the point of departure is a core set of learning principles, then the selection of teaching strategies, mediated, of course, by subject matter, age and grade level, and desired outcome, can be purposeful. The many possibilities then become a rich set of opportunities from which a teacher constructs an instructional program rather than a chaos of competing alternatives.

Perhaps no area stands to gain more from knowledge of how people learn than the area of assessment, a persistent concern in the educational process. Assessing educational outcomes is not as straightforward as measuring height or weight; the attributes to be measured are mental representations and processes that are not outwardly visible. Thus, an assessment is a tool designed to observe students' behavior and produce data that can be used to draw reasonable inferences about what students know. Another recent National Academy of Sciences report, *Knowing What Students Know* (Pellegrino et al., 2001), emphasizes that the targets of inference should be determined by cognitive models of learning that describe how people represent knowledge and develop competence in the domain of interest. The cognitive models suggest the most important aspects of student achievement about which one would want to draw inferences and provide clues about the types of assessment tasks that will elicit evidence to support those inferences.

The process of collecting evidence to support inferences about what students know represents a chain of reasoning from evidence about student learning that characterizes all assessments, from classroom quizzes and standardized achievement tests to computerized tutoring programs to the conversation a student has with his or her teacher as they work through an experiment. The process of reasoning from evidence can be portrayed as a triad of three interconnected elements known as the *assessment triangle*. The vertices of the assessment triangle represent the three key elements underlying any assessment: a model of student *cognition* and learning in the domain; a set of beliefs about the kinds of *observations* that will provide evidence of students' competencies; and an *interpretation* process for making sense of the evidence. These three elements may be explicit or implicit, but an assessment cannot be designed and implemented without some consideration of each. The three are represented as vertices of a triangle because each is connected to and dependent on the other two. A major tenet of *Knowing What Students Know* (Pellegrino et al., 2001) is that for an assessment to be effective, the three elements must be in synchrony. The assessment triangle provides a useful framework for analyzing the underpinnings of current assessments to determine how well they accomplish the goals we have in mind, as well as for designing future assessments.

The *cognition* corner of the triangle refers to a theory or set of beliefs about how students represent knowledge and develop competence in a subject domain (e.g., fractions). In any particular assessment application, a theory of learning in the domain is needed to identify the set of knowledge and skills that is important to measure for the task at hand, whether that be characterizing the competencies students have acquired thus far or guiding instruction to further increase learning. A central premise is that the cognitive theory should represent the most scientifically credible understanding of typical ways in which learners represent knowledge and develop expertise in a domain. These findings should derive from cognitive and educational research about how people learn, as well as the experience of expert teachers. Use of the term *cognition* is not meant to imply that the theory must necessarily come from a single cognitive research perspective. Theories and data on student learning and understanding can take different forms and encompass several levels and types of knowledge representation that include social and contextual components.

Depending on the purpose for an assessment, one might distinguish from one to hundreds of aspects of student competence to be sampled. These targets of inference for a given assessment will be a subset of the larger theory of how people learn the subject matter. Targets for assessment could be expressed in terms of numbers, categories, or some mix; they might be conceived as persisting over long periods of time or apt to change at the next problem step. They might concern tendencies in behavior, conceptions of phenomena, available strategies, or levels of development.

IMPLICATIONS FOR THE DESIGN OF LEARNING ENVIRONMENTS

How do we take the knowledge about how people learn, as well as the implications for curriculum, instruction, and assessment, and use it productively to design effective learning environments? What role is there for information and communication technologies in this process? These questions do not have simple answers and at least one implication is that to achieve the higher level thinking and learning outcomes we want for our students, we will need to build learning environments that more carefully and consistently implement design principles that foster an effective integration of curriculum, instruction, and assessment. Furthermore, all three elements must be driven by theories, models, and empirical data on domain-specific learning. There is of course a tension in the juxtaposition of general principles of instructional design with matters of domain-specific knowledge and understanding. This tension cannot be avoided and requires that broader principles must always be tailored to specific cases of subject matter learning. Furthermore, it is likely to be the case that learning environments sensitive to such matters will be more complex than those designed and implemented in the past. Some of that complexity will be enabled and/or supported by information and communication technologies.

To address the design challenges alluded to previously, we need to ask what the findings from contemporary research on cognitive and social issues in learning and assessment, such as those described earlier and in the *How People Learn* (Bransford et al., 1999; Donovan et al., 1999) and *Knowing What Students Know* (Pellegrino et al., 2001) reports, suggest about general characteristics of powerful learning environments. Four such characteristics have been identified which in turn overlap with four major design principles for instruction that are critically important for achieving the types of learning with understanding that are espoused in contemporary educational standards. The four characteristics of powerful learning environments are as follows:

1. *Effective learning environments are knowledge centered.* Attention is given to what is taught (central subject matter concepts), why it is taught (to support "learning with understanding" rather than merely remembering), and what competence or mastery looks like.

2. *Effective learning environments are learner centered.* Educators must pay close attention to the knowledge, skills, and attitudes that learners bring into the classroom. This incorporates preconceptions regarding subject matter, and it also includes a broader understanding of the learner. Teachers in learner-centered environments pay careful attention to what students know as well as what they don't know, and they continually work to build on students' strengths.

3. *Effective learning environments are assessment centered.* Especially important are efforts to make students' thinking visible through the use of frequent formative assessment. This permits the teacher to grasp the students' preconceptions, understand where students are on the "developmental corridor" from informal to formal thinking, and design instruction accordingly. They help both teachers and students monitor progress.

4. *Effective learning environments are community centered.* This includes the development of norms for the classroom and school, as well as connections to the outside world, that support core learning values. Teachers must be enabled and encouraged to establish a community of learners among themselves. These communities can build a sense of comfort with questioning rather than knowing the answers and can develop a model of creating new ideas that builds on the contributions of individual members.

Consistent with the ideas about the multiple and interacting elements of a powerful learning environment, all driven by concerns about how people learn, are four principles for the design of instruction within such a contextual perspective:

1. To establish knowledge-centered elements of a learning environment, *instruction is organized around meaningful problems with appropriate goals.*
2. To support a learner-centered focus, *instruction must provide scaffolds for solving meaningful problems and supporting learning with understanding.*
3. To support assessment-centered activities, *instruction provides opportunities for practice with feedback, revision, and reflection.*
4. To create community in a learning environment, *the social arrangements of instruction must promote collaboration and distributed expertise, as well as independent learning.*

We consider each principle in turn and briefly describe how technology can support its realization. A more complete discussion of these ideas and the variety of technology-based tools available to support these design principles can be found in Goldman et al. (1999, 2002). The present focus is on specific technology tools and applications rather than technology in general or its general or specific effects on student learning outcomes. For those interested in learning outcomes, a variety of analyses have appeared in recent years of the impact of technology on instruction, including discussions and evidence of when technology applications appear to be most effective in producing student learning gains (see, e.g., Cognition and Technology Group at Vanderbilt [CTGV], 1996; Kulik, 1994; Schacter & Fagnano, 1999; Wenglinsky, 1998).

Instruction Is Organized Around the Solution of Meaningful Problems

When students acquire new information in the process of solving meaningful problems, they are more likely to see its potential usefulness than when they are asked to memorize isolated facts. Meaningful problems also help students overcome the "inert knowledge" problem, defined by Whitehead (1929) as knowledge previously learned but not remembered in situations where it would be potentially useful. Seeing the relevance of information to everyday problems helps students understand when and how the information may be useful.

When students see the usefulness of information, they are motivated to learn (McCombs, 1991, 1994). Research on the relationship between interest and learning indicates that personal interest in a topic or domain positively impacts academic learning in that domain (Alexander, Kulikowich, & Jetton, 1994). New approaches to motivation emphasize motivational enhancement through authentic tasks that students perceive as real work for real audiences. This emphasis contrasts with earlier emphases on elaborate extrinsic reinforcements for correct responding (for discussion, see Collins, 1996).

Problem solving is at the core of inquiry- or project-based learning. Students will work on problems that are interesting and personally meaningful (Brown & Campione, 1994; CTGV, 1997; Hmelo & Williams, 1998; Resnick & Klopfer, 1989). Several contemporary educational reform efforts use dilemmas, puzzles, and paradoxes to "hook" or stimulate learners' interests in the topic of study (Brown & Campione, 1994, 1996; CTGV, 1997; Goldman et al., 1996; Lamon et al., 1996; Scardamalia, Bereiter, & Lamon, 1994; Secules et al., 1997; Sherwood et al., 1995).

One major challenge for inquiry-based learning environments is developing problems that are rich and complex enough to engage students in the kinds of sustained inquiry that will allow them to deeply understand important new concepts. Bringing complex problems into the classroom is an important function of technology. Unlike problems that occur in the real world, problems that are created with graphics, video, and animation can be explored again and again. These multimedia formats capture children's interest and provide information in the form of sound and moving images that is not available in text-based problems and stories. Multimedia formats are more easily understood and allow the learner to concentrate on high-level processes such as identifying problem-solving goals or making important inferences (Sharp et al., 1995).

Although technology-based problem environments come in many forms, an important characteristic is that they are under the learner's control: Stories on interactive videodisc, CD-ROM, or DVD can be reviewed many times and specific frames or pictures can be frozen and studied. Problems presented via the World Wide Web or in hypermedia allow students to search easily for the parts that interest them most. Exploratory environments called *microworlds* or simulations allow students to carry out actions, immediately observe the results, and attempt to discover the rules that govern the system's behavior. No matter what form of technology is involved, the student is primarily responsible for deciding how to investigate the problem, and the technology creates an environment in which flexible exploration is possible.

The cumulative work on *The Adventures of Jasper Woodbury Problem Solving Series* (CTGV, 1994, 1997, 2000) is one example of an attempt to develop meaningful problems and use instructional design principles based on cognitive theory. The Jasper series consists of 12 interactive video environments that invite students to solve authentic challenges, each of which requires them to understand and use important concepts in mathematics. For example, in the adventure known as *Rescue at Boone's Meadow* which focuses on distance–rate–time relations, Larry is teaching Emily to fly an ultralight airplane. During the lessons, he helps Emily learn about the basic principles of flight and the specific details of the ultralight she is flying, such as its speed, fuel consumption, fuel capacity, and how much weight it can carry. Not long after Emily's first solo flight, her friend Jasper goes fishing in a remote area called Boone's Meadow. Hearing a gunshot, he discovers a wounded bald eagle and radios Emily for help in getting the eagle to a veterinarian. Emily consults a map to determine the closest roads to Boone's Meadow, then calls Larry to find out about the weather and see if his ultralight is available. Students are challenged to use all the information in the video to determine the fastest way to rescue the eagle.

After viewing the video, students review the story and discuss the setting, characters, and any unfamiliar concepts and vocabulary introduced in the video. After they have a clear understanding of the problem situation, small groups of students work together to break the problem into subgoals, scan the video for information, and set up the calculations necessary to solve each part of the problem. Once they have a solution, they compare it with those that other groups generate and try to choose the optimum plan. Like most real-world problems, Jasper problems involve multiple correct solutions. Determining the optimum solution involves weighing factors such as safety and reliability, as well as making the necessary calculations. The Jasper series focuses on providing opportunities for problem solving and problem finding. It is not intended to replace the entire mathematics curriculum.

**Instruction Provides Scaffolds
for Achieving Meaningful Learning**

In the previous section, we briefly described the benefits of giving students the opportunity and responsibility of exploring complex problems on their own. This is clearly a way to support the implementation of knowledge-centered elements in a learning environment. The mere presence of these opportunities, however, does not lead to learning with understanding, nor will they enhance a learner-centered approach. Because of the complexity of the problems and the inexperience of the students, scaffolds must be provided to help students carry out the parts of the task that they cannot yet manage on their own. Cognitive scaffolding assumes that individuals learn through interactions with more knowledgeable others, just as children learn through adult–child interactions (Bakhtin, 1935/1981; Bruner, 1983; Vygotsky, 1962). Adults model good thinking, provide hints, and prompt children who cannot "get it" on their own. Children eventually adopt the patterns of thinking reflected by the adults (Brown, Bransford, Ferrara, & Campione, 1983; Wood, Bruner, & Ross, 1976). Cognitive scaffolding can be realized in a number of ways. Collins, Brown, and Newman (1989) suggested modeling and coaching by experts, and providing guides and reminders about the procedures and steps that are important for the task.

Technologies can also be used to scaffold the solution of complex problems and projects by providing resources such as visualization tools, reference materials, and hints. Multimedia databases on CD-ROM, videodisc, or the World Wide Web provide important resources for students who are doing research. Technology-based reference materials provide several advantages over those in book format. Most important, they allow the presentation of information in audio or video format. In many cases, students can see an actual event and create their own analysis rather than reading someone else's description. Electronic references are easy to search and provide information quickly while students are in the midst of problem solving. For example, definitions of words and their pronunciations are readily available while a student is reading or writing a story. Hints and demonstrations can be effortlessly accessed when a student is stuck while setting up a math problem. The knowledge that is acquired in these "just in time" situations is highly valued and easily remembered, because learners understand why it is useful to them.

Technology can help learners visualize processes and relations that are normally invisible or difficult to understand. For example, students might use spreadsheets to create a graph that demonstrates a trend or shows if one result is out of line with the rest. These graphs are useful in initial interpretations of numerical data and also valuable for reporting it to others. Graphs, maps, and other graphic representations can be created by students or automatically generated by simulation programs to depict the changes brought about by student actions.

Instruction Provides Opportunities for Practice
With Feedback, Revision, and Reflection

Feedback, revision, and reflection are aspects of metacognition that are critical to developing the ability to regulate one's own learning. Many years ago, Dewey (1933) noted the importance of reflecting on one's ideas, weighing one's ideas against data and predictions against obtained outcomes. In the context of teaching, Schon (1983, 1988) emphasized the importance of reflection in creating new mental models. Content-area experts exhibit strong self-monitoring skills that enable them to regulate their learning goals and activities. Self-regulated learners take feedback from their performance and adjust their learning in response to it. Self-monitoring depends on deep understanding in the domain because it requires an awareness of one's own thinking, sufficient knowledge to evaluate that thinking and provide feedback to oneself, and knowledge of how to make necessary revisions. In other words, learners cannot effectively monitor what they know and make use of the feedback effectively (in revision) unless they have deep understanding in the domain. The idea that monitoring is highly knowledge dependent creates a dilemma for novices. How can they regulate their own learning without the necessary knowledge to do so? Thus, the development of expertise requires scaffolds for monitoring and self-regulation skills so that deep understanding and reflective learning can develop hand-in-hand.

Analyses of expert performance indicate that the development of expertise takes lots of practice over a long period of time (e.g., Bereiter & Scardamalia, 1993; Glaser & Chi, 1988). Cycles of feedback, reflection, and opportunities for revision provide students with opportunities to practice using the skills and concepts they are trying to master. Cognitive theories of skill acquisition place importance on practice because it leads to fluency and a reduction in the amount of processing resources needed to execute the skill (e.g., Anderson, 1983; Schneider, Dumais, & Shiffrin, 1984; Schneider & Shiffrin, 1977). Practice with feedback produces better learning than practice alone. Thorndike (1913) provided a simple but elegant illustration of the importance of practice with feedback for learning. He spent hundreds of hours trying to draw a line that was exactly 4 inches long. He did not improve—until he took off his blindfold. Only when he could see how close each attempt had come to the goal was Thorndike able to improve. Unless learners get feedback on their practice efforts, they will not know how to adjust their performance to improve.

An early and major use of technology was providing opportunities for extended practice of basic skills. It is important to distinguish between two stages of basic skill development: acquisition and fluency. *Acquisition* refers to the initial learning of a skill, and *fluency* refers to being able to access this skill in a quick and effortless manner (such as math facts). If basic skills are not developed to a fluent level then the learning process is incomplete and the student will not be able to function well in the real world.

Although there is no question that the nature of a drill-and-practice application makes it ideal for providing endless practice in almost any curricular area, the use of drill-and-practice is inappropriate when a student is in an acquisition phase of learning. As the name implies, computer-based drill-and-practice is designed to reinforce *previously learned information* rather than provide direct instruction on new skills. If technology is to be used during the acquisition phase of a new skill or concept, the tutorial is more appropriate than drill-and-practice. A technology-based tutorial differs from a drill-and-practice application in that a tutorial attempts to play the role of a teacher and provide direct instruction on a new skill or concept. The tutorial presents the student with new or previously unlearned material in an individualized manner, providing frequent corrective feedback and reinforcement.

It is important to remember that tutorials and drill-and-practice software came into existence at a time when teacher-led lecture and recitation was widely accepted and that these applications frequently mirror this instructional approach. For some, the mere mention of this type of software evokes a negative response; however, when students encounter difficulties in the process of solving meaningful problems, the opportunity for individualized instruction and practice can be very valuable. This is especially true when the curriculum provides students a chance to apply what they have learned by revising their solutions to the problem that caused them difficulty.

Fortunately, there are now multiple examples that support a wide range of formative assessment practices in the classroom. They include exciting new technology-based methods such as the Diagnoser software for physics and mathematics (Hunt & Minstrell, 1994), Latent Semantic Analysis for scoring essays (e.g., Landauer, Foltz, & Laham, 1998), the IMMEX system for providing feedback on problem solving (Hurst, Casillas, & Stevens, 1998), as well as the Curriculum Based Measurement system (Fuchs, Fuchs, Hamlett, & Stecker, 1991) and Knock Knock environments (CTGV, 1998) for feedback on literacy skills to young children. Such software can also be used to encourage the kind of self-assessment skills that are frequently seen in expert performance.

The Social Arrangements of Instruction Promote Collaboration and Distributed Expertise, as Well as Independent Learning

The view of cognition as socially shared rather than individually owned is an important shift in the orientation of cognitive theories of learning. It reflects the idea that thinking is a product of several heads in interaction with one another (Bereiter, 1990; Hutchins, 1991). In the theoretical context of "cognition as socially shared," researchers have proposed having learners work in small groups on complex problems as a way to deal with complexity. Working together facilitates problem solving and capitalizes on distributed expertise (Barron, 1991; Brown & Campione, 1994, 1996; CTGV, 1992a, 1992b, 1992c, 1993a, 1993b, 1994, 1997; Pea, 1993; Salomon, 1993; Yackel, Cobb, & Wood, 1991). Collaborative environments also make excellent venues for making thinking visible, generating and receiving feedback, and revising (Barron et al., 1995; CTGV, 1994; Hatano & Inagaki, 1991; Vye et al., 1997, 1998).

A number of technologies support collaboration by providing venues for discussion and communication among learners. Through the use of computer networks, many schools today are connecting their computers to other computers often thousands of miles away. By networking computers within a room, building, or larger geographic area, students can send and receive information to and from other teachers or students not in their physical location. By networking computers, teachers and students are freed from the constraints of location and time. For example, students can log on to a network at any time that is convenient to send or receive information from any location attached to their network. Also, given the heavy dependence on text in most networked systems, students have a reason to use text to read, write, and construct thoughts and ideas for others to read and respond to. In addition, a vast amount of information is available through the Internet.

A vast array of communications services are rapidly becoming available to schools. For example, two-way video and two-way audio systems are now being used to allow students and teachers at remote sites to see and hear each other. In this way, face-to-face interactions can take place over great distances in real time. Communal databases and discussion groups make thinking visible and provide students with opportunities to give and receive feedback, often with more reflection, because the comments are written rather than spoken. Networked and Web-based communications technologies such as e-mail, List Serves, and more sophisticated knowledge-building software such as Knowledge Forum (Scardamalia & Bereiter, 1994) can also help students form a community around important ideas. Such technology helps capture ideas that otherwise can be ephemeral, and it supports communication that is asynchronous as well as synchronous.

FINAL COMMENTS: MAKING IT ALL WORK

Although the design principles mentioned earlier can be described individually, it is important to recognize that they need to work together. Thus, it is worth noting that various methods to incorporate knowledge-centered, learner-centered, assessment-centered, and community-centered elements in the overall instructional design have been explored in working with the Jasper Adventures and a related set of science materials known as the *Scien-*

tists In Action series. For more complete descriptions of this body of work and data, see CTGV (1992a, 1992b, 1992c, 1993a, 1993b, 1994, 1997, 2000); Goldman, Zech, Biswas, et al. (1999); Pellegrino et al. (1991); Vye et al. (1997, 1998); and Zech et al. (1994, 1998).

With regard to learner-centered and assessment-centered issues, efforts were made to provide frequent and appropriate opportunities for formative assessment (Barron et al., 1995, 1998; CTGV, 1994, 1997, 2000). These include assessment of student-generated products at various points along the way to problem solution such as blueprints or business plans, and assessment facilitated by comparing intermediate solutions with those generated by others around the country who are working on similar problem-based and project-based curricula. In these examples, assessment is both teacher and student generated, and it is followed by opportunities to revise the product that has been assessed. The revision process is quite important for students and seems to lead to changes in students' perspectives of the nature of adult work as well as conceptual growth.

Advantage was also taken of the fact that different ways of organizing classrooms can also have strong effects on the degree to which everyone participates, learns from one another, and makes progress in the cycles of work (e.g., Brown & Campione, 1996; Collins, Hawkins, & Carver, 1991). It has proven beneficial to have students work collaboratively in groups, but to also establish norms of individual accountability. One way to do this is to set up a requirement that each person in a group has to reach a threshold of achievement before moving on to collaborate on a more challenging project, for example, to be able to explain how pollution affects dissolved oxygen and hence life in the river, or to create a blueprint that a builder could use to build some structure. Under these conditions, the group works together to help everyone succeed. The revision process is designed to ensure that all students ultimately attain a level of understanding and mastery that establishes a precondition for moving from the problem-based to project-based activity.

The larger model that emerged is known as SMART, which stands for Scientific and Mathematical Arenas for Refining Thinking (Schwartz, Brophy, Lin, & Bransford, 1999; Schwartz, Lin, Brophy, & Bransford, 1999). The SMART model incorporates a number of design features to support all four features of an effective learning environment. For example, a variety of scaffolds and other technology-based learning tools were developed to deepen the possibilities for student learning. They included (a) Smart Lab, a virtual community for students in which they are exposed to contrasting solutions to problems in the context of being able to assess the adequacy of each; (b) Toolbox, various visual representations that can be used as tools for problem solving; and (c) Kids-on-Line, which features students making presentations. By using actors who make presentations based on real students' work, we were able to seed the presentations with typical errors. This design feature allows students to engage in critical analysis of the arguments and see same-age peers explaining their work in sophisticated ways.

In the context of developing the SMART model, it has proven useful to provide students and teachers with access to information about how people outside their classroom have thought about the same problem that they are facing (CTGV, 1994, 1997, 2000). Such access can help students be more objective about their own view and realize that even with the same information other people may come to different conclusions or solutions. In addition, discussion of these differences of opinion can support the development of shared standards for reasoning. This can have a powerful effect on understanding the need for revising one's ideas and as a motivator for engaging in such a process. Internet and Web-based environments now provide excellent mechanisms to incorporate these processes within the overall SMART model. Some of these mechanisms include interactive websites with database components that are dynamically updated as students from multiple classrooms respond to items or probes on the website.

In summary, it is only through the process of designing complex learning environments such as the Jasper Adventures and the accompanying SMART model and implementing them in multiple classrooms that we can develop a truly rich and useful understanding of the complexities of connecting learning theory, instructional design, and technology. Such attempts to work in Pasteur's Quadrant (Stokes, 1997) put theory into practice, provide the feedback we need about what works and why, and thus provide the basis for much richer and evolving theories of learning and instructional design.

REFERENCES

Alexander, P. A., Kulikowich, J. M., & Jetton, T. L. (1994). The role of subject-matter knowledge and interest in the processing of linear and non-linear texts. *Review of Educational Research, 64,* 201–252.

Anderson, J. R. (1983). A spreading activation theory of memory. *Journal of Verbal Learning and Verbal Behavior, 22,* 261–296.

Bakhtin, M. (1981). Discourse in the novel. In M. Holquist (Ed.), *The dialogic imagination* (pp. 259–422). Austin: University of Texas Press. (Original work published 1935)

Barron, B. (1991). *Collaborative problem solving: Is team performance greater than what is expected from the most competent member?* Unpublished doctoral dissertation, Vanderbilt University, Nashville, TN.

Barron, B. J., Schwartz, D. L., Vye, N. J., Moore, A., Petrosino, A., Zech, L., Bransford, J. D., & the Cognition and Technology Group at Vanderbilt. (1998). Doing with understanding: Lessons from research on problem and project-based learning. *Journal of Learning Sciences, 7,* 271–312.

Barron, B., Vye, N. J., Zech, L., Schwartz, D., Bransford, J. D., Goldman, S. R., Pellegrino, J., Morris, J., Garrison, S., & Kantor, R. (1995). Creating contexts for community-based problem solving: The Jasper Challenge Series. In C. N. Hedley, P. Antonacci, & M. Rabinowitz (Eds.), *Thinking and literacy: The mind at work* (pp. 47–71). Hillsdale, NJ: Lawrence Erlbaum Associates.

Bereiter, C. (1990). Aspects of an educational learning theory. *Review of Educational Research, 60,* 603–624.

Bereiter, C., & Scardamalia, M. (1993). *Surpassing ourselves: An inquiry into the nature and implications of expertise.* Chicago: Open Court.

Bransford, J. D., Brown, A. L., & Cocking, R. R. (1999). *How people learn: Brain, mind, experience, and school.* Washington, DC: National Academy Press.

Brice-Heath, S. (1981). Toward an ethnohistory of writing in America. In M. F. Whiteman (Ed.), *Writing: The nature, development, and teaching of written communication* (Vol. 1, pp. 25–45). Hillsdale, NJ: Lawrence Erlbaum Associates.

Brice-Heath, S. (1983). *Ways with words: Language, life and work in communities and classrooms.* Cambridge, England: Cambridge University Press.

Brown, A. L., Bransford, J. D., Ferrara, R., & Campione, J. (1983). Learning, remembering, and understanding. In J. H. Flavell & E. Markman (Eds.), *Handbook of child psychology: Vol. 3. Cognitive development* (4th ed., pp. 77–166). New York: Wiley.

Brown, A. L., & Campione, J. C. (1994). Guided discovery in a community of learners. In K. McGilly (Ed.), *Classroom lessons: Integrating cognitive theory and classroom practice* (pp. 229–272). Cambridge, MA: MIT Press/Bradford Books.

Brown, A. L., & Campione, J. C. (1996). Psychological theory and the design of innovative learning environments: On procedures, principles, and systems. In L. Schauble & R. Glaser (Eds.), *Innovations in learning: New environments for education* (pp. 289–325). Mahwah, NJ: Lawrence Erlbaum Associates.

Bruner, J. S. (1983). *Child's talk: Learning to use language.* New York: Norton.

Carey, S., & Gelman, R. (1991). *The epigenesis of mind: Essays on biology and cognition.* Hillsdale, NJ: Lawrence Erlbaum Associates.

Clement, J. (1982). Student preconceptions of introductory mechanics. *American Journal of Physics, 50,* 66–71.

Cognition and Technology Group at Vanderbilt. (1992a). An anchored instruction approach to cognitive skills acquisition and intelligent tutoring. In J. W. Region & V. J. Shute (Eds.), *Cognition approaches to automated instruction* (pp. 135–170). Hillsdale, NJ: Lawrence Erlbaum Associates.

Cognition and Technology Group at Vanderbilt. (1992b). The Jasper experiment: An exploration of issues in learning and instructional design. *Educational Technology Research and Development, 40,* 65–80.

Cognition and Technology Group at Vanderbilt. (1992c). The Jasper series as an example of anchored instruction: Theory, program description, and assessment data. *Educational Psychologist, 27,* 291–315.

Cognition and Technology Group at Vanderbilt. (1993a). The Jasper series: Theoretical foundations and data on problem solving and transfer. In L. A. Penner, G. M. Batsche, H. M. Knoff, & D. L. Nelson (Eds.), *The challenge in mathematics and science education: Psychology's response* (pp. 113–152). Washington, DC: American Psychological Association.

Cognition and Technology Group at Vanderbilt. (1993b). Toward integrated curricula: Possibilities from anchored instruction. In M. Rabinowitz (Ed.), *Cognitive science foundations of instruction* (pp. 33–55). Hillsdale, NJ: Lawrence Erlbaum Associates.

Cognition and Technology Group at Vanderbilt. (1994). From visual word problems to learning communities: Changing conceptions of cognitive research. In K. McGilly (Ed.), *Classroom lessons: Integrating cognitive theory and classroom practice* (pp. 157–200). Cambridge, MA: MIT Press/Bradford Books.

Cognition and Technology Group at Vanderbilt. (1996). Looking at technology in context: A framework for understanding technology and education research. In D. C. Berliner & R. C. Calfee (Eds.), *The handbook of educational psychology* (pp. 807–840). New York: Simon & Schuster Macmillan.

Cognition and Technology Group at Vanderbilt. (1997). *The Jasper Project: Lessons in curriculum, instruction, assessment, and professional development.* Mahwah, NJ: Lawrence Erlbaum Associates.

Cognition and Technology Group at Vanderbilt. (1998). Designing environments to reveal, support, and expand our children's potentials. In S. A. Soraci & W. McIlvane (Eds.), *Perspectives on fundamental processes in intellectual functioning* (pp. 313–350). Norwood, NJ: Ablex.

Cognition and Technology Group at Vanderbilt. (2000). Adventures in anchored instruction: Lessons from beyond the ivory tower. In R. Glaser (Ed.), *Advances in instructional psychology: Vol. 5. Educational design and cognitive science* (pp. 35–99). Mahwah, NJ: Lawrence Erlbaum Associates.

Collins, A. (1996). Design issues for learning environments. In S. Vosniadou, E. DeCorte, R. Glaser, & H. Mandl (Eds.), *International perspectives on the psychological foundations of technology-based learning environments* (pp. 347–362). Mahwah, NJ: Lawrence Erlbaum Associates.

Collins, A., Brown, J. S., & Newman, S. E. (1989). Cognitive apprenticeship: Teaching the crafts of reading, writing, and mathematics. In L. B. Resnick (Ed.), *Knowing, learning, and instruction: Essays in honor of Robert Glaser* (pp. 453–494). Hillsdale, NJ: Lawrence Erlbaum Associates.

Collins, A., Hawkins, J., & Carver, S. M. (1991). A cognitive apprenticeship for disadvantaged students. In B. Means, C. Chelemer, & M. S. Knapp (Eds.), *Teaching advanced skills to at-risk students* (pp. 216–243). San Francisco: Jossey-Bass.

Dewey, J. (1933). *How we think, a restatement of the relation of reflective thinking to the educative process.* Boston: Heath.

Donovan, M. S., Bransford, J. D., & Pellegrino, J. W. (1999). *How people learn: Bridging research and practice.* Washington, DC: National Academy Press.

Fuchs, L. S., Fuchs, D., Hamlett, C. L., & Stecker, P. M. (1991). Effects of curriculum-based measurement on teacher planning and student achievement in mathematics operations. *American Educational Research Journal, 28,* 617–641.

Gardner, H. (1991). *The unschooled mind: How children think and how schools should teach.* New York: Basic Books.

Glaser, R., & Chi, M. T. H. (1988). Introduction: What is it to be an expert? In M. T. H. Chi, R. Glaser, & M. J. Farr (Eds.), *The nature of expertise* (pp. xv–xxix). Hillsdale, NJ: Lawrence Erlbaum Associates.

Goldman, S. R., Petrosino, A., Sherwood, R. D., Garrison, S., Hickey, D., Bransford, J. D., & Pellegrino, J. W. (1996). Anchoring science instruction in multimedia learning environments. In S. Vosniadou, E. De Corte, R. Glaser, & H. Mandl (Eds.), *International perspectives on the psychological foundations of technology-supported learning environments* (pp. 257–284). Mahwah, NJ: Lawrence Erlbaum Associates.

Goldman, S. R., Williams, S. M., Sherwood, R. D., Hasselbring, T. S., & the Cognition and Technology Group at Vanderbilt. (1999). *Technology for teaching and learning with understanding: A primer.* Boston: Houghton Mifflin.

Goldman, S. R., Williams, S. M., Sherwood, R. D., Pellegrino, J. W., Plants, R., & Hasselbring, T. S. (2002). Technology for teaching and learning with understanding. In J. M. Cooper (Ed.), *Classroom teaching skills* (pp. 181–224). Boston: Houghton Mifflin.

Goldman, S. R., Zech, L. K., Biswas, G., Noser, T., & the Cognition and Technology Group at Vanderbilt. (1999). Computer technology and complex problem solving: Issues in the study of complex cognitive activity. *Instructional Science, 27,* 235–268.

Harvard–Smithsonian Center for Astrophysics, Science Education Department. (1987). *A private universe* [Video]. Cambridge, MA: Science Media Group.

Hatano, G. (1990). The nature of everyday science: A brief introduction. *British Journal of Developmental Psychology, 8,* 245–250.

Hatano, G., & Inagaki, K. (1991). Sharing cognition through collective comprehension activity. In L. Resnick, J. M. Levine, & S. D. Teasley (Eds.), *Perspectives on socially shared cognition* (pp. 331–348). Washington, DC: American Psychological Association.

Hmelo, C. E., & Williams, S. M. (Eds.). (1998). Learning through problem solving [Special issue]. *Journal of the Learning Sciences, 3 & 4.*

Holyoak, K. J. (1984). Analogical thinking and human intelligence. In R. J. Sternberg (Ed.), *Advances in the psychology of human intelligence* (Vol. 2, pp. 199–230). Hillsdale, NJ: Lawrence Erlbaum Associates.

Hunt, E., & Minstrell, J. (1994). A cognitive approach to the teaching of physics. In K. McGilly (Ed.), *Classroom lessons: Integrating cognitive theory and classroom practice* (pp. 51–74). Cambridge, MA: MIT Press.

Hurst, K. C., Casillas, A. M., & Stevens, R. H. (1998). *Exploring the dynamics of complex problem-solving with artificial neural network-based assessment systems* (CSE Tech. Rep. No. 387). Los Angeles: University of California–Los Angeles, National Center for Research on Evaluation, Standards, and Student Testing.

Hutchins, E. (1991). The social organization of distributed cognition. In L. Resnick, J. M. Levine, & S. D. Teasley (Eds.), *Perspectives on socially shared cognition* (pp. 283–307). Washington, DC: American Psychological Association.

Hutchins, E. (1995). *Cognition in the wild.* Cambridge, MA: MIT Press.

Kulik, J. (1994). Meta-analytic studies of findings of computer-based instruction. In E. L. Baker & H. F. O'Neill (Eds.), *Technology assessment in education and training* (pp. 9–33). Hillsdale, NJ: Lawrence Erlbaum Associates.

Lamon, M., Secules, T., Petrosino, A. J., Hackett, R., Bransford, J. D., & Goldman, S. R. (1996). Schools for thought: Overview of the project and lessons learned from one of the sites. In L. Schauble & R. Glaser (Eds.), *Innovation in learning: New environments for education* (pp. 243–288). Mahwah, NJ: Lawrence Erlbaum Associates.

Landauer, T. K., Foltz, P. W., & Laham, D. (1998). Introduction to latent semantic analysis. *Discourse Processes, 25,* 259–284.

McCombs, B. L. (1991). Motivation and lifelong learning. *Educational Psychologist, 26,* 117–127.

McCombs, B. L. (1994). Alternative perspectives for motivation. In L. Baker, P. Afflerback, & D. Reinking (Eds.), *Developing engaged readers in school and home communities* (pp. 67–87). Hillsdale, NJ: Lawrence Erlbaum Associates.

National Council of Teachers of Mathematics. (2000). *Principles and standards for school mathematics.* Reston, VA: Author.

National Research Council. (1996). *National science education standards.* Washington, DC: National Academy Press.

Novick, L. R., & Holyoak, K. J. (1991). Mathematical problem solving by analogy. *Journal of Experimental Psychology: Learning, Memory, and Cognition, 17*(3), 398–415.

Palincsar, A. S., & Brown, A. L. (1984). Reciprocal teaching of comprehension-fostering and comprehension monitoring activities. *Cognition and Instruction, 1,* 117–175.

Pea, R. D. (1993). Practices of distributed intelligence and designs for education. In G. Salomon (Ed.), *Distributed cognitions: Psychological and educational considerations* (pp. 47–87). New York: Cambridge University Press.

Pellegrino, J. W., Chudowsky, N., & Glaser, R. (2001). *Knowing what students know: The science and design of educational assessment.* Washington, DC: National Academy Press.

Pellegrino, J. W., Hickey, D., Heath, A., Rewey, K., Vye, N. J., & the Cognition and Technology Group at Vanderbilt. (1991). *Assessing the outcomes of an innovative instructional program: The*

1990–91 implementation of the "Adventures of Jasper Woodbury" (Tech. Rep. No. 91-1). Nashville, TN: Vanderbilt University, Learning Technology Center.

Resnick, L. B., & Klopfer, L. E. (Eds.). (1989). *Toward the thinking curriculum: Current cognitive research.* Alexandria, VA: Association for Supervision and Curriculum Development.

Salomon, G. (Ed.). (1993). *Distributed cognitions: Psychological and educational considerations.* New York: Cambridge University Press.

Scardamalia, M., & Bereiter, C. (1994). Computer support for knowledge-building communities. *Journal of the Learning Sciences, 3,* 265–283.

Scardamalia, M., Bereiter, C., & Lamon, M. (1994). The CSILE project: Trying to bring the classroom into world 3. In K. McGilly (Ed.), *Classroom lessons: Integrating cognitive theory and classroom practice* (pp. 201–228). Cambridge, MA: MIT Press.

Scarmadalia, M., Bereiter, C., & Steinbach, R. (1984). Teachability of reflective processes in written composition. *Cognitive Science, 8,* 173–190.

Schacter, J., & Fagnano, C. (1999). Does computer technology improve student learning and achievement? How, when, and under what conditions? *Journal of Educational Computing Research, 20,* 329–343.

Schneider, W., Dumais, S. T., & Shiffrin, R. M. (1984). Automatic and controlled processing and attention. In R. Parasuraman & D. R. Davies (Eds.), *Varieties of attention* (pp. 1–27). Orlando, FL: Academic Press.

Schneider, W., & Shiffrin, R. M. (1977). Controlled and automatic human information processing: Detection, search, and attention. *Psychological Review, 84,* 1–66.

Schoenfeld, A. H. (1983). Problem solving in the mathematics curriculum: A report, recommendation and annotated bibliography. *Mathematical Association of America Notes,* No. 1.

Schoenfeld, A. H. (1984). *Mathematical problem solving.* Orlando, FL: Academic Press.

Schoenfeld, A. H. (1991). On mathematics as sense making: An informal attack on the unfortunate divorce of formal and informal mathematics. In J. F. Voss, D. N. Perkins, & J. W. Segal (Eds.), *Informal reasoning and education* (pp. 331–343). Hillsdale, NJ: Lawrence Erlbaum Associates.

Schon, D. A. (1983). *The reflective practitioner: How professionals think in action.* New York: Basic Books.

Schon, D. A. (1988). Coaching reflective teaching. In P. P. Grimmett & G. L. Erickson (Eds.), *Reflection in education* (pp. 17–29). New York: Teachers College Press.

Schwartz, D. L., Brophy, S., Lin, X., & Bransford, J. D. (1999). Flexibly adaptive instructional design: A case study from an educational psychology course. *Educational Technology Research and Development, 47,* 39–59.

Schwartz, D. L., Lin, X., Brophy, S., & Bransford, J. D. (1999). Toward the development of flexibly adaptive instructional designs. In C. M. Reigeluth (Ed.), *Instructional design theories and models: Vol. 2. A new paradigm of instructional theory* (pp. 183–213). Mahwah, NJ: Lawrence Erlbaum Associates.

Secules, T., Cottom, C. D., Bray, M. H., Miller, L. D., & the Cognition and Technology Group at Vanderbilt. (1997). Schools for thought: Creating learning communities. *Educational Leadership, 54*(6), 56–60.

Sharp, D. L. M., Bransford, J. D., Goldman, S. R., Risko, V. J., Kinzer, C. K., & Vye, N. J. (1995). Dynamic visual support for story comprehension and mental model building by young, at-risk children. *Educational Technology Research and Development, 43,* 25–42.

Shepard, L. A. (2000, April). *The role of assessment in a learning culture.* Presidential address presented at the annual meeting of the American Educational Research Association, New Orleans, LA.

Sherwood, R. D., Petrosino, A. J., Lin, X., Lamon, M., & the Cognition and Technology Group at Vanderbilt. (1995). Problem-based macro contexts in science instruction: Theoretical basis, design issues, and the development of applications. In D. Lavoie (Ed.), *Towards a cog-*

nitive-science perspective for scientific problem solving. Manhattan, KS: National Association for Research in Science Teaching.

Stokes, D. R. (1997). *Pasteur's Quadrant: Basic science and technological innovation.* Washington, DC: Brookings Institution Press.

Suina, J. H., & Smolkin, L. B. (1994). From natal culture to school culture to dominant society culture: Supporting transitions for Pueblo Indian students. In P. M. Greenfield & R. R. Cocking (Eds.), *Cross-cultural roots of minority child development* (pp. 115–130). Hillsdale, NJ: Lawrence Erlbaum Associates.

Thorndike, E. L. (1913). *Educational psychology.* New York: Columbia University Press.

Vosniadou, S., & Brewer, W. F. (1989). *The concept of the earth's shape: A study of conceptual change in childhood.* Unpublished paper, Center for the Study of Reading, University of Illinois, Champaign.

Vye, N. J., Goldman, S. R., Voss, J. F., Hmelo, C., Williams, S., & the Cognition and Technology Group at Vanderbilt. (1997). Complex mathematical problem solving by individuals and dyads. *Cognition and Instruction, 15,* 435–484.

Vye, N. J., Schwartz, D. L., Bransford, J. D., Barron, B. J., Zech, L., & the Cognition and Technology Group at Vanderbilt. (1998). SMART environments that support monitoring, reflection, and revision. In D. Hacker, J. Dunlosky, & A. Graesser (Eds.), *Metacognition in educational theory and practice* (pp. 305–346). Mahwah, NJ: Lawrence Erlbaum Associates.

Vygotsky, L. S. (1962). *Thought and language.* Cambridge, MA: MIT Press.

Wenglinsky, H. (1998). *Does it compute? The relationship between educational technology and student achievement in mathematics.* Princeton, NJ: Educational Testing Service.

White, B. C., & Frederiksen, J. (1998). Inquiry, modeling, and metacognition: Making science accessible to all students. *Cognition and Instruction, 16*(1), 3–118.

Whitehead, A. N. (1929). *The aims of education.* New York: Macmillan.

Wood, S. S., Bruner, J. S., & Ross, G. (1976). The role of tutoring in problem solving. *Journal of Child Psychology and Psychiatry, 17,* 89–100.

Yackel, E., Cobb, P., & Wood, T. (1991). Small group interactions as a source of learning opportunities in second-grade mathematics. *Journal for Research in Mathematics Education, 22,* 390–408.

Zech, L., Vye, N., Bransford, J., Goldman, S., Barron, B., Schwartz, D., Hackett, R., Mayfield-Stewart, C., & the Cognition and Technology Group at Vanderbilt. (1998). An introduction to geometry through anchored instruction. In R. Lehrer & D. Chazan (Eds.), *New directions in teaching and learning geometry* (pp. 439–463). Mahwah, NJ: Lawrence Erlbaum Associates.

Zech, L., Vye, N. J., Bransford, J. D., Swink, J., Mayfield-Stewart, C., Goldman, S. R., & the Cognition and Technology Group at Vanderbilt. (1994). Bringing geometry into the classroom with videodisc technology. *Mathematics Teaching in the Middle School Journal (MTMS), 1*(3), 228–233.

Chapter 2

Model-Centered Learning Environments: Theory, Instructional Design, and Effects

Norbert M. Seel
Albert-Ludwigs-University of Freiburg, Germany

Schooling, especially in mathematics and science, has been criticized for decades. Actually, despite the increase of budgets, the implementation of new programs, the lengthening of school days and years, and the addition of new subjects and the deletion of others, the results of these efforts have been disappointing. Thus, with regard to mathematics education, Peterson (1988) criticized the elementary school mathematics curriculum "as based on the assumption that computational skills must be learned before children are taught to solve even simple word problems" (p. 7). The curriculum also reflects this sequence at the secondary level: Students generally take arithmetic, then algebra, then geometry, and it is common to view higher order objectives as more appropriate later in the sequence. Thus, proofs are expected in geometry but not in algebra, and mathematical reasoning is more appropriate in algebra than arithmetic. As students progress through the grades, only the more capable students are able to keep up with the academic mathematics curriculum, so that most fall away before they encounter higher order instructional objectives, such as mathematical problem solving. Raudenbush, Rowan, and Cheong (1993) pointed out that although current conceptions of learning encourage the pursuit of higher order objectives, many teachers lack adequate preparation for teaching higher order thinking, and, additionally, organizational conditions at schools often discourage the pursuit of higher order objectives. From the perspective of Raudenbush et al., the pervasive influence of behaviorism in curriculum and instruction provides a potential explanation for the link between academic tracks (especially of math and science education) and the pursuit of instructional objectives. Shepard (1991) demonstrated that behaviorist theories imply that students learn best when complex learning tasks are broken down into smaller parts that are learned sequentially. Only when the earlier, simple steps are mastered is the learner ready for more complex tasks requiring analysis, hypothesis testing, and evaluation.

An alternative conception, the approach of *model-centered learning and instruction*, is described in this chapter. This approach is based on theories of mental models (cf. Johnson-Laird, 1983; Seel, 1991) and focuses on *self-organized discovery learning*. Therefore, the learner has to search continuously for information in a learning environment in order to complete or stabilize a mental model that corresponds to an a priori understanding of the material to be learned. Discovery learning is guided by exploratory models designed with a specific endpoint in mind. Students explore these models by developing hypotheses and then varying input parameters to investigate how well their conjectures align with the models.

With regard to mathematics education, the National Council of Teachers of Mathematics (1994) has formulated the precept that the primary role of algebra at the school level should be to develop confidence and facility in using variables and functions to *model* numerical patterns and quantitative relationships. For science education, Schauble (1996) formulated such an approach in the following manner: "The goal of scientific reasoning is not primarily the formulation of inductive generalizations, but rather the *construction of explanatory models*, that . . . account for the observed phenomena" (p. 103). Lesh and Doerr (2000) argued that helping students to develop explanatory models in order to make sense of their experiences of light, gravity, electricity, and magnetism should be among the most important goals of science instruction; otherwise, students invent models of their own that are often incomplete and incorrect (cf. D. E. Brown & Clement, 1989). Clement and Steinberg (2002) described how conventional approaches to electricity instruction in physics start with electrostatics and quickly introduce the concept of "potential difference," which is defined mathematically. As the concept of electric potential generally remains unlearned when this instructional approach is implemented, Clement and Steinberg advocated the construction of a mental model that helps to develop a qualitative conception of electric potential, based on an analogy with pressure in compressed air that is compelling to most students, before introducing distant action and mathematical representation. Actually, students often do not (and cannot) develop appropriate symbol systems to make sense of mathematical entities such as directed quantities (negatives), multivalued quantities (vectors), ratios of quantities, changing or accumulating quantities, or locations in space (coordinates). However, they can invent significant mathematical solutions when confronted with the need to create meaningful models of real situations.

Model-centered learning and instruction is not simply an add-on activity to the curriculum. Rather, it involves a reformulation of the curriculum that gives primacy to students' constructions of content knowledge through an inquiry process of experimentation, simulation, and analysis (cf. Doerr, 1996). In the following sections of this chapter, several aspects of model-centered learning and instruction are discussed: The psychological foundations of model-centered learning are described, then important conclusions for instructional design are derived. Following this, research on model-centered instruction is summarized, and, finally, problems of the assessment of mental models are described.

THE PSYCHOLOGY AND EPISTEMOLOGY
OF MODEL-CENTERED LEARNING

Model-centered learning is both a new and old paradigm of psychology and education (see, e.g., Chapanis, 1961; Karplus, 1969). According to the paradigm of social *model learning*, developed in accordance with Bandura (1971), behavioral changes can also occur when a person is not engaged directly in a learning process but rather merely observing the behavior of another person. Similarly, in several instructional conceptions, such as the cognitive apprenticeship approach of Collins, Brown, and Newman (1989), learning is situated in the observation of an expert's problem-solving behavior.

Actually, model-centered learning is an important kind of cognitive learning and focuses "on the symbolic activities that human beings employed in constructing and in making sense not only of the world, but of themselves" (Bruner, 1990, p. 2). Cognitive psychology is concerned with the construction of symbolic models of information processing, understood here as the capacity of the human mind to construct knowledge, to interpret the world, and to reason in a deductive or inductive manner (Seel, 2000). Cognitive learning occurs when people actively construct meaningful representations, such as coherent *mental models*, that represent and communicate subjective experiences, ideas, thoughts, and feelings (cf. Mayer, Moreno, Boire, & Vagge, 1999). By means of mental representations, an individual is able to simulate real actions in imagination. However, several authors, such as Brewer (1987) and Rips (1987), have criticized the lack of conceptual differentiation between mental models and schemas.

The notion of a *schema* is one of the central concepts of modern cognitive psychology and is common to the work of Kant, Bartlett, Piaget, Abelson, Norman, and others. In the terms of Piaget (1943), a schema of an action is defined as the structured totality of the characteristics of this action that may be generalized, that is, of those characteristics that allow one to repeat the same action and apply it to new contexts. For some cognitive theorists (e.g., Rumelhart, 1980), schemas are the basic building blocks of the psychological understanding of cognition. Mandl, Friedrich, and Hron (1988) defined them as cognitive structures that represent general knowledge in memory. Schemas (or frames and scripts) are understood as generic data structures that play a central role in the interpretation of perceptions, the regulation of behavior, and the storage of knowledge in memory. However, according to Rumelhart, Smolensky, McClelland, and Hinton (1986) there is no representational object in the mind that *is* a schema. Rather, a schema emerges at the moment it is needed from the interaction of many simpler elements all working in concert with one another in order to interpret the given environment as well as to assimilate new information into existing knowledge structures. The fundamental mechanism for this process is *pattern matching*. It enables individuals to quickly "settle" on an interpretation of an input pattern.

Schemas constitute the fundamental basis for the construction of models of the world. Such models can be understood as "tools" of accommodation (Seel, 1991). Incidentally, Rumelhart et al. (1986) divided the cognitive system into two modules or sets of units. One part—called an *interpretation network*—is concerned with the activation of schemas, the other one is concerned with constructing a "model of the world." It takes as input some specification of the actions we intend to carry out and produces an interpretation of "what would happen if we did that." Part of this specification could be a specification of what the new stimulus conditions would be like (appearance modeling). Thus, the interpretation network (i.e., a schema) takes input from the world (to be explained) and produces relevant reactions, whereas the second module, that is, the constructed "model" of the world, predicts how the input would change in response to these reactions. In the literature it is common to talk about a *mental model* that would be expected to be operating in any case, insofar as it is generating expectations about the state of the world and thereby "predicting" internally the outcomes of possible actions. However, it is not necessary that world events have happened. In case they have, the cognitive system replaces the stimulus inputs from the world with inputs from the mental model. This means that a "mental simulation runs" envisioning in the imagination the events that would take place in the world if a particular action were to be performed. Thus, mental models allow one to perform actions entirely internally and to judge the consequences of actions, interpret them, and draw appropriate conclusions.

This theoretical conception by Rumelhart et al. (1986) corresponds with the theory of mental models that emerged in the 1980s to capture (deductive and inductive) reasoning by "settling" computations of the human mind in a solution rather than applying logical operations (Johnson-Laird, 1983). More generally, it has been argued that comprehension and reasoning in specific situations (e.g., in schools and real-life situations) necessarily involves the use of mental models of different qualities in order to understand the world (Greeno, 1989). Accordingly, the theory of mental models has been applied successfully in different domains such as human–computer interaction (Ackermann & Tauber, 1990), text and discourse processing (Rickheit & Habel, 1999), the operation of complex (technical) systems (Kluwe & Haider, 1990), and so on.

> Mental models play a central and unifying role in representing objects, states of affairs, sequences of events, the way the world is, and the social and psychological actions of daily life. They enable individuals to make inferences and predictions, to understand phenomena, to decide what action to take and to control its execution, and, above all, to experience events by proxy. (Johnson-Laird, 1983, p. 397)

The theory of mental models is based on the assumption that an individual who intends to give a rational explanation for something must develop practicable methods in order to generate appropriate explanations on the basis of principally restricted domain-specific knowledge and a limited information-processing capacity. Therefore, the individual constructs a model that both integrates the relevant domain-specific knowledge and meets the requirements of the phenomenon to be explained—then the model works. Mental models are higher order constructions of the mind insofar as they presuppose bits of knowledge that are integrated step by step into a model of the world in order to explain a specific phenomenon. They represent the structure of the world because they are generated to structure it and not to reproduce or copy a given external structure. In sum, mental models *represent* the subject's knowledge in such a way that even complex phenomena become plausible.

It is interesting that this argumentation largely corresponds with the model theory of semantics (Stachowiak, 1973; Wartofsky, 1979), which focuses on the construction of models and their thoughtful use in various fields of interest. Coming from semantics, Chapanis (1961) classified models into *reproduction models* (i.e., material-semantic models) and *symbolic models.* The former may consist of physical objects or diagrams that serve the purpose of communication (e.g., in the context of instruction), whereas the latter serve the purpose of *mental representation* of knowledge. Reproduction models are to be considered as external models that serve the purpose of communication, and this presupposes an externalization of corresponding mental models. External models, on the other side, can be internalized to mental models, which will be discussed further on.

From both a psychological and epistemological point of view, models are constructed in accordance with specific intentions of the model-building person. Models are always representations of something; they represent natural or artificial objects, so-called originals, which can be again models of something. Accordingly, talking about models implies, first of all, asking for the original to be modeled. Every model is constructed in accordance with specific intentions in order to simplify its original in many respects. From a formal point of semantics this can be illustrated as in Fig. 2.1. Here, modeling is defined as a homomorphism $\Phi: O \rightarrow M$ with

O $= (O, R_i^O, f_j^O, c)$, that is, a structure with the individuals O, relations R_i, specific functions f_j, and constant factors c;

M $= (M, R_i^M, f_j^M, c)$, that is, a structure with the individuals M, relations R_i, specific functions f_j, and constant factors c.

Modeling corresponds to the function Φ with

(a) $(R_i^O(o_1, \ldots, o_n) \supset R_i^M(\Phi(o_1), \ldots, \Phi(o_n))$ for $i \in I$, and
(b) $(f_j^O(o) = o' \supset f_j^M(\Phi(o)) = \Phi(o')$ for all $j \in J$.

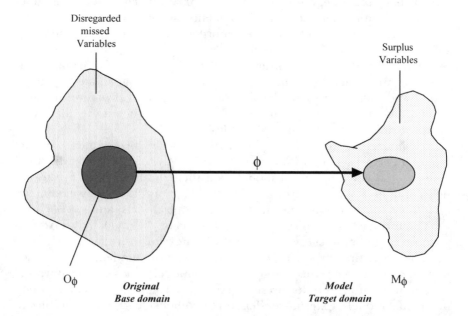

FIG. 2.1.   Model building as a structure-mapping function.

Φ is a homomorphism insofar as it does not imply that Φ must be defined with regard to all elements of O but rather only to particular elements. Accordingly, M contains fewer elements and substructures than O.

To illustrate this, one can refer to globes, which are models of the earth. Naturally, a particular globe is not a reduced earth, but rather it is supposed to give answers to questions concerning the locations of different places or distances between places. However, with regard to the chemical composition of the earth, a globe is not relevant. Other examples to demonstrate the different features of modeling of mapping, reduction, and pragmatics can be taken from the field of physics, such as Rutherford's atomic model or Newton's models of gravitation.

The functionality of a model is defined exclusively on the basis of the intentions of the model-building person. Therefore, in sciences the term *model* is generally used to serve different functions:

1. Models aid in the *simplification* of an investigation to particular and relevant phenomena in a closed domain.

2. Models aid in the *envisioning* (or visualization) of a structure and its relationships.

3. Models aid in the *construction of analogies* that help to identify the structure of an unknown domain with the help of the structure of a known domain. In this way a well-known explanation (e.g., Rutherford's atomic model) can be mapped onto a phenomenon to be explained (e.g., quantum mechanisms). Such models are called *analogy models*. Here, the aspect of envisioning is not applied or is relegated to the background.

4. Finally, models may aid the *simulation* of a system's processes. This occurs when an individual interacts with the objects involved in a situation in order to manipulate them mentally in such a way that the cognitive operations simulate specific transformations of these objects that may occur in real-life situations. These *simulation models* operate as thought experiments that produce qualitative inferences with respect to the situation to be mastered (cf. Greeno, 1989).

Up to now, the emphasis has been on mental models and external models, but an analysis of the literature indicates that a distinction is often made between mental models and conceptual models (Norman, 1983). But, what is a "conceptual model"? To give an answer to this question it is useful to refer to Kluwe and Haider (1990), who distinguished between different semantic models with which instructional psychology currently works. Kluwe and Haider start with a more or less complex system S of the physical world to be understood or explained. To explain this particular system S, individuals develop distinctive internal representations, which are called *mental models* of the system, MM(S) for short. They represent the individuals' distributed knowledge with regard to the system S. Based on their own mental models, scientists develop *conceptual models*, CM(S), which represent the shared knowledge of a discipline with regard to the system to be explained. For their part, cognitive psychologists develop *psychological models* of the construction of mental models: PM[MM(S)]. In addition, from an instructional point of view, so-called *design and instructional models*, DIM[CM(S)], are of special interest. They are instruction-oriented descriptions of the conceptual models of the system that are used for the construction of interfaces (e.g., programmed communications about learning tasks, manuals, and training) and aid in guiding the learners' construction of mental models.

In the following section, the focus is on instruction that helps students to develop adequate mental models in various educational sectors, such as mathematics and physics education.

MODEL-CENTERED LEARNING AND INSTRUCTION

The question of how one can influence model-building activities of learners through instruction has long been at the core of various educational approaches (see, e.g., Karplus, 1969), and in the field of research on mental models we can find a strong pedagogical impetus from the very beginning (Anzai & Yokoyama, 1984; Norman, 1983). Johnson-Laird (1989) formulated his pedagogical verdict as follows: "What is at issue is how such models develop as an individual progresses from novice to expert, and whether there is any pedagogical advantage in providing people with models of tasks they are trying to learn" (p. 489).

Rumelhart et al. (1986) pointed out that people are not only good at pattern matching (by means of schema activation) but also at modeling their world and manipulating their environment. Actually, the feature of modeling as a central manner of creating expectations by *internalizing* experiences is just as crucial to learning as the skill of manipulating the environment, because it allows us to reduce very complex problems to simpler ones. From an instructional point of view, the suggestion has been made (Norman, 1983) that mental models are constructed from the significant properties of external situations, such as designed learning environments and the subject's interactions with them. According to this view, the external environment becomes a key extension of the human mind and its processing is *real* symbol processing that people are capable of. Actually, imagination is highly dependent on our experiences with external representations, which therefore play a crucial role in thought and its communication. The idea that people learn and think on the basis of mental models resulting from the *internalization of external representations* is especially relevant for instruction insofar as external representations provide the means to influence the learners´ construction of mental models.

Accordingly, Johnson-Laird (1989) identified three different sources for constructing mental models: (a) the learner's ability to construct models in an inductive manner, either from a set of basic components of world knowledge or from analogous models that the learner already possesses; (b) everyday observations of the outside world; and (c) other people's explanations (see also Gibbons, 2002). This differentiation corresponds to different general paradigms of instruction, such as self-organized discovery and exploratory learning, externally guided discovery learning, and learning oriented toward an expert's behavior or a teacher's explanation.

Actually, instructional programs can present clearly defined concepts followed by clear examples. A designed conceptual model may be presented ahead of the learning tasks in order to direct the learner's comprehension of the learning material. On the other hand, there might exist environments that can initiate free explorations by invention, but in instructional contexts we regularly operate with well-prepared and designed learning environments that constrain the student's learning processes to various extents. This paradigm of model-centered instruction is concerned with the learning-dependent progression of mental models, defined as a specific kind of transition between preconceptions (i.e., the initial states of the learning process) and causal explanations (i.e., the desired end states of learning) (Seel, Al-Diban, & Blumschein, 2000).

According to Carlson (1991), instruction can be designed to involve the learner in an inquiry process in which facts are gathered from data sources, similarities and differences among facts noted, and concepts developed. In this process, the instructional program serves as a facilitator of learning for students who are working to develop their own answers to questions (cf. Penner, 2001). The learner has to search continuously for information in a given learning environment in order to complete or stabilize an initial mental model that corresponds to an a priori understanding of the material to be learned. The goal of instruction is to create microworlds in which objects follow specific sets of rules. One example is a microworld in which balls fall in accordance with Newton's laws of motion (cf. White, 1993). Students explore this model by developing hypotheses and then varying input parameters to investigate how well their conjectures align with the model. In mathematics education, the defining characteristic of this kind of discovery learning is that students explore conventional mathematical symbolizations in experientially real settings. Kaput (1994) suggested that one might facilitate this kind of learning by supporting the students' efforts to explore the linkages between the mathematical symbolizations and their own experiences and to generate new hypotheses. Moreover, he argued that "as the model develops . . . the mental model based in the mathematical representations comes to relate more directly to conceptualizations of the setting" (p. 390).

With regard to the various settings of self-guided discovery learning, Doerr (1996) stated that students develop *expressive models* to explain phenomena using a variety of tools. Here, students invent models on their own that express their developing interpretations of the phenomena in question. Doerr determined that this model-building approach begins with students' informal understanding and progressively builds on it. Self-guided learning occurs as a multistep process of model building and revision (Penner, 2001). Johnson-Laird (1983) conceived this process as a "fleshing out" procedure, which can be understood as a *reductio ad absurdum* that continuously examines whether a model can be replaced with an alternative model or not (Seel, 1991). Self-guided discovery learning is a very ambitious process that even an expert might sweat over sometimes. It requires from the learner sophisticated problem-solving skills as well as metacognitive competencies. Novices, therefore, often lapse back into trial-and-error instead of achieving deep understanding. Thus, Briggs (1990) demonstrated in a case study that an instructional strategy aiming at discovery learning may dramatically increase the probability of stabilizing faulty initial mental models. Consequently, a substantial conceptual change does not take place, and relatively stable intermediate states of causal understanding often precede the conceptual mastery intended by instruction.

If teachers intend to initiate model-centered learning they have to take into consideration the preconceptions with which learners enter a given learning environment and their motivation to engage in learning. Furthermore, they also have to take into consideration the quality of the learning material and the information which must be understandable, coherent, plausible, and so on in order to persuade the students to engage in the learning environment. Actually, the learners' preconceptions and motivational states as well as the quality of the learning materials strongly influence the patterns of participation and persuasion (Dole & Sinatra, 1998), understood here as central factors of effective model-centered instruction. By combining these factors with the theoretical framework of model-based learning and instruction developed by Buckley and Boulter (1999), one may depict the interplay between model-centered learning and instruction as follows.

Model-based teaching focuses on the patterns of participation, persuasion, and model building that individuals follow in the classroom to construct their understanding of some phenomenon. This is accomplished mainly through discourse with and about external representations provided and guided by the teacher, who facilitates negotiation between the discourse participants—including those not present, such as the scientists who developed the conceptual models in the domain and the instructional designers who developed the materials and activities to facilitate the learners' understanding of the phenomenon. *Model-based learning* focuses on individuals' construction of mental models of the phenomenon under study. During the course of this process, learners form an initial model of the phenomenon, either intentionally to meet some learning goal or spontaneously in response to some task. If the model is used successfully, it is reinforced and may eventually become a stable model. If it turns out that the model is unsatisfactory, it may be revised or rejected in a progression of mental models.

RESEARCH ON MODEL-CENTERED LEARNING AND INSTRUCTION

Research on model-centered learning and instruction generally follows one of two approaches, emphasizing either the *internalization of conceptual models* the students are provided with in the course of learning or the *use of devices for discovery learning.*

Research on Providing Students With Conceptual Models

The history of mental-model research in the field of instruction indicates a clear predominance of studies aiming at learning explicitly directed by a teacher or an instructional program. Mayer (1989) expressed the pedagogical idea of this approach, commenting that "students given model-instruction may be more likely to build mental models of the systems they are studying and to use these models to generate creative solutions to transfer problems" (p. 47). Accordingly, the learners are provided with a *conceptual model* that illustrates the main components and relations of a complex system. In accordance with Mayer's (1989) definition of a conceptual model "as words and/or diagrams that are intended to help learners build mental models of the system being studied" (p. 43), many educators and researchers are convinced of the influence of graphical diagrams or even of "helpful video" on the construction of mental models. They consider these instructional media to be effective tools for creating dynamic images that constitute the frame of reference for the construction of mental models (see, e.g., Hegarty & Just, 1993; Schnotz & Kulhavy, 1994; Sharp et al., 1995). However, this presupposes that the learner is sensitive to characteristics of the learning environment, such as the availability of certain information at a given time, the way the information is structured and mediated, and the ease with which it can be found in the environment (Seel, 2000).

It has been argued that it is often easier for a novice learner to assimilate an explanation (provided through a conceptual model) than to induce one independently. In this case, the conceptual model provided will be incorporated into the thinking process functionally, and related information can be progressively integrated in a more or less consistent manner to achieve substantial conceptual changes. Meanwhile, there are numerous studies that have demonstrated that the presentation of a conceptual model actually affects the construction of a task-related mental model, depending on the stage in the learning process at which a conceptual model is presented (Mayer, 1989; Seel, 1995; Seel & Dinter, 1995). However, more recent investigations (Al-Diban & Seel, 1999; Seel et al., 2000) indicated that the subjects exhibited only a minor tendency to adopt the conceptual models they were provided with in an instructional program, preferring instead to extract information from the learning environment in order to construct their own explanatory models. These models displayed only minor similarities with the provided conceptual models. Thus, mental models are not fixed structures of the mind, but rather constructed "just in time" when needed. Therefore, it can be assumed that learners construct idiosyncratic mental models if no other preconceptions are available (for more details, see Seel, 2001).

The early research on mental models has been critized by several authors (e.g., Royer, Cisero, & Carlo, 1993; Snow, 1990) because it has typically been performed piecemeal, in small-scale, specialized contexts. In order to overcome these shortcomings of experimental research, Seel et al. (2000) looked for a more comprehensive instructional approach as a fundamental basis for initiating and directing model-centered learning. Three main topics were investigated (see Al-Diban & Seel, 1999; Seel & Schenk, 2002): (a) the investigation of the learning-dependent progression of mental models in the course of a comprehensive instructional program; (b) how this progression can be guided by way of a particular instructional intervention designed as a multimedia environment in accordance with principles of the cognitive apprenticeship approach; and (c) how to assess mental models and their learning-dependent progression as influenced by model-centered instruction.

In the cognitive apprenticeship approach of Collins et al. (1989), students are provided with an expert's conceptual model. Collins et al. postulated 18 features belonging to four broad dimensions, namely *content, methods, sequencing,* and the *sociology of teaching,* to build effective learning environments. Seel et al. (2000) investigated the *methods* (modeling, coaching, scaffolding, articulation, reflection, and exploration) in the proposed sequence within a multimedia learning environment. In modeling, an expert demonstrates a problem's solution, and the students acquire a conceptual model of this process by observing the expert's approach. In coaching, the students are supervised and given guidance as they try to find solutions to a given task in an adaptive manner. In scaffolding, a special problem-solving heuristics (analogical reasoning) is taught. Articulation and reflection have been realized in the form of a "teach back" procedure (Jih & Reeves, 1992) in a social learning situation. Finally, in exploration, the learners have to solve two transfer tasks (cf. Seel et al., 2000; Seel & Schenk, 2002). These methods are summarized in Fig. 2.2.

In five replication studies with 17-year-old students, Seel et al. (2000) studied (a) the effects of providing a conceptual model at the beginning of the learning process on the construction of a corresponding mental model, and (b) the long-term effectiveness of the multimedia learning program on both the acquired domain-specific knowledge and the stability of the initially constructed mental models. One of the main conclusions of the formative evaluation is that the cognitive apprenticeship approach might be an appropriate framework for the instructional design of environments that focus on instructionally guided model-centered learning. These results correspond with empirical results of other studies (Casey, 1996; Chee, 1995). Taken together, these studies agree that the learners who accomplish the learning tasks of coaching come out on top. This method, which aims at controlled, *content-oriented learning*, encourages the learners to imitate the expert model they are provided with in modeling. Successful learners made fewer mistakes in task solutions and applied adequately the knowledge acquired in coaching.

Research on Model-Centered Discovery Learning

Since the 1990s a new movement in instructional research has been concerned with the investigation of the construction of models as a means of discovery and exploratory learning (cf. Penner, 2001). Sometimes this re-

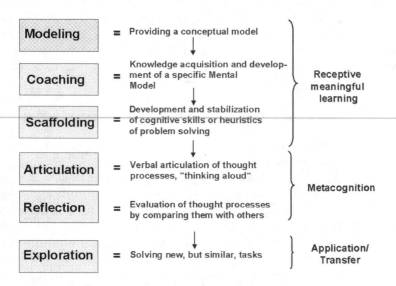

FIG. 2.2. The methods of cognitive apprenticeship implemented in the instructional intervention of Seel et al. (2000).

search is associated with the notion of "Learning by Design" (see Kolodner et al., chap. 4, this volume), which is based on the idea that students make a sketch or model of an object, such as "designing the elbow" (Penner, Giles, Lehrer, & Schauble, 1997). This partially corresponds with studies in the field of mental-model research in which students were asked to produce diagrams or three-dimensional models of phenomena to be explained (May, 1991; McCloskey, Caramazza, & Green, 1980). However, there are some differences between these lines of research: First, approaches of learning by design regularly do not refer to the theory of mental models but rather are integrated into the field of instructional investigations, with an emphasis on the curriculum of different subjects, such as mathematics and science. Second, whereas the instructional research on mental models is strongly associated with the *internalization* of conceptual models, this approach emphasizes the *externalization* of mental models by means of diagrams and conversation. Instead of showing students models designed by others, many modeling initiatives support students in constructing their own models (Jackson, Stratford, Krajcik, & Soloway, 1994; Penner, Lehrer, & Schauble, 1998). During this process, a *conversation* unfolds in which spirited interaction occurs among students, between students and the teacher, and among students, their model, and the materials they work with as they attempt to create meaning through and from their constructions. This conversation guides the students in the evaluation of their methodologies (*how they construct models*), their justifications (*does a model reflect the real system adequately?*), and their perceptions (*did they recognize the true problem under study?*). Students move beyond the simple discovery of facts and become involved in a reciprocal action in which they develop, test, and revise models as a means to promote deep understanding. Actually, such "modeling is seldom a one-shot process; rather, model testing and evaluation are most often followed by model revision" (Penner et al., 1998, p. 433).

A third characteristic of these inquiry-oriented approaches of model-centered learning and instruction is an emphasis on collaborative learning as well as on epistemic discourse and argumentation. However, to date only a few studies have investigated the quality of epistemic discourse of students and its effects on the deep understanding of problems. A. L. Brown and Kane (1988) and Coleman (1998) found that successful learners make an *explanation-seeking effort.* However, it remains unclear whether and to what degree argumentation is associated with an improvement of conceptual knowledge and understanding. Other studies (King, 1990; King & Rosenshine, 1993) demonstrated that students do not spontaneously generate effective explanations. That is, reflection does not occur automatically. Rather, it presupposes the thoughtful design of an intervention that requires to apply explanations demonstrating the comprehension of phenomena.

A strong implication of inquiry-oriented approaches of model building is their emphasis on the curriculum of different subjects, such as mathematics and physics education. Stewart, Hafner, Johnson, and Finkel (1992) delineated the central idea of these approaches, commenting that "a science education should do more than instruct students with respect to the conclusions reached by scientists; it should also encourage students to develop insights about science as an intellectual activity" (p. 318). Accordingly, advocates of this approach argue that "given that we wish to involve students in the practices of scientists, we focus primarily on model building" (Penner et al., 1998, p. 430). Indeed, in physics education some of the most important goals of instruction are helping students develop powerful models so that they can make sense of their experiences involving light, gravity, electricity, and magnetism; it has also become evident that young students invent models of their own and that changing students' ways of thinking must involve challenging and testing these models.

A similar argumentation can be found with regard to the learning of mathematics. Several authors, such as Hodgson (1995) and Lesh and Doerr (2000), understand mathematics as a particular form of modeling, as the development of mathematical descriptions and explanations usually involves the use of specialized languages, symbols, graphs, pictures, concrete materials, and other notational systems. This obviously constitutes a heavy demand on learners' representational capabilities. Accordingly, Lesh and Doerr (2000) discussed models that students should develop to produce mathematical descriptions or explanations of systems of the physical world. Helping students to develop powerful models should be among the most important goals of science and mathematics instruction. When confronted with the need to create meaningful models of experientially real situations, students can invent significant mathematical solutions on the basis of model constructions.

An analysis of the literature shows good examples of the model-centered approach, but unfortunately there is a considerable lack of empirical research including quantitative data that could be interpreted in accordance with the theoretical assumptions in the literature. This leads to the next section of this chapter, which focuses on the third corner of the curriculum–instruction–assessment triad.

ASSESSMENT OF MENTAL MODELS AND RELATED LEARNING ACTIVITIES

According to Pellegrino (chap. 1, this volume), assessment is a necessary component of instruction, insofar as it *provides opportunities for feedback, revision, and reflection on learning*. It includes formal methods of testing, such as large-scale state assessments, or less formal classroom-based procedures, such as quizzes, class projects, and teacher questioning. Accordingly, cognitive science as well as instructional research have at their disposal a remarkably wide and varied pool of methods to assess knowledge and cognitive artifacts, such as mental models, that range from naturalistic observation to computer simulation, from traditional experimental methods to performing linguistic analyses, from recording electrical impulses of the brain to collecting reaction times or verbal protocols (cf. Seel, 1999). Thus, a review of the related literature reveals some standard methods for the assessment of mental models, such as (a) experimental methods based on the systematic observation of learners' overt behavior when dealing with learning tasks; (b) protocol analysis including verbal reports, "think-aloud" data, and content analysis; and (c) computer modeling and simulation.

In the following subsections, three examples of the assessment of mental models in instructional settings are discussed: (a) causal diagrams, (b) analysis of model-building behavior, and (c) "teach back" procedures involving epistemic dialogue.

Causal Diagrams

The idea of causal diagrams goes back to Funke (1985) and has been applied successfully by Seel and colleagues (Al-Diban, 2002; Seel et al., 2000) to assess the learning-dependent progression of analogy models of economics. A causal diagram is a technique that demands of the learners that they externalize their mental models by actively spreading a causal structure on the table. Figure 2.3 shows two examples of causal diagrams constructed by the same subject at two different measurement points in the course of the instructional program.

The investigations of Al-Diban (2002), Seel (1999), and Seel et al. (2000) indicate that causal diagrams are reliable and valid methods of measuring learners' subjective assumptions about the causality of a dynamic system as well as of appropriate external representations of the learners' mental models of that system. The results of various replication studies reported by Seel et al. (2000) support the assumption that the causal diagrams constructed at different times of measurement are representations of the mental models the subjects have constructed in the current test situation. Actually, the subjects' causal diagrams turned out to vary according to the different demands of these situations (for more details, see Seel, 2001). The assessment studies on the learning-dependent progression of mental models support the argument that model building produces not a single correct solution but rather there are often several competing models, each of which may represent a particular aspect of the situation. This observation

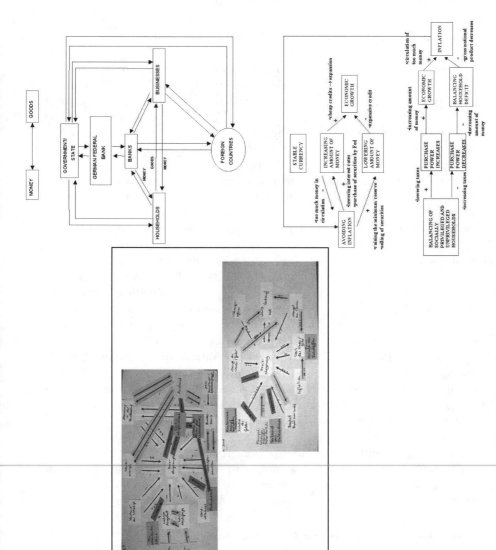

FIG. 2.3. Examples of causal diagrams (Seel et al., 2000).

65

corresponds with Hodgson's (1995) argumentation concerning the assessment of modeling in the field of mathematics education.

Analysis and Categorization of Model-Building Behavior

Hodgson (1995) argued that each model constructed by a learner is correct insofar as it allows the model builder to apply, for example, mathematics in order to investigate a given situation in the physical world. The correctness of these models must be evaluated with regard to the objectives of the model-constructing individual. The starting point is the construction of a simplified version of the initial problem situation, then a mental model of that simplified version is constructed and applied to solve the problem. The next step consists of the interpretation of the various solutions with regard to the simplified problem situation, and, finally, it is verified that the solutions produced are also solutions for the initial situation.

Hodgson (1995) argued that due to the nature of model building in mathematics—the complexity of its process and the relative value of a model—one must apply alternative assessment procedures, such as *qualitative scales,* to classify students' observable behavior for each component of the model-building process. He distinguished between different dimensions of model building: *simplification, mathematizing* (i.e., the construction of a mathematical model), *transformation* (i.e., the application of the mathematical model), and *validation* of the model. Each dimension is characterized by four different levels. For example, simplification contains the following levels: At the first level, the student does not understand the problem situation and is not able to construct a meaningful simplified version of the situation. At the second level, the student comprehends the problem situation but is not able to take into consideration the influence of one or more essential components. At the third level, the student demonstrates an understanding of the problem situation and is able to take into consideration all relevant components of the problem. And at the fourth level, the student is able to address features of the situation, indicating that he or she has a deep understanding of the problem situation.

"Teach Back" Procedures and Epistemic Dialogues

Jih and Reeves (1992) and Sasse (1991) suggested assessing mental models by means of a "teach back" procedure as an epistemic discourse in which a student communicates an *explanation model* to another student. This procedure is a form of the *epistemic discourse.* It is characterized by several components, such as description, explanation, prognosis, and argumentation (Ohlsson, 1995). To explain something implies externalizing, clarifying, organizing, and restructuring one's own knowledge. Thereby, one can experience deficiencies in knowledge as well as the necessity of searching for more information. In the case that the communication partner does not understand the explanation given, the explaining person can try to create comprehension by means of familiar words, examples, or prior knowledge about similar tasks. According to de Vries, Lund, and Baker (2002), this kind of epistemic discourse is especially characterized by *argumentation* that involves a reconstruction of new arguments as well as the search for new and more convincing arguments in a given learning and communication environment. De Vries et al. developed a particular schema for the analysis of dialogues that contains four main categories, of which *explanation* and *argumentation* are especially important for the communication of mental models. Explanation includes the subcategories "explicate" and "understand," whereas argumentation is divided into the units "thesis," "attack," "defense," "concession," "compromise," and "outcome" (for more details, see de Vries et al., 2002). In a further step, the resulting qualitative data could be analyzed by means of specific techniques, such as AQUAD 5 (Huber, 2000 [http://www.aquad.de]), which is a software program for the fine-grained analysis of qualitative data.

INSTRUCTIONAL DESIGN OF MODEL-CENTERED LEARNING ENVIRONMENTS

Successful model-centered instruction presupposes effective learning environments to be designed in accordance with two different conceptions: First, there is a goal-oriented design of learning environments that has to be done by instructional designers and aims at the internalization of conceptual models the students are provided with. Second, there is an approach of "learning by design," which emphasizes the construction and revision of models by the students in the course of discovery.

In accordance with Dörner's (1976) distinction between epistemic and heuristic structures of knowledge to be constructed in learning, the design of model-centered instruction can be distinguished correspondingly.

Design of Model-Centered Instruction Aiming at Epistemic Knowledge

The events of instruction, which are the structures we design, serve human learning processes under the ultimate control of the individual. Instruction, therefore, does not *cause* learning but *supports* learning intentions the learner commits. . . . Some of these processes (such as the initial processing of visual or auditory information) are involuntary, but many of them (focusing attention, finding and selecting associations, etc.) are completely voluntary. (Gibbons, 2002, p. 3)

In accordance with this precept, Gibbons formulated seven principles of model-centered instruction, such as "experience" (i.e., learners should be given maximum opportunity to interact with one or more self-constructed models of systems for learning purposes), problem solving, goal orientation, resourcing, and instructional augmentation. These principles are to be considered as a fundamental basis for the instructional design of effective learning environments.

Evidently, most approaches of expository teaching, such as the cognitive apprenticeship approach or, more specifically for math education, Schoenfeld's (1985) approach and Gravemeijer's (Gravemeijer, Cobb, Bowers, & Whitenack, 2000) approach, correspond with these principles. So, for example, one of the most challenging aspects of Gravemeijer's approach is finding problem situations that might support progressive mathematization. An important heuristic method for instructional design focuses on the role that *emergent models* play in individual students' learning and in the collective mathematical development of the classroom community. The notion of emergent models encompasses some aspects of the exploratory approach in that both aim to make it possible for students to use conventional symbolizations in powerful ways, and the emergence of taken-as-shared models involves both the judicious selection of instructional activities and the negotiation of the ways of symbolizing that students create as they participate in communities of practice. In this process, the teacher attempts to achieve the instructional agenda by capitalizing on students' contributions and by introducing ways of symbolizing that fit with their reasoning. Students are still encouraged to develop their own models, but they do so in situations that are chosen to support the realization of a proposed learning trajectory. It is possible for the designer to lay out a proposed developmental route for the classroom community in which students first model situations in an informal way (this is called a *model of the situation*) and then mathematize their informal modeling activity (this produces a *model for reasoning*; see Sfard, 1991).

Design-Based Modeling Aiming
at Heuristic Structures of Knowledge

This movement of instructional research is closely related to the idea of model-based discovery learning. Bhatta and Goel (1997) developed an interesting approach of "Integrated Design by Analogy and Learning (IDEAL)" within a theory of adaptive design. Similarly, Smith and Unger (1997) emphasized *conceptual bootstrapping* as a conception of analogy-based learning and problem solving. Both approaches are based on the assumption that new designs are created by learners through the retrieval of and adaptation to known designs in order to achieve competence of transfer between more complex domains. Bhatta and Goel discussed *task-guided learning*, which is dependent on the specific learning tasks and related domain-specific prior knowledge. Accordingly, the instructional design of learning tasks are at the core of IDEAL, which has as its goal the construction of device designs (in the fields of electrics, electronics, and heat exchangers). Bhatta and Goel argued that designing a device implies constructing a model of how the device should operate, that is, how its structure may serve the desired functions. They assumed that the model necessarily presupposes (a) knowledge about the functions, causal relations, and structure of the design, as well as (b) knowledge about the composition of the functions and the structure. Learners should carry out model- and similarity-based learning related to retrievable knowledge (about primitive functions within the known domain).

Another approach of device- and design-based modeling was developed by Erickson and Lehrer (1998). They distinguished between the design components *planning, transforming, evaluation*, and *revision*. Each of these components involves various model-building activities. For example, planning includes defining the nature of the problem (asking questions) and project management (e.g., composition of the learning group, decision making concerning tasks and roles), whereas transforming consists of information search, information extraction, organization, and so on. It is easy to find several realizations of this approach in the work of Lehrer and Schauble.

REFERENCES

Ackermann, D., & Tauber, M. J. (Eds.). (1990). *Mental models and human–computer interaction 1*. Amsterdam: Elsevier.

Al-Diban, S. (2002). *Diagnose mentaler Modelle* [Diagnosis of mental models]. Hamburg, Germany: Kovac.

Al-Diban, S., & Seel, N. M. (1999). Evaluation als Forschungsaufgabe von Instruktionsdesign—Dargestellt am Beispiel eines multimedialen Lehrprogramms [Evaluation as a research task of instructional design—exemplified by the example of a multimedia learning program]. *Unterrichtswissenschaft, 27*(1), 29–60.

Anzai, Y., & Yokoyama, T. (1984). Internal models in physics problem solving. *Cognition and Instruction, 1*, 397–450.

Bandura, A. (1971). *Social learning theory.* New York: General Learning Press.

Bhatta, S. R., & Goel, A. (1997). Learning generic mechanisms for innovative strategies in adaptive design. *Journal of the Learning Sciences, 6*(4), 367–396.

Brewer, W. F. (1987). Schemas versus mental models in human memory. In P. Morris (Ed.), *Modelling cognition* (pp. 187–197). Chichester, England: Wiley.

Briggs, P. (1990). The role of the user model in learning as an internally and externally directed activity. In D. Ackermann & M. J. Tauber (Eds.), *Mental models and human–computer interaction 1* (pp. 195–208). Amsterdam: Elsevier.

Brown, A. L., & Kane, M. J. (1988). Preschool children can learn to transfer: Learning to learn and learning from example. *Cognitive Psychology, 20*(4), 493–523.

Brown, D. E., & Clement, J. (1989). Overcoming misconceptions via analogical reasoning: Abstract transfer versus explanatory model construction. *Instructional Science, 18*, 237–261.

Bruner, J. (1990). *Acts of meaning.* Cambridge, MA: Harvard University Press.

Buckley, B. C., & Boulter, C. J. (1999). Analysis of representation in model-based teaching and learning in science. In R. Paton & I. Neilsen (Eds.), *Visual representations and interpretations* (pp. 289–294). London: Springer.

Carlson, H. L. (1991). Learning style and program design in interactive multimedia. *Educational Technology Research and Development, 39*(3), 41–48.

Casey, C. (1996). Incorporating cognitive apprenticeship in multi-media. *Educational Technology Research and Development, 44*(1), 71–84.

Chapanis, A. (1961). Men, machines, and models. *American Psychologist, 16*, 113–131.

Chee, Y. S. (1995). Cognitive apprenticeship and its application to the teaching of Smalltalk in a multimedia interactive learning environment. *Instructional Science, 23*, 133–161.

Clement, J. (2000). *Model construction in scientists and students: Case studies of imagery, analogy, and physical intuition.* Mahwah, NJ: Lawrence Erlbaum Associates.

Clement, J. J., & Steinberg, M. S. (2002). Step-wise evolution of mental models of electric circuits: A "learning-aloud" case study. *Journal of the Learning Sciences, 11*(4), 389–452.

Coleman, E. B. (1998). Using explanatory knowledge during collaborative problem solving in science. *Journal of the Learning Sciences, 7*(3 & 4), 387–427.

Collins, A., Brown, J. S., & Newman, S. E. (1989). Cognitive apprenticeship: Teaching the crafts of reading, writing, and mathematics. In L. B. Resnick (Ed.), *Knowing, learning, and instruction* (pp. 453–494). Hillsdale, NJ: Lawrence Erlbaum Associates.

de Vries, E., Lund, K., & Baker, M. (2002). Computer-mediated epistemic dialogue: Explanation and argumentation as vehicles for understanding scientific notions. *Journal of the Learning Sciences, 11*(1), 63–103.

Doerr, H. M. (1996). Integrating the study of trigonometry, vectors, and force through modeling. *School Science and Mathematics, 96*, 407–418.

Dole, J. A., & Sinatra, G. M. (1998). Reconceptualizing change in the cognitive construction of knowledge. *Educational Psychologist, 33*(2/3), 109–128.

Dörner, D. (1976). *Problemlösen als Informationsverarbeitung* [Problem solving as information processing]. Stuttgart, Germany: Kohlhammer.

Erickson, J., & Lehrer, R. (1998). The evolution of critical standards as students design hypermedia documents. *Journal of the Learning Sciences, 7*(3 & 4), 351–386.

Freudenthal, H. (1973). *Mathematics as an educational task.* Dordrecht, Netherlands: Reidel.

Funke, J. (1985). Steuerung dynamischer Systeme durch Aufbau und Anwendung subjektiver Kausalmodelle [Steering of complex systems by means of the construction and application of causal models]. *Zeitschrift für Psychologie, 193*(4), 443–465.

Gibbons, A. S. (2002). *Model-centered instruction.* Paper presented at the annual meeting of the American Education Research Association, New Orleans, LA.

Gravemeijer, K., Cobb, P., Bowers, J., & Whitenack, J. (2000). Symbolizing, modeling, and instructional design. In P. Cobb, E. Yackel, & K. McClain (Eds.), *Symbolizing and communicating in mathematics classrooms: Perspectives on discourse, tools, and instructional design* (pp. 225–273). Mahwah, NJ: Lawrence Erlbaum Associates.

Greeno, J. G. (1989). Situations, mental models, and generative knowledge. In D. Klahr & K. Kotovsky (Eds.), *Complex information processing* (pp. 285–318). Hillsdale, NJ: Lawrence Erlbaum Associates.

Hegarty, M., & Just, M. A. (1993). Constructing mental models of machines from text and diagrams. *Journal of Memory and Language, 32*, 717–742.

Hodgson, T. (1995). Secondary mathematics modeling: Issues and challenges. *School Science and Mathematics, 95*(7), 351–358.

Huber, G. L. (2000). AQUAD Version 5.8 (Computer software). Available: http://www.aquad.de

Jackson, S., Stratford, S., Krajcik, J., & Soloway, E. (1994). Making dynamic modeling accessible to pre-college science students. *Interactive Learning Environments, 4*(3), 233–257.

Jih, H. J, & Reeves, T. C. (1992). Mental models: A research focus for interactive learning systems. *Educational Technology Research and Development, 40*(3), 39–53.

Johnson-Laird, P. N. (1983). *Mental models: Towards a cognitive science of language, inference, and consciousness.* Cambridge, England: Cambridge University Press.

Johnson-Laird, P. N. (1989). Mental models. In M. I. Posner (Ed.), *Foundations of cognitive science* (pp. 469–499). Cambridge, MA: MIT Press.

Kaput, J. J. (1994). The representational roles of technology in connecting mathematics with authentic experience. In R. Biehler, R. W. Scholz, R. Sträßer, & B. Winkelmann (Eds.), *Didactics of mathematics as a scientific discipline* (pp. 379–397). Dordrecht, Netherlands: Kluwer.

Karplus, R. (1969). *Introductory physics: A model approach.* New York: Benjamins.

King, A. (1990). Enhancing peer interaction and learning in the classroom through reciprocal questioning. *American Educational Research Journal, 27*, 664–687.

King, A., & Rosenshine, B. (1993). Effects of guided cooperative questioning on children's knowledge construction. *Journal of Experimental Education, 61*, 127–148.

Kluwe, R. H., & Haider, H. (1990). Modelle zur internen Repräsentation komplexer technischer Systeme [Models of internal representations of complex technical systems]. *Sprache & Kognition, 9*(4), 173–192.

Lesh, R., & Doerr, H. M. (2000). Symbolizing, communicating, and mathematizing: Key components of models and modeling. In P. Cobb, E. Yackel, & K. McClain (Eds.), *Symbolizing and communicating in mathematics classrooms: Perspectives on discourse, tools, and instructional design* (pp. 361–383). Mahwah, NJ: Lawrence Erlbaum Associates.

Mandl, H., Friedrich, H. F., & Hron, A. (1988). Theoretische Ansätze zum Wissenserwerb [Theoretical approaches to the acquisition of knowledge]. In H. Mandl & H. Spada (Eds.), *Wissenspsychologie* (pp. 123–160). Munich, Germany: Psychologie Verlags Union.

May, M. (1991). *Mentale Modelle von Städten. Wissenspsychologische Untersuchungen zum Beispiel der Stadt Münster* [Mental models of cities]. Münster, Germany: Waxmann.

Mayer, R. E. (1989). Models for understanding. *Review of Educational Research, 59*(1), 43–64.

Mayer, R. E., Moreno, R., Boire, M., & Vagge, S. (1999). Maximizing constructivist learning from multimedia communication by minimizing cognitive load. *Journal of Educational Psychology, 91*(4), 638–643.

McCloskey, M., Caramazza, A., & Green, B. (1980). Curvilinear motion in the absence of external forces: Naive beliefs about the motion of objects. *Science, 210*, 1139–1141.

National Council of Teachers of Mathematics. (1994). *Curriculum and evaluation standards for school mathematics.* Reston, VA: Author.

Norman, D. A. (1983). Some observations on mental models. In D. Gentner & A. L. Stevens (Eds.), *Mental models* (pp. 7–14). Hillsdale, NJ: Lawrence Erlbaum Associates.

Ohlsson, S. (1995). Learning to do and learning to understand: A lesson and a challenge for cognitive modeling. In P. Reimann & H. Spada (Eds.), *Learning in humans and machines* (pp. 37–62). Oxford, England: Elsevier.

Penner, D. E. (2001). Cognition, computers, and synthetic science: Building knowledge and meaning through modeling. *Review of Research in Education, 25*, 1–35.

Penner, D. E., Giles, N. D., Lehrer, R., & Schauble, L. (1997). Building functional models: Designing an elbow. *Journal of Research in Science Teaching, 34*(2), 125–143.

Penner, D. E., Lehrer, R., & Schauble, L. (1998). From physical models to biomechanics: A design-based modeling approach. *Journal of the Learning Sciences, 7*(3 & 4), 429–449.

Peterson, P. L. (1988). Teaching for higher-order thinking in mathematics: The challenge for the next decade. In D. A. Grouws, T. J. Cooney, & D. Jones (Eds.), *Perspectives on research on effective mathematics teaching* (Vol. 1, pp. 2–26). Reston, VA: Lawrence Erlbaum Associates.

Piaget, J. (1943). *Le développement mental de l'enfant* [The mental development of children]. Zürich, Switzerland: Rascher.

Raudenbush, S. W., Rowan, B., & Cheong, Y. F. (1993). Higher order instructional goals in secondary schools: Class, teacher, and school influences. *American Educational Research Journal, 30*(3), 523–553.

Rickheit, G., & Habel, C. (Eds.). (1999). *Mental models in discourse processing and reasoning.* Amsterdam: Elsevier.

Rips, L. J. (1987). Mental muddles. In M. Brand & R. M. Harnish (Eds.), *The representation of knowledge and belief* (pp. 259–286). Tucson: University of Arizona Press.

Royer, J. M., Cisero, C. A., & Carlo, M. S. (1993). Techniques and procedures for assessing cognitive skills. *Review of Educational Research, 63*(2), 201–243.

Rumelhart, D. E. (1980). Schemata: The building blocks of cognition. In R. Spiro, B. Bruce, & W. Brewer (Eds.), *Theoretical issues in reading comprehension* (pp. 33–58). Hillsdale, NJ: Lawrence Erlbaum Associates.

Rumelhart, D. E., Smolensky, P., McClelland, J. L., & Hinton, G. E. (1986). Schemata and sequential thought processes in PDP models. In J. L. McClelland, D. E. Rumelhart, & the PDP Research Group (Eds.), *Parallel distributed processing: Explorations in the microstructure of cognition: Vol. 2. Psychological and biological models* (pp. 7–57). Cambridge, MA: MIT Press.

Sasse, M. (1991). How to t(r)ap users' mental models. In M. J. Tauber & D. Ackermann (Eds.), *Mental models and human–computer interaction 2* (pp. 59–79). Amsterdam: North-Holland.

Schauble, L. (1996). The development of scientific reasoning in knowledge-rich contexts. *Developmental Psychology, 32*(1), 102–119.

Schnotz, W., & Kulhavy, R. W. (Eds.). (1994). *Comprehension of graphics.* Amsterdam: North-Holland.

Schoenfeld, A. H. (1985). *Mathematical problem solving.* New York: Academic Press.

Seel, N. M. (1991). *Weltwissen und mentale Modelle* [World knowledge and mental models]. Göttingen, Germany: Hogrefe.

Seel, N. M. (1995). Mental models, knowledge transfer, and teaching strategies. *Journal of Structural Learning and Intelligent Systems, 12*(3), 197–213.

Seel, N. M. (1999). Educational diagnosis of mental models: Assessment problems and technology-based solutions. *Journal of Structural Learning and Intelligent Systems, 14*(2), 153–185.

Seel, N. M. (2000). *Psychologie des Lernens* [Psychology of learning]. Munich, Germany: Reinhardt.

Seel, N. M. (2001). Epistemology, situated cognition, and mental models: "Like a bridge over troubled water." *Instructional Science, 29*(4–5), 403–427.

Seel, N. M., Al-Diban, S., & Blumschein, P. (2000). Mental models and instructional planning. In M. Spector & T. M. Anderson (Eds.), *Integrated and holistic perspectives on learning, instruction and technology: Understanding complexity* (pp. 129–158). Dordrecht, Netherlands: Kluwer.

Seel, N. M., & Dinter, F. R. (1995). Instruction and mental model progression: Learner-dependent effects of teaching strategies on knowledge acquisition and analogical transfer. *Educational Research and Evaluation, 1*(1), 4–35.

Seel, N. M., & Schenk, K. (2002). Multimedia environments as cognitive tools for enhancing model-based learning and problem solving: An evaluation report. *Evaluation and Program Planning, 26*(2), 215–224.

Sfard, A. (1991). On the dual nature of mathematical conceptions: Reflections on processes and objects as different sides of the same coin. *Educational Studies in Mathematics, 22*, 1–36.

Sharp, D. L. M., Bransford, J. D., Goldman, S. R., Risko, V. J., Kinzer, C. K., & Vye, N. J. (1995). Dynamic visual support for story comprehension and mental model building by young, at-risk children. *Educational Technology Research and Development, 43*(4), 25–42.

Shepard, L. (1991). Psychometricians' beliefs about learning. *Educational Researcher, 20*(7), 2–9.

Smith, C., & Unger, C. (1997). What's in dots-per-box? Conceptual bootstrapping with stripped-down visual analogies. *Journal of the Learning Sciences, 6*(2), 143–181.

Snow, R. E. (1990). New approaches to cognitive and conative assessment in education. *International Journal of Educational Research, 14*(5), 455–473.

Stachowiak, H. (1973). *Allgemeine Modelltheorie* [General model theory]. Vienna: Springer.

Stewart, J., Hafner, R., Johnson, S., & Finkel, E. (1992). Science as model building: Computers and high-school genetics. *Educational Psychologist, 27*(3), 317–336.

Volet, S. E. (1991). Modelling and coaching of relevant, metacognitive strategies for enhancing university students' learning. *Learning and Instruction, 1*(4), 319–336.

Wartofsky, M. W. (1979). *Models: Representation and the scientific understanding.* Dordrecht, Netherlands: Reidel.

White, B. (1993). ThinkerTools: Causal models, conceptual change, and science education. *Cognition and Instruction, 10*(1), 1–100.

Chapter 3

Epistemological Development: An Implicit Entailment of Constructivist Learning Environments

David Jonassen
Rose Marra
University of Missouri

Betsy Palmer
Montana State University

Since the beginning of the constructivist movement in instructional design (Jonassen, 1991), researchers and theorists have provided a number of rich conceptions of constructive learning. For example, rich environments for active learning (REALs) are instructional systems that engage learners in realistic, authentic, complex, and information-rich learning contexts; support intentional, self-regulated learning; support cooperative efforts in learning; and engage learners in complex problem solving (Grabinger, 1996). REALs emphasize authentic learning contexts for anchoring the meaning-making processes. They are student centered and learner controlled, emphasizing student responsibility and initiative in determining learning goals and regulating their performance toward those goals, not just determining the path through a prescribed set of learning activities.

Open-ended learning environments (OELEs) stress the use of manipulable objects to support experiential learning and student model building (Land & Hannafin, 1996). OELEs provide rich contexts, friendly interfaces, manipulation tools, supporting resources, and guidance to facilitate learner understanding. They support identifying, questioning, and testing personal models of phenomena as learners develop theories-in-action.

In goal-based scenarios (GBSs), students become active participants in complex systems. They employ a "learning by doing" architecture (Schank, Fano, Bell, & Jona, 1993/1994) in which learners are immersed in a focused, goal-oriented situation and required to perform authentic, real-world activities. They are supported with advice in the form of stories that are indexed and accessed using case-based reasoning. Skills are acquired through practice in an authentic environment. Learning is driven by acceptance of a meaningful goal beyond the requirements of a particular task.

Constructivist learning environments (CLEs) represent another generic model for designing authentic, complex learning environments. CLEs consist of a number of integrated and interdependent components: the problem space (including context, representation, and manipulation spaces), related cases, information resources, cognitive tools, and collaborative tools (Jonassen, 1999). The problem and its multimodal representation is the focus of learning, and the other components assist learners to understand and manipulate the problem. Jonassen, Prevish, Christy, and Stavurlaki (1999) demonstrated how CLEs could be used to support learning in operations management.

PROBLEMS IN LEARNING IN LEARNING ENVIRONMENTS

Although educators are devoted to the development and implementation of these complex and constructivist environments, there are many psychological and personological impediments to effective implementation. Here are a few that we have observed in secondary and higher education.

Scriptless in Schools

Schank and Abelson (1977) described mental structures called *scripts*. Scripts are schemas for common events; they function as archetypal scenarios. They help us to set up expectations about what will happen during typical events. Schank and Abelson described a restaurant script that includes a series of events with certain actors fulfilling expected roles. In a restaurant, we wait and are seated; we select food to eat from menus of options; the server takes our order and disappears into a back room where (we believe) some chefs prepare our food, which is served to us by the server. After eating, we pay the check, leave a tip, and depart. We are able to refine that script for various kinds of restaurants. For instance, in a fast-food restaurant, we wait in line to order food, which is prepared in front of us. We pay for the food, move to a table, eat the food, and clean up after ourselves. Each script determines our expectations about the experience. When the experience violates our expectations (e.g., no server in a sit-down restaurant), we have a story. Our scripts also tell us how to behave in those experiences.

Students of all ages construct scripts for school-based learning. Based on years of similar experiences, they develop scripts in higher education that include listening to lectures, predicting what ideas will be examined on the test, cramming information into working memory, and completing examinations before forgetting most of what was studied. In universities in the United States, students use strategic supports to ameliorate those scripts, including note-taking services, fraternity test files, summaries, on-line paper-writing services, and others to fulfill the expectations of their scripts. Their scripts guide their study processes in order to maximize their productivity.

The focus of nearly every kind of constructivist learning environment is problem solving (Jonassen, 2002). Problem solving requires learners to deal with multiple sources of information, seek and provide evidence, judge that evidence, and decide between multiple solution alternatives, all of which require self-directed learning skills. The study methods that students normally apply to learning are ineffective while attempting to function in constructivist learning environments; that is, they violate students' well-developed scripts. For example, in a course on interactive dynamics, where students were required to interact and solve problems using complete dynamic systems rather than simply solving static equations about a single system aspect, many of the students perceived the innovative environment to require too much work (Yaeger, Marra, Costanzo, Gray, & Sathianathan, 1999). It did require more intellectual effort because meaningful learning certainly requires effortful engagement. Successful functioning in constructivist learning environments requires intentional conceptual change efforts (Sinatra & Pintrich, 2003). Expecting intentional conceptual change in students will require dramatic changes in students' learning scripts, which will further require fairly extensive educational reform with expectations set at the beginning of a university career ("so this is what college will be like"). Those experiences need to be carried through their careers consistently so that they are manageable for students. When constructive learning is not required, students readily revert to their preferred and better instantiated learning scripts.

Undermotivated in Universities

Because expectations are violated and scripts do not work, students often become frustrated by their lack of immediate success in constructivist learning environments. Their frustrations are manifested in motivation problems. Unable to succeed, students are unwilling to exert effort and persist on tasks (i.e., they lack tenacity), and so are unwilling to engage in the environments intentionally (willingness), all of which are important but often unrecognized learning outcomes (Jonassen & Tessmer, 1996/1997). These deficiencies further erode and preclude any meaningful learning. The relation between motivation and meaningful learning is inviolable.

Epistemologically Challenged in Education

Why are students frustrated by constructivist learning environments? Why do they lack motivation? An important causal factor is the students' levels of epistemological development relative to the levels of epistemological development required by constructivist learning environments. Also known as intellectual maturity, epistemic beliefs, and intellectual development, *epistemological development* describes one's beliefs about the meaning of epistemological constructs such as knowledge and truth and how those beliefs change over time (Hofer & Pintrich, 1997). Although the theories differ in detail and scope, they suggest a common pattern of development that progresses from simple, black–white thinking, through an exploration of multiple perspectives, to complex, relativistic thinking. The developmental aspect contrasts this line of research with that on epistemological beliefs that seeks to identify categories of beliefs, such as externally controlled learning, simple knowledge, quick learning, and certain knowledge (Schommer, Crouse, & Rhodes, 1992).

There are several stage theories for describing learners' levels of epistemological development, including epistemological reflection (Baxter-Magolda, 1987), reflective judgment (King & Kitchner, 1994), and Perry's levels of intellectual development (Perry, 1970). We briefly describe Baxter-Magolda's and Perry's work and refer the reader to Hofer and Pintrich (1997) for a review of epistemological developmental theories.

Epistemological reflection, according to Baxter-Magolda (1987), progresses through the following stages:

- *Absolute knowing:* Knowledge is certain and obtained from authorities (receiving, then mastery through practice).
- *Transitional knowing:* Knowledge is partially certain and requires understanding (interpersonal resolving of ideas or impersonal—using logic, debate, research).
- *Independent knowing:* Knowledge is uncertain and requires independent thinking (interindividual [open-mindedness] or individual challenging).
- *Contextual knowing:* Knowledge is contextual, based on evidence in context.

Perry's (1970) scheme of intellectual development, developed by William Perry during the late 1950s based on interviews with approximately 100 Harvard and Radcliffe students, describes nine stages (positions) that students move through during their intellectual development (see Table 3.1).

TABLE 3.1
Perry's Scheme of Epistemological Development

Perry Position	Knowledge	Learning
1—Basic dualism (hypothetical)	Knowledge is right or wrong, a collection of facts.	Receive right answers from authority.
2—Multiplicity pre-legitimate	Knowledge is generally right or wrong. Complexity or uncertainty is either an error or a teaching tool.	Authorities are the source of right answers or give us problems so we can learn to find the Truth.
3—Multiplicity legitimate but subordinate	Knowledge is right or wrong, and some knowledge is unknown temporarily.	Authority is the source of answers or the source of method to find the answers.
4—Multiplicity	Some knowledge is right or wrong, but most is not yet known. Where authorities do not know, everyone is entitled to their own opinion.	Authorities are the source of ways to think.
5—Contextual relativism	Most knowledge is contextual and can be judged qualitatively.	Student learns methods and criteria of his/her discipline. Metacognition begins.
6—Commitment foreseen	Knowledge is not absolute but student accepts responsibility for making judgments.	Student accepts responsibility for making a commitment based on his/her values.
7, 8, and 9—Commitment within relativism	Commitments made within a relativistic world as an affirmation of one's own identity.	Choices made in the face of legitimate alternatives and after experiencing genuine doubt.

Note. Adapted from Perry (1970).

Position 1 is *basic dualism*, in which students believe that if ideas are right, they are facts. Otherwise they are wrong. Position 2 reasoning, called *multiplicity pre-legitimate*, exhibits a view of the world that is bifurcated. Students at Positions 1 and 2 see things as us-versus-them, right-versus-wrong, and good-versus-bad. First-year college students who are often at this level (Eaton, McKinney, Trimble, & Andrieu-Parker, 1995; Pavelich & Moore, 1993) recognize that multiple points of view may exist but generally attribute this to a shortcoming in the authority. Students at this level working on an open-ended design project may be disturbed or shocked that neither the client nor the professor has a definite answer to the problem at hand.

At Position 3, *multiplicity subordinate*, students acknowledge diversity of ideas as legitimate but believe that this uncertainty is temporary. In Position 3, students still believe that Truth[1] is out there, but we just haven't found it yet. Although this change in thinking does not affect students' view of

---

[1]Truth is capitalized here to indicate a perspective that something is absolutely or universally true.

truth—things are still right and wrong—it does raise questions about authority's relationship to truth. Now, instead of grading students on whether their work is right or wrong, students perceive the evaluation of their work as based on adherence to a procedure for finding the Truth that, of course, is learned from authority. In working through an open-ended problem, students in Position 3 may be willing to temporarily suspend their desire for a right answer, but will still search for the right procedure for finding the answer (e.g., "Professor Smith wants me to do the problem *this* way!").

In Position 4, called *multiplicity*, students accept multiple points of view and the absence of concrete answers. Knowledge is divided into two realms: (a) things that are definitely known as right or wrong, and (b) things that are uncertain or that are represented by a multiplicity of views. Students in Position 4 become more adept at using evidence. They do not see evidence as a consequence of knowledge and its sources, however, but rather as an exercise in "how we should think." Students may believe that all opinions are equally valid and, therefore, do not develop a commitment to one particular decision or course of action.

Students make a significant transition in thinking as they move from Position 4 to Position 5. In Position 5, students relinquish their earlier dualistic views of the world and accept knowledge as, for the most part, transient and contextual. Simultaneously, students transform their perspective on authority and on themselves as learners. Students can now accept themselves as one among many legitimate sources of knowledge. In doing so, they forgo their former view of instructors as absolute authorities. Students now see teachers as fellow seekers in a relativistic world who have legitimate claims to authority based on experience and expertise. In this position, students become comfortable making qualitative judgments among a variety of alternatives.

In Position 6, the fluidity of this newfound relativism begins to dissolve into an uneasy sense of personal disorientation. If knowledge is in a continual state of flux, who am I as a knower? At this position, students become aware that they must affirm their own place within the changing contexts of a relativistic world, and that there is a need for commitment to decisions one is making. Students want to make a commitment, although they have not yet reached the point of declaring a choice. As they move into Position 7, then, students make an initial, self-affirming decision. In Positions 8 and 9, this initial commitment gives way to a cycle of commitments, where students learn to prioritize various types of commitments, balancing stability and flexibility. Students may reach these positions as they progress through college.

Multiple research projects conducted at several universities have found that first-year college students are most often at Position 2, multiplicity prelegitimate (Eaton et al., 1995; Marra, Palmer, & Litzinger, 2000; Pavelich &

Moore, 1993). These students recognize that multiple points of view may exist but generally attribute this to shortcomings in authority. For instance, engineering students at this level working on an open-ended design project may be disturbed or shocked that neither the client nor the professor has a definite answer to the problem at hand.

Why are students' epistemological beliefs so naive? Traditional approaches to K–12 and undergraduate instruction systemically reinforce naive epistemological beliefs. The teach-and-test ontology used in most education requires learners to assume absolutist beliefs about knowledge. Teachers and administrators establish a curriculum that describes the objective content that learners are required to assimilate. Truth is defined by the teacher, and knowledge is a process of memorizing and attempting to comprehend what the teacher or professor says. Questioning the beliefs of a teacher or professor is often punished. Students are clearly rewarded for employing naive beliefs. In the next section, we review limited research on the relations among epistemic beliefs, learning, and instruction.

EFFECTS OF EPISTEMOLOGICAL BELIEFS ON LEARNING

In this chapter we propose a two-way relation between levels of epistemic beliefs and instruction. Specifically, instructional interventions can have an impact on students' epistemic beliefs, and students' epistemic beliefs can, in turn, affect the success of certain kinds of instruction.

Effects of Instruction on Epistemological Beliefs

A small body of research has examined the relationship of epistemological development and different instructional methods. Some research has confirmed that instructional methods can affect learners' levels of epistemic beliefs. For example, Stephenson and Hunt (1977) developed a course-based intervention around the Perry scheme to encourage first-year students to move from dualist positions to a more relativistic stage. This type of intervention assumes that intellectual development occurs as a result of "cognitive conflict or dissonance which forces individuals to alter the constructs they have used to reason about certain situations" (Widick, Knefelkamp, & Parker, 1975, p. 291). The freshman social science course was designed to emphasize content that challenged students' typically dualistic values in a supportive teaching environment and move them toward relativistic thinking. On pre- and posttests on the Perry scale, the students in the experimental course section showed substantially greater movement than their counterparts in the control group.

Pascarella and Terenzini (1991) described two other studies that examined whether course interventions specifically aimed at students' cognitive development encourage advancement on the Perry scale (Knefelkamp, 1974; Widick, Knefelkamp, & Parker, 1975; Widick & Simpson, 1978). Similar to the Stephenson and Hunt (1977) study, both of these course interventions designed instruction to match and advance students' current intellectual development stages; they found that there was a pre- to postcourse gain of slightly more than 0.75 of a Perry stage and that a greater percentage of the students in the experimental section showed growth on the Perry scale than those in the control group.

Marra, Palmer, and Litzinger (2000) also reported a statistically significant impact on Perry ratings from a single course. Although this research was not designed to intentionally affect Perry ratings, their Perry ratings were statistically higher than their counterparts who listened to lectures (3.29 vs. 2.9). Marra et al. noted that the first-year design course is a project-focused, active-learning course where students spend time during class working in their teams and interacting with their instructors in a student–coach-type relationship. Even though the course may not have been designed to specifically promote intellectual development, Marra et al. concluded that the challenges inherent in an open-ended design project and team-based curriculum may provide the type of intellectual environment that stimulates students' natural progression toward more complex thinking.

Effects of Epistemological Beliefs on Instruction

The underlying assumption of this chapter is that successful use of constructivist learning environments presumes more advanced levels of epistemic beliefs. A very small amount of empirical research supports our assumption. Windschitl and Andre (1998), for instance, found that college students with higher levels of epistemological beliefs experienced more conceptual change when learning in an exploratory, constructivist learning environment than when working in a directed, objectivist learning environment. Conversely, students with lower levels of epistemological beliefs benefited more from working in the objectivist environment. Similar results were described by Angeli (1999), who found an interaction between epistemic beliefs and situated (immersion) and nonsituated (preteach) instructional treatments.

Further support for our assumption comes from a study on problem solving. Because most constructivist learning environments engage learners in some form of problem solving, the relation of epistemic beliefs to problem solving is important. Schraw, Dunkle, and Bendixen (1995) found that epistemic beliefs had a greater effect on ill-structured problem-solving tasks than on well-structured tasks. Students' strong belief in the certainty of knowledge prevents a thorough analysis of alternative solutions, whereas belief in omniscient authority may limit the set of viable solutions to those suggested by experts. Clearly, more empirical support is needed.

Epistemological Requirements of Constructivist Learning Environments

We propose that functioning most effectively in constructivist learning environments requires a higher level of epistemological beliefs than Position 2, the standard for most college students. We propose that functioning effectively in constructivist learning environments requires epistemological beliefs of at least Position 4, multiplicity, if not Position 5, cultural relativism, on the Perry scale. In constructivist learning environments, learners must be able to:

1. question and evaluate information sources;
2. analyze material intentionality;
3. represent problems qualitatively and quantitatively in multiple modalities;
4. generate and evaluate alternative hypotheses;
5. resolve and integrate multiple perspectives (personal, thematic, and theoretical);
6. justify their conclusions and beliefs through argumentation, including warrants and multiple sources of evidence; and
7. question the contextual and cultural assumptions, beliefs, and history of information sources.

What levels of epistemic beliefs do these skills require? Using the Perry scale, we have analyzed each of these entailments and propose the following epistemic orientations required by the learner:

1. Questioning and evaluating information sources engages at least Position 4, multiplicity. Authorities are sources of ways to think, but those sources must be critically examined.
2. Analyzing intentionality of the author or purveyor of information entails Position 5, contextual relativism. Without understanding the context surrounding an author's beliefs, it is difficult to understand the author's intentions.
3. Representing problems qualitatively and quantitatively in multiple modalities probably only requires Position 3, multiplicity subordi-

nate. Different representations can be different representations of the same truth.

4. Generating and evaluating alternative hypotheses requires at least Position 3, multiplicity subordinate. To be successful, Position 4, multiplicity, is really required.

5. Resolving and integrating multiple perspectives is an archetype of Position 4, multiplicity.

6. Justifying one's conclusions and beliefs through argumentation is best described by Position 6, commitment foreseen. Students must commit to values by arguing for them.

7. Questioning the contextual and cultural assumptions, beliefs, and history of information sources clearly requires at least Position 5, contextual relativism.

Scaffolding Epistemic Beliefs

How do we support epistemologically underdeveloped learners in constructivist learning environments? How do we move students from dualistic to more multiplistic positions? Kloss (1994) suggested providing concrete experiences where two or three conflicting or paradoxical points of view exist, or simply reinforcing the legitimacy of students' personal views. Determining how to help students develop to Position 3 and beyond in order to function effectively in constructivist learning environments is more challenging. We believe that a potential solution for supporting the use of more mature epistemic beliefs in constructivist learning environments is to scaffold that performance. Scaffolding provides temporary frameworks to support learning and student performance beyond their capacities. In order to distinguish scaffolding from other kinds of supports, including modeling and coaching, we argue that scaffolding represents some manipulation by the teacher or the learning system of the task itself. Scaffolding may involve adjusting the difficulty of the task, providing tools to engage and support task performance, altering the assessment methods to focus task performance, adapting the task requirements to cultural or historical needs, or performing a task or parts of a task for the learner. Designing scaffolds requires explication of the activity structure required to complete a task (using activity theory or cognitive task analysis; Jonassen, Tessmer, & Hannum, 1999) and identifying those parts of the task for which learners are not ready (defining the learner's zone of proximal development). Scaffolding may initially provide learners with an easier task that they know how to perform and gradually add task difficulty until they are unable to perform alone. This form of task regulation is an example of black-box scaffolding (Hmelo

& Guzdial, 1996), which facilitates student performance but will not be faded out while learners are using the environment.

Another approach to scaffolding learners' performance is to redesign the task in a way that supports learning, that is, supplanting task performance (Salomon, 1979). Task performance may be supplanted by providing cognitive tools to help learners represent or manipulate the problem. These forms of scaffolding are examples of glass-box scaffolding (Hmelo & Guzdial, 1996) because they are faded after a number of cases. Having learned to perform desired skills, students must learn to perform without the scaffolds that support their performance.

Addressing the seven previously proposed entailments of constructivist learning, we propose the following means of scaffolding those behaviors:

1. Questioning and evaluating information sources can be scaffolded by (a) requiring students to articulate goals and intentions as well as a search strategy prior to searching, (b) evaluating the source of any message, (c) assessing the integrity and viability of any information found, and (d) triangulating resources (Colaric & Jonassen, 2001).

2. Analyzing intentionality of the author or purveyor of information can be scaffolded using the methods described in No. 1.

3. Representing problems qualitatively and quantitatively can be scaffolded using a variety of cognitive tools such as concept-mapping tools, expert system shells, systems dynamics tools, and others (Jonassen, 2000). These tools provide alternative formalisms that require learners to represent their understanding of the problem at hand in different ways. For instance, representing a problem space using a concept map focuses the learner on the semantic relations between concepts in the problem domain, whereas expert systems and systems dynamics tools require learners to explicitly define the causal relations between problem-space components.

4. Generating and evaluating alternative hypotheses. Too often, the hypotheses that students generate are impoverished, and the students usually overestimate the completeness of their hypotheses (Fisher, Gettys, Manning, Mehle, & Baca, 1983). A potential scaffold is to provide learners with a lengthy list of hypotheses, one of which is correct, and require them to select the correct one. When they do, students disconfirm significantly more incorrect hypotheses and find the highest percentage of correct hypotheses (Adsit & London, 1997). Another useful scaffold may be a structured hypothesis scratchpad, which enables learners to use a larger number of variables in their hypotheses and to search the hypothesis space before conducting experiments (van Joolingen & de Jong, 1991).

5. Resolving and integrating multiple perspectives may be scaffolded by requiring learners to assume a higher order goal and structuring that goal with information in the form of a cognitive flexibility hypertext. Cognitive

flexibility hypertexts are intended to facilitate the advanced acquisition of knowledge to serve as the basis for expertise in complex and ill-structured knowledge domains (Spiro & Jehng, 1990).

6. Justifying conclusions and beliefs through argumentation can be scaffolded through computer-supported collaborative argumentation (CSCA; Jonassen & Carr, 2000). CSCA uses technological tools such as Belvedere (Suthers, 1998), Sense Maker in the Knowledge Integration Environments, CaMILE, Questmap, and the Collaboratory Notebook to constrain students' asynchronous discussion by requiring them to respond to claims with warrants and evidence. Most of these tools provide a graphical argumentation structure to support students' construction of coherent arguments.

7. Questioning the contextual and cultural assumptions, beliefs, and history of information sources can be scaffolded using a combination of methods described in No. 2 and No. 5.

CONCLUSION

Epistemological growth is essential for functioning in professional positions, because everyday and professional roles are replete with ill-structured problems (Culver, 1982). Doctors must diagnose tricky cases; engineers must create designs that are safe, cost-effective, and socially responsible; computer technicians must solve their clients' problems quickly and without disruption. To solve these problems, learners becoming practitioners must grow from their naive and dualistic worldviews to a more contextualized view of problem solving. Working with open-ended design problems and processing the many sources of design ideas developed within their teams necessarily challenges students' views on absolute answers and authority figures. Professionals must be able to engage in open-ended, team-based design projects while seeing that multiple solutions are possible, and that their task is to evaluate the many potential solutions based on criteria that they must define. Constructivist learning environments may be able to scaffold the epistemological development required to function in everyday and professional contexts. In this chapter we have assessed the levels of epistemological beliefs required to successfully use constructivist learning environments and have suggested ways to scaffold their epistemological development.

REFERENCES

Adsit, D. J., & London, M. (1997). Effects of hypothesis generation on hypothesis testing in a rule-discovery task. *Journal of General Psychology, 124,* 19–34.

Angeli, C. M. (1999). Examining the effects of context-free and context situated instructional strategies on learners' critical thinking. *Dissertation Abstracts International, 60*(5A), 1447.

Baxter-Magolda, M. B. (1987). Comparing open-ended interviews and standardized measures of intellectual development. *Journal of College Student Personnel, 28,* 443–448.

Colaric, S., & Jonassen, D. H. (2001). Information equals knowledge; searching equals learning; and hyperlinking is good instruction; and other myths about learning from the Internet. Part I. *Computers in Schools, 17*(3/4), 159–169.

Culver, R. S. (1982). Perry's model of intellectual development. *Engineering Education, 73*(3), 221–226.

Eaton, M. D., McKinney, G. R., Trimble, J. E., & Andrieu-Parker, J. M. (1995). *Portfolio analysis and cognitive development at Fairhaven College* (Tech. & Research Rep. No. 1995-01). Bellingham, WA: Western Washington University.

Fisher, S. D., Gettys, C. F., Manning, C., Mehle, T., & Baca, S. (1983). Consistency checking in hypothesis generation. *Organizational Behavior and Human Performance, 31,* 233–254.

Grabinger, R. S. (1996). Rich environments for active learning. In D. H. Jonassen (Ed.), *Handbook of research for educational communications and technology.* New York: Macmillan.

Hmelo, C. E., & Guzdial, M. (1996). Of black and glass boxes: Scaffolding for doing and learning. In *Proceedings of the Second International Conference on the Learning Sciences* (pp. 128–133). Charlottesville, VA: Association for the Advancement of Computers in Education.

Hofer, B. K., & Pintrich, P. R. (1997). The development of epistemological theories: Beliefs about knowledge and knowing and their relation to learning. *Review of Educational Research, 67*(1), 88–140.

Jonassen, D. H. (1991). Objectivism vs. constructivism: Do we need a new paradigm? *Educational Technology: Research and Development, 39*(3), 5–14.

Jonassen, D. H. (1999). Designing constructivist learing environments. In C. M. Reigeluth (Ed.), *Instructional design theories and models: A new paradigm of instructional technology* (Vol. 2, pp. 215–240). Mahwah, NJ: Lawrence Erlbaum Associates.

Jonassen, D. H. (2000). *Computers as mindtools for schools: Engaging critical thinking.* Columbus, OH: Prentice-Hall.

Jonassen, D. H. (2002). Integration of problem solving into instructional design. In R. A. Reiser & J. Dempsey (Eds.), *Trends and issues in instructional design and technology* (pp. 107–120). Upper Saddle River, NJ: Prentice-Hall.

Jonassen, D. H., & Carr, C. (2000). Mindtools: Affording multiple knowledge representations in learning. In S. P. Lajoie (Ed.), *Computers as cognitive tools: Vol. 2. No more walls* (pp. 165–196). Mahwah, NJ: Lawrence Erlbaum Associates.

Jonassen, D., Prevish, T., Christy, D., & Stavurlaki, E. (1999). Learning to solve problems on the Web: Aggregate planning in a business management course. *Distance Education: An International Journal, 20*(1), 49–63.

Jonassen, D. H., & Tessmer, M. (1996/1997). An outcomes-based taxonomy for instructional systems design, evaluation, and research. *Training Research Journal, 2,* 11–46.

Jonassen, D. H., Tessmer, M., & Hannum, W. H. (1999). *Task analysis methods for instructional design.* Mahwah, NJ: Lawrence Erlbaum Associates.

King, P. M., & Kitchner, K. S. (1994). *Developing reflective judgment: Understanding and promoting intellectual growth and critical thinking in adolescents and adults.* San Francisco: Jossey-Bass.

Kloss, R. J. (1994). A nudge is best: Helping students through the Perry scheme of intellectual development. *College Teaching, 42*(40), 151–158.

Knefelkamp, L. (1974). *Developmental instruction: Fostering intellectual and personal growth in college students.* Unpublished doctoral dissertation, University of Minnesota, Minneapolis–St. Paul.

Land, S. M., & Hannafin, M. J. (1996). A conceptual framework for the development of theories-in-action with open-ended learning environments. *Educational Technology Research & Development, 44*(3), 37–53.

Marra, R. M., Palmer, B., & Litzinger, T. A. (2000). The effects of a first-year engineering de-
sign course on student intellectual development as measured by the Perry scheme. *Journal
of Engineering Education, 89*(1), 39–46.
Pascarella, E. T., & Terenzini, P. T. (1991). *How college affects students.* San Francisco: Jossey-
Bass.
Pavelich, M. J., & Moore, W. S. (1993, November). *Measuring maturing rates of engineering stu-
dents using the Perry model.* Paper presented at the Frontiers in Education annual meeting,
Washington, DC.
Perry, W. G. (1970). *Intellectual and ethical development in the college years: A scheme.* New York:
Holt, Rinehart & Winston.
Salomon, G. (1979). *The interaction of media, cognition, and learning.* San Francisco: Jossey-Bass.
Schank, R., & Abelson, R. (1977). *Scripts, plans, goals, and understanding.* Hillsdale, NJ: Law-
rence Erlbaum Associates.
Schank, R. C., Fano, A., Bell, B., & Jona, M. (1993/1994). The design of goal-based scenarios.
Journal of the Learning Sciences, 3(4), 305–345.
Schommer, M., Crouse, A., & Rhodes, N. (1992). Epistemological beliefs and mathematical
text comprehension: Believing it is simple does not make it so. *Journal of Educational Psychol-
ogy, 84*(4), 435–443.
Schraw, G., Dunkle, M. E., & Bendixen, L. D. (1995). Cognitive processes in well-defined and
ill-defined problem solving. *Applied Cognitive Psychology, 9*, 523–538.
Sinatra, G. M., & Pintrich, P. R. (2003). *Intentional conceptual change.* Mahwah, NJ: Lawrence
Erlbaum Associates.
Spiro, R. J., & Jehng, J. C. (1990). Cognitive flexibility and hypertext: Theory and technology
for the non-linear and multi-dimensional traversal of complex subject matter. In D. Nix &
R. J. Spiro (Eds.), *Cognition, education, and multimedia: Explorations in high technology* (pp.
163–202). Hillsdale, NJ: Lawrence Erlbaum Associates.
Stephenson, B., & Hunt, C. (1977). Intellectual and ethical development: A dualistic curricu-
lum intervention for college students. *Counseling Psychologist, 6*, 39–42.
Suthers, D. (1998, April). *Representations for scaffolding collaborative inquiry on ill-structured prob-
lems.* Paper presented at the annual meeting of the American Educational Research
Association, San Diego, CA.
van Joolingen, W. R., & de Jong, T. (1991). Supporting hypothesis generation by learners ex-
ploring and interactive computer simulation. *Instructional Science, 20*, 389–404.
Widick, C., Knefelkamp, L., & Parker, C. (1975). The counselor as developmental instructor.
Counselor Education and Supervision, 14, 286–296.
Widick, C., & Simpson, D. (1978). Developmental concepts in college instruction. In C. Parker
(Ed.), *Encouraging development in college students* (pp. 27–59). Minneapolis: University of
Minnesota Press.
Windschitl, M., & Andre, T. (1998). Using computer simulations to enhance conceptual
change: The roles of constructivist instruction and student epistemological beliefs. *Journal
of Research in Science Teaching, 35*(2), 145–160.
Yaeger, P. M., Marra, R. M., Costanzo, F., Gray, G. L., & Sathianathan, D. (1999). Interactive
dynamics: Effects of student-centered activities on learning. In D. Budny & G. Bjedov
(Eds.), *29th ASEE/IEEE Frontiers in Education Conference 1999* (pp. 12–17). New York: Frontiers in Education.

Chapter 4

Promoting Deep Science Learning Through Case-Based Reasoning: Rituals and Practices in Learning by Design™ Classrooms

Janet L. Kolodner, Paul J. Camp, David Crismond,
Barbara Fasse, Jackie Gray, Jennifer Holbrook,
and Mike Ryan
Georgia Institute of Technology, College of Computing

Learning by Design (Hmelo, Holton, & Kolodner, 2000; Kolodner, Crismond, et al., 2003; Kolodner et al., 1998; Kolodner, Gray, & Fasse, 2003) is a project-based inquiry approach to science education for middle school (ages 12–14; grades 6–8) where students learn science content and skills in the context of achieving design challenges. For example, to learn about erosion, its sources, and ways of managing it, students design an erosion-management solution for a basketball court to be built at the bottom of a hill. To learn about forces and motion, they design a miniature vehicle and its propulsion system that can navigate several hills on its own power. The approach is highly collaborative and highly reflective. Students engage in much "doing"; they also spend much time discussing their reasoning, justifying their decisions, and articulating the ways to engage skillfully in the practices of scientists. A variety of approaches to scaffolding are embedded in the approach to promote successful interpretation of experiences, extraction of science content and practices embedded in their experiences, and the kinds of reflection that result in transfer. All units focus on skills learning—learning the skills and practices that scientists and engineers engage in on a regular basis—in addition to learning science content.

Learning by Design (LBD) has been piloted and field-tested with over 3,500 students and two dozen teachers in the Atlanta area, covering a full spectrum of student backgrounds and capabilities. Formative assessments have helped us refine our design-based approach so that students can successfully engage and learn and so that teachers feel comfortable with the approach. Summative assessments show that LBD students learn science content at least as well as matched comparison students and that their ability to engage in science and collaboration skills is quite a bit more advanced than the abilities of their comparisons. Indeed, average-ability LBD students engage in science and collaboration skills as well as or better than non-LBD honors students, and LBD honors students engage quite expertly (Kolodner, Crismond, et al., 2003; Kolodner, Gray, & Fasse, 2003).

The goal of this chapter is to provide an example of how what we know about cognition can be used to design learning environments that promote deep and lasting learning. We begin with discussion of case-based reasoning as a cognitive model of transfer, then present Learning by Design as an enactment of case-based reasoning's suggestions. We present some learning results, and then a discussion of the lessons that might be learned from our endeavor about designing effective project-based curriculum units.

THE COGNITIVE MODEL IMPLIED BY CASE-BASED REASONING

A Model of Reasoning

Case-based reasoning (CBR) means solving a new problem based on lessons learned or procedures followed in an old situation or interpreting a new situation like an old one that it is similar to. We might, for example, create a new recipe by adapting one we've made previously.

Case-based reasoning (see, e.g., Kolodner, 1993; Schank, 1982, 1999) was developed as a way of enhancing the reasoning capabilities of computers; it is a kind of analogical reasoning in which problems are solved by reference to previously experienced situations and the lessons learned from them. Experiences implementing computer systems that could reason and learn based on their experience have allowed the CBR community to extract principles about learning from experience—for example, the kinds of interpretations of experience that are important to reach a reusable encoding of an experience, the kinds of interpretations of experience that promote accessibility, and triggers for generating learning, explanation goals, and revising previously made encodings.

The basic premise underlying CBR is the preference to reason using the most specific and most cohesive applicable knowledge available. Inferences made using specific knowledge are relatively simple to make. Inferences made using cohesive knowledge structures—those that tie together several aspects of a situation—are relatively efficient. Cases, which describe situations, are both specific and cohesive. In addition, they record what is possible, providing a reasoner with more probability of moving forward in a workable way than is provided by using general knowledge that is merely plausible. Reasoning based on previous experience seems natural in people; an understanding of how it is done well and effectively can provide guidelines for helping people to effectively use this natural reasoning process.

A Model of Learning

Learning, in the CBR paradigm, means extending one's knowledge by interpreting new experiences and incorporating them into memory, by reinterpreting and reindexing old experiences to make them more usable and accessible, and by abstracting out generalizations over a set of experiences. Interpreting an experience means creating an explanation that connects one's goals and actions with resulting outcomes. Such learning depends heavily on the reasoner's ability to create such explanations, suggesting that the ability and desire to explain are key to promoting learning.

CBR thus gives failure a central role in promoting learning because failure promotes a need to explain. When the reasoner's expectations fail, it is alerted that its knowledge or reasoning is deficient. When some outcome or solution is unsuccessful, the reasoner is similarly alerted of a deficiency in its knowledge. Crucial to recognizing and interpreting failure is useful feedback from the world allowing indexing that discriminates usability of old cases and allowing good judgments later about reuse.

A Model of Learning for Transfer

A case-based reasoner is constantly engaging in transfer—that is, applying lessons learned in old situations to new ones. It learns by adding new cases, reencoding and reindexing old cases, and abstracting out generalizations. CBR defines *transfer* as spontaneously reusing some past experience productively, and it points out three steps involved in reuse: remembering (access), deciding on applicability, and application (Kolodner, Gray, & Fasse, 2003). Computational models we have built show that "getting to productive transfer," or being able to carry out all three steps, is a developmental process, requiring practice and explanation, articulation of lessons learned, and iterative and reflective application of those lessons (Hammond, 1989; Kolodner, 1993; Schank, 1982, 1999).

These computer implementations provide insights into the processes involved in "getting to productive transfer." Remembering, they tell us, requires interpreting at encoding time and at retrieval time, and matching. The better one encodes, the more chance there is of noticing relevant similarities that allow remembering of applicable cases to happen. Productive interpretation means making connections between goals, what one decided to do to achieve them, and what happened when the plan was carried out; extracting lessons that can be learned; and making conditions of applicability of those lessons explicit. The better a reasoner is at extracting lessons and conditions of applicability from a situation, the better he or she will be able to see connections between an old and a new situation. This means for the classroom that we should help learners interpret their experiences to extract what can be learned from them; anticipate the kinds of situations in which those lessons might be applied; and abstract across a variety of experiences to extract general principles.

Implications for Education

Case-based reasoning gives much advice about promoting deep and transferable learning (Kolodner, 1997):

1. We should ask learners to achieve engaging goals that provide interpretable feedback—so that they will have the motivation to take part in learning activities, the opportunity to misunderstand and make mistakes, the desire to explain, and a need to engage in several iterations to achieve success.

2. We should help learners turn their experiences into accessible and productively usable cases in their memories—by helping them interpret their experiences so as to explain results and extract out lessons that can be learned and conditions of applicability of those lessons.

3. We should make sure learners get both the feedback and help they need so that they know the effects of their decisions and can explain those effects. That means helping them recognize and explain mistakes and/or poor predictions, and helping them revise memory's encodings and interpretations as those explanations suggest.

4. We should give learners practice reusing and debugging what they've learned—that is, retrieving applicable cases from memory; judging which of several potential cases might be most applicable in a situation; and merging, adapting, and applying the lessons learned in new situations.

5. We should help learners notice similarities across their own experiences and those of others and extract out general rules and draw out abstractions to use for more sophisticated encoding.

FROM COGNITIVE MODEL
TO CLASSROOM ENACTMENT

A central aim in science education is to help students learn content and skills in ways that allow them to transfer what they have learned to new situations; that is, to apply what they've learned in situations that weren't directly targeted in the learning. The suggestions of CBR are consistent with much in the learning-sciences literatures (see, e.g., Bransford, Brown, & Cocking, 1999; Collins, Brown, & Newman, 1989). But CBR cannot explain what the teacher's and the students' roles would be. What should we use the computer for? How many times can learners iterate before they become bored? How do you help learners become interested in discussing what they are learning? We therefore sought out an approach to education that would be consistent with CBR's suggestions and that would provide us with guidance in designing ways to enact those suggestions. Two approaches were interesting to us: problem-based learning (Barrows, 1985) and project-based inquiry learning (Blumenfeld et al., 1991).

Problem-based learning (PBL) has students learn both content and skills by solving authentic, real-world problems and reflecting on their experiences. Because the problems are complex, students work in groups, where they pool their expertise and experience and together grapple with the complexities of the issues that must be considered. Coaches guide student reflection on their problem-solving experiences, asking students to articulate both the concepts and skills they are learning, and helping them identify the cognitive skills needed for problem solving, the full range of skills needed for collaboration and articulation, and the principles behind those skills. But students decide how to go about solving problems and what they need to learn, while coaches question students to force them to justify their approach and explain their conclusions. Students learn the practices of the profession they are learning and the content professionals need to know, as well as skills needed for lifelong learning.

In project-based inquiry, students investigate scientific content and learn science skills and practices in the context of attempting to address challenges in the world around them. Students investigate as scientists would, through observations; designing and running experiments; designing, building, and running models; reading written material; and so on, as appropriate. They make presentations to each other as scientists do, for purposes of learning more, informing peers so that they can be successful, and having the opportunity to build on each other's contributions. They also apply what they are learning to address the project challenge, and in project-based science, there is emphasis not only on being able to articulate the science but also being able to use it appropriately and know when it is applicable.

LEARNING BY DESIGN

Learning by Design builds on these insights. It is a project-based inquiry approach to science education with project challenges in the form of design challenges, usually design of working devices. Design challenges are naturally iterative. That is, one almost never is able to fulfill the criteria of a design challenge in one try; usually, what is designed doesn't work as well as expected, and successive iterations of identifying why the device is behaving the way it is and then redesigning it are needed. Design challenges can thus play two roles in a project-based inquiry classroom: providing an engaging context for generating questions, investigating, and learning content and skills, as well as providing a natural context for iteratively constructing better understandings of content and skills while iteratively working toward a solution to the project challenge.

Design challenges can also provide social affordances for promoting learning, if they are chosen to be complex enough so that students feel they can be more successful if they share findings and experiences with each other. PBL suggests times for reflection and interpretation, and CBR suggests the content of that reflection. But it is far more fun to work on a project than to interpret and reflect on one's experiences. If, however, students feel they can learn from each other, they will see reason to report to each other, to listen to each other, and to advise each other. Presenting to others provides students a reason to think back on what they've done, organize their thoughts about it, and present it in ways others can understand. It also provides opportunities for students to experience several different ways of using the same knowledge and carrying out the same skills.

LBD's cycle of activities is shown in Fig. 4.1. Within this framework are myriad opportunities for students to share their work with others, hear their questions and ideas, and extract scientific principles and practices from their experiences. Presentations are made at each place in the cycle where students can benefit from hearing about the work of others and from taking the time to reflect back on their own experience to make connections. This is generally at three points: after investigations are complete ("poster sessions"), after generating design ideas ("pin-up sessions"), and after each attempt to try out ideas ("gallery walks"). In poster sessions, students present the design of their investigation, their results, and their interpretations of those results, and discussion after a poster session usually focuses on experimental methodology, identifying trends in data, and explaining trends in data scientifically. In pin-up sessions, students focus on the design decisions they've made, justifying those design decisions using evidence from experiments, rules of thumb generated from data, and scientific principles discussed earlier. Gallery walks follow design testing, usually contain the finished artifact, and describe the consequences of design decisions, frequently through performance. In their presentations, students focus on explaining how they think their designs work, using science and engineering concepts and vocabulary and the evidence that comes from the investigations they and their classmates have carried out.

Not seen in this cycle are the many scaffolding tools provided to help students succeed at their design and investigative activities. The most important ones are Design Diary pages (Puntambekar & Kolodner, 1998, 2003) in sup-

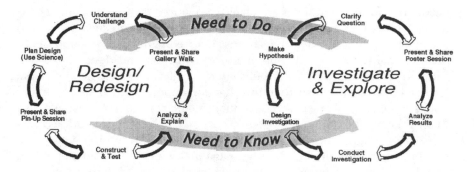

FIG. 4.1. Learning by Design's cycles. From "Promoting Transfer Through Case-Based Reasoning: Rituals and Practices in Learning by Design Classrooms," by J. L. Kolodner, J. Gray, and B. B. Fasse, 2003, *Cognitive Science Quarterly*, *3*(2), p. 199. Copyright 2003 by Lavoisier. Reprinted with permission.

port of small-group activities and SMILE software (Kolodner & Nagel, 1999; Nagel & Kolodner, 1999) in support of planning for small-group work and putting presentations together. Although class discussions provide pointers about the how-to's of activities students are engaging in, it is the rare learner who can use pointers well, even after several discussions and attempts at use. Both the Design Diary and SMILE software are designed to provide reminders about the most important points touched on in class discussions.

A Sample Walkthrough

The Balloon Car Challenge comes 2 months into the school year and is a subchallenge of our Vehicles in Motion unit. In this unit, students learn about forces and motion in the context of designing a vehicle and its propulsion system that can navigate several hills and beyond. The Vehicles unit helps students develop a deep understanding of the effects of forces on motion. In the early part of the Vehicles Challenge, students "mess about" with toy cars and notice that some are better able than others to navigate hills and bumpy terrain, that some start easier than others, and that some go farther, faster, and/or straighter than others. They generate a variety of questions about effects of forces on motion, for example, "What affects how far a vehicle will go?" "How can we apply enough force to a car to make it go over a hill?" "What kind of engine will get a vehicle started easily and keep it going?" This is followed by four modules. In the first, the Coaster Car Challenge, we ask them to construct and redesign a coaster car that can go as far and as straight as possible after being let go at the top of a ramp. In this module, they investigate how to keep things going and learn about combining forces, two particular forces (gravity and friction), and the skill of explaining behavior of a device scientifically. In the second module, which we go through in detail, they construct and design a balloon-powered engine for their vehicle that will allow it to go as far as possible on flat ground, investigating how to get things moving and learning more about combining forces and about forces in pairs. In the third module, they construct and design a rubber-band-powered engine for their vehicle that will allow it to go as far as possible on flat ground, doing further investigations about getting and keeping things going and moving from conceptions to the language of Newton's laws. In the final module, they pull together what they've learned in previous modules to design and construct a vehicle and its hybrid propulsion system that can go over several hills and beyond. Each module ends with a competition and discussion explaining the varying behaviors of the different vehicles.

The Balloon Car Challenge is the second part of the Vehicles Challenge, and students are challenged here to design and build a propulsion system from balloons and straws that can propel their coaster car as far as possible on flat ground. Figure 4.2 shows students racing a set of balloon-powered cars. Notice in the walkthrough how iteration toward better solutions provides opportunities for iteration toward better understanding; how sharing experimental results, design ideas, and design experiences promotes focus on learning of scientific reasoning; how Design Diary pages and SMILE

FIG. 4.2.   Racing balloon-powered vehicles. From "Problem-Based Learning Meets Case-Based Reasoning in the Middle-School Science Classroom: Putting Learning by Design™ Into Practice," by J. L. Kolodner et al., 2003, *Journal of the Learning Sciences, 12*(4), p. 530. Copyright 2003 by Lawrence Erlbaum Associates. Reprinted with permission.

software provide scaffolding for doing and reflection; how activities students engage in are "ritualized" to fit needs at that stage of the design cycle; and the many different opportunities students have in the course of a 2-week challenge to engage in and learn a variety of science, communication, collaboration, planning, reflection, and design skills as they are learning and applying science content.

Understanding the Challenge.   Addressing the challenge begins with gaining a better understanding of it (top of the design/redesign cycle), first through "messing about" in small groups and then "whiteboarding" as a class to identify ideas. Messing about is exploratory activity with materials or devices with mechanisms similar to what will be designed to quickly identify important issues that will need to be addressed. For this challenge, students mess about with a variety of balloon-and-straw engines. By the time students are working on the Balloon Car Challenge, they have experienced messing about several times, and they are becoming adept at it. They know that they should quickly try out several different possible ways of using the materials and eyeball how each seems to work. Thus, it is not uncommon during this session to see students comparing engines with shorter and longer straws attached, bigger and smaller balloons, and so on, and also trying out such things as using more than one engine.

After 20 minutes of messing about, the class gathers together for whiteboarding. Whiteboarding, taken from PBL, is a whole-class discussion where students record their observations and identify facts they know, suggest ideas and hypotheses for addressing the challenge, and identify issues they need to learn more about (learning issues). Having participated in whiteboarding several times earlier in the year, students are familiar with expectations. They eagerly volunteer what they've observed (e.g., "It seems like a wider straw makes the car go farther," "We attached two straws to our balloon, and it went really far"), argue about what they saw and how to interpret it (e.g., "Our car seemed to go farther with a shorter straw," "Ours went farther with a longer straw," "I don't think we can compare across those cars because they didn't go exactly the same distance off the ramp. We'll need to run fair tests to really know"), try to explain what they observed (e.g., "I think the wider straw makes it go farther because more air comes out of it, and that must mean more force"), and identify variables whose effects they want to know about conclusively (e.g., effects of length of straw, number of straws in a balloon, diameter of straw, extra engines, bigger balloons, amount of air in the balloon). During this public session, the teacher helps the class see what their peers have done, helps them articulate questions and hypotheses, and helps them turn their initial questions into questions that can be answered through well-controlled experiments (e.g., what effect does the size of a balloon have on the distance the car will travel?).

Investigate and Explore.   Next the teacher helps the class decide which of the issues they've identified as important for investigation are the most important. They might then have a discussion about the ins and outs of good experimentation, reminding themselves of what they've learned about experimentation during earlier activities (e.g., the need to vary only one variable at a time, the need to run procedures exactly the same way each time). Indeed, there may be a poster on the wall with "fair test rules of thumb" generated during previous activities and with such entries as "To insure a fair test, make sure to run procedures exactly the same way each time," and "To insure a fair comparison, keep everything the same except for one variable."

Each group of students now takes responsibility for investigating one of the questions that has been generated and then designs and runs an experiment (investigates) to find an answer. It is usually the end of a class period at this point, and for homework the teacher assigns individuals the responsibility of designing an experiment that will assess the effects of the variable they are investigating. As they are designing their experiments, students use a Design Diary page that prompts them on what to pay attention to in designing and running an experiment and collecting data (Fig. 4.3).

Students get together in small groups the next day, comparing and contrasting the experiments they have each designed as individuals and designing an experiment that takes the best of each. One student may have remembered that multiple trials are needed, while another grappled with which variables to control. It is rare for a single student to consider everything needed for a fair test. The teacher also makes his or her way around the room, providing help as groups need it.

Students spend a day or two designing and running their experiments and collecting and analyzing their data, and at the beginning of the following day, each group prepares a poster to present to the class. They show their experimental design, data, and data interpretations, and they try to extract out advice for the class from their results. Each group presents to the class in a poster session. Because students need each other's investigative results to be successful balloon-car designers, they listen intently and query each other about experimental design and procedures and gathering and interpretation of data (much as in a professional poster session). This provides an opportunity to discuss the ins and outs of designing and running experiments well. For example, in running balloon-car experiments, groups often fail to make sure that they blew up their balloons exactly the same amount each time. The class might discuss ways of making sure that balloons are inflated the same way each time—by counting breaths, by measuring diameter of the balloon, and so on. Often, even though students have already had some previous experience designing and running experiments, some groups' results are not trustworthy yet, and they redo their experiments and the cycle of activities just described. Figures 4.4 and 4.5 show typical posters.

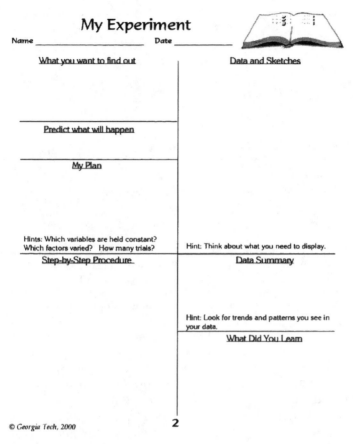

My Experiment

Name _____   Date _____

What you want to find out   Data and Sketches

Predict what will happen

My Plan

Hints: Which variables are held constant?
Which factors varied?   How many trials?   Hint: Think about what you need to display.

Step-by-Step Procedure   Data Summary

Hint: Look for trends and patterns you see in
your data.

What Did You Learn

© *Georgia Tech, 2000*   **2**

FIG. 4.3. Design Diary page: My Experiment. From "Problem-Based Learning Meets Case-Based Reasoning in the Middle-School Science Classroom: Putting Learning by Design™ Into Practice," by J. L. Kolodner et al., 2003, *Journal of the Learning Sciences, 12*(4), p. 520. Copyright 2003 by Lawrence Erlbaum Associates. Reprinted with permission.

When the class agrees that the results most groups have come up with are believable, the teacher helps students abstract over the full set of experiments and experimental results to notice abstractions and extract out "design rules of thumb" (e.g., "By using double-walled balloon engines, the car goes farther because a larger force is acting on the car"). Experiments provide learners the opportunity to experience and record phenomena, but they don't necessarily understand why those phenomena are happening. To learn the explanations behind these phenomena, the teacher makes some relevant reading available about the science content involved, performs demonstrations that exemplify the science concept in another context, and reviews and discusses student-generated examples of the science

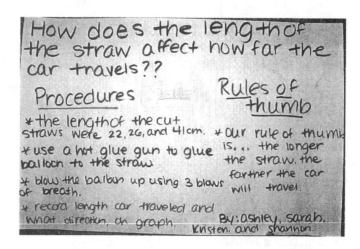

FIG. 4.4. Poster from balloon-car investigation—Length of straw. From "Problem-Based Learning Meets Case-Based Reasoning in the Middle-School Science Classroom: Putting Learning by Design™ Into Practice," by J. L. Kolodner et al., 2003, *Journal of the Learning Sciences, 12*(4), p. 531. Copyright 2003 by Lawrence Erlbaum Associates. Reprinted with permission.

concept, usually from everyday life experiences. Here the issue is why a bigger force would cause the vehicle to go farther if the total amount of air coming out of the balloon is the same no matter how many balloons are used. The balloon car works best when a high velocity is achieved because most of the distance gained is during coasting (after the balloon engine has exhausted its air). If you are coasting to zero velocity, then the higher your velocity is when you start to coast, the greater the distance you will travel, provided that the floor has low, near-constant friction during coasting. Thus, students need to obtain high acceleration with their engines. To understand this, the class spends time discussing both Newton's Third Law— equal and opposite forces—and Newton's Second Law—about how changes in force and mass can change motion—and use that science to explain how their balloon-powered vehicles behave. Later iterations to the rule of thumb produce more informed and complete statements (e.g., "By using double-walled balloon engines, the car goes farther because a larger force is acting on the air inside, so then an equally large force from the air acts on the car").

Design Planning. Upon returning to the design/redesign cycle, the class briefly revisits the whiteboard and specifies the constraints and criteria of this challenge (understanding the challenge). Next, students plan their balloon-car designs, using the combination of experimental results the class has produced, design rules of thumb extracted out, and scientific prin-

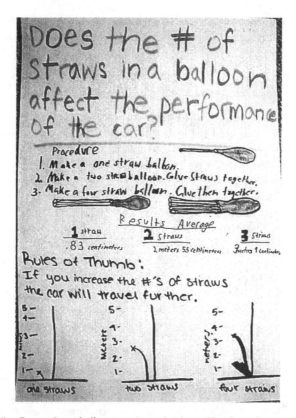

FIG. 4.5. Poster from balloon-car investigation—Number of straws. From "Problem-Based Learning Meets Case-Based Reasoning in the Middle-School Science Classroom: Putting Learning by Design™ Into Practice," by J. L. Kolodner et al., 2003, *Journal of the Learning Sciences, 12*(4), p. 531. Copyright 2003 by Lawrence Erlbaum Associates. Reprinted with permission.

ciples read about and discussed as a class. Generally, the teacher has each individual plan his or her design for homework and bring the designs to the group. The group then discusses the ins and outs of each individual design decision that has been made and decides on a group design. Often, one person's design will be chosen as the "best" one, and it will be refined based on some of the design decisions other group members suggested. In general, students tend to design cars with two or three balloon engines, often the balloons are doubled, and they tend to use wide straws or several narrow ones attached to each balloon. They justify these decisions based on the experimental results they've seen and what they know about forces.

Each group prepares another poster, this time presenting their design ideas along with the evidence that justifies each decision and their predictions about how it will perform. They present to their peers in a pin-up session. During this activity, the primary foci are justifying decisions using evidence and making predictions, and after groups present to their peers and entertain their peers' questions and suggestions, the class as a group discusses not only the ideas that everyone has presented, but also the practice of justifying, what it means to identify and use good evidence, and making predictions.

Justifications during this pin-up session tend to refer to both the experiments that have been done and the principles about combining forces that were discussed earlier: "We didn't use more than two because we couldn't figure out how to blow up more than two balloons at a time. We also decided to double the balloons on each engine because Group 4's experiment showed that double balloons make the car go farther. We think this is because a double balloon exerts more force on the air inside the balloon, providing more force in the direction we want the car to go." If justifications are truly qualitatively better than during a previous pin-up session, the teacher might point that out to the class and ask them if they know why they were better and use the results of that discussion to update "justification rules of thumb" or the "justification working definition" (e.g., "Justifications can refer to experimental results or to scientific principles; if they refer to both, they will convince people more than if they refer to just one").

Construct and Test; Analyze and Explain; Gallery Walks. Students now move to the construction and testing phase, modifying their designs based on what they've discussed in class and heard from their peers, and then constructing and testing their first balloon-powered engine. They use another Design Diary page here, this time with prompts helping them to keep track of their predictions, the data they are collecting as they test, whether their predictions are met, and explanations of why not (Fig. 4.6).

None of their balloon cars work exactly as predicted, sometimes because of construction problems and sometimes because of incomplete understanding of scientific principles and the results of experiments. Some students can explain why their balloon cars didn't work well enough; some can't. After working in small groups to try to explain their results, the class engages in a gallery walk, with each group's presentation focused on what happened when their design was constructed and tested, why it worked the way it did, and what to do next so that it will perform better. Some students can explain quite well, but some students have not understood the science well and need help explaining. The teacher helps students state their explanations scientifically and calls on others in the class to help as well. Hearing the explanations students are generating allows the teacher to identify misconceptions and gaps in student knowledge, and discussions about those conceptions and gaps might follow the gallery walk, along with readings or a short lecture or set of demos to help promote better understanding. This

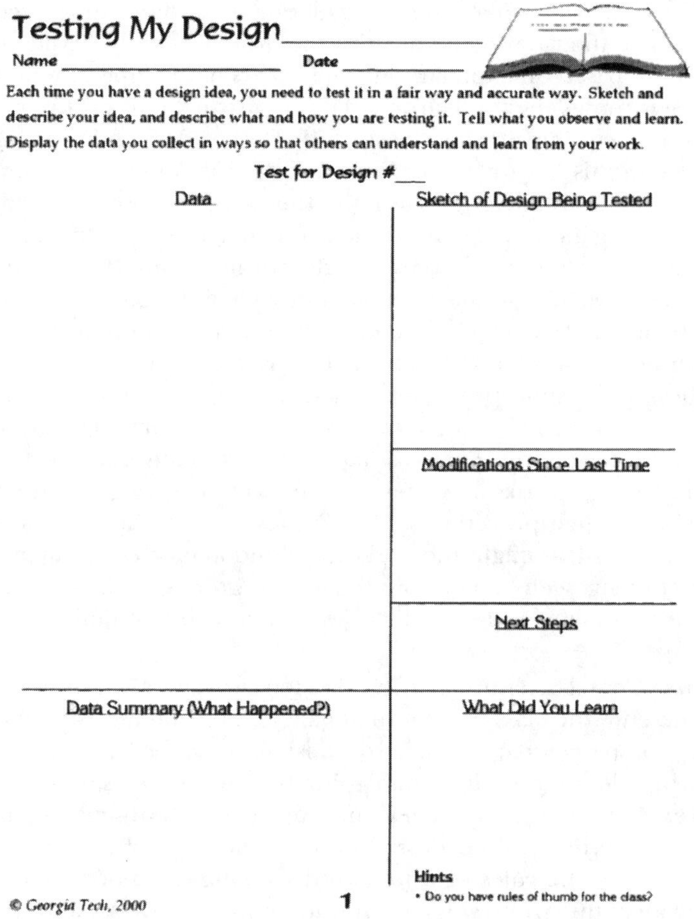

Testing My Design_____

Name _____ Date _____

Each time you have a design idea, you need to test it in a fair way and accurate way. Sketch and describe your idea, and describe what and how you are testing it. Tell what you observe and learn. Display the data you collect in ways so that others can understand and learn from your work.

Test for Design #___

Data	Sketch of Design Being Tested
	Modifications Since Last Time
	Next Steps
Data Summary (What Happened?)	**What Did You Learn**
	Hints
	• Do you have rules of thumb for the class?

© Georgia Tech, 2000   1

FIG. 4.6. Design Diary page: Testing My Design. From "Problem-Based Learning Meets Case-Based Reasoning in the Middle-School Science Classroom: Putting Learning by Design™ Into Practice," by J. L. Kolodner et al., 2003, *Journal of the Learning Sciences, 12*(4), p. 522. Copyright 2003 by Lawrence Erlbaum Associates. Reprinted with permission.

gallery walk is also followed by classroom discussion abstracting over the set of experiences presented, and revisiting and revising design rules of thumb, correcting them and doing a better job of connecting them to explanations of why rules of thumb work. Discussion also focuses on the explanations students made, and the class might generate the beginning of a working definition of "scientific explanation," for example, "Explaining scientifically means providing reasons why something happened that use science terminology and include the science principles we learned about earlier."

Iterative Redesign.   Following the gallery walk and ensuing discussions, students make their way again around the design/redesign cycle, revising their designs, based on explanations their peers have helped them develop and the new things they've learned. They construct and test their new designs, each time using another "Testing My Design" Design Diary page, and they iterate in this way toward better and better solutions until they or the teacher decide they have gotten as far as they need to. Discussions after second and third gallery walks often focus on "fair testing," this time in the context of comparing results across different iterations of balloon-car designs. Students will not be able to explain why a new design works better than an old one if they have changed more than one thing in their design since the earlier time. Nor will they be able to believe their own results if they don't follow the same testing procedures each time. Sometimes teams discover these issues as they are testing a later design and report them to the class; sometimes a peer notices that a test was done differently than last time or, if results are confusing, asks how a test was done and helps a group discover inconsistencies in their procedures. The "fair test rules of thumb" may be consulted and refined, as might the working definition of scientific explanation. Once all students seem aimed toward success, groups work independently, refining their designs without gallery walks between iterations.

Finishing Up.   The entire activity takes ten to twelve 45-minute class periods. At the end, the class holds a final gallery walk and a competition, and then they compare and contrast across designs to better understand the scientific principles they are learning, going back to the rules of thumb to revise and explain them better. They finish up, as well, by discussing their collaboration experience, their design process, their use of evidence, and so on, and revising the rules of thumb and working definitions about each. Following all of this group work, each student writes up and hands in a project report—including a summary of the reasoning behind their group's final design and what they've learned about collaboration, design, use of evidence, and so on.

Learning by Design's Novel Features

Although it integrates features of PBL and project-based inquiry, LBD has many novel features of its own.

Iteration.   Iteration serves several purposes in LBD. First, because students have several chances to address the challenge, they are more likely to succeed, promoting better engagement. Second, because LBD is explicit about the need for explanation between cycles and explicit about the activities that must be carried out between iterations, it promotes more productive reflection than one normally finds in a project-based classroom. Third, the attempts to explain and replan between iterations provide opportunities to recognize where conceptions and/or skills are deficient or missing, prompting a desire to learn those things as well as the opportunity to try out what's been learned. Students have the opportunity not only to do a better job of achieving the challenge but also to revise and refine their understandings and capabilities. On the downside, too much iteration can make a project long and/or boring. Our experience shows that it is important for teachers to make sure that progress is made between each iteration and to provide extra help to those having trouble so that the whole class does not have to engage in extra iterations because one or two groups are far behind.

Public Presentations. The literature suggests that when learners are asked to organize their thoughts to explain to others, it aids their own learning (Scardamalia, Bereiter, & Steinbach, 1984; Palincsar & Brown, 1984). Public presentations play a major role in LBD, and LBD includes three kinds, each focusing on a different set of skills that have recently been used during project work. Presentations that focus on investigation skills can aid learning of investigation skills; presentations that focus on the decisions a group has made and why they've made them provide affordances for learning well how to make decisions and justify them; presentations that focus on explaining what happened have affordances for learning the skills involved in explaining. We've found that the need to make a public presentation encourages students to reflect on what they've just done and make sense of it in a way that others can understand. We've found, as well, that if we are very explicit in defining requirements for a particular kind of presentation *and* if we provide scaffolding to help with achieving those requirements, then students will become more seriously engaged in preparing for their presentations, and teachers and students will be able to be focused as they interpret what others are saying and draw lessons from across the experiences of several groups.

But simply making a presentation does not go far enough toward ensuring productive learning. Students differ in their abilities (e.g., reasoning, organizing, argumentation), thus each of the public presentations done in the context of LBD is followed by a whole-class discussion that takes advantage of the opportunities presented by groups' presentations to each other. Exceptional reasoning can be noted and rules of thumb derived from it. Poor reasoning can be noted and the class can give advice about how to do better. The reasoning of several groups can be compared and/or contrasted to allow the group to notice some other rule of thumb for performing a skill well.

Ritualizing Classroom Activities. LBD routinizes or ritualizes the repeated activities of the classroom, making them into scripts. In LBD, we've created classroom "rituals" and sequences of rituals to correspond to each of the important skill sets we want students to learn. For example, students learn experimental methodology through an extended sequence of rituals. First, they use SMILE or a Design Diary page to remind them of what they need to take into account in designing an experiment. Then they run the experiment, collect their data, interpret them, and make a poster of their results, again using either a Design Diary page or SMILE to remind them about what needs to be included in a poster session presentation. They then present as part of a poster session, where they are expected to present their question, investigative plan, data, and data interpretations. Their peers read their posters and ask questions about how trustworthy the results are. The ins and outs of experimental design are discussed if necessary, and they are helped by the class to redesign their experiment. After all presentations are done, rules of thumb are extracted, both about experimental design and about the phenomena being investigated. Experiments are redesigned and repeated if results are not trustworthy. Repeating rituals over time systematizes practices to make them methodical, situates them in several contexts, and engages students in public practice as collaborators. The whole set of rituals and their purposes are listed in Table 4.1 (from Kolodner, Gray, & Fasse, 2003).

Design Diary and Software Scaffolding. There is much independent work done in a project-based classroom. The teacher can only be with one group at a time. It is easy for groups to become disengaged or forget what they should be doing. LBD's Design Diary pages and software scaffolding are designed for the purpose of augmenting the help the teacher can provide to a group. Design Diary pages (Figs. 4.3 and 4.6) are specialized to the kinds of activities students work on as individuals and small groups, and they provide reminders about the things the group should be doing and/or thinking about during any activity. Design Diary pages don't have much detail; they are designed to augment the discussions that take place in the classroom and the rules of thumb and working definitions posted on the walls. But these pages work if the teacher does a good job of modeling skills before students engage in them and if whole-class discussions are used to articulate the how-to's and debug those skills. SMILE's scaffolding is more specific than what is found in Design Diary pages—because it is easier to organize materials on the computer than on paper so that they are not overwhelming. But SMILE's scaffolding also is designed to augment the modeling and drawing out of lessons learned led by the teacher in the classroom.

TABLE 4.1
LBD's Rituals and Their Purposes

LBD Ritual	Placement in Cycle	Purpose
Pin-up session	Design: Present & Share	Presentation of design ideas and design decisions and their justifications for peer review
Gallery walk	Design: Present & Share	Presentation of design experiences and explanation of design's behavior for peer review
Poster session	Investigate: Present & Share	Present procedures, results, and analysis of investigations for peer review
Messing about	Design: Understand challenge	Exploration (in small groups) of materials or devices to identify phenomena, promote question asking, and see connections between science and the world; followed by whiteboarding
Whiteboarding	Design: Understand challenge Investigate: Clarify question	A forum for sharing what peers know, their ideas, and what they need to learn, and to keep track of class's progress and common knowledge
Creating and refining design rules of thumb	Design: Analyze & Explain, Present & Share (gallery walk), Understand challenge Investigate: Analyze results, Present & Share (poster session)	Identify trends in data and behaviors of devices; connect scientific explanations so as to know when the trends apply

Note. From "Promoting Transfer Through Case-Based Reasoning: Rituals and Practices in Learning by Design Classrooms," by J. L. Kolodner, J. Gray, and B. B. Fasse, 2003, *Cognitive Science Quarterly, 3*(2), p. 201. Copyright 2003 by Lavoisier. Reprinted with permission.

Getting Ready for LBD. A big challenge in working on projects is getting students (and teachers) ready to engage in the skills needed for success. It is difficult, we've found, for students to learn all of those skills from scratch at the same time they are trying to learn difficult content. We therefore had to design activities for early in the year that introduced students to the skill sets they would be engaging in in the context of simple science. LBD's launcher units (Holbrook & Kolodner, 2000) introduce the full set of other skills that students need to be successful in learning from design activities. A simple early challenge introduces collaboration and gallery walks and the notions of criteria, constraints, and tradeoffs in design. Another activity introduces the need for procedures to be run exactly the same way every time to get results that can be trusted, and that is followed up by another activity that makes clear the need to control variables well to make a test fair. Each launcher unit ends with a design challenge that requires messing about, investigation, and several iterations for success. Physical science students design and build a parachute; earth science students design and model (in a stream table) an erosion management system to keep a hill from eroding onto a basketball court. Launcher units spend approximately 4 weeks introducing important skills and put more emphasis on skills than content. At the end of a launcher unit, students are ready to use the skills they've learned to achieve design challenges that require deep understanding of science content.

LEARNING THROUGH LBD: EVALUATION AND ASSESSMENT RESULTS

One of our goals when we began the design of LBD was to get more students more engaged in science. Our observations and discussions with students, teachers, and parents show that students enjoy LBD and remain engaged throughout as long as teachers draw good connections between the modules in a unit and are excited about what they are doing. Teachers have reported to us that discipline in class is qualitatively improved over previous years, and we see that students who begin the year sure that they will not like science become quite engaged. Students report to us that they enjoy the fact that their verbal, planning, and collaboration skills are valued. Many tell us that they didn't know science required those skills.

But are students learning? We are aiming for them to learn science more effectively than other students and to learn the skills and practices of science and project work. We have evaluated learning among LBD students in a variety of classroom venues. Our most interesting results come from our evaluations of Vehicles in Motion done over a wide range of eighth-grade classrooms (age 13–14; Kolodner, Gray, & Fasse, 2003; Holbrook et al., 2001).

Learning of Science Content

We tested students on physical science content knowledge and general science skill knowledge using a standardized written test format. It was administered in a pre-/post-implementation design in LBD and comparison classrooms. Items on the test were drawn from a number of normed and tested sources, including the National Assessment of Educational Progress

(NAEP), released items from the Third International Mathematics and Science Study (TIMSS), the Force Concept Inventory, and the Force and Motion Conceptual Evaluation, as well as items of our own.

Comparing LBD students to matched comparisons, we found in two separate years of data collection that LBD students do at least as well as comparison students in content mastery and sometimes better. When we analyze the results from individual teachers, we find that the largest gains among our LBD students were in those classes that are the most socioeconomically disadvantaged and who tested lowest on the pretest. Interestingly, these classes also had teachers with less background in physical science. We also see a trend toward reengaging girls in science. Preliminary scoring on our 1998–1999 data shows that although girls score lower than boys, as a rule, on pretests, they are equal with boys or ahead of them on posttests. Although we would have liked to have seen LBD students master the content far better than non-LBD students, and we believe they have, we don't yet have the data to show that, as the short-answer and multiple-choice questions we were using did not allow us to distinguish different levels of content mastery.

Learning of Science and Collaboration Skills

Our more interesting results are on the learning of skills, a major focus in LBD. To learn about students' skill competence, we assessed their capabilities when working in groups on a set of performance tasks. One assessment was done after 5 weeks of LBD; another was done after completion of the Vehicles unit, after a total of 13 to 18 weeks of LBD. Each performance task has three parts to it. In Part 1, students design an experiment or procedure for fair testing. In Part 2, they run an experiment or a procedure that we specify for them and collect data. In Part 3, they analyze the data and use it to make recommendations. Our friction task, modified from PALS (SRI, 1999), is the simplest to explain. Here, we put students in the position of learning enough about the braking performance of several kinds of rubber to be able to make recommendations about materials to use for tires on school buses. In Part 1, we provide them with a block that has two kinds of rubber on it and ask them to design an experiment that would provide information about braking performance of each. The most successful students consider what they need to test, how to measure it, and what conditions to test for. In Part 2, we provide them with surfaces and provide a procedure they should use to collect data. In Part 3, we ask them to analyze the data and make a recommendation about what kind of rubber to use and explain why.

We videotape groups of four students working on a performance task and analyze it on seven dimensions: negotiations during collaboration, distribution of the task, attempted use of prior knowledge, adequacy of prior knowledge mentioned, science talk (use of science vocabulary), science practice (appropriate to the task), and self-checks. Scoring is by group, and each group is scored on a Likert scale of 1 to 5, with 5 being the highest score. Typically, and a score of 1 represents no attempt to even participate in the targeted activity, and a score of 5 means that almost all students are consistently engaging in the activity over the episode; a score of 2 shows that at least one member of the group is consistently trying to engage, 3 shows that two or more students are consistently engaging, and 4 shows that over half are engaging. Table 4.2 shows rubrics for several of those dimensions. Notice that the coding captures the extent to which students in a group participate in practicing a skill. If more students use the skill, the group gets a higher rating.

TABLE 4.2
Two Example Items From the Video Coding Rubric

Students use science practice to decide on method/procedures.

Not at all	At least one of the members of the group suggests a method to test at least one variable	At least one of the members suggests a method and indicates an understanding of fair testing	At least one of the members suggests a method and indicates an understanding of fair testing and controlling for variables	Most of the team agree that the method used will fairly test the important variables and their decisions would actually be a reasonable experiment
1	2	3	4	5

Answers to the questions are negotiated based on data.

Not at all	At least one of the members of the group refers back to the data	At least one of the members of the group refers back to the data and the group uses the data	At least two of the members of the group refer back to the data and the group uses the data accurately to respond	Most of the group recognize the need to look back at the data and discuss the data to reach an answer that is appropriate
1	2	3	4	5

Comparing LBD students to matched comparisons on performance tasks, our data show that LBD students consistently perform significantly better than non-LBD students at collaboration skills and metacognitive skills (e.g., those involved in checking work) and that they almost always perform significantly better than matched comparisons on science skills (those involved in designing fair tests, justifying with evidence, and explaining). Non-LBD students treat the tasks we give them as simply writing something down, never really addressing them as a challenge needing distributed effort. LBD students, on the other hand, negotiate a solution and see the tasks as requiring an experimental design. Indeed, in the year when we collected performance data early in the year (after the launcher unit for LBD students) and later in the year (in December or January, after the Vehicles unit for LBD students, and at the end of the school year for comparisons), we saw not only that LBD students performed better than comparison students, but that, though early in the year they performed better than comparisons in just a few categories (generally collaboration and self-checks), later in the year they performed better in a much larger range. Most interesting, perhaps, is that when we compare across mixed-achievement LBD students and honors non-LBD students, we found that mixed-achievement LBD students performed as well or better than non-LBD honors students on skills, meaning that LBD brings normal-achieving students to a level of capability usually found only among gifted or honors students. Table 4.3 shows the data that support these results.

DISCUSSION

We would like to see more deep understanding of science among our LBD students, and we are revising our units so that connections can more easily be made between science content and design-project experiences. We are also administering more in-depth content tests to get at the depth of understanding of LBD students. Anecdotal reports show us that students are learning science deeply, and we believe that with only a bit more revision of the units and with better assessment procedures, we will be able to show that. We are delighted by student engagement and by LBD students' learning of science and collaboration skills and practices. We believe there are several reasons for this success. LBD provides motivating activities that keep students' attention. It helps them reflect on their experiences in ways that promote abstraction from experience, explanation of results, and understanding of conditions of applicability. Repeated use of concepts, repeated practice of skills, and experience with those skills and concepts over a variety of circumstances seem to be important. LBD gives students reason to reflect on their experiences (they have to explain to others; others need their results; they want to improve their own results). LBD's sequencing provides

TABLE 4.3

Results of Performance Assessments for 1999–2000 and 2000–2001:
Means (and Standard Deviations) for Comparison and Learning by Design Students After the Unit

Coding Categories	1999–2000 Typical Comparison	1999–2000 Typical LBD	2000–2001 Typical Comparison	2000–2001 Typical LBD	1999–2000 Honors Comparison	1999–2000 Honors LBD	2000–2001 Honors LBD
Self-checks	1.50 (.58)	3.00 (.82)** $t(6) = 3.00$	1.30 (.67)	3.88 (1.03)* $t(7) = 5.548$	2.33 (.58)	4.25 (.50)*** $t(5) = 4.715$	5.00 (.00)*** $t(3) = 6.197$
Science practice	2.25 (.50)	2.75 (.96)	1.40 (.89)	3.75 (1.32)* $t(7) = 3.188$	2.67 (.71)	4.75 (.50)*** $t(4) = 4.648$	4.75 (.35)** $t(3) = 4.443$
Distributed efforts	2.25 (.50)	3.25 (.50)* $t(6) = 2.828$	1.70 (.84)	3.00 (.00)* $t(7) = 3.064$	3.00 (1.00)	4.00 (1.15)	4.25 (.35)
Negotiations	1.50 (.58)	2.50 (1.00)	1.40 (.65)	2.88 (1.03)* $t(7) = 2.631$	2.67 (.58)	4.50 (.58)*** $t(5) = 4.158$	4.00 (.00)* $t(3) = 3.098$
Prior knowledge adequate	1.50 (.58)	2.75 (.96)	1.60 (.89)	3.88 (.75)* $t(7) = 4.059$	2.67 (1.15)	3.50 (1.00)	4.25 (.35)
Prior knowledge	1.75 (.50)	2.25 (.50)	1.60 (.89)	3.75 (.87)* $t(7) = 3.632$	3.0 (.00)	3.75 (1.50)	3.75 (.35)
Science terms	1.75 (.50)	2.75 (.96)	1.50 (.87)	2.88 (.63)* $t(7) = 2.650$	2.67 (.71)	3.50 (1.00)	4.00 (.00)

Note. N = groups, where most groups consisted of 4 students each. Means are based on a Likert scale of 1 to 5, with 5 being the highest rating. Reliability for the coding scheme ranged from 82% to 100% agreement when two coders independently rated the tapes. For this set of data, a random sample of four or five tapes was coded for each teacher from one class period. Approximately 60 group sessions are represented in this table, representing 240 students. From "Promoting Transfer Through Case-Based Reasoning; Rituals and Practices in Learning by Design Classrooms," by J. L. Kolodner, J. Gray, and B. B. Fasse, 2003, *Cognitive Science Quarterly, 3*(2). p. 222. Copyright 2003 by Lavoisier. Reprinted with permission.

*$p < .03$. **$p < .02$. ***$p < .01$.

many different ways of helping students be successful at reflecting on their experiences productively, remembering, judging applicability, applying, and explaining. We believe there are six classroom practices to keep in mind in designing PBL environments for deep and lasting learning (adapted from Kolodner, in press):

1. Iterative refinement of concepts and skills being learned.
3. Consistent, continuous, reflective practice of targeted skills in contexts consistent with authentic use.
4. Giving students a need to use targeted content, skills, and practices.
5. Making recognition of applicability automatic through ritualizing important packages of skills.
6. Establishing and enforcing expectations about rigorous thinking and collaboration.
7. Liberal modeling and scaffolding—by teacher, peers, public displays, and Design Diary–type pages or software.

REFERENCES

Barrows, H. S. (1985). *How to design a problem-based curriculum for the preclinical years*. New York: Springer.

Blumenfeld, P. C., Soloway, E., Marx, R. W., Krajcik, J. S., Guzdial, M., & Palincsar, A. (1991). Motivating project-based learning: Sustaining the doing, supporting the learning. *Educational Psychologist, 26*(3 & 4), 369–398.

Bransford, J. D., Brown, A. L., & Cocking, R. R. (1999). Learning and transfer. In *How people learn: Brain, mind, experience, and school* (pp. 39–66). Washington, DC: National Academy Press.

Collins, A., Brown, J. S., & Newman, S. E. (1989). Cognitive apprenticeship: Teaching the crafts of reading, writing, and mathematics. In L. B. Resnick (Ed.), *Knowing, learning, and instruction: Essays in honor of Robert Glaser* (pp. 453–494). Hillsdale, NJ: Lawrence Erlbaum Associates.

Hammond, K. J. (1989). *Case-based planning*. New York: Academic Press.

Hmelo, C. E., Holton, D. L., & Kolodner, J. L. (2000). Designing to learn about complex systems. *Journal of the Learning Sciences, 9*(3), 247–298.

Holbrook, J. K., Gray, J., Fasse, B. B., Camp, P. J., & Kolodner, J. L. (2001). *Assessment and evaluation of the Learning by Design™ physical science units, 1999–2000: A document in progress* [Online]. Available: http://www.cc.gatech.edu/projects/lbd/pubtopic.html#assess

Holbrook, J., & Kolodner, J. L. (2000). Scaffolding the development of an inquiry-based (science) classroom. In *Proceedings, International Conference of the Learning Sciences 2000 (ICLS)* (pp. 221–227). Mahwah, NJ: Lawrence Erlbaum Associates.

Kolodner, J. L. (1993). *Case-based reasoning*. San Mateo, CA: Morgan Kaufmann.

Kolodner, J. L. (1997). Educational implications of analogy: A view from case-based reasoning. *American Psychologist, 52*(1), 57–66.

Kolodner, J. L. (in press). Facilitating the learning of design practices: Lessons learned from an inquiry into science education. *Journal of Industrial Teacher Education*.

Kolodner, J. L., Crismond, D., Fasse, B. B., Gray, J. T., Holbrook, J., Ryan, M., & Puntambekar, S. (2003). Problem-based learning meets case-based reasoning in the middle-school science classroom: Putting a Learning by Design curriculum into practice. *Journal of the Learning Sciences, 12*(4), 495–547.

Kolodner, J. L., Crismond, D., Gray, J., Holbrook, J., & Puntambekar, S. (1998). Learning by Design from theory to practice. In *Proceedings of ICLS 98* (pp. 16–22). Charlottesville, VA: AACE.

Kolodner, J. L., Gray, J. T., & Fasse, B. B. (2003). Promoting transfer through case-based reasoning: Rituals and practices in Learning by Design™ classrooms. *Cognitive Science Quarterly, 3*(2), 119–170.

Kolodner, J. L., & Nagel, K. (1999). The design discussion area: A collaborative learning tool in support of learning from problem-solving and design activities. In *Proceedings of CSCL '99. Palo Alto, CA* (pp. 300–307). Mahwah, NJ: Lawrence Erlbaum Associates.

Nagel, K., & Kolodner, J. L. (1999). SMILE: Supportive Multi-user Interactive Learning Environment [Poster summary]. Available http://www.cc.gatech.edu/projects/lbd/htmlpubs/SMILE. html

Palincsar, A. S., & Brown, A. L. (1984). Reciprocal teaching of comprehension monitoring activities. *Cognition and Instruction, 1*, 117–175.

Puntambekar, S., & Kolodner, J. (1998). The Design Diary: A tool to support students in learning science by design. In *Proceedings of the International Conference of the Learning Sciences (ICLS 98)* (pp. 35–41). Charlottesville, VA: AACE.

Puntambekar, S. & Kolodner, J. L. (2003). *Distributed scaffolding: Helping students learning science from design.* Manuscript submitted for publication.

Scardamalia, M., Bereiter, C., & Steinbach, R. (1984). Teachability of reflective processes in written composition. *Cognitive Science, 8*, 173–190.

Schank, R. C. (1982). *Dynamic memory.* New York: Cambridge University Press.

Schank, R. C. (1999). *Dynamic memory revisited.* New York: Cambridge University Press.

SRI International, Center for Technology in Learning. (1999). *Performance Assessment Links in Science website* [On-line]. Available: http://www.ctl.sri.com/pals

Children as Instructional Designers: Apprenticeship and Evaluation in the Learning Science by Design Project

Yasmin B. Kafai
UCLA Graduate School of Education & Information Studies

Cynthia Carter Ching
University of Illinois, Urbana–Champaign

Many would argue that the purpose of instructional design is to develop a body of knowledge that prescribes instructional actions to optimize instructional outcomes for the learner. Few would consider an approach in which learners themselves are engaged as instructional designers for the purpose of developing their content knowledge and skills. This unusual approach, however, is exactly what we advocate and describe in this chapter. Our model, called *learning science by design*, is situated within a curricular tradition of project-based learning approaches. Common features of these curricular approaches are that they provide students with "long-term, problem-focused, integrative and meaningful units of instructions" (Blumenfeld et al., 1991, p. 370). Design projects, such as our Learning Science by Design project, emphasize the construction of meaningful and complex artifacts (physical or virtual), which serve as driving vehicles for students' and teachers' classroom activities. Design-project activities have been developed and examined for a variety of subject matters, such as mathematics (e.g., Harel, 1991; Kafai, 1995), sciences (Brown, 1992; Kafai, Ching, & Marshall, 1998; Penner, Lehrer, & Schauble, 1998), engineering (Hmelo, Holton, & Kolodner, 2000; Roth, 1998), and social studies (Carver, Lehrer, Connell, & Erickson, 1992). In this chapter we examine various aspects of students' participation within the Learning Science by Design project, including students' apprenticeship interactions with one another and their development of evaluation criteria for themselves and others.

The context for our study of students as instructional designers is as follows. A class of 31 students composed of seven teams of fourth and fifth graders participated with their teacher in a science project for 3 months. They designed and implemented instructional software about neuroscience to teach younger students in their school. In creating the teams and examining their interactions, we used a software design model that emulated professional perspectives of software users, designers, and consultants (Kafai & Harel, 1991). We distinguished between *users* (third-grade students who used and evaluated the software), *newcomers* (fourth-grade students who designed software for the third graders), and *oldtimers* (fifth-grade students who had previously been newcomers and then apprenticed newcomers by coparticipating with them in software design practices). This model spans three classroom grade levels and introduces all participants into forms of legitimate software design practice, albeit with different levels of access. Other studies have attempted to replicate some aspects of this development by having the same students either participate in repeated design projects (e.g., Brown & Campione, 1994; Erickson & Lehrer, 1998) or in different design activities (e.g., Barron et al., 1998).

Apprenticeship interactions within teams were one focus of our investigation, because apprenticeship has been supported as one of the best ways for learners to become expert in a given domain. Proponents of this approach to learning argue that part of the reason for educational failure stems from school's lack of resemblance to other apprenticeship-style environments where learning takes place naturally (Lave & Wenger, 1991). There has been no small difficulty, however, in applying an apprenticeship model to formal schooling. Earlier attempts focused on apprenticing students into the cognitive practices of thinking in academic domains (e.g., Collins, Brown, & Newman, 1989; Scardamalia, Bereiter, & Lamon, 1994); however, they neglected to address the physical environment, activities, and tool use that make up the culture of learning in a particular subject (cf. Roth, 1995). Furthermore, these cognitive approaches focused largely on a dialogic relationship between learners and the teacher; other students were not included in the equation. The goal of this study was to address both of these issues within the context of learning science through design (Kafai, 1996). What distinguishes our approach from other design studies is the presence of both experienced and inexperienced designers in the same classroom, who coparticipate in creating science software together.

Unlike formal schooling, in documented studies of apprenticeships explicit instruction almost never happens (Rogoff, 1990). Rather than engaging in "how to," oldtimers and newcomers (as termed by Lave & Wenger, 1991) jointly participate in a common task. The way in which labor is divided in an apprenticeship may vary based on the participants' skill levels (Hutchins, 1993); however, they work together toward the same goal. Studies examining the role of relevant artifacts in learning environments with or without an apprenticeship structure have found that tools and artifacts can constrain the tasks at hand by providing structure for newcomers (Rogoff, 1993), or they can create additional possibilities for activity depending on the users' design flexibility (Roth, 1996). The computer in particular, as an artifact being jointly used by students with varying skill levels, can enable learning and mutual respect on the one hand (Harel, 1991) and can alternately be used by more capable students to restrict others' participation. Based on the literature just cited, we wanted to investigate the nature of the apprenticeship relationship among more and less experienced student designers, how this relationship might change as the project progressed, the role of computer and nonelectronic design artifacts in that apprenticeship relationship, and how roles of particular artifacts might change over time.

We wanted to complement these investigations of apprenticeship interactions with an analysis of students' perceptions of their design skills and their evaluations of the finished products. A critical aspect in design projects is a continuous evaluation of the progressively evolving artifact. This evaluation demands that the student designers have developed some criteria to judge the success. Erickson and Lehrer (1998) called these criteria "critical evaluation standards," whereas Roth (1998) spoke about "final product knowledge." In the context of human–computer interaction work, interface designers call these principles user-centered design (e.g., Norman & Draper, 1986). Educational software as such represents a particular challenge because it requires the designer to take into account the knowledge background, interests, and motivations of learners who are often distinct from professional users (Soloway, Guzdial, & Hay, 1994). In terms of evaluation, we were thus interested not only in students' perceived software design competencies, but also in the kinds of software evaluation standards they employed. In the Learning Science by Design project, students were introduced to software design practices, which involved mastering a programming tool. For that reason, it is important to understand in which ways the young designers perceived themselves as competent tool users and what their programming competencies were. Furthermore, we chose students' own evaluation standards because these have been recognized as one essential component in design projects (Erickson & Lehrer, 1998).

Taken together, these avenues of research—apprenticeship processes and students' evaluations of their skills and final software designs—represent crucial phases in the process of instructional design for learning. In this chapter we examine how students enter a community of instructional design as both learners and designers as well as how they collaborate with others in that community, and how they reflect on and evaluate their design skills and final instructional design products.

THE LEARNING SCIENCE BY DESIGN PROJECT

One classroom with 31 fourth- and fifth-grade students (14 boys and 17 girls) and their classroom teacher from a school in metropolitan Los Angeles participated in the study. Eleven of the 31 students had participated in a similar research project the previous year. The group of experienced students, or oldtimers, consisted of 10 fifth-grade girls and 1 fifth-grade boy. These experienced students were distributed throughout the seven teams of designers; groups were also matched for grade level and gender. The classroom consisted of different areas: a "rug" area in front of a whiteboard and seven table clusters, each of which had a Macintosh PowerPC workstation connected to the Internet. In addition, there were four other computers in the classroom against the walls, one of which was used mostly by the teacher to demonstrate projects or activities on a large-screen TV display, the other served as a scanner station. All the computers contained Microworlds™ Logo software, which students used to program their science software.

The science intervention and related design-project activities lasted 10 weeks (Galas, 1997–1998). In general, the class spent 75 minutes, 4 days per week, on science- and software-design-related activities. The introduction to the science unit started with an all-class discussion in which students generated all the questions they had about the science topic of neuroscience. Some examples of individual research questions are: "What controls our dreams?" "How do your eyes see?" "How does your brain know to turn around the picture you see?" "How does memorizing things and memory work?" A central information source for the neuroscience simulation project was a website called Neuroscience for Kids,[1] which contains a variety of resources such as background information in text and graphics, online memory and vision experiments, and game activities. In addition, students visited the neuroscience laboratory on the university campus, conducted a dissection of a sheep eye, and a brain surgeon (the father of one of the students) came to talk about his work and brought a human brain and a cow brain for comparison purposes. Parallel to the generation of research questions, all teams participated in a 3-hour introduction to basic graphic and software design functionalities of their programming environment. During this introduction, the teacher asked the oldtimers to help newcomers learn the basic programming functions while creating their first animation.

Several kinds of evaluation activities took place throughout the project. Twice, at Weeks 5 and 8, a group of 14 third graders came to visit and use the developing instructional simulations. The student instructional designers conducted these "usability sessions" themselves. Before the usability visit, design teams met and discussed the questions they wanted to ask the

---

[1]URL: http://weber.u.washington.edu/~chudler/neurok.html.

third graders in regard to their liking and understanding of the software. Informal evaluations and demonstrations also occurred throughout the project, as students visited different teams' workstations to view others' computer screens. At the end of the project, the whole class met to discuss criteria for final software evaluations and generated a list of evaluation questions. The next day, each team visited three other software simulations and tested the software. (Examples of students' instructional screen designs can be found in Fig. 5.1.) Each team received a summary report of other teams' evaluations that listed the ratings received and comments provided by students. Students' participation in *all* of these activities provides the context for their integrative learning of software design, collaboration, project management, and science. It is important to note that although the outline of activities might suggest a lockstep sequencing, most activities are scheduled based on a perceived need by the teacher or the researchers to address student questions or emerging problems.

Research Documentation

We used a variety of methods to document student learning, classroom activities, and group work. Student teams were videotaped as they met during class time to plan, research, and implement their software. Each team was captured for at least 30 minutes on tape approximately once a week. We videotaped the class session at the end of the project in which students generated criteria for the final evaluation activity, and we collected all the final evaluations and student comments. Finally, we also interviewed all the students at the end of the project. The interview questions varied depending on whether students were newcomers or oldtimers to the project. The questions asked students about their design-project experiences by examining their collaborative and individual contributions, the development and application of project-management strategies, their generation and implementation of research questions, and their expectations for prospective design projects. All interviews were videotaped and then transcribed in preparation for coding.

We decided to use a case-study approach for the examination of instructional design apprenticeship. The case-study team was the most normative: It contained no uniquely skilled (or unskilled) students, did not have any unusually difficult problems getting along, and was not characterized by frequent or extended absences on the part of one or more members. Each of the four team members seemed typical of the different kinds of students in the classroom as a whole. Caren,[2] a female oldtimer, was a good planner and organizer as well as a competent, but not superb, programmer. Naisha,

---

[2]All student names have been changed.

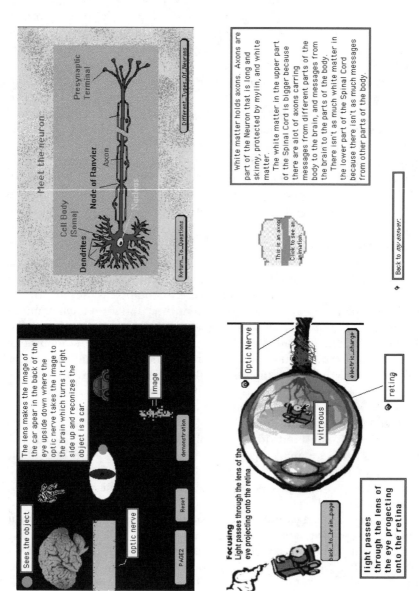

FIG. 5.1. Examples of instructional software screens.

also a female oldtimer, was less interested in organization and still needed to master some aspects of programming. Brian, a male newcomer, had computer experience and skills surpassing that of Naisha and Caren, but he had never used Logo before. Finally, Jiao, a male newcomer, was also a competent computer user but was somewhat shy and appeared to be confused by the open-endedness of the design task. The fact that both of the case-team oldtimers were girls was not atypical; most of the students who repeated the design experience in fifth grade were female.

Results

In the following sections, we provide an overview of different complementary aspects of the Learning Science by Design project: apprenticeships among experienced and inexperienced instructional designers/learners, and evaluative criteria derived and employed by students in reflecting on their design skills and final products.

Apprenticeship Into an Instructional Design Community. One of the key questions in our research deals with how students learn to become instructional designers. We were interested in not only how students learn to represent knowledge for the benefit of younger learners (as in traditional instructional design), but also how they master the use of various tools and artifacts specific to the learning-through-design process. In this project, these tools were comprised mainly of the Logo software, which students used to create simulations, and "planning boards": freestanding posters that served as storyboards for the emerging software designs, central message centers, and project calendars for each design team. In our study, students' mastery of these tools took place largely in the realm of apprenticeship interactions between newcomers and oldtimers. We were interested in how both the apprenticeship interactions and tool use would change over time as newcomers became more expert instructional designers. Overall, we found that apprenticeship relationships, working patterns, and tools that appeared to serve particular functions at the project outset were changed to suit new goals and circumstances as the project progressed and the developing software took shape.

Apprenticeship Structures. At the beginning of the 10 weeks of designing, all groups were informed that they would have to divide their group in half and pick working partners, since on certain days half of the group members would be doing instructional science activities with the teacher in another part of the classroom. The resulting partnerships in our case-study group were (1) Caren and Brian and (2) Naisha and Jiao. These pairings were particularly interesting in that they allowed the maximum distance in skill and assertiveness between the oldtimers and newcomers involved. For example, had Naisha been paired with Brian, she would not have been much more skilled than he was and therefore not able to help him a great deal with programming. The maximum-distance pairings of oldtimers and newcomers that occurred in the case-study group seemed to facilitate good working relationships, group harmony, and productivity during the first half of the project. A few other groups who did not use maximum-distance pairings had trouble getting along, and the newcomers learned slowly due to floundering when working without the presence of an oldtimer.

Role of Artifacts.   During the first 4 weeks of working on the software, the case-study group members were largely occupied with planning and researching their product; not a great deal was actually made yet. Consequently, the foam storyboard, or planning board, and its components played the important role of documenting what was going to be implemented. All group members contributed to the board, although Caren was in charge of determining how it should be organized. Initially, the relation between the computer and the planning board was directly related to the apprenticeship structure. For example, when Naisha and Jiao were paired together for computer work, Naisha would do most of the programming while Jiao checked the board to make sure they were working according to plan, as in the following segment:

Naisha: Okay, so I'm doin' the background. What color?
Jiao: I don't know. (*gets up to look at the board*) Ben has it brown on here.
Naisha: It's brown on his sheet?
Jiao: Yeah, I'm looking at it right now.
Naisha: Okay.

This division of responsibility in the group served to enforce the notion with newcomers of the need to stay focused and follow the group's plans. In a few other groups, when newcomers were left to their own devices, they played with Logo, making nonscience animations and ignoring the planning boards, behavior that was detrimental both to their own learning and to group productivity.

Change Over Time.   As the project progressed and the newcomers became more skilled in Logo, the case-study group found that the maximum-distance pairings were no longer necessary. Working pairs became much more flexible, and who was working on the computer together was determined more by common interests (such as Naisha and Ben's screen about brain waves during dreaming) than by a need for assistance. The role of various design artifacts changed as well. Though the planning board was crucial in the beginning, its use tapered off during the second half of the project. As the emerging software took shape and the group accumulated a number of half-finished screens in their folder on the hard drive, the developing product itself seemed to dictate what needed to be completed, making the planning boards obsolete. Likewise, Caren's role as the group organizer also waned when her control of the planning board was no longer as relevant. In the end, group members behaved much more like equals than oldtimers and newcomers—which was appropriate since the fourth graders were no longer inexperienced in software design.

Instructional Designers' Self-Evaluations

Designing software, and for that matter any kind of artifact, is a complex enterprise. We examined how students' perspectives on their programming expertise expressed themselves and what kind of criteria or evaluation standards students had developed. One central feature of the Learning Science by Design project is that students learn to program in Logo not just for the sake of learning how to program but also for the purposes of knowledge reformulation and personal expression (Harel & Papert, 1990). The goal is to introduce students to a tool that facilitates their creation of dynamic, interactive representations in science.

All students participate in the basic programming introduction, with oldtimers taking the lead in their teams in the beginning. Over the course of 10 weeks, newcomers get introduced to more sophisticated aspects of software design by either their team members or other students. Some newcomers very quickly become the programming experts in their teams. Yet when we look at interview results, 50% of all newcomers report mastery of the software design environment as one of the hardest parts in the project, whereas only 10% of the oldtimers listed this as a challenge. All oldtimers listed this as one aspect that was different from their first design-project experience. Later, when asked whether they considered themselves "junior software designers," 72% of oldtimers agreed compared to only 55% of newcomers.

The students' explanatory statements shed some light on the different ways in which oldtimers and newcomers saw themselves as junior software designers. Oldtimers saw their programming expertise relative to where they started from and to others, *and* to what they still had to learn:

> Heidi: Well I'm not like the best programmer software maker and I'm
>   not the worst programmer software maker, so I'm sort of in the
>   middle.

Jade: Probably last year I don't think I would have thought myself but
         this year I think that I am.

Elisa: I know that I can do much more and I know that there are peo-
         ple that know much more than me, but kind of. And if I think of
         the next project, I will do much better.

Newcomers situated their understanding of programming only in regard to
where they were in the beginning:

John: I know more than the first time.

Katia: Because I know what Microworlds is, how to program it, how to
         make animations, how to make buttons, how to do all the stuff.

Sven: I think of myself as more experienced than when we started.

All students became more competent in programming, which was also
indicated in their use of programming terminology. Newcomers and oldtimers alike used terms such as "pages," "buttons," "back buttons" (when referring to buttons linking pages back to the table of contents or previous
pages), and "textboxes" and actions such as "making things move," "finding
where the turtle is," or "putting them into order" (when referring to the sequencing of procedures) to describe their science software.

Instructional Designers' Product Evaluations

During the design project, the software development was evaluated not
only by the third graders but also by their peers in informal reviews on a
day-to-day basis. Furthermore, in official classroom demos, designers presented their science simulation designs to the whole class. During the review sessions, students would not only comment on screen designs but also
on information content. In the context of the debriefing interview, we
posed several questions that asked students to evaluate and review their
own educational software.

The results are not surprising given the different ways oldtimers and
newcomers judged features of their software. Students used several evaluation criteria to judge the software content and organization:

- *Liking/entertainment value:* Students referred to page organization and
  content presentation as "I thought it was cute," "I liked my animation,"
  "This was interesting," or "This was fun."

- *Information value:* Students focused on the information content in relation to science or media forms. For example, students commented: "And we just had this dinky animation and it wasn't very good, and it had a lot of words. Like words pretty much the whole page"; "We had too much text, we didn't give enough information"; "The picture doesn't explain what you are supposed to do . . ."
- *Navigational structure and performance:* Students evaluated the operation of various software features, such as: "It was kind of jerky . . . like I say it didn't work"; "Maybe we could make another little table of contents and that little table of contents would lead to games about the senses"; or "I would change the buttons cause they're pretty plain."
- *Audience consideration:* Students included in their considerations of navigation and content their expected users by stating: "And if you are saying a hard word say it slowly"; "I would probably put it more not so you can push buttons, not so make it is easy to learn. Some things you have to make hard to learn"; or "We just showed what the brain did and it wasn't a simulation so the kids didn't learn anything . . ."
- *Production value:* Students evaluated the relationship between quantity and quality of information production by stating: "It is better to have more pages that are pretty good because than you have a variety of things to do," or "They should make the project smaller but the pages better."

In comparing newcomers and oldtimers, we found several differences in how they used criteria such as information and navigational organization for evaluating their science simulation (see Table 5.1). More newcomers used entertainment values in their evaluations. Both groups considered information and navigation features in their evaluations. The most striking difference was in the near absence of audience considerations of software features among the newcomers. Only two newcomers (10%) made any reference to their potential users, whereas five oldtimers (45%) included this factor in their considerations. In a later question in the interview, we asked the designers how they would change their software when designing it for

TABLE 5.1
Software Evaluation Standards by Newcomers and Oldtimers

Category	Oldtimers	Newcomers
Entertainment/interest	9%	33%
Information	64%	50%
Navigational performance	18%	33%
Audience consideration	45%	10%
Production value	27%	10%

older students. Here we found no differences between newcomers and oldtimers in considering different aspects such as different wording or more text, based on the assumption that their older audiences know how to read. This result may point out that newcomers are able to include the audience in their software design considerations when specifically asked to do so. But it appears not to be a systematic factor in considering information and navigational organization of their software.

These results reflect those found by Erickson and Lehrer (1998) in their comparisons of students' changes in hypermedia development over 2 years, with the exception of audience consideration and production value. In the Learning Science by Design project, students designed software for actual users who visited them twice, and one half of the newcomers were previous users. Consequently, it is not surprising that this evaluation standard was included in their considerations for information presentation and software organization.

These analyses present a complex picture of apprenticeships within a school classroom. From the observational analyses, we learned that collaborative interactions between oldtimers and newcomers shifted over the course of the project. The interview analyses indicated that oldtimer students evaluated their instructional software tool use and instructional design products according to different criteria. In the following section, we discuss what these findings tell us about the feasibility and benefits of curriculum designed around students as instructional software designers.

Discussion

Students' apprenticeship interactions and differences between oldtimers and newcomers were focal points of our analysis of children as instructional designers. Our particular approach within the Learning Science by Design project provided an apprenticeship model within a school context. The accounts of successful apprenticeships in traditional societies describe the social networks involved as complex, changing structures in which participants move fluidly from one stage to the next (Lave & Wenger, 1991). This investigation found that student apprenticeships are dynamic systems as well. Oldtimers and newcomers inside the classroom, within the context of learning through design, do not stay constant in their respective roles or their relationship with various tools and artifacts in the environment. Existing studies have documented the fact that in design projects, the student designs eventually become artifacts in the environment (Roth, 1996). Here, however, the emerging design was not only added to the artifact arsenal, but it actually affected the utility value of other artifacts. As the gradual shift in the importance of the storyboard took place, a shift in the group control structure also occurred. As the collaborative product emerged, student roles shifted to be more equal.

The interviews conducted with students at the project's end required students to do "talking about design" rather than "talking within design," as they had practiced with their team members during the 10 weeks of the project. Schön (1986) pointed out one of the inherent problems in design: the difficulties of getting designers to articulate their thinking and doing— not just a step-by-step description of design activities but an articulation of principles that carry over from project to project. All the students were articulate about the many aspects of software evaluation and design. Students referenced their statements with multiple examples describing the design and operations of particular software screens or interactions with other students. Their statements were grounded in experience of the particular design-project case or cases (for the oldtimers). The issue at hand is to what extent the students' own descriptions are representative of actual mindful practice within a project. What we heard students describe resonates with descriptions and analyses of mindful practice in action such as provided by Roth (1998) and Hall and Stevens (1995). Furthermore, within the particular case of project management, we had actually documented and analyzed students' performances during the project (Marshall, 2000).

The comparison between newcomers and oldtimers gave us a first view of what it might mean to become an instructional software designer for learning. The observed differences between newcomers and oldtimers should not come as a surprise as we would expect oldtimers with time and experience to become more sophisticated. The differences between newcomers and oldtimers were not of a conceptual nature (as it is often pointed out in the research literature focusing on expert–novice differences). The difference was that the repertoire of oldtimers was more expanded. The ability to consider multiple standards for software evaluation and to understand one own's programming competence were features of the oldtimers' expanded repertoire. We should note that there was also a substantial degree of shared understanding between newcomers and oldtimers of which standards to apply for evaluating software products.

To conclude, we see a particular benefit in our version of the apprenticeship model in that it sustains learning over several classroom years and thus provides the essential experiential component. It sustains a classroom environment not only with teachers' careful and knowledgeable guidance and facilitation but also with students who know and understand classroom activities and apprentice others into it. This model begins with the third-grade students who get introduced to software design practice through the perspective of being a user. It continues with the newcomer students who move from users to codesigners under the guidance of the oldtimers. The oldtimers are the students who apprentice the newcomers to the various aspects of instructional software design practice. This apprenticeship model not only gradually moves responsibility from teacher to student (as reciprocal teaching does), it also moves responsibility from student to student over years. Both teachers and students have to be cognizant of learning practices to make a classroom intervention work and sustain over time.

Future directions for this work include an increasing focus on the teacher's role and on individual student differences. The role the teacher plays in such collaborative environments—how he or she interacts with teams and individual students, in which ways he or she provides assistance—is definitely a complex one and deserves further investigation. It is also clear that our description and investigation of newcomer and oldtimer students provides us with only a beginning understanding of the cognitive and social differences between them and of how these differences impact team interactions (Ching, 2000). Existing collaborative research provides us with little understanding of the multiple factors that come into play in such a long-term learning environment. Our analyses presented in this chapter are a first step in coming to understand the complexities of implementing such collaborative instructional design models in school classrooms.

ACKNOWLEDGMENTS

An Early CAREER Award from the National Science Foundation to the first author (REC-9632695) supported this research. The ideas expressed in this chapter do not necessarily reflect the positions of the funding agency. This chapter is based on previous presentations by both authors at the annual meetings of the American Educational Research Association in 1998, 1999, and 2000. We thank the teacher, Cathleen Galas, and her science students at UCLA's Seeds University Elementary School for their participation. Sue Marshall and numerous UCLA undergraduates assisted in collecting, transcribing, coding, and analyzing the data.

REFERENCES

Barron, B. J. S., Schwartz, D. L., Vye, N. J., Moore, A., Petrosino, A., Zech, L., Bransford, J. D., & the Cognition and Technology Group at Vanderbilt. (1998). Doing with understanding: Lessons from research on problem- and project-based learning. *Journal of the Learning Sciences, 7*(3/4), 271–311.

Blumenfeld, P., Soloway, E., Marx, R., Krajcik, J., Guzdial, M., & Palincsar, A. (1991). Motivating project-based learning: Sustaining the doing, supporting the learning. *Educational Psychologist, 26,* 369–398.

Brown, A. (1992). Design experiments: Theoretical and methodological challenges in creating complex interventions in classroom settings. *Journal of the Learning Sciences, 2*(2), 141–178.

Brown, A., & Campione, J. (1994). Guided discovery in a community of learners. In K. McGilly (Ed.), *Classroom lessons: Integrating cognitive theory and classroom practice* (pp. 229–272). Cambridge, MA: MIT Press.

Carver, S., Lehrer, R., Connell, T., & Erickson, J. (1992). Learning by hypermedia design: Issues of assessments and implementation. *Educational Psychologist, 27*, 385–404.

Ching, C. C. (2000). *Apprenticeship, learning and technology: Children as oldtimers and newcomers in the culture of learning through design.* Unpublished doctoral dissertation, University of California, Los Angeles.

Collins, A., Brown, J. S., & Newman, S. (1989). Cognitive apprenticeship: Teaching the crafts of reading, writing, and mathematics. In L. Resnick (Ed.), *Knowing, learning, and instruction: Essays in honor of Robert Glaser* (pp. 453–494). Hillsdale, NJ: Lawrence Erlbaum Associates.

Erickson, J., & Lehrer, R. (1998). The evolution of critical standards as students design hypermedia documents. *Journal of the Learning Sciences, 7*(3 & 4), 351–386.

Galas, C. (1997–1998). From presentation to programming: Designing something different, not the same thing differently. *Learning and Leading With Technology, 25*(4), 18–21.

Hall, R., & Stevens, R. (1995). Making space: A comparison of mathematical work in school and professional design practices. In S. L. Star (Ed.), *The cultures of computing* (pp. 118–145). London: Blackwell.

Harel, I. (1991). *Children designers.* Norwood, NJ: Ablex.

Harel, I., & Papert, S. (1990). Software design as a learning environment. *Interactive Learning Environments, 1*(1), 1–30.

Hmelo, C. E., Holton, D. L., & Kolodner, J. L. (2000). Designing to learn about complex systems. *Journal of the Learning Sciences, 9*(3), 247–298.

Hutchins, E. (1993). Learning to navigate. In S. Chaiklin & J. Lave (Eds.), *Understanding practice: Perspectives on activity and context* (pp. 35–63). New York: Cambridge University Press.

Kafai, Y. B. (1995). *Minds in play: Computer game design as context for children's learning.* Hillsdale, NJ: Lawrence Erlbaum Associates.

Kafai, Y. B. (1996). *Learning science by design: Developing information-rich learning environments in science for young software designers* (National Science Foundation No. REC-9632695). Los Angeles: University of California, Los Angeles.

Kafai, Y. B., Ching, C. C., & Marshall, S. (1998). Children as designers of educational multimedia software. *Computers and Education, 29*, 117–126.

Kafai, Y. B., & Harel, I. (1991). Children's learning through consulting: When mathematical ideas, programming knowledge, instructional design, and playful discourse are intertwined. In I. Harel & S. Papert (Eds.), *Constructionism* (pp. 85–110). Norwood, NJ: Ablex.

Lave, J., & Wenger, E. (1991). *Situated learning: Legitimate peripheral participation.* New York: Cambridge University Press.

Marshall, S. (2000). *Planning in context.* Unpublished doctoral dissertation, University of California, Los Angeles.

Norman, D. A., & Draper, S. W. (Eds.). (1986). *User-centered system design.* Hillsdale, NJ: Lawrence Erlbaum Associates.

Penner, D. E., Lehrer, R., & Schauble, L. (1998). From physical models to biomechanics: A design-based modeling approach. *Journal of the Learning Sciences, 7*, 429–502.

Rogoff, B. (1990). *Apprenticeship in thinking: Cognitive development in social context.* New York: Oxford University Press.

Rogoff, B. (1993). Observing sociocultural activity on three planes: Participatory appropriation, guided participation, and apprenticeship. In J. Wertsch, P. del Rio, & A. Alvarez (Eds.), *Sociocultural studies of mind* (pp. 139–164). Boston: Cambridge University Press.

Roth, W. M. (1995). Inventors, copycats, and everyone else: The emergence of shared resources and practices as defining aspects of classroom communities. *Science Education, 79,*
475–502.

Roth, W. M. (1996). Art and artifact of children's designing: A situated cognition perspective.
Journal of the Learning Sciences, 5, 129–166.

Roth, W. M. (1998). *Designing communities.* Dordrecht, Netherlands: Kluwer.

Scardamalia, M., Bereiter, C., & Lamon, M. (1994). The CSILE project: Trying to bring the
classroom into World 3. In K. McGilly (Ed.), *Classroom lessons: Integrating cognitive theory and
classroom practice* (pp. 201–228). Cambridge, MA: MIT Press.

Schön, D. (1986). *The reflective practitioner: How professionals think in action.* New York: Basic
Books.

Soloway, E., Guzdial, M., & Hay, K. (1994). Learner-centered design. *Interactions, 1*(2), 36–48.

CURRICULUM DEVELOPMENT, INSTRUCTIONAL DESIGN, AND INFORMATION TECHNOLOGY

Norbert M. Seel
Albert-Ludwigs-University of Freiburg, Germany

The contents of the chapters of Part II are concerned with the relationships between curriculum development and instructional design (ID). Accordingly, processes of curriculum development and their impact on ID are discussed. Before the chapters are briefly outlined, a framework to integrate the contents is proposed.

WHAT IS THE ESSENCE OF CURRICULUM DEVELOPMENT?

To answer this question it is necessary to define the term *curriculum*. A useful definition is given by Glatthorn (1987): "The curriculum is the plans made for guiding learning in schools, usually represented in retrievable documents of several levels of generality, and the implementation of those plans in the classroom; those experiences take place in a learning environment that also influences what is learned" (p. 6). Some years earlier, Beauchamp (1968) defined a curriculum as a document describing contents of subject matter domains, such as history, science, math; aims; and learning situations. This definition is still common, especially in the various German approaches of didactics. Accordingly, several

131

authors, such as Pellegrino (chap. 1, this volume), define curriculum as consisting of the knowledge and skills in subject matter areas that teachers teach and students are supposed to learn. The curriculum generally consists of a scope or breadth of content in a given subject area and a sequence for learning. Standards, such as those developed in mathematics and science, typically outline the goals of learning, whereas curriculum sets forth the more specific means to be used to achieve those ends.

The central issue of curriculum development is to allocate the contents and methods that are seen as relevant for the challenges in the students' present and future life. Curriculum development yields a set of decisions about objectives, learner characteristics, instructional contents and strategies, learning assessments, and learning resources (such as information technology [IT] and media) that must be cast into a usable formulation or structure. More specifically, curriculum development regularly starts with challenges: (a) Are the selected contents and methods appropriate to improve the acquisition of particular qualifications, and (b) does the acquisition of a qualification allow one to master a particular situation of life? As a consequence, curriculum development grounds on the assessment of *qualifications* or proficiencies as well as of knowledge and skills that result from an analysis of situations to be mastered in everyday life.

This argumentation characterized the early curriculum research. Its central goal consisted of the identification of those qualifications that are considered relevant for the learner to "master" situations of present and future life. Robinsohn (1969), for example, started with the assumption that if the accomplishment of the life situation L_x was to be realized, the learner must acquire the qualification $Q_1, Q_2, \ldots, Q_x$ in advance. According to this argumentation we can formulate more specifically: There are contents to be taught $I_1, I_2, \ldots, I_n$ that allow the acquisition of a particular qualification Q_x and we can formulate the hypothesis to be falsified, "If the qualification Q_x should be acquired, then the content $I_1, I_2, \ldots, I_n$ must be delivered." In accordance with this argumentation, Lenzen (1971) suggested a strategy of curriculum development with the following steps:

1. Identification of content units $I_1, I_2, \ldots, I_n$ to be taught.
2. Identification of those instructional methods that are considered as effective for the transmission of the contents in question: $I_1 + M_1, M_2, \ldots, M_k; I_2 + M_1, M_2, \ldots, M_k; I_n + M_1, M_2, \ldots, M_k$.
3. Testing whether Step 2 facilitates or impedes the acquisition of qualifications $Q_{e1}, Q_{e2}, \ldots, Q_{el}$.
4. Analysis of qualifications $Q_{me1}, Q_{me2}, \ldots, Q_{mel}$ that can be additionally acquired.

5. Analysis of life situations that can be designed on the basis of Steps 3 and 4.
6. Testing whether these life situations are desired by the society.

In the field of ID, some of these steps are central components of needs assessment and task analyses. As a consequence, both curriculum development and ID are concerned to a great extent with similar or even identical issues. Actually, curriculum development as well as ID are concerned with the intentional planning, design, and evaluation of effective arrangements for learning in different settings and environments. Accordingly, they similarly aim at (a) the careful description of results of education and teaching; (b) reflective thinking about alternatives of acting, on the one hand, and about the construction of learning environments, on the other; and (c) working-out of conditioned prescriptions for the design of the curriculum and learning environments in the sense of anticipative decision making. However, curriculum development is more restricted than ID, which entails all steps of the planning and construction of learning environments, whereas the focus of curriculum development is on the determination of contents and objectives of instruction. On the other hand, curriculum development is more far-reaching than ID, which is concerned with the design of concrete learning environments with a limited range, whereas curriculum development is concerned with educational activities that span time and space insofar as a curriculum is regularly assigned to grade levels or years of learning in schools. Actually, the curriculum is a central factor for both the continuation and further development of the various educational sectors of organizations and nations. More specifically, the impact of the curriculum on instructional planning can be described as in Fig. II.1 (cf. Seel, 1999).

A *curriculum* may be defined as a plan for a sustained process of teaching and learning. Any curriculum owes its origin to human needs or interests that are expressed in a demand for education and training and educational change. These needs and interests may derive from various fields, including economic, political, cultural, or intellectual from academic fields. Actually, there is widespread agreement among curriculum scholars that the fundamental basis and justification for curriculum development is human needs. A need is generally defined as "a gap between a current and a desired state" (Kaufman, Herman, & Watters, 1996). Kaufman et al. argued that needs assessment is at the core of educational planning in general—in ID as well as in curriculum development and management. Suarez (1991) defined *needs assessment* as "an information gathering and analysis process which results in the identification of the needs of individuals, institutions, communities, or societies" (p. 433). A central goal of needs assessment is the identification

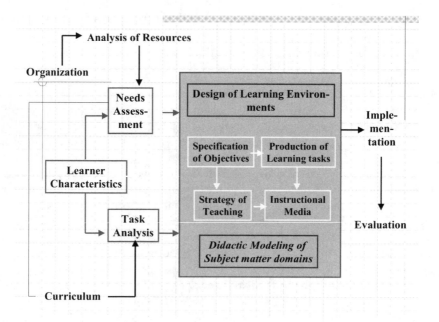

FIG. II.1.   The impact of the curriculum on instructional planning.

of the educational needs of different clients: individual as client, organization as client, and society as client. Closely related to needs assessment is task analysis, whereby an endeavor such as an occupational skill is divided into its component tasks.

THE ADDED VALUE OF CURRICULUM DEVELOPMENT TO ID

Putman's (1987) analysis of teachers' instructional planning as well as Rowland's (1992, 1993) analysis of design procedures of ID experts indicate the importance of a *curriculum script* as an ordered set of goals and actions for teaching a particular topic by taking into account the skills and concepts students are expected to learn. The exact nature of a curriculum script may vary for different subject matter areas (cf. Raudenbush, Rowan, & Cheong, 1993) and for different topics, but, at a minimum, it regularly contains a loosely ordered set of goals and objectives for what students are to learn, activities and examples to be used in teaching for these goals, and likely misconceptions or difficulties in learning a particular domain.

In most ID models, it is commonplace that the topics of a subject matter first must be transformed into *learning goals and instructional contents* (Psillos

& Koumaras, 1992; Tait, 1992), which emerge from the analysis of those subject matter topics that seem to be relevant to the instructional goals and, especially, to the learners' predispositions and characteristics (cf. Schott, 1992). This line of argumentation corresponds to the pioneering approach of Tyler (1949), who emphasized the fact that intentional learning is strongly associated with "objects" of possible experience. In the context of teaching, these "objects of learning" usually are represented as chemical formulas, historical data, texts, graphics, and so on. However, they do not correspond to the topics of the subject matter in a one-to-one mapping but rather are the products of transforming subject matter topics into *learnable contents* and *learning tasks* (cf. Seel, 1981, 1998) that mediate the "structure of knowledge" of a discipline. More pragmatically, Dick and Reiser (1989) emphasized the relevance of textbooks to the instructional designer's content decisions. Actually, they suggested that "textbooks drive the curriculum," that is, that most instructional content decisions are based on the textbooks that are used in subject areas. Often this causes difficulties for many students to understand which reality is depicted by the texts that are written in an "instructional manner," which may complicate its understanding for the learner.

In contrast to this pragmatic view, Shulman (1986) argued that besides a basic knowledge of educational goals and learner characteristics, the instructional designer must synthesize different knowledge sources into the *pedagogical content knowledge*, which includes the knowledge about the subject matter with its substantive structures, and the related *curriculum contents* as well as the general pedagogical knowledge about teaching methods. Furthermore, the pedagogical content knowledge incorporates the designer's experiences with most regularly taught topics, most useful forms of their representations, a basic understanding of what makes topics easy or difficult to learn, and, finally, the designer's knowledge about preconceptions that students of different ages and backgrounds bring along. The added value of curriculum development consists of its substantial contribution to this synthesis of the pedagogical content knowledge and the general pedagogical knowledge relevant for planning and structuring instruction.

Curriculum development gives preference to processes of decision making by linking objectives, organizational constraints, and the purposeful use of means and instruments on the basis of theoretically sound prescriptions. It entails multiple situations demanding decisions that are mutually dependent but must be made in different phases or periods of planning. Each of them has different *premises*, which constitute the "information field" of pedagogical decision making:

- *Normative premises* involve, first, *goals and objectives* as they become effective through the preferences of the designer of a curriculum. These normative premises result in expectancies that are related to the learners' characteristics that should be modified by instruction. Second, this group of premises involves societal and organizational constraints that limit the designer's freedom to design learning environments. Third, there are important curriculum constraints that must be taken into account when making pedagogical decisions. Actually, the question of what the learner should know or should be able to do after instruction is the starting point of instructional planning. However, the knowledge or skill to be acquired is determined, to a great extent, by the demands of society or the organization, and, especially in schooling, the syllabi of subject matter domains constitute the content-oriented framework of curriculum constraints.

• *Factual premises* refer to the context of instruction, to the physical and psychological constraints of a specific educational setting, and to the expected results of instructional activities. Obviously, the learner characteristics are the most important psychological constraints of instruction. A second main group of factual premises includes the situational and organizational conditions of different instructional settings.

• *Methodical premises* include appropriate methods for solving decision problems by selecting an optimal procedure whereby the quality of this procedure will be determined by its outcomes. In order to attain optimal procedures, and a procedure is optimal whenever an outcome corresponds to the normative and factual premises, we need a methodology of selecting appropriate strategies and methods of decision making. That is the main issue of ID.

Curriculum development is concerned with planning of education and related pedagogical decision making in the same way as ID, but it differs from it in the scope and bandwidth of activities related to the determination of the objects of planning, the organization of planning, the instruments of planning, and the way of mastering the implementation problem. In general, the spectrum of planning activities reaches from the prognosis of global trends of educational development as well as the binding determination on future actions in detail. From this perspective, curriculum development and ID are two sides of the same coin that entail both *planning as process* (i.e., the preparation and construction of a plan) and *planning as the creation of a result* (i.e., the formulation of a concrete plan for educational practice or of a syllabus). Clearly, the result of planning consists of a plan. The way to reach the plan is labeled "planning" and it contains various procedures, such as brainstorming, preliminary sketches, decision making in groups, and so on. The label "planning" is also used for the procedure for the development of a plan in a time period, but in each case the term "planning" is applied for labeling of distinct facts combined with a forecasting coordination of competing alternatives of activities to realize a plan. In accordance with the length of the time period to which the planning is oriented, we can distinguish between short-term, medium-term, and long-term planning. Accordingly, educational planning can be related to the global trends of educational development (e.g., the entire educational program of a state) or it can be disaggregated and related to specific aspects of teaching and learning in restricted areas of application, such as instruction in the classroom. In the first case—the case of curriculum development—we speak about "global planning"; in the second case—the field of ID—we speak about "detailed planning." In both cases the starting point is the determination of differences between objectives (i.e., the desired end states) and the given initial states. However, long-term planning is usually global and it becomes difficult to minimize these differences between objectives and initial states. Here, ID mediates between the global plan of a curriculum and the specific learning environment constructed with the aim to initiate the accomplishment of clearly defined but limited learning tasks.

Actually, a problem of educational planning is finding a proper balance between the intended generality of a curriculum and the necessary specificity of a concrete learning environment. A truly general curriculum must say something about a wide range of situations and individuals. But it is nearly impossible for a curriculum to be this generally applicable, yet specific enough to make unambiguous predictions. A completely specified general curriculum would contain so many details that it would be hopeless to clarify and realize all of it at once. Thus, the breadth of a curriculum, which is one of its most important aspects, is widely incompatible with great specificity. On the one hand, detail is necessary to make exact, testable, and useful prescriptions; on the other hand, this detail is impossible to achieve with consistency. One solution is to separate the generality from the detail. That means there is a general curriculum, which may remain broad and covers many aspects of instruction, and there are more precise representations of its central parts that include greater levels of detail. One possibility to bridge the gap between generality and specificity of instructional planning may consist in open approaches of curriculum development (such as school-focused curriculum planning); another possibility is to combine curriculum development with strategies and methods of ID. Actually, an important characteristic of most ID models is that they are sufficiently concrete and clear so that their properties are well defined and predictions become exact. From my point of view, this combination of curriculum development and ID supports a kind of planning that occurs strategically: First, long-term trends of educational development must be anticipated in order to prevent that momentary decisions are insufficient and counterproductive with regard to future options of behavior. On the other side, commitments for future actions should be restricted to a minimum. Rather, they should be open for alternative realizations and options for acting in concrete learning environments (see Dijkstra, chap. 6, this volume).

CURRICULUM DEVELOPMENT AS DESIGN

Because a curriculum is an artifact that spans time and space, a plan needs to be designed to show how the various decisions and components of a curriculum are organized and justified in relation to one another. The design bridges both the substance (content?) of a curriculum and its temporal and material constraints. For example, structural decisions need to be made about what portion of a curriculum is to be assigned to each grade level or year of learning. The combination of objectives, content, and learning activities must also be determined. The goal of structural design is to avoid fragmentation and elements or components that do not contribute to the whole. A well-structured curriculum design provides a map for all participants to education (students, teachers, parents) who may enter a program at a certain point but who wish to understand how that segment fits in with all that went before or comes after.

Certain criteria have been identified as being useful in creating and evaluating an appropriate structural design for a curriculum (Pratt & Short, 1994; Short, 1987)—for example, conceptual integrity and structural unity. The first criterion means that all concepts must be intelligibly defined, consistently employed, and coherently, systematically, and semantically related to each other in ways that assure integrity throughout the design. Structural unity can be achieved by assuring that the elements in a curriculum are contributing to some overall purposes.

CORE ISSUES OF CURRENT CURRICULUM DEVELOPMENT

Although curriculum development and research was a main field of educational research in the 1970s, in the following decades other educational movements, such as ID, became more prominent. That is why Achtenhagen (1992) pleaded for a "renaissance of curriculum discussion." Other authors, such as Hameyer (1992, 1994), shared this opinion and distinguished between several core issues in curriculum theory and development:

1. *Profiling the core curriculum: the changing needs of basic education.* School learning, as well as the curriculum, is subject to often rapid changes in society. The changes call for an adaptive school using an adaptive curriculum.

2. *Reorganizing subject matter knowledge.* New domains of learning, such as new technologies, health education, maintaining peace, and biotechnology, must be considered in curriculum development.

3. *Enhancing computer literacy.* Since the 1980s, various countries have begun to integrate information and communication technologies into the curriculum. As a consequence, computer and technology literacy became a central issue of schooling and other educational fields (cf. Seel & Casey, 2003).

4. *Changing processes of syllabus work.* Following Hameyer (1994), syllabus revision is a core concern in several countries around the world. Syllabi used in schools have been challenged as new subjects emerged.

5. *Expanding the experiential curriculum.* New educational movements, such as approaches of situated learning, as well as the revival of different approaches of reform pedagogy have inspired the revision of curriculum aiming at activity-based and explorative learning. Good examples of this approach that emphasizes experiential learning are given by Kafai and Ching (chap. 5) and Kolodner et al. (chap. 4) in Part I of this volume.

6. *Changing patterns of teaching and learning.* This core issue of curriculum development is almost self-evident because we can observe worldwide new approaches of teaching and learning aiming at the development and implementation of hybrid learning environments.

When we take into consideration the various movements of curriculum development and research on instruction, we can observe interesting intersections between these fields of educational science since the mid-1980s. As Achtenhagen (1992) pointed out, research on instruction increasingly involves components of the curriculum whereas curriculum development is influenced to a great extent by the results of research on learning and teaching. Achtenhagen summarized the interconnection of curriculum development and research on instruction across the past decades as shown in Fig. II.2.

The lower part of Fig. II.2 can be considered as an appropriate framework for integrating the following chapters of this volume: Dijkstra's introductory chapter (chap. 6) addresses the relations among curriculum design, instructional design, and media choice. He argues that all sectors of the education system have to solve the curriculum problem, which means the selection of knowledge and skills that the students should acquire. The solution of a curriculum problem is temporary, because of the continuous change of knowledge. The highlight of the chapter is that the main steps of curriculum design are integrated with instructional design in one comprehensive model. From this model the instructional design is outlined. It is shown how problem-based instruction can help to understand the concepts

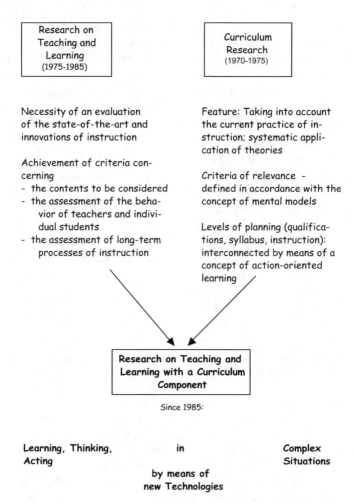

FIG. II.2.   The connection between curriculum research and research in instruction (Achtenhagen, 1992, p. 204).

of a domain and how multiple representations are used to prevent the isolation of subjects. Technology and media selection are considered as central problems of adequate curriculum design and ID.

In the next chapter (chap. 7), Grabowski takes into consideration the central issue of needs assessment and describes its impact on instructional decision making in a large technology-based project. She argues that one of the initial steps of instructional systems design is assessing performance needs. The main purpose of this step is to systematically study a problem from a variety of perspectives so that appropriate decisions can be made about whether instruction or training is necessary, and, if so, what type. Often little attention is paid to this step either in the form of making assumptions without data or ignoring the data when the design and development are underway—not by blatant disregard, but rather from a lack of funding or from a lack of understanding about how and why this phase is important to instructional decision making. Conducting a needs assessment is critical to developing a scientific understanding of a performance problem. The purpose of the chapter is to describe and discuss the goals and steps of conducting a needs assessment. A needs assessment from one large technology-based project is provided as an example case.

Achtenhagen (chap. 8) considers curriculum development as modeling of complex reality. Besides the fact that this approach corresponds with ideas of model-centered learning and instruction (see also Seel, chap. 2 in Part I), Achtenhagen deals with two major topics of curriculum development: (1) How can curriculum theory be used to develop curricular goals and content units for commercial apprenticeships at vocational schools and training firms? (2) Which theoretically based means for the development and implementation of instructional design might help to solve practical curriculum problems? These topics are treated in five steps: (a) discussion of curricular goals and content units for a commercial apprenticeship; (b) the presentation of criteria of instructional design for solving curriculum problems; (c) the introduction of a virtual enterprise as a practical example; (d) the discussion of how to use this instructional design for teaching–learning purposes; and (e) conclusions and possible perspectives on further research and development to close the discussion.

The following chapters are especially concerned with applications of curriculum development and ID on schooling and higher education. Abs (chap. 9) works on curriculum development and ID as different perspectives on teaching. He emphasizes the curriculum aspect and instructional design is looked at from this perspective: First, the type of curriculum is explained. Second, the political context of a recent curriculum evaluation is given. Third, results of this curriculum evaluation are reported. Starting from these results, some basic differences between curriculum work and the approach of instructional design to teaching and learning are described. As a last step, some consequences are suggested.

Cornu (chap. 10) describes the infusion of ICT in diverse educational sectors, such as schools, and the changes that result from the extensive use of ICT. First, he emphasizes that knowledge as well as the access to knowledge is changing due to ICT. Second, disciplines are changing under the influence of ICT, and, as a consequence, teaching is also changing. Another point of Cornu's argumentation is concerned with the need for a changed role of teachers and teacher training. Finally, Cornu underlines the importance of the ethical dimension of these changes as well as the need for appropriate policies.

Lowyck and Elen (chap. 11) focus on linking information technology, knowledge domains, and learning support for the design of learning environments in the field of higher education. First, evolutions in the field of information and communication technology, knowledge domains, and learning support are used as a knowledge base to understand more concrete endeavors in university innovation. The next section focuses on a case study that exemplifies innovative approaches in university teaching and learning. Both sections reveal the increasing importance of instructional design in university settings. In line with student-centered approaches, it is concluded that educational innovation at research-based universities and ID are confronted with similar issues. Instructional design may indeed offer general but beneficial principles to the development of education at universities. Acting in line with these principles may help to avoid major problems.

REFERENCES

Achtenhagen, F. (1992). Zur Notwendigkeit einer Renaissance der Curriculumdiskussion [On the renaissance of curriculum discussion]. *Unterrichtswissenschaft, 20*(3), 200–208.

Beauchamp, G. A. (1968). *Curriculum theory* (2nd ed.). Wilmette, IL: Kagg.

Dick, W., & Reiser, R. A. (1989). *Planning effective instruction.* Englewood Cliffs, NJ: Prentice-Hall.

Glatthorn, A. A. (1987). *Curriculum renewal.* Alexandria, VA: Association for Supervision and Curriculum Development.

Hameyer, U. (1992). Stand der Curriculumforschung—Bilanz eines Jahrzehnts [Curriculum research—State of the art]. *Unterrichtswissenschaft, 20*(3), 209–232.

Hameyer, U. (1994). Curriculum theory. In T. Husén & T. N. Postlethwaite (Eds.), *The encyclopedia of education* (2nd ed., Vol. 3, pp. 1348–1355). Oxford, England: Pergamon.

Kaufman, R., Herman, J., & Watters, K. (1996). *Educational planning: Strategic, tactical, operational.* Lancaster, PA: Technomic.

Lenzen, D. (1971). Eine "eduktive" Strategie für Curriculum-Konstruktion [An "eductive" strategy for curriculum construction]. In H. Blankertz (Ed.), *Curriculumforschung—Strategien, Strukturierung, Konstruktion* (pp. 118–150). Essen, Germany: Neue Deutsche Schule Verlagsgesellschaft.

Pratt, D., & Short, E. C. (1994). Curriculum management. In T. Husén & T. N. Postlethwaite (Eds.), *The international encyclopedia of education* (2nd ed., Vol. 3, pp. 1320–1325). Oxford, England: Pergamon.

Psillos, D., & Koumaras, P. (1992). Transforming knowledge into learnable content. In S. Dijkstra, H. P. M. Krammer, & J. J. G. van Merriënboer (Eds.), *Instructional models in computer-based learning environments* (pp. 83–96). Berlin: Springer.

Putman, R. T. (1987). Structuring and adjusting content for students: A study of live and simulated tutoring of addition. *American Educational Research Journal, 24*(1), 13–48.

Raudenbush, S. W., Rowan, B., & Cheong, Y. F. (1993). Higher order instructional goals in secondary schools: Class, teacher, and school influences. *American Educational Research Journal, 30*(3), 523–553.

Robinsohn, S. B. (1969). *Bildungsreform als Revision des Curriculum* [Educational reform as revision of the curriculum]. Neuwied, Germany: Luchterhand.

Rowland, G. (1992). What do instructional designers actually do? An initial investigation of expert practice. *Performance Improvement Quarterly, 5*(2), 65–86.

Rowland, G. (1993). Designing and instructional design. *Educational Technology: Research and Development, 41*(1), 79–91.

Schott, F. (1992). The useful representation of instructional objectives: A task analysis of task analysis. In S. Dijkstra, H. P. M. Krammer, & J. J. G. van Merriënboer (Eds.), *Instructional models in computer-based learning environments* (pp. 43–59). Berlin: Springer.

Seel, N. M. (1981). *Lernaufgaben und Lernprozesse* [Learning tasks and processes of learning]. Stuttgart, Germany: Kohlhammer.

Seel, N. M. (1998). Instruktionspsychologische Rezeption der didaktischen Reduktion [Instructional psychological reception of the didactic reduction]. In H. Ahlborn & J. P. Pahl (Eds.), *Didaktische Vereinfachung. Eine kritische Reprise des Werkes von Dietrich Hering* (pp. 237–260). Seelze-Velber, Germany: Kallmeyer.

Seel, N. M. (1999). Instruktionsdesign—Modelle und Anwendungsgebiete [Instructional design and fields of application]. *Unterrichtswissenschaft, 27*(1), 2–11.

Seel, N. M., & Casey, N. C. (2003). Changing conceptions of technological literacy. In P. Attewell & N. M. Seel (Eds.), *Disadvantaged teens and computer technologies* (pp. 35–55). Münster, Germany: Waxmann.

Short, E. (1987). Curriculum decision making in teacher education: Policies, program development, and design. *Journal of Teacher Education, 38*, 2–12.

Shulman, L. S. (1986). Those who understand: Knowledge growth in teaching. *Educational Researcher, 15*(2), 4–14.

Suarez, T. M. (1991). Needs assessment studies. In A. Lewy (Ed.), *The international encyclopedia of curriculum* (pp. 433–435). Oxford, England: Pergamon.

Tait, K. (1992). The description of subject matter and instructional methods for computer-based learning. In S. Dijkstra, H. P. M. Krammer, & J. J. G. van Merriënboer (Eds.), *Instructional models in computer-based learning environments* (pp. 127–141). Berlin: Springer.

Tyler, R. W. (1949). *Basic principles of curriculum and instruction* (13th ed.). Chicago: University of Chicago Press.

Chapter 6

The Integration of Curriculum Design, Instructional Design, and Media Choice

Sanne Dijkstra
University of Twente, The Netherlands

THE INFINITE AMOUNT OF INFORMATION AND THE CURRICULUM PROBLEM: A SHORT HISTORICAL REVIEW

The Storage of Information

In general, the curriculum consists of the knowledge and skills that teachers are teaching. However, this is only a small part of all the information and methods that are available for human beings. Moreover, the information and methods change and increase regularly. From the early beginnings of the storage of information, a long-lasting and slow development followed by an exponential increase in the amount of information in the 19th and 20th centuries can be observed. For a long time, human beings have developed new knowledge and skills, which they tried and try to impart to future generations. Much the same is true for other products of the mind such as literature and laws. As soon as they were able to store these achievements by using signs, engraved in information carriers such as stone and clay tablets or written on papyrus and parchment, the idea of bringing together a collection of documents led to the establishment of libraries. This happened from about 2700 B.C. in Mesopotamia (Stellingwerf, 1971), an area in which complete libraries have been excavated. From this period on, more libraries were established in other areas, in ancient Egypt and Greece. Local rulers, scientists, and religious leaders owned the libraries.

The documents, which were stored in special buildings and temples, represented the culture of a group. These documents make an assessment of the quality of the scientific and literary activity in a certain period possible. The increase of knowledge and skills as a result of creative intellectual work, especially in certain periods and regions such as Greece between 700 and 300 B.C., led to the enlargement of libraries. But often the documents that were stored were lost because of the ravages of time or the short life of the information carrier that was used (e.g., papyrus). Sometimes political or religious troubles caused the destruction of the libraries and thus of whole cultures. Sometimes the documents could no longer be read. The development of the script between about 3000 and 1000 B.C. from picture script to the symbols of an alphabet (Seel & Winn, 1997) caused the disuse of some scripts. The meaning of pictures, icons, and symbols that were used in such scripts got lost. Nevertheless, the content of many ancient documents, especially from the Greek, Roman, and Jewish cultures, that have been of tremendous importance for the Western culture has been preserved. Different rulers of the Roman Empire and somewhat later the religious leaders of Christianity in that Empire did preserve many documents of the Greek, Roman, and Jewish–Christian cultures in libraries. After, in about 500 A.D., Christianity became fully dominant in the territory of the former Western Roman Empire, the church became the keeper of the products of the Greek and Roman cultures. Though some schools of law and medicine remained active in the use of existing knowledge, much of the Greek and Roman cultures disappeared. A few religious leaders assigned monks to copy the documents, both those of the Greek and Roman cultures and of course those of Christianity. The ownership of and the responsibility for the libraries went to the church and monasteries. The publications of medieval scholars were added to the libraries. The amount of information stored increased, but the rate of increase was slow. This started to change somewhat in the beginning of the 2nd millennium A.D. and changed strongly in the Renaissance. The change took place in the "academic" world and concerned several aspects of the process of knowledge development. The change also influenced the ownership and organization of libraries.

The Development of Knowledge

For a substantial part, the development of knowledge is a social process. Human beings of all ages discuss their assumptions and hypotheses with others and try to find support for them. In the development and verification of scientific knowledge, this social process became controlled by accepted rules, such as isolation of objects, careful observation of changes, discussion with colleagues, logical reasoning, and publication of results, that are integrated in the task the research workers do. In the 2nd millennium, the following five changes, which improved the quality of the scientific work and did increase the information to be stored, can be observed.

The first milestone is the organization of scientists and students into guilds that led to the establishment of universities, which started in the 12th century in Italy, France, and England. In the next 4 centuries, the organizational model of this institution and the structure of the curriculum were copied in all European countries. The universities developed programs for the arts ("artes liberales"), theology, law, and medicine. After about 4 centuries, by the end of the 16th century, over 60 universities were established. Nearly all of them still exist. In the following centuries, the number of universities all over the world has increased until the present day. During the first 5 centuries of the existence of universities, all scientists used the Latin language. That one language guaranteed mutual communication and shared knowledge. It also guaranteed access to the precious written Latin documents. The libraries were a necessary condition for a university. The invention of the printing press in the 15th century made access to the documents easier. First all the medieval documents that were in use were printed, but soon new, original texts appeared from the printing press and debates about these could start, which was leading to new knowledge.

A second milestone in the organization of scientists was the establishment of academies of science, mainly in the beginning of the 17th century. These were strongly related to the national governments and rulers. Gradually the national languages took over the task, which thus far had been done in the Latin language.

A third milestone was the release of the first two scientific journals in 1665 by members of academies of science, one in France, *Le Journal des Sçavants,* and one in England, *Philosophical Transactions.* These journals started to publish articles on experiments in the sciences, book reviews, and information that were supposed to be relevant for the community of scientists. From then on, scientific journals became relevant for the academic community and gradually gained weight in these communities. After the review procedures became accepted, the journals finally became "authorities" in the domains. The content of the journals strongly motivated the scientists to reflect on the domain knowledge and stimulated new experiments and thus the development of new knowledge.

A fourth milestone was the substantial funding of scientific work by monarchs and national governments. Not only the funding of the universities as such, but also special activities such as the voyages of discovery and the determination of living organisms were paid for. The importance of these for geography, astronomy, and biology is evident.

Next to these organizational milestones, a fifth milestone is the development of the experimental method and of technical devices that allowed better observations of reality and made the test of predictions of future events possible. These developments in the 17th century were crucial for the establishment of the empirical sciences and their applications.

The organization of scientists, the funding, and the development and acceptance of ways of valid reasoning and methods to test hypotheses had tremendous influence. As a result of the systematic application of these methods together with the invention and improvement of instruments for observation, such as microscopes, telescopes, microphones, and amplifiers, the development of knowledge expanded enormously. From the 17th through the 20th century, the development of both mathematics and the technical sciences supported and sometimes boosted the empirical research. Finally, in the 20th century, the invention of the computer made it possible to control complex experiments and to process huge amounts of data in a very short time. Scientific research became done on a daily basis. The applications of scientific knowledge led to many changes in human society.

The result of all the scientific work was and is a tremendous increase in new knowledge and skills, which all should be stored in libraries, real or virtual. Each year the number of scientific journals increases and librarians' concerns are where and how to store all the texts that contain new information and problem-solving methods. The storage problem can still be solved adequately. But a second problem is much more difficult to solve. How much of all this information and problem-solving methods should be acquired by the students in our educational system, or what should be the ends that determine the content of the curricula of primary and secondary education? Moreover, the increase in information and methods often replaces existing concepts and theories. What should be kept and what should be replaced? How often is a revision needed? These questions are the core of the curriculum problem.

GOALS OF EDUCATION AND CURRICULUM DESIGN

Goals of Education

The general goal of education is the impartment, preservation, and renewal of a culture for those who belong to it. A first subgoal for individual human beings and for families and their representatives (in parliaments and churches) is the education of the child in becoming an adult with a personal identity. This is the leading goal in a family and in primary and secondary education. A second subgoal human beings have is to transmit their knowledge and skills to members of future generations and to prepare the members of those generations to adapt themselves to the demands of the natural and public reality in which they live. This includes adaptation to the changing knowledge and to new applications with which they are confronted. Both subgoals are fundamental for adaptation to reality and for the survival of both the individual and the group. To realize these goals, curricula will be designed.

Curriculum

A curriculum is a plan to realize a goal of education that prescribes (a) the content of the information and problem-solving methods of a domain; (b) the objectives the students should reach in the cognitive, affective, and motor domains; and (c) the sequence in which these can be learned by students of a certain group in an estimated period of time. A curriculum has to be designed. The label *curriculum* is used to denote either the total of all courses given in a school or the content of the course program in a particular domain. The rationales of curriculum design include assumptions about the physical, cognitive, and affective development of learners and other characteristics of the group of learners involved, public or societal requirements, and features of the subjects (Posner & Rudnitsky, 2001). Goodlad (1979) and Kuiper (1993) specified different forms in which a curriculum can be understood and realized.

1. An *ideal curriculum* is that which a scientist, who works at the frontier of a domain and who is reflecting on how students of secondary and tertiary education can acquire the newly developed knowledge, can imagine as valuable and useful.

2. A *written curriculum* is a document that specifies the learning goal, the content of the domain(s) involved, the exam requirements, and the criteria the achievement has to meet. The written curriculum can be more or less detailed. It varies from a global description, such as in an official document of a government, to the actual text- and exercise books.

3. The *interpreted curriculum* is the teachers' interpretation of the written curriculum document.

4. The *executed curriculum* comprises the way the teachers structure the content, provide information, and describe the problems the students should solve.

5. The *evaluated curriculum* represents the students' achievement as measured by exams, formal tests, and attitude questionnaires (see also Pellegrino, chap. 1, this volume).

Curriculum designers have to solve the problem of which content of the domain knowledge should be selected, how to sequence the different concepts and methods in a plausible order, and how to describe the objectives in a way that meets the students' developmental age. Different groups, such as families, nations, churches, industrial companies, sports leagues, and others, are authorized to approve a curriculum. These groups appoint committees of curriculum designers who select and describe the content of the domain in the format of general descriptions of the subjects to be studied and descriptions of the exam requirements. From these documents the design and development of textbooks, computer-based instructions, and other instructional programs are made.

Curriculum designers need a framework in which they can categorize both existing and newly developed information and problem-solving methods and their qualities such as the level of complexity. This framework is the categorization of information and methods into domains and subjects, which is discussed in the next section. In that section and in the following sections of this chapter, the labels *information* and *problem-solving methods* are used if their content is publicly available as written curriculum documents in libraries. If part of this content is cognized by a human being, the labels *knowledge* and *skills* are used.

Categorizations of Information and Methods

In this chapter, three broad categories of information and methods are distinguished: (a) philosophy, religion, and anthropology; (b) empirical sciences and their applications; and (c) formal sciences, such as logic, mathematics, and information science. The categorization is based on the "truth criterion," or the way to find evidence for the scientific content that is presented. For the first category, the truth criterion is the—temporary—consensus of arguments among scholars; for the second, it is the accuracy of predictions that are made about future events; and, for the third, it is the proof of the correctness of formal statements.

The categorization of all the available information and methods into three categories with many subcategories is useful for the design of curricula. It may help to delineate a domain or group of domains into so-called subjects. The categorization serves the design of curricula for the education of children as individual human beings with their personalities. And it is useful for the design of curricula that describe the content of the domains of the empirical and formal sciences. A curriculum has a certain number of components or chunks of conceptions and methods. For the first category, the components from anthropology and religion will correspond with the cognitive, affective, and social development of the child. For the second and third categories, the components or modules of a curriculum are broad categories of information (or conceptual systems) and methods that belong together.

Curriculum Design

For solving a curriculum design problem, a general heuristic is suggested that comprises the needs analysis, the description of the goal and the knowledge and skills to be acquired, and the selection, description, analysis, and sequencing of the main components of the domain. The description includes the outcomes that should be realized and the criteria that the knowledge and skills should meet.

1. For elementary and secondary education, the needs analysis is carried out by representatives of relevant groups, who decide which domains are important to include in a curriculum. They describe the knowledge and skills the students will need in a global way. For example, "The students should learn to use the operating system of a computer and a word-processing program." For tertiary education, the information and methods of a domain are analyzed in order of importance for the goal that should be reached.

2. The goals of elementary education, for example, comprise the coaching of the child's developing personality, the education of the "whole" person, and education for literacy. If the goal is to coach the child's developing personality, the components of the curriculum are selected from anthropology, religion, philosophies of life, social science, and ideologies. Such components imply the relationships between humans (e.g., fellowship, cooperation), the ethics of a group, and the rules for how to deal with others and with nature. Important personality characteristics such as honesty, sociability, and a pleasing disposition are discussed and practiced. Later the goal is extended to educate the child in becoming a cooperative adult in a complex democratic society. This means that behaviors such as compliance with the laws and reliability in business are discussed and shown. If the goal is to educate the whole person, the total curriculum includes different subdomains, each with their own components: (a) arts (e.g., drawing, music, dance); (b) sports, physical performance, and hygiene; (c) the social skills; and (d) history and culture. If the goal is education for literacy, the total curriculum includes subjects from the "empirical" and formal domains such as spelling, writing, reading, elementary arithmetic, use of maps, and use of a computer. For these subjects, relevant conceptions and methods will be selected.

For secondary education, the general educational goals described in the previous paragraph still apply for the design of the curriculum. Next to these, different rationales are leading the design of the curriculum. These comprise (a) the introduction to the culture and to the empirical and formal sciences, usually labeled *general education*; (b) the preparation for either vocational training or for a succeeding academic subject; and (c) adaptation to the students' level of intelligence and other individual differences. The rationales are used in combination and their application can be recognized in the designed curricula.

3. The structure of the information and methods of a domain is mostly leading the design of the curriculum, as well as if the context or adventurous stories are emphasized. How does one analyze the content and design a structure of the curriculum that will help students understand the information of a domain such that it will become useful knowledge? To design the structure of the curriculum, the concepts, theories, and methods of a domain are analyzed and sequenced from simple to complex in such a way that the hierarchical structure is taken into account.

For many domains, the general features and phenomena of change of the objects of study lead to the categorizations that determine the design of the curriculum components. For the empirical and formal sciences, the hierarchical structure of the content of the information and the methods is leading the design of the curriculum. Often a textbook is designed for a curriculum. Before the book is written, the author makes a global plan that is based on general principles that structure the information of the domain. Such principles are, for example, "from simple to complex," "from features to category," "the life cycle of a living organism," "from general to detail," "from general category to subcategories," and so on. Atkins (1989), for example, who designed a textbook for freshmen on general chemistry, first used the general concept "matter and its properties" and "change of matter (chemical reactions)" (150 pages). Then the general concept is detailed into three subconcepts: atoms, molecules, and ions (230 pages). The change of matter is outlined in rate of change and equilibrium (220 pages). It can be seen that the author works from general to detail and from general category to subcategory. Such general concepts are the components of the curriculum. They are detailed into simple concepts, hypotheses for the interpretation of change, and methods to solve problems. In native language education, for example, the general components are writing, grammar and spelling, design (letters, memos, and stories), and interpretation and entertainment (literature).

The components of a curriculum follow the broad categories with increasing levels of difficulty in subsequent years (Bruner, 1977). For many subjects, the components are determined by the hierarchical structure of the subject. Requiring the students to solve problems in which they can show they are able to both use the method and apply the knowledge should lead the assessment.

Concluding Remarks

In education, the goals and the design of the curriculum show the most intense debates, especially for the curriculum of secondary education. Only a fixed amount of time is available for a subject. As has been shown in the previous sections, the debate is especially caused by the increase, sometimes accelerated, in information and methods and, as a consequence, the development of new occupations. It doesn't make much sense to increase the content of the curricula for the domains simply if new information becomes available. It will only lead to overload. A better solution is to regularly revise the content and if possible integrate the new information with existing subjects (see Grabowski, chap. 7, this volume). The students need time to master the concepts, hypotheses, theories, and methods of a domain. There are individual differences in the time they need and the executed curriculum should adapt to these differences. The number of subjects and their content should be within the limit of what is possible for the students to master in a given amount of time.

THE RELATION BETWEEN CURRICULUM AND INSTRUCTIONAL DESIGN

The way in which the curriculum is designed, especially how the content is structured, influences the instructional design. The structure of the content is leading the design regardless of the story that leads the communication between the expert and the student. That structure can be embedded in the instructional design, for example, designs that emphasize the context such as in "situated cognition" (Brown, Collins, & Duguid, 1989), or the design of "anchor" situations in anchored instruction, which provide the students with many motivating problems, the solution of which contributes to the learning of the knowledge and skills required (Cognition and Technology Group at Vanderbilt [CTGV], 1992). The acquisition of these is part of the goal of the curriculum. The planning of the curriculum, instruction, implementation, and assessment is depicted in a model and shown in Fig. 6.1. It is adapted from Seel (1999) and Achtenhagen (2001). For the design of the written curriculum, the needs analysis and the analysis of the structure of the information and methods of a domain is crucial. What do the students need? The answer to this question leads to the global structure of the curriculum. For the design of the curriculum of secondary education, the three rationales mentioned before are taken into account. In Fig. 6.1 this task is included in the target-group analysis. As previously mentioned, the needs analysis is often executed by a committee of curriculum designers who are authorized to do this job and who have an overview of the domain knowledge.

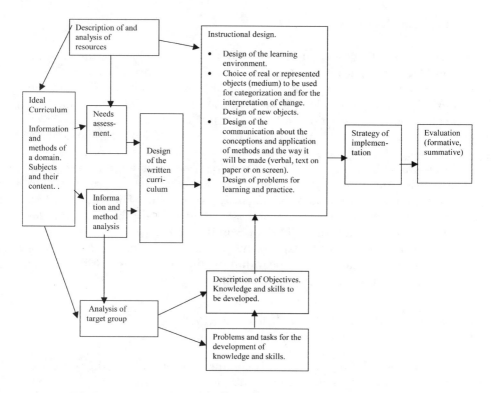

FIG. 6.1. A model of curriculum and instructional design (a modification of Seel's, 1999, components of instructional design and Achtenhagen's, 2001, extension of the model).

Once the global structure or outline of the curriculum is designed, the learning environment, the information, and the problems for the acquisition of the conceptions of the domain have to be designed. For this process, the theory and rules of instructional design apply (see the next section). If the curriculum comprises many components, the instructions for these can be designed and developed by a group of experts. This often happens with textbooks for secondary education.

The learning is strongly influenced by the time the students have available and how the instructor can vary this. The module system with flexible time for mastering the content is to the advantage of the students. The content can be cognized and practiced in the time period the student needs. The execution of a domain curriculum in a year class system with a fixed amount of time for the subjects may lead to overload of content and have adverse effects on productive learning for some students. It easily leads to cognitive overload. In vocational training, the learning should always be situated and coached by experts. This situation is paramount and is motivating for the students.

PROBLEM-BASED INSTRUCTIONAL DESIGN

Assumptions on the Development of Knowledge and Skills

The taxonomy of human goals (or motives) developed by Ford (1992) encompasses the subcategory of cognitive goals, which includes, among others: (a) exploration, (b) understanding, and (c) intellectual creativity. *Exploration* means satisfying curiosity about personally meaningful events. *Understanding* means the development of knowledge that can be used. And *intellectual creativity* means original thinking and coming up with novel ideas. In other taxonomies of goals or needs, comparable descriptions will be found for the cognitive domain. In this chapter, it is assumed that all human behavior is motivated and that the motive or goal of understanding and mastering the environment and the self is often initiating and controlling human activity. It is assumed that the three cognitive goals are basic for the development of knowledge and practicing skills. Generally, a feeling of admiration about the richness and complexity of the real world accompanies the motives. The three goals are basic for human problem solving and scientific work.

A second assumption is that human beings are prepared for regularity. They explore the outside world and try to bring order into the chaos of reality. Concepts and hypotheses do this. Based on that order, humans expect what will happen later. If the order is well described, they will make accurate predictions of what will happen in the near and far future. The exploration leads to the development of knowledge.

A third assumption is that human beings nearly always try to verify the correctness or truth of newly developed knowledge in a social process. For preschool children, parents and other adults are at the center of activating this process. They provide necessary help from the first moment of exploration. They help by providing control, making corrections, and providing answers to the frequently asked *why* questions of children between 3 and 6 years old. In the later phases of development, teachers and the students' peers will help to verify the correctness of students' newly developed knowledge. And ultimately, if human beings continue to work in the process of knowledge development, colleagues and referees of scientific journals consult about the correctness of new knowledge.

The Process of Knowledge Development
and Practicing Skills

It is assumed that human beings act and reflect on the reality they perceive and that they learn to distinguish or infer objects. The actions on and reflections about the perceived or imagined objects are needed for the development of knowledge. The objects can be natural or designed and developed by human beings. The label *object* can mean any entity that is perceived or imagined. Instructions are about objects and "what to do" with them. These include (a) real objects such as plants, birds, houses, cars, the earth; (b) inferred objects, such as atoms, the psyche, a group; and (c) systems of objects, such as the solar system. The increase of knowledge influences the observation of objects and is used to develop new categories and systems of objects. How do human beings develop knowledge? It is a conditional and complex process. The condition is the level of language needed. Some components of the process are (a) exploration and discovery of an unknown reality; (b) perception of objects and observation of their features and phenomena of change; (c) imagination of a possible process and reflection on cause and effect; and (d) creative thinking and design. A main feature of these components is executing certain actions on and with objects followed by asking questions (problems) to the perceived or imagined reality. A problem is a question, the answer of which can be given by applying or finding a method. A problem can be formulated in such a way that new knowledge develops and the method to solve it also will be learned and practiced. Those questions or problems guide the development of knowledge, they cause and support the students' thinking and learning. It is these activities that students should do, so they will be able to think, reflect on what they do, make errors, change their preliminary constructs by reasoning, and thus develop new knowledge. Knowledge consists of conceptions about objects expressed in the symbols of a language. The conceptions comprise how objects are categorized, how they change, and how to make new objects to satisfy a need. The conceptions can be partly told to the students, but for the development of knowledge that will be understood and used, the students should answer questions (problems) for which actions with the objects are needed. These actions or operations support the imagination of the objects and become organized in the problem-solving procedure or method. They lead to a categorization, a prediction, or to the design of a new object. If the result is not confirmed or shows errors, the action or conception should be changed. This can mean observing different features for categorization. Or it can mean the change of existing cognitive constructs. Or the design may be changed in order to adapt it to the laws of the domain or to better satisfy the program of requirements. If the actions are repeated they become automated and form skilled actions or simply a skill. In education, the teachers control the questions and tasks in order to make progress in a curriculum, though the students regularly check what is told to them or what they read. The teachers interact with the students about their answers and require the students to practice a method. The process of knowledge development is accompanied and strongly controlled by the acquisition of language. Knowledge is expressed in a language and the quality of the language that is acquired will support the children's knowledge development. The development of new knowledge as such can enrich the language. Language is the key to cognitive development and a rich vocabulary will help cognitive growth. Bruner (1966) marked cognitive growth into three stages; the enactive, the iconic, and the symbolic. In the first two stages, the child learns from experience with objects. For the preschool child, in the enactive stage the actions with objects do represent them. In the iconic stage the objects can already be represented in visual imagery. In elementary and secondary education, the transition from the iconic to the symbolic stage is conditional for the acquisition of knowledge. In this stage the understanding of the world through symbol systems such as language becomes dominant, though in this stage further cognitive development is found. Language makes it possible to describe and manipulate the objects that are given or shown to the child. As knowledge develops, language also becomes enriched. This makes it possible for reality to be described increasingly in a more general way, independent of the particular object available. The representation of objects, both by a medium or mentally, can take on different codes, such as a pictorial representation, a schematic (iconic) representation (e.g., a map, a schema of an atom), and, later, a fully symbolic form. The whole process of knowledge development is marked by continually asking new questions or problems leading to new actions and change of existing conceptions.

Foundations of Instructional Design

It is supposed that students need coaching and help for the acquisition of knowledge, skills, and attitudes in all forms of obligatory education. Sometimes they can learn independently for a long period. The coaching and help is labeled *instruction*, which is any intended activity to make learning possible or easier to accomplish. This activity may be designed either instantaneously (i.e., during the learning process) or in advance of the learning process (Dijkstra & van Merriënboer, 1997). Instruction is one part of a communication between a teacher (teacher, tutor, instructional program, etc.) and a learner about objects in a reality and conceptions about those objects, such as how they can be categorized, why they change, and how to design them, as well as what the students should do for learning, which questions about the objects they should answer, how to manipulate the objects, and which tasks to do. The other part of this communication is the learner's action to the instruction, such as observing, giving answers, asking questions, or performing a task (Dijkstra, 2001). Both the sender's and the receiver's actions can change; both parties can learn from the communication. The communication is a continuing process in which the learner can take initiatives and ask for help and needs feedback at the right time. The teacher should wait for the students' questions and for the moment they wish feedback. Interrupting the students' cognitive activity is irritating to them (Quintillianus, trans. 2001). Different variables in the communication influence the learning, such as complexity of the content that can increase mental load and the saliency of the features represented that help to reach insight. The students' task and the communication are realized in a learning environment in which the objects to be studied and manipulated are available and accessible for all the students or in which the media that represent those objects are available. Of course, the learning environment can be outside the walls of the school.

If instruction is a communication to realize that the students develop knowledge and practice skills, how should this communication be designed? Is there one design heuristic that can be used for all instructional design? If not, how many design heuristics have to be distinguished, based on what features? The answers to these questions depend on the conceptions about learning and the content of the knowledge. If learning is conceived as a uniform process, independent of content and psychological development of the child, only one design heuristic is enough. If different learning processes are distinguished, different design models are needed. If different contents correspond with different learning processes, many design models are needed, dependent on the domain knowledge. Is there a limit to the number of models? For many instructional designers, the conception of the needed learning model causes uncertainty, and confusing discussions with colleagues. The issue should be addressed in the years to come.

Since the label *instructional design* is used, different instructional design theories and models were distinguished. An *instructional design theory* is a set of statements that interpret why an instructional program leads to the acquisition of knowledge, skills, and attitudes. A model is a heuristic or plan that summarizes the phases and steps of the design. All theories and models of instructional design were founded in theories and models of learning. A typical design issue strengthened the relationship: Is it possible to automate the communication? The idea of an "industrial revolution" in education by using "teaching machines" strongly fostered the reflection on theories of learning and instructional design. The teaching machines did not bring the revolution, but the invention of the computer, digitalization of all kinds of information, and the integration of information and communication technology had a substantial influence on theory of cognition and cognitive processes (including learning) and on instructional design and education in general. There is still a strong need for extension of these theories.

All theories and models of instructional design provide a description of the learning outcomes. Dijkstra (1997) and Dijkstra and van Merriënboer (1997) used three categories of learning outcomes: (a) categorization, (b) interpretation, and (c) design. The outcomes correspond with different kinds of contents of a curriculum, which are the result of different kinds of problems that have been solved by experts. It is supposed that if the students are requested, stimulated, and supported to acquire knowledge and skills that will be retained for a long time and that are transferable to many new situations, the students should solve problems of a domain. It is supposed that asking the right questions in a domain leads to the development of knowledge. The problem-solving process has different components: use of the senses (perception of features and their change), imagination of objects (also if they cannot be perceived), manipulation of objects, hypothesizing the cause of the change of reality, logical reasoning if the feedback shows that a prediction is wrong. Based on the theory of cognition, especially problem solving and thinking, a model of instructional design was developed that can be used for the construction of knowledge and for the training of a skill simultaneously. It will help to analyze and integrate the content of a curriculum into categories of information (knowledge) that are general: concepts, laws, models, explanations (hypotheses and theories). The content of the instructions is part of curricula in the empirical, formal, and applied sciences.

Problem-Based Instructional Design

The challenge for education is to help students acquire an integrated body of knowledge and skills in a domain that can be deployed in subsequent school and work settings in meaningful and productive ways. The process of knowledge development is marked by continually asking new questions (problems) about the objects of a domain, leading to new actions and change of existing conceptions. For the persons involved, these activities and changes of conceptions are the development of knowledge and skills, which leads to improved understanding of reality. Many studies support this claim that problem solving fosters the development of new knowledge and methods (e.g., Anderson, 1982; Duncker, 1945; Polya, 1954). Obviously, results can be repeatedly used and improved. Therefore, problem solving means learning. The problems, which result in new information and methods, are grouped into three main types: (a) problems of categorization, (b) problems of interpretation, and (c) problems of design (Dijk-

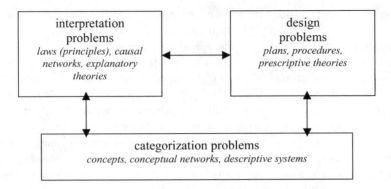

FIG. 6.2.   Three types of problems and their relationships.

stra, 1997; Dijkstra & van Merriënboer, 1997). The problems and their relations are shown in Fig. 6.2 (Dijkstra, 2000).

The result of solving a new problem is both knowledge and a problem-
solving method. Different labels have been and are used for this result. The
label *knowledge* is general. For the reflection on reality and the construction
of the cognitive content of this reflection, the labels *cognitive construct, declarative knowledge,* or *conception* are used. For the problem-solving method, the labels *procedural knowledge* or *procedure* are used. The latter can be either an algorithm or a heuristic, depending on the well- or ill-structuredness of the
problem. The labels in the boxes of Fig. 6.2 correspond with the content of
a curriculum and the description of the cognitive constructs. The instructional design rules are developed for the categories of problems (Dijkstra,
2000). In the short description of the categories, examples of instructional
design for these categories are given.

Categorization Problems.   In case of categorization or description problems, instances must be assigned to categories or relations between entities
have to be found. The knowledge resulting from this activity is labeled *concepts, relationships, conceptual networks,* and *descriptive systems.* It is supposed
that the content of the formal sciences (e.g., mathematics and programming languages) is included as descriptive knowledge and problem-solving
methods. The acquisition of concepts is intensely studied (e.g., Rosch,
1978). The model of learning is used for detailed heuristics for the design
of instruction (e.g., Merrill, Tennyson, & Posey, 1992).

Interpretation Problems.   In case of solving an interpretation problem, the
cognitive constructs are labeled *principles, causal networks,* and *explanatory theories.* The core of the problem is the explanation of the process of change of
an object. The general method to solve such problems is: (a) formulate a hy-

pothesis about a supposed relation between an independent and a dependent variable; (b) make a prediction concerning what will happen in a specified situation after a certain time lapse; (c) test the prediction, indicating whether it is confirmed or falsified, and, if relevant, specify the range of the probability of occurrence of a certain event. Explanatory theories predict changes of objects and relations and lead to an understanding of the causal mechanisms involved. The use of mathematical relations supports accurate prediction. The content of interpretations belongs to the empirical sciences (e.g., physics, neurology, psychology, etc.) and their applications. Different labels are used to designate the interpretations, such as *explanation, causality, law, model, hypothesis, assumption,* and *theory.* The finding of evidence for learning can be done in experiments (see next section) or in "ecologically valid" projects. Explanations can refer to complex changes over centuries, such as erosion of soil, or to complex processes, such as the spread of epidemics and others. The use of computer technology may help to design an interactive learning environment that includes the basic model and simulates the changes (Spector, Christensen, Sioutine, & McCormick, 2001). Stevens and Collins (1980) used the label *functional model,* in which they depicted the variables that cause the change in graphic form (and/or graphs). In a later publication, Collins and Stevens (1983) showed how the student's answers to the teacher's questions are dependent on the student's cognitive constructs and that the students interpret change from the fragmentary knowledge they have at the moment. If the student remembered isolated bits of knowledge or showed misconceptions, the way of questioning and providing some information made the constructs more complete and corresponding to the knowledge of the expert. Collins and Stevens developed detailed rules for the design of inquiry teaching.

Design Problems. For solving design problems, an artifact must be imagined and a first sketch, outline, or plan has to be created and made. Concepts and interpretations form the knowledge that is used to solve design problems. The cognitive constructs are the images of the artifact and the rules and criteria that have to be met in order to achieve a "good" design. If those who requested it accept the design, then it can be realized. This means that it can be produced (a car), constructed (a house, a bridge), interpreted (a composition by an orchestra), developed (an instructional program), or implemented (an organizational structure). A design problem has different subproblems that are dependent on the "life cycle" of the artifact: (a) the design; (b) the realization; (c) the use and maintenance; and (d) archiving, restoring, discarding, or recycling. Objects to be designed and realized should meet four different sets of conditions and criteria: (1) principles and rules of a "good" design, which means that pertinent laws and principles are adequately applied (e.g., a house should not come down, a car should be stable on the road, an instructional program should satisfy recognized principles of learning); (2) functional requirements— designs should be functional and objects should fulfill human needs; (3) aesthetic concerns—the artistic value of a design should satisfy the tastes and preferences of a group of people that often will vary over time; and (4) financial constraints—the financial means that are available should be used efficiently. Though the functional requirements may be detailed, the designer always has to solve an ill-structured problem, and the object that results may surprise many. Depending on the subcategory, the design rules can be general or detailed; for example, the rules for the design of a fugue or a painting are general, the prescriptions for use of an apparatus are detailed. For complex logistic tasks, a virtual environment is useful (Achtenhagen, 2001).

Often, the problems of the subcategories are part of more complex problems. The different subproblems of a complex problem become clear in a process of analysis of the information and methods that are needed to solve the complex problem.

Problem Solving, Knowledge Development, and the Design of Instruction

The description of the development or construction of knowledge as part of a problem-solving process allows the instructional designer to simultaneously emphasize both the knowledge and the procedure of how to solve the problem. This may help the students to construct the knowledge and practice the procedure in an integrated way and as a result makes the knowledge useful. The problems should be designed in such a way that, in the beginning of the learning process, the unknown information is easy to find. In all problems that the students should solve, the development of knowledge and practicing of skills is the objective, not an extreme level of difficulty that allows only the best students to solve them. Van Merriënboer (1990), who studied introductory computer programming, used two instructional strategies that were labeled the completion strategy and the generation strategy. The first strategy emphasized the modification and extension of existing programs. The second strategy emphasized the design and coding of new programs. After finishing a 10-lesson programming course, the students of the first group were superior in measures concerning the construction of programs. Paas (1992) studied the effect of cognitive load. He suggested that the cognitive load that is caused by the complexity of the task should be adapted to the cognitive capacity of the students. High cognitive load has adverse effects on learning (Sweller, 1988).

In the approach to the design of instruction, the models for the acquisition of knowledge are reduced to only three: for the acquisition of concepts, interpretations (assumptions and theories), and design knowledge. These are the basic categories for the design of instruction. The problems of the three main categories mostly appear integrated into complex problems. For example, a physician should learn how to diagnose (categorize) illnesses. Checking visible features and results of lab tests does this (application of an identification algorithm). Based on the interpretation of how the body physiologically reacts to the illness and the appearance of the features (as values on a dimension), the physician interprets the progress of the illness process (change) and predicts which medicine (designed object) might help the patient. A student of medicine can only learn to diagnose by doing this. It means, with the help of an expert, diagnose patients (solve a categorization problem), study the physiological process, and observe and interpret the patient's features; thus find or discover regularities in a pattern of features and interpret them (solve an interpretation problem). The example also shows that the students have to study available information about the physiological processes and apply this as relevant knowledge for diagnosing. They have to practice the skill and simultaneously use the knowledge in a kind of production system. Each category of problems and complex integrated problems can be further distinguished into subcategories, based on the degree of well- and ill-structuredness, complexity, generality, and abstractness (see Dijkstra & van Merriënboer, 1997). The approach of knowledge development from a problem-solving perspective is also found in the four-component instructional design model (van Merriënboer, 1997; van Merriënboer & Dijkstra, 1997). In this model, the development of declarative and procedural knowledge and the training of recurrent and nonrecurrent skills becomes integrated.

REALITY, REPRESENTATIONS, AND MEDIA

The Use of Representations

Because in the empirical and formal sciences the content of instruction is about objects in a reality, the teacher has to solve the problem of whether to use real objects, a representation of those objects, or both. The argument in favor of using the real objects is that students can perceive them with their senses, experience them directly, operate on them to learn how they behave and how they are used, and therefore more easily transfer learning outcomes outside the instructional context. It is clear, however, that real objects are not always available or appropriate. The reasons to use a representation of a reality include the following: (a) The objects are not (easily) perceivable or not available (e.g., bacteria, planets, historic monuments in a foreign country); (b) necessary experiments to determine the structure of reality are inappropriate in an instructional setting; (c) the duration of a process makes it inappropriate for an instructional context (e.g., an evolutionary process might be accelerated using a simulation); and (d) using real objects involves a risk for damage and personal safety. If a representation of objects is used, the teacher has to answer two questions. The first question is whether and how an object should be represented statically (picture, drawing, photograph, slide, transparency), or whether the change of an object or change of its position has to be shown (movie, time-lapse photography, animation, simulation). In the near future, the computer will increasingly be used for these presentations, because of the digitalization of all kinds of information and computer-controlled projection facilities. The second question is whether a demonstration model or a simulator has to be used. In the latter case, the objects may be used in such a way that the risk of damage is minimized and/or experiments can be conducted artificially that would not otherwise be possible.

Medium and Multimedia

The label *medium* has different meanings. The reader is referred to the descriptions that are provided by Seel and Winn (1997). The meanings can be discussed in an isolated way, but they become integrated in education. For the design of instruction, the technical conception and the code-related conception are important.

The technical meaning refers to the technical device (book, projector, video, computer) that is used for the production of signs. The anticipated instructional communication can be made orally and simultaneously supported by a medium; can be presented as text with pictures on paper; or can be presented as text and pictures on a screen. The way the communication is made depends on the content of the subject and the students' preference. For example, for the training of social skills, oral communication and use of video is practiced. The students need it. On the other hand, if text and pictures are presented on a screen connected to a processor, the students mostly make a print of it. The research that compared "classroom" instruction with instruction that used a particular kind of technical medium did not reveal differences in favor of either a technical medium or classroom instruction. The independent variable in such research designs is too ill defined.

The code-related meaning of medium is the rules through which users denote messages by signs (pictures, icons, symbols) in a communication. This is the important conception of medium in education. It makes the representation of the reality in signs possible. It is the meaning of the signs, how they relate to the reality that is acted upon in problem solving, that the students should understand. New conceptions use new representations. In addition to the first representation, the computer makes it possible to interactively study the change of objects as the change in a representation. The label *multimedia* means the combination of stored information that is prepared for different codes (e.g., pictures, icons, symbols) and for different sense organs (visual, auditory). Digital storage makes a mix of representations for educational purposes possible. Though much research has yet to be done, there is a strong idea that multiple representations will support integration of concepts. Figures 6.3 and 6.4 show examples.

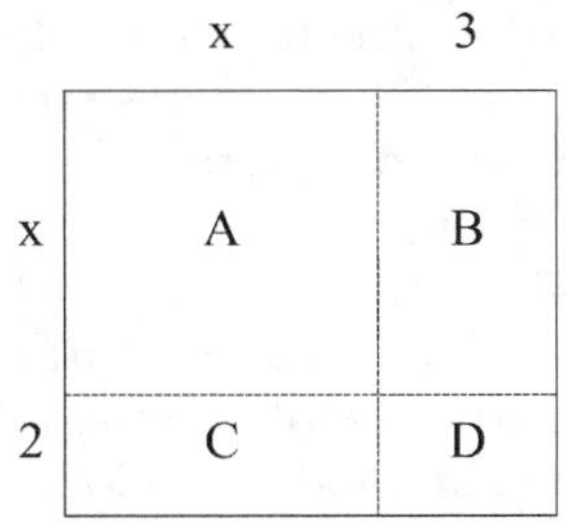

	x	3
x	A	B
2	C	D

Surface of the complete rectangle:

$$y = (x + 3) * (x + 2) =$$

$$x * x + x * 2 + 3 * x + 3 * 2 =$$

$$x^2 + 2x + 3x + 6 =$$

$$y = x^2 + 5x + 6$$

FIG. 6.3.   An iconic and a symbolic representation of a quadratic function.

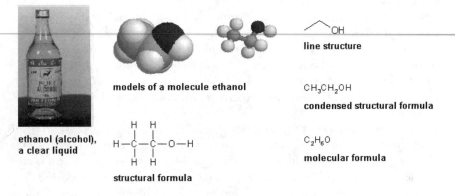

FIG. 6.4.   Different representations for ethanol.

Figure 6.3 shows a surface. This object can easily be used as a "real" object, such as a classroom floor, a kitchen floor, a carpet, and so on. The size of the surface can be calculated as the product of two terms:

$$(x + 3) * (x + 2).$$

Figure 6.3 also shows an iconic and a symbolic representation of a quadratic equation. Because the icon shows a square (Latin: *quadrum*) and three rectangles, the meaning of the label *quadratic* will quickly be grasped. Moreover, the representation of the size of a surface as a quadratic function becomes clear. Many instructional problems can be designed from simple to complex and from realistic to abstract (Bruner, 1966).

Figure 6.4 shows the representation of ethanol (alcohol). The real substance can be bought in bottles. One molecule can be represented in different ways: as a ball model, a ball-and-stick model, a structural formula, and finally in symbolic form. These representations can help the student to understand the structure of an ethanol molecule, support the knowledge (schema) and mental model development, and prevent the students from making many misconceptions of chemical knowledge (Taber, 2002). The animation of the ball-and-stick model shows the substance from different angles. This manipulation will help students observe the atoms and bonds. A teacher of chemistry can provide several problems to the students in which the substance is used. At what temperature does it boil? Why is the boiling point of ethanol lower than that of water? Wine contains ethanol (alcohol). If wine is distilled, the colorless clear alcohol should result. The students can easily do this experiment and learn the technology of distilling. They also learn the properties of the substance when it is manipulated. Doing this results in strengthening the concepts and theory and, moreover, the task is motivating. If they do the experiment for the first time, they will discover what happens and try to understand why by asking the teacher or using a textbook.

The instructions about the reality and what to do with it need the media in the code-related conception. This will help students to understand the reality, foster the use of the knowledge, strengthen the cognitive constructs, and improve retention of the constructs, which are stored in the semantic memory.

Both the development of knowledge and the training of a skill can profit from contexts and stories that are provided by a medium (CTGV, 1992). *Anchored instruction* provides a complex real-life problem as an interactive movie. The "anchor" is the story in which the problem is embedded. The students can explore the situation, generate subproblems, and use the "embedded data" to solve the subproblems and finally the whole problem. The increase in computing power and the storage of movies on digital videodisks make such complex situations a motivating learning environment that will help the students to use and understand the knowledge.

CONCLUDING REMARKS

This chapter described first the relation between curriculum and instructional design, followed by a discussion of the problem-based instructional design model. A curriculum is a plan to realize a goal of education. The content of a curriculum is the information and methods of a domain or of different domains. The analysis of the information and methods of a domain reveals the concepts, laws, models, explanations (hypotheses and theories), and design rules that should be acquired as knowledge. The analysis also reveals the problem-solving methods that were used. In a curriculum, the information and methods are organized in chunks of information or modules that are primarily based on features of the domain. The curriculum designer can use different features and goals for this. The decision of which subjects and which content of a subject will be part of the written and executed curriculum depends on a complicated process of needs analysis. In this process, the general needs of the students, societal needs, and local needs play their role in relation to the sector of education that is involved. Once these decisions are made, the instructional designer decides about the learning environment, the information that should be provided, and the problems and tasks the students should do. I presume that the students develop knowledge from the observation and manipulation of objects, which results from questions to answer (or problems to solve). The students can formulate the questions themselves or they can be guided in their activity by the problems and tasks that are designed for them. This approach cannot be used for all learning. The amount of information and methods is too extensive. Reading information, rehearsing and remembering it are also necessary. But if the construction or development of knowledge is not practiced, the students will not understand this process and why it is so important for human beings and their society. They then can only remember without understanding. Knowledge can develop in all kinds of environments: at home, in a lecture room, in a library in which a book is read, or in a classroom in which students participate in a discussion, solve a math problem, or work through a multimedia simulation (Dijkstra, 2000). Of importance is what the students have to do in all these situations and whether these activities contribute to imagining the real objects, answering questions about their change, and developing methods in such a way that new knowledge and skills can be developed and new objects designed. All environments can function as learning environments. When a learning environment is designed, it has to be evaluated with regard to whether it has the features that are valuable for the development of desired knowledge and skills.

The choice for a problem-based instructional design model is made in order to provide optimal means to support the imagining, perception, and manipulation of objects as well as the invention and production of objects. The choice is founded on assumptions about how human beings develop knowledge and skills, and it is based on the results of studies of cognition, especially problem solving, thinking, and learning. Problem-solving situations make students work toward a new solution. This necessitates the development of new knowledge and methods. After sufficient practice, the use of a method develops into a skill. Generally speaking, instruction is an activity to support the development of knowledge and skills. For instructional designers and for teachers, this activity includes inventing and constructing objects and situations (or representations of these). It further includes questioning students, and giving tasks to students in such a way that students can find relevant features and see what happens when they manipulate "things," and try to interpret this. Finally, it includes practicing design rules when they have to make "things" themselves. For teachers, the task includes providing guidance and feedback, if this is judged as necessary by both the teacher and the student. The design of instruction is making the plan for and the construction of situations and objects that can be used for the formulation of problems. These problems guide the perception and manipulation of objects, and require the students to make predictions and to design and construct objects themselves.

ACKNOWLEDGMENTS

The author thanks Han Vermaat, Fer Coenders, and Nelly Verhoef for their constructive comments on the example problems.

REFERENCES

Achtenhagen, F. (2001). Criteria for the development of complex teaching–learning environments. *Instructional Science, 29,* 361–380.

Anderson, J. R. (1982). Acquisition of cognitive skill. *Psychological Review, 89,* 369–406.

Atkins, P. W. (1989). *General chemistry.* New York: Freeman.

Brown, J. S., Collins, S., & Duguid, D. (1989). Situated cognition and the culture of learning. *Educational Researcher, 18,* 32–42.

Bruner, J. S. (1966). *Toward a theory of instruction.* Cambridge, MA: Harvard University Press.

Bruner, J. S. (1977). *The process of education.* Cambridge, MA: Harvard University Press.

Cognition and Technology Group at Vanderbilt. (1992). The Jasper series as an example of anchored instruction: Theory, program description, and assessment data. *Educational Psychologist, 27,* 291–315.

Collins, A., & Stevens, A. L. (1983). A cognitive theory of inquiry teaching. In C. M. Reigeluth (Ed.), *Instructional-design: Theories and models* (pp. 247–278). Hillsdale, NJ: Lawrence Erlbaum Associates.

Dijkstra, S. (1997). The integration of instructional systems design models and constructivistic design principles. *Instructional Science, 25,* 1–13.

Dijkstra, S. (2000). Epistemology, psychology of learning and instructional design. In M. Spector & T. Anderson (Eds.), *Holistic and integrative perspectives on learning, instructional design and technology* (pp. 213–232). Dordrecht, The Netherlands: Kluwer.

Dijkstra, S. (2001). The design of multi-media based training. In S. Dijkstra, D. H. Jonassen, & D. Sembill (Eds.), *Multimedia learning. Results and perspectives* (pp. 15–40). Frankfurt, Germany: Peter Lang.

Dijkstra, S., & van Merriënboer, J. J. G. (1997). Plans, procedures, and theories to solve instructional design problems. In S. Dijkstra, N. M. Seel, F. Schott, & R. D. Tennyson (Eds.), *Instructional design: International perspectives* (Vol. 2, pp. 23–44). Mahwah, NJ: Lawrence Erlbaum Associates.

Duncker, K. (1945). On problem solving. *Psychological Monographs, 58*(Whole No. 270).

Ford, M. (1992). *Motivating humans: Goals, emotions, and personal agency beliefs.* Newbury Park, CA: Sage.

Goodlad, J. I. (1979). *Curriculum inquiry: The study of curriculum practice.* New York: McGraw-Hill.

Kuiper, W. A. J. M. (1993). *Curriculumvernieuwing en lespraktijk* [Curriculum reform and teaching practice]. Unpublished doctoral dissertation, University of Twente, The Netherlands.

Merrill, M. D., Tennyson, R. D., & Posey, L. O. (1992). *Teaching concepts: An instructional design guide* (2nd ed.). Englewood Cliffs, NJ: Educational Technology Publications.

Paas, F. G. W. C. (1992). Training strategies for attaining transfer of problem-solving skill in statistics: A cognitive load approach. *Journal of Educational Psychology, 84,* 429–434.

Polya, G. (1954). *How to solve it.* Princeton, NJ: Princeton University Press.

Posner, G. J., & Rudnitsky, A. N. (2001). *Course design: A guide to curriculum development for teachers* (6th ed.). New York: Longman.

Quintillianus, M. F. (trans. 2001). *De opleiding tot redenaar* [Institutio oratoria] (P. Gerbrandy, Trans.). Groningen, The Netherlands: Historische uitgeverij.

Rosch, E. (1978). Principles of categorization. In E. Rosch & B. B. Lloyd (Eds.), *Cognition and categorization* (pp. 28–46). Hillsdale, NJ: Lawrence Erlbaum Associates.

Seel, N. M. (1999). Instruktionsdesign: Modelle und Anwendungsgebiete [Instructional design: Models and applications]. *Unterrichtswissenschaft, 27,* 2–11.

Seel, N. M., & Winn, W. D. (1997). Research on media and learning: Distributed cognition and semiotics. In R. D. Tennyson, F. Schott, N. M. Seel, & S. Dijkstra (Eds.), *Instructional design: International perspectives* (Vol. 1, pp. 293–326). Mahwah, NJ: Lawrence Erlbaum Associates.

Spector, J. M., Christensen, D. L., Sioutine, A. V., & McCormick, D. (2001). Models and simulations for learning in complex domains: Using causal loop diagrams for assessment and evaluation. *Computers in Human Behavior, 17,* 517–545.

Stellingwerf, J. (1971). *Inleiding tot de universiteit* [Introduction to the university]. Amsterdam: Buijten & Schipperheijn.

Stevens, A. L., & Collins, A. (1980). Multiple conceptual models of a complex system. In R. E. Snow, P. A. Frederico, & W. E. Montague (Eds.), *Aptitude, learning and instruction: Cognitive process analysis of learning and problem solving* (pp. 177–197). Hillsdale, NJ: Lawrence Erlbaum Associates.

Sweller, J. (1988). Cognitive load during problem solving: Effects on learning. *Cognitive Science, 12,* 257–285.

Taber, K. (2002). *Chemical misconceptions—Prevention, diagnosis and cure: Vol. 1. Theoretical background.* London: Royal Society of Chemistry.

van Merriënboer, J. J. G. (1990). Strategies for programming instruction in high school: Program completion vs. program generation. *Journal of Educational Computing Research, 6,* 265–287.

van Merriënboer, J. J. G. (1997). *Training complex cognitive skills: A four-component instructional design model for technical training.* Englewood Cliffs, NJ: Educational Technology Publications.

van Merriënboer, J. J. G., & Dijkstra, S. (1997). The four-component instructional design model for training complex cognitive skills. In R. D. Tennyson, F. Schott, N. M. Seel, & S. Dijkstra (Eds.), *Instructional design: International perspectives* (Vol. 1, pp. 427–445). Mahwah, NJ: Lawrence Erlbaum Associates.

Chapter 7

Needs Assessment—Informing Instructional Decision Making in a Large Technology-Based Project

Barbara L. Grabowski
Penn State University

> As [human beings] invented tools, weapons, clothing, shelter, and language, the need for training became an essential ingredient in the march of civilization.
> —Miller (1996, p. 3)

Since the time of early civilization, transfer of knowledge and understanding has played a key role in survival (Miller, 1996). In today's time, knowledge and understanding have become so complex that detailed systematic and systemic analyses are needed to determine what type and through which methods training should be offered. Instructional systems design (ISD) as a process helps designers by *systematically* specifying and describing the steps one would take to create an instructional or learning intervention. Instructional systems design, though systematic in process, is systemic in approach. A *systemic* analysis is specifically required in the needs assessment phase. A holistic understanding of the entire system and how the parts interact and impact each other is needed to design a reasoned instructional solution (Romiszowski, 1981). Several models and processes for designers and developers in business, industry, military, school, and informal learning settings exist (Dick & Carey, 1985; Romiszowski, 1981; Rossett, 1987; Seels & Glasgow, 1990). Andrews and Goodson (1995) and Gustafson (1981) analyzed over 60 models in two separate studies. They found many common steps that distill into five core phases: Analysis, Design, Development, Implementation, and Evaluation, fondly termed the *ADDIE* model.

The entire ISD process is followed only when a performance problem is one that can be resolved by training or instruction. A needs assessment is conducted as the first phase of the process to make this determination. For the purpose of this chapter, *needs assessment* refers to the analysis phase during which many perspectives about a task are gathered to determine the causes of a gap between the ideal performance and the actual performance. The problem is the discrepancy specified by the organization between the desired performance and what actually occurs.

PURPOSE OF THE ANALYSIS PHASE

The purpose of the analysis phase is to gather enough information so that designers can make informed and responsive decisions, first about whether an instructional intervention is needed, and, if so, what type of content should be learned, its sequence, media delivery, and instructional strategies and tactics that would be appropriate for a particular audience in a given context. During this phase, designers form a broad scientific understanding of a performance problem. This understanding is critical in predicting causes, explaining those causes, and then predicting again the actions or interventions that would resolve the problem. This process is like Warries' (1990) description of scientific enterprise in theory and systematic design of instruction. Scientific understanding comes from making data-driven decisions and hypotheses regarding the proposed solutions. These understandings are then confirmed or disaffirmed through the evaluation conducted throughout the entire ISD process. In other words, the designer gathers data during the needs assessment to describe what the actual need is and how that need is placed within the entire organizational system, thereby confirming the performance gap and allowing the designer to recommend interventions.

Kaufman, Rojas, and Mayer (1993) recommended that designers first determine the scope of the problem. Scope is determined by the type of client/beneficiary—that is, society, organization, individual, or small group. The scope warrants different levels of effort: megalevel, macrolevel, microlevel, or quasi needs assessment, respectively. For example, a quasi needs assessment is "methods–means procedures and how to do it" (p. 9) for an individual or organization, whereas a megalevel needs assessment specifies the methods and means for a larger societal problem. Regardless of scope, the nature of the problem is always examined in the analysis phase so that designers can determine the underlying causes (i.e., lack of training or motivation or something that is ergonomically awry in the environment). An instructional intervention is only appropriate if the gap is caused by lack of training, whereas an employee reward system or a change in structure might resolve the latter two underlying causes.

Leshin, Pollock, and Reigeluth (1992) called the front-end needs assessment "the critical link" between the needs of an organization or individual and the instructional development efforts. Each subsequent phase in the ISD process is dependent on the analysis phase first and foremost, and then each phase that precedes it. Although it may seem from this description that ISD is a linear process, it is important to understand its cyclical nature that is defined by a scientific and systemic approach. Many subsequent steps require the designer to reanalyze previous steps to gather a better understanding of current information and decisions. The reanalysis may reveal additional information needed to make appropriate instructional decisions. The approach one takes to the ISD process has implications for the kind of data that must be gathered during the analysis phase. Rossett (1995) believed the needs assessment "drives" the other steps and shapes the design, development, implementation, and evaluation decisions. Without the benefit of a cycle, the needs assessment would need to be broader and unrealistically all-encompassing (Leshin et al., 1992).

In summary, this phase is important because if the designers do not understand what the real problem is, they cannot solve it (Knirk & Gustafson, 1986). Kaufman and English (1979) advised that designers must define where they should be headed, justify why they are going there, and determine the best means for getting there. Given this premise, the process is more systemic and involved than just examining the content and the audience. Often, given constraints in time and budget, this phase is shortened, data not gathered, and assumptions made with regard to the needs of the employees. Offering of inappropriate instruction is one possible consequence, as explained in the case presented later in this chapter.

STEPS FOR CONDUCTING THE NEEDS ASSESSMENT

Once a performance problem has been identified, Step 2 is to write the goal of the needs assessment. The goal of the needs assessment is to understand the context in which a problem exists enough to make recommendations for solving the problem. To be clear, the goal, therefore, should state the problem, the setting, and the desired outcome. If the goal is fuzzy, the results of the analysis may also be fuzzy, or irrelevant effort expended gathering data that is not needed to make recommendations (Kaufman et al., 1993; Rossett, 1987, 1995; Smith & Ragan, 1993).

The rest of the needs assessment, simply stated, validates or revises the client's initial understanding of the ideal and actual using a data-driven approach. Step 3, therefore, is to understand the ideal situation desired by the organization; Step 4, substantiate whether a need for intervention exists by understanding the actual and its difference from the ideal; Step 5, determine possible causes along with prioritized, recommended interventions; and Step 6, communicate the results back to the client.

Although the importance of working with the client to clearly understand the desired situation should not be underestimated, the majority of the effort of a needs assessment is expended in Step 4, analyzing the actual environment and matching it with the ideal to substantiate the existence of the problem and the need for an intervention. There are three parts to this step. Part 1 is planning a clear and concise approach that defines the parameters to be examined and the tools for data collection. This plan serves as a blueprint for collecting appropriate data. Part 2 is to collect and summarize the data, and Part 3 is to explain the gap between the real and the ideal. The scope of the problem determines the extent of the analysis at this point; that is, whether needed data should be internal or external to the organization. If the scope of the needs assessment is broad (i.e., at a mega-level), a broad search for information from a broad audience of internal and external sources is required to describe the environment. It will take more time and effort. The reverse is also true. For quasi needs assessments, a much more narrowly defined effort is necessary.

The data from this step is compared with the ideal to identify the performance gaps. If there are several gaps identified, they should be analyzed for instructional causes, and those causes prioritized. Recommended interventions are generated and communicated back to the client (Kaufman et al., 1993; Rossett, 1987, 1995; Smith & Ragan, 1993).

TOOLS FOR CONDUCTING THE ANALYSIS

Many techniques and tools are available for ferreting out the ideal and actual performance. These tools enable the designer to gather organizational and individual feelings about the causes and solutions to a performance problem. Extant data analysis, subject matter and performance document analyses, observations, focus groups, interviews, and written surveys are the tools generally recommended by needs assessment experts.

Each tool has its advantages and disadvantages (Kaufman et al., 1993; Leshin et al., 1992; Rossett, 1987, 1995; Smith & Ragan, 1993). Extant data analysis examines data from documents that currently exist within an organization. The advantage of using extant data is that it often includes results of performance assessments, but not necessarily what the individual has done to gain those results. The designer must make inferences back to the performance. Subject matter analysis includes interviews with subject matter experts and the examination of documents that contain content and descriptions about performance (Rossett, 1987). Designers seek the "nature and shape of bodies of knowledge which employees need to possess to do their jobs effectively" (p. 26). This analysis is useful for defining the ideal content that should be included in a performance.

Observations involve real-time scrutiny of the performance of the task. Observations allow the designer to watch the task being performed, which may include interactions with others. On the other hand, observation is subjective and time-consuming. Focus groups are small group interviews with several key players. Differing opinions and perspectives and nonverbal interactions can be obtained in a short period of time. However, they can be difficult to arrange, and the varied views difficult to synthesize. Interviews are usually held one-on-one via the telephone or in face-to-face meetings. An interview allows the designer to probe into areas that emerge during the conversation. These are also time-consuming, so that conducting a large number is not reasonable. Relying on a small number may result in making decisions based on a biased sample (Leshin et al., 1992). Written surveys contain a series of questions that are distributed to a broad audience. One of their advantages is reaching a large group of people, thereby generating a large amount of data for the time, effort, and financing expended. Clear surveys, however, are difficult to write and often result in a low response rate (Leshin et al., 1992).

Advances in electronic means of communication and distribution of information have greatly increased the sources of data for instructional designers. Designers can now create on-line electronic surveys sent via e-mail or post them to websites to gather data from more individuals. Also, focus groups can be conducted via chats and listserv discussions, and interviews through videoconferencing. Designers can examine information distributed via the Internet from many sources of experts rather than be limited to those of the organization or print media. These sources of information must be scrutinized for purpose so that the real problem is not lost, or data gathered just because it can be. These means for data collection are more appropriate for Kaufman et al.'s (1993) mega- and macrolevel needs assessments (Kaufman & Herman, 1997).

THE NEEDS ASSESSMENT CASE

The purpose, steps, tools used, and outcomes of a needs assessment are described using the following case. This case was selected because it represents a megalevel needs assessment dealing with the National Aeronautics and Space Administration's (NASA) desire to have their data from the Internet used in public kindergarten through high school and Year 2 of community colleges' (K–14) science, math, and technology classrooms in the United States, and because it represents a classic example of the importance of conducting needs assessments. This needs assessment was conducted over a

5-month period and included 12 designers and several NASA and industry consultants. The results of this case provided the data needed to launch a multiyear effort to conduct research about and develop teacher training and tools for Web-based science, mathematics, and technology instruction.

Case Description—Step 1: Identify the Performance Problem

NASA is recognized internationally for its contributions to science and space exploration. NASA, however, also has a little-known mission to provide service to education. One of their services is translating NASA science into usable educational resources for teachers. Historically, they have provided off-line, tangible materials (workbooks, videos, posters, etc.) through their regional NASA teacher resource centers. An opportunity to expand this face-to-face service into a different, innovative way of diffusing on-line NASA resources of all kinds to the schools presented itself through the World Wide Web. At the time of this case, approximately 300,000 Web pages of various types with the nasa.gov domain name existed. NASA educators felt that helping teachers use NASA Web resources in classrooms would inspire students' interest in science, math, or technology and provide teachers with resources to support their teaching, but they were concerned that many teachers were not using this vast resource. The performance problem as foreseen through the eyes of NASA was that "teachers were not using NASA Web resources available to them." Their conclusion, for reasons that are unclear, was that teachers would be more apt to use NASA Web resources if teachers knew how to create Web pages that used NASA data, and began to offer workshops on this topic. There was little evidence that supported this conclusion. The reality was that no one knew why teachers were not using NASA Web resources. Thus, the design team proposed that NASA management conduct a needs assessment prior to developing further Internet training sessions for teachers to understand if and why teachers were not using their resources.

Step 2: Specify the Goal of the Needs Assessment

Once NASA agreed to engage in a needs assessment, the designers held several probing discussions with NASA educators and scientists through weekly conference calls and other face-to-face meetings to understand the problem that NASA was trying to address with their workshops. The design team presented a rationale for why the current practice of providing training on how to create Web pages may not address the real needs of teachers. Like many cases, the initial selection of content and method of delivering the instruction came from an intuitive rather than a data-driven sense of teachers' needs and selection of content, and from an incomplete understanding of the environment in which the problem existed. They explained that the needs assessment could reveal any number of factors for why teachers were not using their resources in their classrooms—attitude, awareness, motivation, access, knowledge, or skill—only some of which would be addressable by a NASA training solution, and that the purpose of the needs assessment, therefore, should be to study the gap between this ideal and the real situation in the classroom.

Given the NASA-identified problem, McCarthy's statement of purpose in the preface of the needs assessment document described the goal of the needs assessment for this case (Grabowski, McCarthy, & Koszalka, 1998):

> The purpose of the needs assessment was to identify our K–14 customer's [teachers'] needs with regard to using the World Wide Web (WWW) for instruction and to identify the obstacles K–14 teachers face in utilizing NASA Learning Technologies products in the classroom. As our understanding of our customer's needs become clearer, it then becomes possible to define strategies to assist K–14 teachers to effectively use web-based NASA (and non-NASA) materials. (p. ix)

The problem was that teachers were not using NASA resources in the classroom; the setting was K–14 classrooms in which the Web could be used for instruction; and the desired outcome was to understand these teachers' needs with regard to the Web and the obstacles teachers faced in using NASA learning-technology products in their classroom. Ideally, the statement of the problem should be included in the statement prior to the stated purpose.

Just as the goal of any needs assessment is not to judge the value or importance of a stated problem, our job was not to judge whether or not NASA should want to increase teachers' use of their Web materials in the classroom. Rather, the goal was to understand *why* teachers were not using NASA Web resources in their classroom and *in what ways* they could.

Step 3: Specify the Ideal

From these meetings, the design team also determined that NASA's ideal was for teachers to be able to use NASA Web-based resources in their classroom to inspire children to pursue science, math, and technology career interests. NASA saw this as a nationwide problem with their ideal involving teachers on a national scale. The implication of this national ideal was that broad rather than specific understandings needed to be sought, and a national rather than a specific approach to the data collected.

Step 4: Substantiating Need—Understanding
the Use of NASA Web Resources

The next step was to analyze the actual school environment in which NASA
Web resources could be used. The team planned for three phases examining the national school context, content (science, math, and technology),
and teaching and learning processes, representing the "who/where, what,
and how" of the system. Given that NASA's ideal was national in scope, they
had to selectively choose specific parameters and tools that would yield the
most useful data.

Step 4.1: Selecting Parameters and Tools

In Phase 1, context parameters were those areas affecting the integration
and use of computer technology to deliver instruction in an educational
setting—that is, administrative infrastructure, technology infrastructure,
and teacher factors. Given the diversity of the U.S. school curricula, the
team chose to define content by two parameters: school curriculum
through the National Education Standards and existing NASA materials.
Teaching and learning processes meant the ways in which instruction could
be presented most effectively for the teacher and the student. Its parameters were best practices using the Web in the classroom, teacher tutorials,
and learning theories and teaching practices. As a result, eight parameters
were studied in these three phases.

Several different types of needs assessment data-gathering tools were selected. Since the assessment was national in scope, most sources of data
came from extant data and subject matter analysis. Extensive extant data
were available from the Internet and conference meetings. Existing federal, state, and local strategic plans, district policies with regard to technology implementation and support for teachers, United States Department of
Education documents, and the National Center for Educational Statistics
(NCES; 1995a, 1995b, 1996) databases illustrate the type of extant data that
were examined. Comprehensive reviews of the literature for learning theory and teaching practices, school curricula, and the National Education
Standards exemplify the types of subject matter data that were analyzed.
Trade books, magazines, and the Web were also searched for information
and sites representing best practices, existing tutorial types, and categories
of websites to create an understanding of current and potentially effective
practices for Web use.

The design team generated a pool of approximately 50 questions that
were selectively incorporated into interviews, focus groups, and surveys.
The focus groups included two local, convenience samples, whereas several
informal and two formal interviews were conducted at conferences and

through the telephone with technology experts identified by NASA. In addition, educational listservs, teacher chat rooms, and e-mail were used to ask further questions and distribute electronic surveys. The purpose of the focus groups and surveys was to identify how the Web was currently being used by the teachers, how students interacted with the sites, and the types of sites used with different types of activities. The interviews were used to gather information about administrative policies, how and what type of technology currently was supported, and to learn about best practices. Education experts were also interviewed for a perspective of current learning theory and teaching practices.[1] Table 7.1 matches the type of tools employed by each of the eight parameters identified for analysis.

As can be seen from Table 7.1, there were no direct observations of teachers using the Web. Observations are labor intensive and time-consuming, and given the national scope, whatever the team could accomplish would represent a biased sample. This was a limitation in this needs assessment. To accommodate this limitation, the leaders of the design team took opportunities for continued contact with teachers during the development project, as well as continue to gather stories of teacher use (or lack of use) of technology in the classroom.

Step 4.2: Description of the School Environment

The analysis of the data resulted in identifying 30 detailed dimensions or attributes of the eight parameters of the school context, content, and processes that affected Web use in the schools. These dimensions, summarized in Table 7.2, were used to describe the team's understanding of school realities related to this problem. From these dimensions, 41 trends were found. From these trends, the team selected 16 dimensions it felt had the most impact on whether teachers would use Web resources in their classroom. As a system, each parameter was then discussed in relation to the other parameters studied. These were further synthesized into nine problem areas that were described as the realities of the school environment: Web access, teacher skill in using the Web, perception of the best use of the Web, teacher time, changing school-curriculum requirements, type of Web resources available, classroom teaching practices, Web practices, and available instruction about the Web. Because of space limitations, only a summary of the trends for school context, content, and the process of teaching and learning is included in Step 4.3. The resulting realities of the school environment are presented in Table 7.3, column 1, and discussed in Step 5.

---

[1]Providing specific details regarding who was interviewed and the entire list of resources referenced is beyond the scope of this chapter. Those details can be found in the analysis and needs assessment report prepared for NASA (NASA/TP-1998-206547).

TABLE 7.1
Tool Type by Area of Investigation

Type of Tools Used/Areas of Investigation	Extant Data Analysis	Focus Groups	Observations	Interviews	Surveys	Subject Matter Analysis
School Context						
Administrative infrastructure	X			X		X
Technology infrastructure	X			X		X
Teacher factors	X	X			X	X
School Content						
School curriculum						X
Existing NASA materials						X
Teaching and Learning Processes						
Best practices of using the Web	X			X		X
Existing teacher tutorials	X					X
Learning theories and teaching practices				X		X

TABLE 7.2
Defined Dimensions of the School Context, Content, and Processes

Detailed Characteristics	Dimensions or Attributes
School Context	
Administrative infrastructure	Supportive administrators
	Supportive computer technology and services
	Support for teachers
Technology infrastructure	Points of connectivity
	Number of connected instructional rooms
	Type of network connection
	Technology plans
	Technical support
Teacher factors	Technical skill
	Attitude and motivation
	Perception of skills
	Perception of administrative support
	Grade-level assignment
	Subject matter area
	Experience teaching science and math
Content (Science, Math, and Technology)	
School curriculum	Curriculum guidance
	Curriculum support
	Curriculum resources
Existing NASA materials	Databases
	Information and resources
	Lesson plans
	Projects
	Student activities
	References and links
	Tools
	Tutorials
Teaching and Learning Processes	
Best practices of using the Web	Use of the Web during instruction
	Interactivity with the Web
	Types of websites
	Origination of sites
Existing teacher tutorials	Web producers
	Web integrators
Learning theories and teaching practices	Behavioral perspectives
	Cognitive perspectives
	Motivational perspectives
	Sociocognitive perspectives
	Developmental theories

One assumption made during this investigation was that the findings represent the administrative infrastructures at the time and that they could be generalized to school districts across the country. Most of the research included extensive searches and limited discussions with administrators and teachers met during conferences. Another assumption was that technology would eventually become more prevalent in schools, and teachers did want to know more about technology use in their classroom, but did not have the time or staff support to do so.

The most significant limitation was the small number of teachers who were interviewed directly, using only the two local teachers involved with the team. Also, the informal surveys and interviews targeted teachers who had access to the Web (via Web surveys) and were interested in using technology in their classroom. These surveys and interviews served as verification for existing NCES national surveys that provided a more valid and representative source of data capturing national statistics on a wide variety of teachers' uses of technology under several different circumstances, such as limited Web access, rural school, and disadvantaged districts.

Step 4.3: Explain Factors Affecting Teacher's Use of NASA Web Materials in Their Classroom

Administrative Infrastructure Trends.   This parameter referred to the policies and personnel that facilitated the use of computer technology in the classroom. U.S. federal, state, district, or local level policies were examined. Noted administrative personnel included principals, vice-principals, school board members, teachers, secretaries, parents, and outside sponsors. The level of support provided by the administrator in an overall management capacity and in day-to-day activities with teachers and support staff set the pace for the use of computer technology in the classroom. The schools that were most successful in using computer technology and the Web in the classroom had administrators who were highly involved in establishing technology objectives and budgets, actively sought partnerships with outside sources, provided secretarial and administrative support for writing grants, provided an encouraging environment for change and experimentation, and integrated computer technology in their administrative functions. Technical support that included equipment maintenance, system administration, and user support was considered vital in maintaining ongoing, effective use of the computer. Those measures that demonstrated positive and supportive computer technology services included administrator understanding of state-level technology strategic plans, the existence of a local or district plan that included how to acquire, maintain, and use equipment, and the existence of ongoing technical support. Effective teacher support by administrators included those that provided release time, qualified substitute teachers, had developed teacher training plans, and had an expectation that computer technology would be integrated into the curriculum, and had developed standards for computer competency.

Technology Infrastructure Trends.   This referred to the physical characteristics of the Web connection to a school. Not surprisingly, the team noted that in the technology infrastructure area at the time of this investigation, not all teachers had access *in their classroom*. Access, however, is changing rapidly (Becker, 1998; NCES, 1995a, 1995b, 1996). Fourteen percent of the classrooms being wired to the Internet at the beginning of our investigation had become 40%; 65% of schools that were wired had become 90%. With this finding came another reality that six different school configurations of Internet access existed, from those with direct access in their classrooms to those with access in administrative areas or at home. Access speed varied greatly, with most schools not having the latest and fastest access.

Teacher Factor Trends.   Teacher factors, those that facilitated or inhibited the use of the Web in the classroom, included personal characteristics such as attitude, skill, and knowledge, and external characteristics such as assignment and grade level. Teachers in general had limited understanding of the type of resources that exist on the Web, limited search skills, and limited skill in preparing and utilizing Web-based resources in their classroom. Realities also revealed that those teachers who used the Internet in their classroom used it for gaining information (68%), some for e-mail (39%), and only 18% posted messages to the Web. Only 29% had their students using the Web themselves and 7% used e-mail. The most important finding was that only 4% actually published on the Web (Becker, 1998).

Teachers had a limited perception about the best use of the Web, and felt that choosing to use the Web would take too much time in a limited schedule. They were not interested in making a high initial investment for an unknown payoff. As expected, teachers also told us that they feared that the computer would break down in class and they would not know what to do about it (Grabowski et al., 1998).

Curriculum Trends.   Curriculum includes content, methods, and sequence of instruction. Given the diverse nature of the U.S. curriculum being determined at the local level, the team was forced to examine other sources for national trends. They, therefore, focused the investigation on existing science, math, and technology National Standards to search for insights into possible links between NASA resources and the curriculum. Scientific literacy and technological competence were defined. The standards also specified a process-oriented curriculum. One finding was that schools were basing their curriculum and activities on national, state, and local standards; however, the teachers in this sample were not all aware of how these standards linked to what they did.

Existing NASA Materials Trends.   A typology of Web resources was created to summarize the types of materials that would be functional in the classroom. Most of the sites that were available were information rather than instructional or learning sites, but included significant resources for curriculum materials such as lessons, activities, projects, references, tools, and so on. The types of resources were then classified into information and network sites, and further subdivided into databases, information resources, lesson plans, projects, student activities, tools, references and links, and tutorials (Grabowski et al., 1998).

Trends for Best Practices of Using the Web in the Classroom.   Many techniques and activities can be used to enhance learning. Effective learning environments engage learners. In reported best practices, teachers used the Web to facilitate learning through collaborative activities with individuals inside and outside the classroom. These teachers challenged students to use the Web to research content areas that support lesson goals. Students were also using the Web to create new or manipulate existing data to support lesson objectives. The Web was also used successfully in distance education when users had access and were comfortable with technology, instructions were clear, and the instructor maintained a high level of on-line or off-line presence. Many issues still surround the use of the Web, such as privacy, security, and quality of websites; however, these issues were not summarized in this needs assessment.

The findings also noted that using Web resources in the classroom was still a fairly rare occurrence, given that access was lacking in most schools. Lessons that incorporated the Web only as an information resource, with no clear goal in mind, did not generally stimulate the students. However, when there was a clear instructional goal or intent, generated either by the teacher or the student, Web searching was more purposeful and valuable.

Although access in many classrooms was slow, teachers downloaded or cached text, images, and videotape clips prior to class to save loading time. Some teachers started to use website-capturing software to load sites of interest onto non-Internet-connected computers. In these ways, teachers have been able to take advantage of Web resources previously unavailable to them because of time considerations.

Teacher Tutorial Trends.   The team searched for existing tutorials that focused on skills related to both instructional and technical issues of the Web. To use the Web in the classroom, teachers needed varying degrees of technical proficiency combined with strategies and skills relating to designing instruction and writing lesson plans. Adequate teacher tutorials demonstrating methods of incorporating Web-based content into instruction existed; however, teachers had difficulty locating this information because it was embedded in a much larger volume of tutorials on how to design and produce Web pages. Many resources entitled "integration" only covered the topic of "production" of Web content. The result was that teachers were flooded with redundant information on issues of production but few relevant integration strategies. Also, these resources had relatively little structure and required initiative from the teacher to master the skills and knowledge of Web production. Resources for integration were also available outside the Web in the form of facilitated events such as workshops, conferences, in-service programs, and seminars provided for teachers to learn integration skills. These facilitated events tended to have greater structure and were easily accessible, but typically involved a financial cost that limited their general accessibility.

Trends for Learning Theories and Teaching Practices. Broad theoretical perspectives on how learning occurs (behavioral, cognitive, motivational, sociocognitive, and developmental) and how these could be applied in the classroom were researched. These perspectives founded the ideal teaching strategies that incorporated the Web in the classroom (Grabowski et al., 1998). However, most teachers used an eclectic combination of the five theoretical perspectives, matching their approach with the task and the learners.

Step 5: Determining Causes and Prioritizing Recommendations

Although the team inferred from the data that teachers were not using NASA Web resources in their classes, they could not determine the extent of NASA's specific problem, just that a gap did exist. This was inferred from access and use data in general, not just those specific to NASA resources. However, when shown existing NASA Web resources, teachers from the sample responded similarly, "I had no idea that such excellent educational resources were available from NASA!"

From the detailed data collected, nine major inhibiting factors to using *any* Web resources were highlighted. Without access, skill, positive perception, adequate time, curriculum links to standards, useful Web content, classroom activities reflecting effective learning, appropriate use of Web teaching practices, and instruction about Web integration, increased use was not likely. The school realities about these problem areas are summarized in column 1 of Table 7.3. Corresponding recommendations to the nine realities noted in the description of the school environment are listed in Table 7.3, column 2.

TABLE 7.3A
Realities and Recommendations for School Context

School Context Realities	*Recommendations*
	Access
Although Internet access in schools is changing daily, teachers who do not have instructional access cannot even consider the Web as an educational resource.	Prepare teachers for the eventuality that they will one day have Internet access.
Four different configurations of access in the classroom exist: classroom access, lab access, resource room access, and home access only. These access options also vary depending on the number and type of computers available. Each access option presents unique challenges for using the Web in the classroom.	Help teachers determine how the Web can be used within their own school and classroom configuration so that its use is seamless to their instruction, rather than being used solely as a "big-time event."
Speed of access challenges even the most creative and motivated teacher when they only have slow modems.	Help teachers understand that the Web has many options and strategies for addressing slow modem speeds, and that the most glitzy sites may not be the most educationally effective.
	Skill
Teachers have a limited understanding of what resources exist on the Web.	Expose teachers to the many different types of resources that exist on the Web that are classroom appropriate.
Teachers are unaware of efficient search strategies to find materials and resources quickly.	Train teachers about resources and efficient search strategies.
Teachers lack skill in preparing and utilizing Web-based resources in their classroom.	For those teachers with a real interest, provide and encourage training in the areas of how to develop, produce, and integrate Web-based resources.
	Perception
Teachers have a limited and biased perception that the best use of the Web is for the teachers or their students to "program" material to place on the Web.	Educate teachers on other strategies for using the Web in their classroom.
Teachers fear that if they choose to use the Web, it will take a great deal of already limited time for planning and development.	Educate teachers to understand the type of resources that are available on the Web and how to use efficient strategies for finding useful Web resources quickly.
Teachers fear that the computers will break down or things will go wrong in the middle of their lessons.	Administrators should budget technical support for teachers rather than rely on the teachers to have to troubleshoot and do systems administration as well. An analogy is that when teachers use the school car to transport students, they are not expected to maintain it as well.

(Continued)

TABLE 7.3A
(Continued)

School Context Realities	Recommendations
Time	
A teacher's day is already taken up with tremendous amounts of responsibilities just to meet the minimum requirements of teaching and maintaining safety in the school.	Web use should be viewed as another classroom resource. Choosing what and whether to use the Web should be done in the same way as deciding to use other resources. This selection is a natural part of writing lesson plans rather than being an additional task to accomplish.
There is a high initial investment of time that teachers need to invest in learning new techniques to be used in the classroom.	Administrators should view learning the Web in much the same manner as upgrading other skills and provide release time and training that would make teachers aware of the potential of the Web as an instructional resource.

TABLE 7.3B
Realities and Recommendations for School Content

School Content Realities	Recommendations
Curriculum	
Curriculum standards are changing to a more process and problem-solving oriented curriculum.	Web-enhanced lessons can help teachers meet the changing curriculum standards by bringing problems anchored in reality to learners. Instructional resources that are designed specifically for the Web should reflect these changing curriculum standards.
School curriculum is based on National Standards.	Any material that is put on the Web for specific school use should be tied to the National Education Standards for easy linking back to school curriculum.
Not all teachers are aware of the National Standards and, in fact, are sometimes in conflict with understanding how their state and local standards fit into the scheme of things.	Whenever possible, Web resources should also be tied to state and local education standards.
Web Content	
Resources on the Web contain a variety of materials including resources on people, databases, information, lesson plans, projects, student activities, tools, references and links, and tutorials.	This variety of resources makes it even more feasible to incorporate some aspects of the Web in the classroom without it being experienced as an additional responsibility in an already overloaded schedule. Web-enhanced lessons should take into account the variety of materials to offer the most flexible strategies for Web use.

187

TABLE 7.3C
Realities and Recommendations for Teaching and Learning Processes

Teaching and Learning Process Realities	Recommendations
Classroom	
The classroom is being changed from a teacher-centered to a learner-centered environment in which the children become active generators of knowledge rather than passive recipients of information.	Classroom strategies for using the Web should take into account this new perception of the learning environment and the learning process, as well as traditional modes of instruction.
Web Practices	
Interactivity on the Web does not simply mean interaction between the learner and the computer information, but rather that interaction can be viewed in the broadest sense of creating learning partners with the global Web environment.	This broad definition of interactivity needs to be taken into account when any Web-enhanced learning models are created.
The Web offers the classroom a global rather than a local view of information, jobs, science, mathematics, and technology.	Anchoring local classrooms in real-life activities through the Web should be one model of its use in the classroom.
The Web offers information resources for demonstration in the classroom.	Using the Web in the classroom does not always have to mean elaborate or extensive use. Using simple resources of the Web to expand those that are available locally should be another consideration of Web use in the classroom.
The Web can be a source of information, or it can be a repository of teacher- or student-generated content or activities as well.	When students or teachers have the inclination to learn how to create content for the Web, they should be encouraged to do so; however, this should not be the only way the Web is promoted for classroom use.
Teachers use a variety of effective teaching and learning strategies currently in their classrooms.	Strategies for using the Web in the classroom should apply the most prevalent and effective learning strategies currently used by teachers and not be limited to only one approach.
Instruction About the Web	
Instruction exists that teaches teachers how to develop Web resources. Less material exists that assists teachers in the integration of the Web into the classroom. Often, however, these two types of Web use are not differentiated, resulting in the integration lessons being subsumed and lost under production lessons.	Simple-to-use models that stand alone as Web-integration strategies should be developed and disseminated.

Note. From "Web-Based Instruction and Learning, Analysis and Needs Assessment," by B. L. Grabowski, M. McCarthy, and T. A. Koszalka, 1998, NASA Tech. Paper No. NASA/TP-1998-206547, pp. 24–26 (public domain document).

These general areas defining realities and recommended solutions were then distilled into the following conclusions:

1. However the Web is recommended for inclusion into the classroom, it cannot add to the teachers' workload.
2. Given the new curriculum standards, new and innovative strategies for classroom use of the Web should be developed.
3. Administration must acknowledge the Web as an important resource for teachers and provide the necessary support for teachers in terms of learning time, technical support, and training opportunities.
4. Developers of Web-based resources that will be used by teachers need to take into consideration the realities about the school context, content, and teaching and learning processes in the classroom, which focuses on the teacher and learner's need.
5. Teachers need to learn how to use the Web efficiently and effectively in their classroom.

The first four conclusions are not instruction or training issues. These deal with environment, administration, and educator issues. The fourth, however, is. Other details from the needs assessment and performance analysis from teacher realities helped the team make recommendations about that instruction. These are summarized in Table 7.4. As a result, the design team recommended three actions: development of tools, and training for the use of the tools, for teacher reflection about the Web; development of instruction on integrating Web-based resources in the classroom; and development of an exemplary best practice of how the total Web could be used in the classroom as a demonstration project.

TABLE 7.4
Realities and Recommended Training Solutions

Realities	Type of Recommended Solution
Lack of understanding of the Internet itself and what it provides an educator	Reflection tools and training
Lack of understanding of how information on the Internet could be used to help them teach	Reflection tools, training, best practice example
Fear by some	Not directly a training issue, although confidence can be built during training
Lack of understanding about how to use the Internet under various classroom configurations	Training, best practice example
Lack of incentives by some	Motivation, not training
Lack of time	Not directly a training issue, unless teachers learn to become more efficient

Step 6: Communicate Results Back to the Client

The design team kept in constant communication with their client to keep them abreast of the activities of the needs assessment. The final report was written and submitted to the client and edited after substantial feedback was received.

EPILOGUE

Several projects resulted from this needs assessment. The first major one was to develop two tools for teachers to develop an understanding about what exists on the Web and how those resources could be used in the classroom. The first, ID PRISM, which stands for Instructional Design Possibilities, Realities, Issues, Standards, and Multidimensional Perspectives, was a reflection tool for teachers to systematically and systemically reflect on changing their classroom environment to an electronic one (Koszalka, Grabowski, & McCarthy, 1999). The second was the Web-Enhanced Learning Environment Strategies (WELES) reflection tool and lesson planner to help teachers integrate Web resources of all kinds into their classroom (Grabowski, Koszalka, & McCarthy, 1999). Workshops were also developed to train teachers on the use of the tool. The paper-based model was eventually converted into an electronic search tool, NASA Ed Finder, to assist teachers in finding usable resources efficiently.

As a demonstration project, a problem-based learning environment was created on the Web that used existing NASA resources to demonstrate the feasibility of the WELES reflection tool and planner. This project, called Kids as Airborne Mission Scientists, was funded by NASA under their Learning Technologies Projects (Devon & Grabowski, 1999; Koszalka, Grabowski, & Kim, 2001).

Finally, a distance education course entitled Internet in the Classroom was developed from the content and performance analysis of this study with support from the Pennsylvania State University World Campus. Modules and cases were created to help teachers think about the three major ways they could use the Internet in their classroom—as a planner, integrator, or producer (Grabowski, 2001).

CONCLUSION

The information gathered during the needs assessment and performance analysis flowed into informing decisions at each stage in designing, developing, evaluating, and implementing the teacher training, course, and tools.

Each time another product was produced, the information gathered at that stage was fed back into our initial understanding and modified our thinking. In this case, the needs assessment performed an important function in making strategic instructional decisions for addressing this problem.

ACKNOWLEDGMENTS

This project was made possible through funding from the National Aeronautics and Space Administration (NASA Grant NAG 4-113). The author would like to acknowledge the team of designers who conducted this investigation: Dr. Tiffany A. Koszalka, Dr. Marianne McCarthy, James Lloyd, Angel Hernandez, Connie Garrett, Leah Iwinski, Tom Iwinski, Ellen Kendall, Chih-Lung Lin, Natalie Tiracorda, Felipe Vazquez, Dr. Marchelle Canright, Jeff Ehman, Rebecca Beaty, and E. Lee Duke. Any opinions, findings, and conclusions or recommendations expressed in this material are those of the authors and do not necessarily reflect the views of the National Aeronautics and Space Administration.

REFERENCES

Andrews, D. H., & Goodson, L. A. (1995). A comparative analysis of models of instructional design. In G. Anglin (Ed.), *Instructional technology: Past, present and future* (2nd ed., pp. 161–182). Englewood, CO: Libraries Unlimited.

Becker, H. (1998). Internet use by teachers and students. *Teaching, Learning and Computing.* Retrieved from http://www/critouci/TLC/findings/Internet-Use

Devon, R., & Grabowski, B. L. (1999). *Learning using ERAST aircraft for understanding remote sensing (LUAUII—Kids as airborne mission scientists, KAAMS)* (Grant No. NCC5-432). Washington, DC: NASA Goddard Flight Research Center, Learning Technologies Project.

Dick, W., & Carey, L. (1985). *The systematic design of instruction* (2nd ed.). Glenview, IL: Scott, Foresman.

Grabowski, B. L. (2001, June). *E-learning: Instructional design considerations.* Paper presented at the ED-Media 2001 World Conference, Tampere, Finland.

Grabowski, B. L., Koszalka, T. A., & McCarthy, M. (1999). *Web-enhanced learning environment strategies handbook* (10th ed.). (Available from the Instructional Systems Program, 315 Keller Building, The Pennsylvania State University, University Park, PA 16802)

Grabowski, B. L., McCarthy, M., & Koszalka, T. (1998). *Web-based instruction and learning: Analysis and needs assessment* (NASA Tech. Publ. No. 1998-206547). Hanover, MD: NASA Center for Aerospace Information. Available: http://www.dfrc.nasa.gov/DTRS/1998/index.html

Gustafson, K. L. (1981). *Survey of instructional development models.* Syracuse, NY: ERIC Clearinghouse on Information Resources.

Kaufman, R., & English, F. W. (1979). *Needs assessment: Concept and application.* Englewood Cliffs, NJ: Educational Technology Publications.

Kaufman, R., & Herman, J. (1997). Strategic planning, schooling and the curriculum for tomorrow. In S. Dijkstra, N. Seel, F. Schott, & R. D. Tennyson (Eds.), *Instructional design: International perspectives* (Vol. 2, pp. 45–59). Mahwah, NJ: Lawrence Erlbaum Associates.

Kaufman, R., Rojas, A. M., & Mayer, H. (1993). *Needs assessment: A user's guide.* Englewood Cliffs, NJ: Educational Technology Publications.

Knirk, F. G., & Gustafson, K. L. (1986). *Instructional technology: A systematic approach to education.* New York: Holt, Rinehart & Winston.

Koszalka, T. A., Grabowski, B. L., & Kim, Y. (2001). Kids as airborne mission scientists: Designing PBL to inspire kids. *Proceedings for the 2001 Association for Educational Communications and Technology, 1,* 217–221.

Koszalka, T. A., Grabowski, B. L., & McCarthy, M. (1999, February). *ID-PRISM: Reflecting on the electronic classroom.* Paper presented at the annual meeting of the K–12 Consortium for School Networking, Washington, DC.

Leshin, C. B., Pollock, J., & Reigeluth, C. R. (1992). *Instructional design, strategies and tactics.* Englewood Cliffs, NJ: Educational Technology Publications.

Miller, V. A. (1996). The history of training. In R. L. Craig (Ed.), *The ASTD training and development handbook: A guide to human resource development* (pp. 3–18). New York: McGraw-Hill.

National Center for Educational Statistics. (1995a). *Advanced teleconferencing in public schools K–12* (Fast Response Survey System, FRSS No. 56). Washington, DC: U.S. Department of Education.

National Center for Educational Statistics. (1995b). *Advanced teleconferencing in public elementary and secondary schools* (Fast Response Survey System, FRSS No. 57). Washington, DC: U.S. Department of Education.

National Center for Educational Statistics. (1996). *Advanced teleconferencing in public elementary and secondary schools* (Fast Response Survey System, FRSS No. 61). Washington, DC: U.S. Department of Education.

Romiszowski, A. J. (1981). *Designing instructional systems: Decision making in course planning and curriculum design.* London: Kogan Press.

Rossett, A. (1987). *Training needs assessment.* Englewood Cliffs, NJ: Educational Technology Publications.

Rossett, A. (1995). Needs assessment. In G. Anglin (Ed.), *Instructional technology: Past, present and future* (2nd ed., pp. 183–196). Englewood, CO: Libraries Unlimited.

Seels, B., & Glasgow, S. (1990). *Exercises in instructional design.* Columbus, OH: Merrill.

Smith, P. L., & Ragan, T. J. (1993). *Instructional design.* New York: Merrill.

Warries, E. (1990). Theory and the systematic design of instruction. In S. Dijkstra, B. Van Hout Wolters, & P. C. Van Der Sijde (Eds.), *Research on instruction: Design and effects* (pp. 1–19). Englewood Cliffs, NJ: Educational Technology Publications.

Chapter 8

Curriculum Development as Modeling of Complex Reality

Frank Achtenhagen
Georg-August-University, Göttingen, Germany

This chapter deals with two major topics:

1. How can curriculum theory be used to develop curricular goals and content units for commercial apprenticeships at vocational schools and training firms?
2. Which theoretically based means for the development and implementation of instructional design might help to solve practical curriculum problems?

These topics are treated in five steps: a discussion of curricular goals and content units for a commercial apprenticeship; the presentation of criteria for instructional design for solving curriculum problems; the introduction of a virtual enterprise as a practical example; the discussion of how to use this instructional design for teaching–learning purposes; and conclusions and possible perspectives on further research and development to close the discussion.

CURRICULAR GOALS AND CONTENT UNITS FOR A COMMERCIAL APPRENTICESHIP

Our research focused on commercial apprenticeships for industrial clerks (*Industriekaufleute*). Such apprenticeships take place under the following conditions:

1. The apprenticeship takes 3 years.
2. The apprentices attend the commercial part-time school (*Berufsschule*) 1.5 days per week and are trained 3.5 days per week in their individual industrial enterprise.
3. There are state curricula for the commercial schools and federal training schedules for the enterprises. Both together define the goals and content of the apprenticeship.
4. Intermediate and final examinations are run outside the schools by the Chambers of Industry and Commerce.
5. At the beginning, the apprentices are at least in their 10th year of schooling (after a minimum of 9 years of compulsory school).

State curricula and the federal training schedules have been under pressure to be changed in recent years—as so-called megatrends have been causing new and difficult challenges for the apprenticeship system (cf. Achtenhagen & Grubb, 2001; Achtenhagen, Nijhof, & Raffe, 1995; Buttler, 1992; Castells, 2001). The megatrends, which include processes of globalization and Europeanization or the increasing use of information and communication technologies, influence the shape of production and business processes. Traditional tasks and process structures are disappearing or becoming more complex and dynamic. Consequently, the preparation for the adequate and efficient fulfillment of business tasks and processes also has to be changed. Therefore, the development of new curricula for the corresponding apprenticeships is urged.

The State of Lower Saxony—as a consequence—has changed the curriculum for industrial clerks

(a) by using theoretical knowledge about curriculum construction (cf. Achtenhagen et al., 1992; Reetz, 1984; Tramm, 1997),
(b) by using empirical knowledge won by field studies (cf. reports in Achtenhagen & Grubb, 2001), and
(c) by using aspects of management concepts and software engineering concepts (cf. Gomez & Probst, 1987; Wigand, Picot, & Reichwald, 1998).

Our Göttingen project group was involved in all these processes and could define the main principles, goals, and content units of the new curricula for the school subjects "business administration," "accounting," and "computer training." One very special effect was the possibility to formulate curricular goals and content units for the teaching and learning possibilities provided by our complex learning environments.

One example out of the Lower Saxonian Curriculum for Commercial Schools (*Berufsschule für Industriekaufleute*) is presented in the following:

Learning Area 1: The enterprise as a complex economic and social system

Central goals:

* Exploration, analysis, and presentation of market-oriented business processes of an industrial enterprise.
* Understanding the interdependency of material-, information-, money-, and value-chains.
* Understanding the underlying information, accounting, and controlling systems.
* Working with a (virtual) model enterprise and exploring the individual (real) training firm.

. . .

Learning Area 8: Recording and documentation of value-chains

Central goals:

* Recording and documenting value-chains with regard to the business processes (financial and cost accounting).
* Running the accounting and controlling systems by approaching adequate software.

. . .

The main overall goals for the whole apprenticeship with its learning processes in the enterprises and in the part-time commercial school were:

→ Understanding complex and dynamic business processes.
→ Understanding and working with complex software systems (like SAP) that are supposed to help manage the complex and dynamic business processes efficiently and effectively.

CRITERIA FOR INSTRUCTIONAL DESIGN THAT HELP TO SOLVE PRACTICAL CURRICULUM PROBLEMS

A preliminary remark is necessary: Instructional design (ID) applications are very often run selectively and isolatedly (which makes sense for certain computer-based training programs, e.g., training for a job on an assembly line). But such approaches do not work well with the increased complexity and dynamics of business and production processes.

As learning normally takes place within contexts (school curricula, firm training programs), each ID application should be embedded in a curricular context. Necessary steps are, therefore, the development of ID applications with this context in mind—this means directing the ID applications to central curricular goals and content units in order to support them. It is also necessary to provide links to the following teaching/training–learning/working processes and to their context. The ID applications should cover longer teaching/training–learning/working periods (preferably 6–12 months).

One central point is that the ID application reported on here is modeled with special attention to the fostering of "deep understanding" processes (Pellegrino, 2002). We therefore have to adapt the ID application optimally to given/modified goal-content structures; this also includes the modification of those structures. This especially concerns the mutual dependency of the construction of the ID application and its implementation on the one hand and the goal-content structure of the curriculum on the other.

By trying to fit the ID application, instruction, and the curriculum to each other, one can refer to the principles of the report *How People Learn* (Bransford, Brown, & Cocking, 2000), which focuses on

(a) learner-centered processes,

(b) knowledge-centered processes,

(c) assessment-centered processes, and

(d) community-centered processes.

When we considered how to launch an instructional design according to curricular goals (and their necessary change) and also to the summarizing aspects of *How People Learn*, we decided to develop a virtual enterprise and work with it.

Especially the following goals of the curriculum should be achieved by this virtual enterprise:

1. The exploration, analysis, and presentation of market- and client-oriented business processes.
2. Understanding the interdependency of material-, information-, money-, and value-chains.

As these goals have to be realized by the use of the *virtual* enterprise, all information won has to be checked and compared to the business processes in the *real* training firms; the results of comparison and reflection are communicated in the vocational classroom.

The central endeavor in this enterprise is to educate and train a clerk with regard to deep understanding of the business and production processes in an industrial enterprise so that he or she is able to work conscientiously and use complex firm software packages (such as SAP) effectively.

For developing and constructing the virtual enterprise, we used a set of criteria (cf. Achtenhagen, 2001) that was checked against the criteria of other projects (mainly the anchored instruction approach; cf. Cognition and Technology Group at Vanderbilt, 1997; also see criteria in Bransford, Brown, & Cocking, 2000; Pellegrino, 2002):

1. The students must obtain the opportunity to have school experiences with relatively complex facts and problems that can be related to "reality."

2. The teaching should explicitly take into account the prior and everyday knowledge and the interests of the students.

3. Teaching should start with a complex goal and content structure that can serve principally as an advance organizer for all topics to be taught within the course.

4. There must be a concentration on the intension and extension of terms and concepts. The decisive point for successful decontextualization is given here. For example, the general concept of devaluation (the intension of that term) also has to be used for the solution of more specific tasks (e.g., devaluation of machines, trucks, etc.) or for alternative procedures (e.g., linear or degressive devaluation)—the extension of the term.

5. The teaching–learning processes should foster a clear and distinctive action and activity orientation. Learners should develop knowledge by solving meaningful problems and developing a deep understanding.

6. In this action-oriented sense, illustrative clarity is more than pictorial demonstration. For the development of adequate mental models, learning objects are expected to be accessible and open to the experience of the students.

7. The conflict between casuistic and systematic procedures has to be balanced by the use of a systems and action-oriented perspective.

8. The instruction should also foster a metacognitive perspective: The conditions, necessities, and restrictions of the environment should be thematized and reflected on by a "learning about the model."

9. Unstructured, ill-defined problems that cannot be easily solved by merely additive teamwork should be offered with the ongoing instruction. The students can experience the importance of integrated work during the course of this process as well as the advantages and problems of distributed cognition.

10. The complex teaching–learning environment should also provide tasks similar to those that have to be fulfilled at the workplace—as direct preparation for the labor market, but also as a possibility to understand and perform similar or even new tasks at the workplace: the aspect of transferability and mobility.

11. These overall criteria for didactic modeling take into account the fact that different dimensions of knowledge should be considered: declarative, procedural, and strategic knowledge. Declarative knowledge is related to facts, concepts, and network-like structures of facts and concepts that might give a first illustration of the systems character of an enterprise. Procedural knowledge is related to operations with facts, concepts, and structures (e.g., to count purchase and production data), which may be related to each other to find optimal pathways. Strategic knowledge is defined by what one can do and why and when one does it. It is mainly present in the form of mental models in one's process of comprehending certain phenomena; this helps to integrate the declarative and procedural knowledge in a way in which both can be used in specific situations and enable and support processes of deep understanding and corresponding actions and activities.

A VIRTUAL ENTERPRISE AS A PRACTICAL EXAMPLE

We constructed the virtual enterprise "Arnold & Stolzenberg GmbH" (cf. Siemon, 2001) with a strong relation to a real enterprise "Arnold & Stolzenberg GmbH." Figure 8.1 shows some central goals of the construction of the virtual enterprise.

While modeling the complex learning environment "Arnold & Stolzenberg," we were confronted with a specific problem that has not yet been suf-

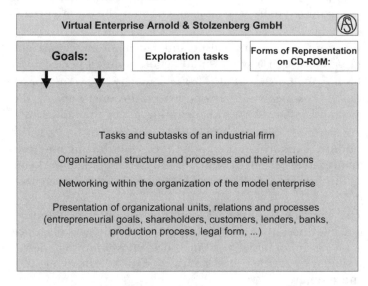

FIG. 8.1. Central goals of the virtual enterprise.

ficiently discussed (cf. Achtenhagen, 2001): Usually it is overlooked that didactic modeling processes have to consist of two steps:

1. modeling reality, and
2. modeling models of reality from a didactic perspective.

Modeling Reality

The central question is which elements (and their relations) of a real enterprise should be visualized by the virtual enterprise. As the apprentices are trained in different (real) firms that are very different with regard to products, size, branch, organizational structure, and so on, the complex learning environment—the virtual enterprise—must offer a prototype of an industrial firm that helps to promote a deep understanding of the underlying systems structure of very different industrial enterprises.

Our model of reality, the virtual enterprise, was based on a real enterprise that is not particularly large (it has about 500 workers and employees) and exceptional, but successful (it serves one quarter of the world market), and produces goods (industrial chains) with a relatively simple parts list (of pieces) and a clearly organized production structure.

The managers, employees, and workers were interviewed and filmed—together with the production and administrative processes. The learner can enter the different departments of the virtual enterprise by clicking on the names of the specific departments, which are shown by an aerial view of the real enterprise (Fig. 8.2) or by its organogram (Fig. 8.3).

Clicking on "Produktion" (production) or "Beschaffung" (purchase) will bring Fig. 8.4 or 8.5 onto the screen. The pictures are part of videoclips that can be started. The workers and employees report on their tasks. It is also possible to get the spoken text simultaneously in a written form (Fig. 8.5).

The modeling process of the virtual enterprise took into account (a) the comprehension modes and needs of the apprentices, (b) the strategies of actual business behavior, (c) the delivery of a certain product to a defined client, and (d) the demonstration of the systems character of the business and production processes.

According to standards of curriculum theory, these conditions correspond to the leading literature in the fields of business and economy. Figure 8.6 is one example of the description and a first operationalization of the systems character of the business and production processes, which forms the basis for the redefinition of curricular goals (cf. Preiss, 1994).

This approach is directed against the very traditional structure of curricula and learning material, such as textbooks, since it is widely spread over

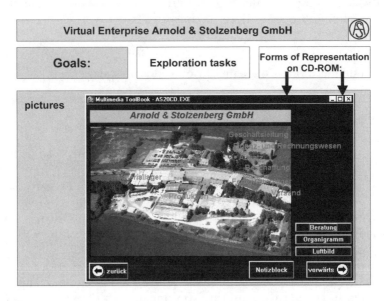

FIG. 8.2. Aerial view of the real enterprise.

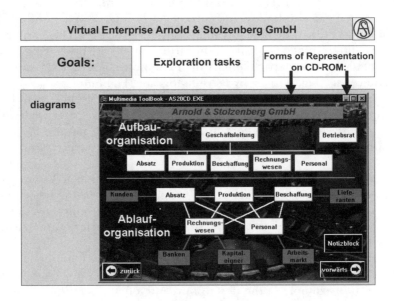

FIG. 8.3. Organogram of the real enterprise.

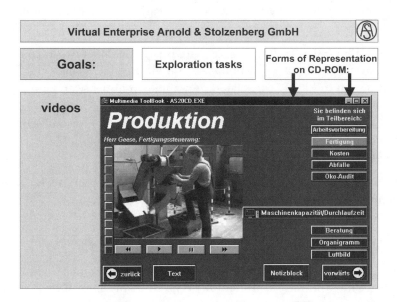

FIG. 8.4. Videoclip about a production process in the real enterprise.

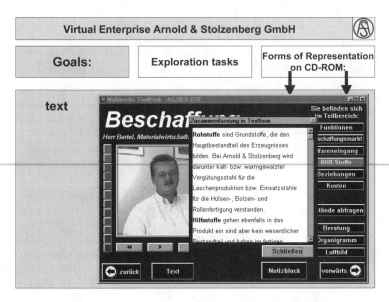

FIG. 8.5. Videoclip (and additional text) about the purchase of raw material in the real enterprise.

the fields of economic and commercial education (cf. Achtenhagen, 1992, pp. 323–324):

1. Content units (including goals) are not defined by situational aspects and are thus not operationalized on all possible levels.
2. Content units are not related to usability in industry and administration.
3. Content units are linearized, chopped into pieces, distant from economic needs, distant from personal needs and abilities, and wrongly mixed.

Exactly these three strands of criticism were the starting points for the development of the virtual enterprise and its underlying network structure of goals and content—as demonstrated by Fig. 8.6.

Modeling Models of Reality From a Didactic Perspective

The overall didactic perspective ("didactic" in the German or Scandinavian languages has a positive connotation) is given by the 11 criteria presented previously. The means by which instructional processes are supported is decisive: One means is to run so-called exploration tasks, by which the learners are forced to navigate through the CD-ROM (on which the virtual enterprise is stored) to get all information necessary to solve these tasks. One example is given in narrative form by a videoclip: A client phones and asks an apprentice: "When can you deliver 200 chains of a certain type?"; the learners have to help the apprentice solve this task. They have to detect and collect relevant information—if they come to the right department and, once there, to the right screen or videoclip. Figure 8.7 gives one example: The learners see that there are no "Innenlaschen" and "Außenlaschen" (flaps) in stock. That means that raw material has to be bought to produce the flaps. We also see that for "Hülsen" (tubes), raw material for the production of only 140 m of the special chain is in stock. Specific purchase and production activities must also start here.

The time for purchase and production time have to be considered simultaneously, following a network-like structure of reasoning. One example:

> To solve the task "When can we deliver?," the apprentices collect the information that it will take 12 days until the necessary machines are available. They also know that raw material must be bought, which takes 3 days. The only accepted solution for the total time needed is 12 days: The learners have to find out that the waiting time for the machines principally can (and must) be used to run the purchase, and so on—that means developing an integrated view on production and purchase processes. This example is related to the curriculum goal "Understanding the interdependency of material-, information-, money-, and value-chains."

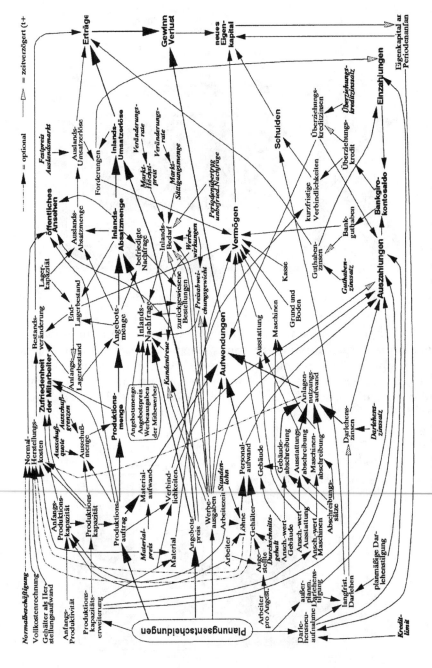

FIG. 8.6. Basic goal and content structure for business instruction.

203

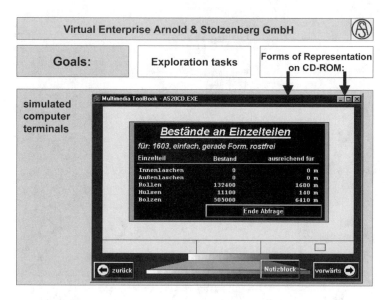

FIG. 8.7.   Simulated computer terminal of the virtual enterprise.

Another very important curriculum goal is "Understanding the escorting information, accounting, and controlling processes." We can follow this goal by running the accounting and controlling systems with adequate software. Figures 8.8 and 8.9 demonstrate the changed view on the business and production processes: from function orientation (Fig. 8.8) to process orientation (Fig. 8.9).

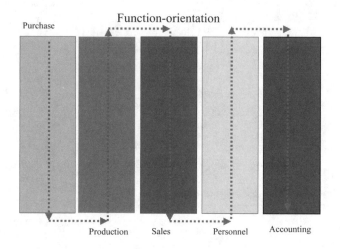

FIG. 8.8.   Function orientation of business and production processes.

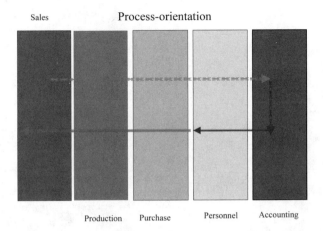

FIG. 8.9.   Process orientation of business and production processes.

We demonstrate the process orientation of business and production processes by modeling in detail processes within the virtual enterprise by using a special software: the ARIS toolset. This software leads to the application of SAP—providing an integrated view on events (*Ereignisse*), functions (*Funktionen*), and data (*Daten*). Figure 8.10 shows working steps according to the ARIS procedure that led to the structure in Fig. 8.11.

Another curricular goal is "Recording and documenting value-chains with regard to business processes (financial and cost accounting)." This goal is related to Learning Area 8, "Recording and documentation of value-chains," which starts together with Learning Area 1, "The enterprise as a complex economic and social system." All instructional units in the field of accounting are related to the virtual enterprise, which also functions as the model enterprise for accounting (we developed corresponding material that covers about 1 year of instruction in accounting; cf. Getsch & Preiss, 2001; Fig. 8.12).

USE OF THE VIRTUAL ENTERPRISE
FOR TEACHING–LEARNING PROCESSES

We follow central categories of corresponding teaching–learning processes from *How People Learn* (for a short description, see Bransford, Brown, & Cocking, 2000, pp. 131ff.).

Learner Centered

We run the virtual enterprise from a (modified) mastery learning perspective—taking into account the great heterogeneity of the apprentices with regard to school socialization, age, and prior knowledge (in one classroom

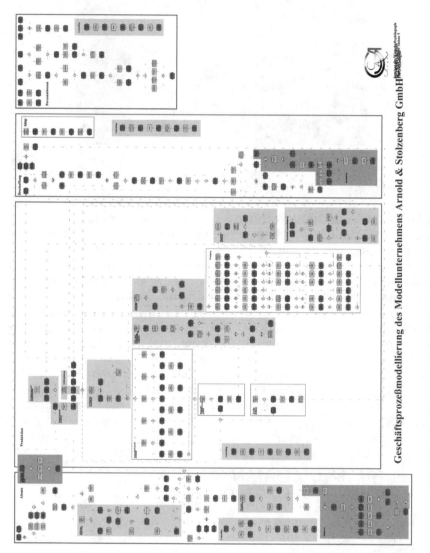

Geschäftsprozeßmodellierung des Modellunternehmens Arnold & Stolzenberg GmbH

FIG. 8.10.   Working steps for modeling the business and production process structure.

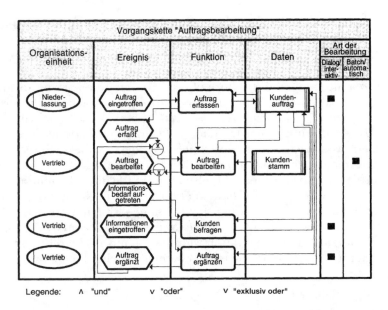

FIG. 8.11. Modeling the business and production processes of the virtual enterprise (partial view).

FIG. 8.12. Introductory course in accounting based on the virtual enterprise.

of the commercial school, we found apprentices with 11 different years of birth). Our major goal is to harmonize the knowledge of the learners for the following teaching–learning processes. The central problem of the mastery learning approach—the distribution of additional learning time—was solved by a differentiated structure of tasks (for an overview on the advantages and disadvantages of the mastery learning approach, cf. the discussion in *Review of Educational Research*, 1987, pp. 175–235, and 1990, pp. 265–307). As the individual learners need different amounts of time to solve their tasks, each student gets a new task that cannot be solved in the same day, immediately after having solved a previous task. These new tasks, therefore, have to be finished and solved later in the firms or at home; thus, all students have to prepare their solution for the beginning of the next school day. In this way, all learners get the same tasks; they are always busy and reach the same stage of knowledge for the next school day. This procedure was developed in cooperation with the trainers of the different firms (cf. Achtenhagen, Bendorf, Getsch, & Reinkensmeier, 2000).

Knowledge Centered

We mainly concentrated the instruction on the development of declarative, procedural, and strategic knowledge. Because we interpret strategic knowledge as an operationalization of "deep understanding," we developed a set of additional tasks that are related to the business and production processes of the virtual enterprise and have to be solved together with navigation processes in the CD-ROM or independently. One example:

> The apprentices have to demonstrate a way in which the whole production program could/must be changed to provide shorter delivery time. They have to prepare possible solutions, and judge and compare its intended main effects and unintended side effects: Changing the production program causes higher costs and also has the consequence that chains are delivered to another client later than agreed upon (negative effects), versus earlier delivery to the client who urgently needs his chains (positive effect with regard to better client relations in the future).

Assessment Centered

Our mastery learning approach urges a lot of formative assessment (cf. the discussion in Pellegrino, Chudowsky, & Glaser, 2001). We use a lot of formats: from multiple-choice items (used for the external examinations of the apprentices by the Chambers for Industry and Commerce) to essay-like assessment. The summative evaluation showed a mastery level of about 90%.

Community Centered

The apprentices have to work in teams in the commercial school classroom. We also fostered their cooperation in the training firms by giving them an exploration task that was identical to the first exploration task to be worked out on the CD-ROM: The apprentices have to solve the task of determining a delivery term in their individual enterprise—by walking to and through the different departments and by collecting information on their firm network. The apprentices have to compare different business concepts in this process: that of their real firm and that of the virtual enterprise, which is developed according to the scientific literature as an "average" model or prototype. After having solved this "real" exploration task, the apprentices have to report on it in the school classroom—also presenting their individual firm and its products.

An evaluation of the whole approach shows a high amount of motivation and interest, but also an increase of deep understanding (operationalized by items for the testing of strategic knowledge). The retention rate after 18 months (measured by unannounced tests) is remarkably high (about 80% of the test results collected immediately after the instruction phase).

CONCLUSION

We conducted experiments in different schools, over different years, and in different classrooms and were able to achieve similar results. We are therefore starting a project for nearly all commercial schools in the State of Lower Saxony. The major task at the moment, therefore, is to develop comparable complex learning environments and the corresponding materials—proposals for instruction included—for the whole period of 3 years. We are cooperating with voluntary teachers and institutions of further teacher training (*Studienseminare*). The whole project also includes new modes of teacher training, as complex learning environments are not "self-runners" for instruction.

ACKNOWLEDGMENTS

The work reported on was supported by a grant from the German Research Foundation (Ac 35/15-1). Besides the author, the main researchers were Michael Bendorf, Ulrich Getsch, Peter Preiss, and Sandra Reinkensmeier.

REFERENCES

Achtenhagen, F. (1992). The relevance of content for teaching–learning processes. In F. Oser, A. Dick, & J.-L. Patry (Eds.), *Effective and responsible teaching: The new synthesis* (pp. 315–328). San Francisco: Jossey-Bass.

Achtenhagen, F. (2001). Criteria for the development of complex teaching–learning environments. *Instructional Science, 29,* 361–380.

Achtenhagen, F., Bendorf, M., Getsch, U., & Reinkensmeier, S. (2000). Mastery Learning in der Ausbildung von Industriekaufleuten [Mastery learning in the training of industrial clerks]. *Zeitschrift für Pädagogik, 46,* 373–394.

Achtenhagen, F., & Grubb, W. N. (2001). Vocational and occupational education: Pedagogical complexity, institutional diversity. In V. Richardson (Ed.), *Handbook of research on teaching* (4th ed., pp. 604–639). Washington, DC: AERA.

Achtenhagen, F., Nijhof, W., & Raffe, D. (1995). *Feasibility study: Research for vocational education in the framework for COST social sciences.* European Commission: Directorate General: Science, Research and Development. Brussels, Luxembourg: ECSC-EC-EAEC.

Achtenhagen, F., Tramm, T., Preiss, P., Seemann-Weymar, H., John, E. G., & Schunck, A. (1992). *Lernhandeln in komplexen Situationen* [Learn-acting in complex situations]. Wiesbaden, Germany: Gabler.

Bransford, J. D., Brown, A. L., & Cocking, R. R. (Eds.). (2000). *How people learn: Brain, mind, experience, and school.* Washington, DC: National Academy Press.

Buttler, F. (1992). Tätigkeitslandschaft bis 2010 [Job landscape until 2010]. In F. Achtenhagen & E. G. John (Eds.), *Mehrdimensionale Lehr-Lern-Arrangements* [Multidimensional teaching–learning arrangements] (pp. 162–182). Wiesbaden, Germany: Gabler.

Castells, M. (2001). *Der Aufstieg der Netzwerkgesellschaft. Teil 1 der Trilogie Das Informationszeitalter* [The rise of network society]. Opladen, Germany: Leske + Budrich.

Cognition and Technology Group at Vanderbilt. (1997). *The Jasper project: Lessons in curriculum, instruction, assessment and professional development.* Mahwah, NJ: Lawrence Erlbaum Associates.

Getsch, U., & Preiss, P. (2001). *Modellunternehmen Arnold & Stolzenberg GmbH: Grundkurs Rechnungswesen, belegorientiert* [Virtual enterprise Arnold & Stolzenberg GmbH: Introductory course for accounting] [CD-ROM]. Bad Homburg v.d.H., Germany: Gehlen.

Gomez, P., & Probst, G. (1987). *Vernetztes Denken im Management* [Networked reasoning of the management]. Bern, Switzerland: Schweizerische Volksbank.

Pellegrino, J. W. (2002). Connecting learning theory and instruction: Principles, practices, and possibilities. In F. Achtenhagen & E. G. John (Eds.), *Milestones in vocational and occupational education and training* (Vol. 1, pp. 17–43). Bielefeld, Germany: Bertelsmann.

Pellegrino, J. W., Chudowsky, N., & Glaser, R. (Eds.). (2001). *Knowing what students know.* Washington, DC: National Academy Press.

Preiss, P. (1994). Schema-based modeling of complex economic situations. In W. J. Nijhof & J. N. Streumer (Eds.), *Flexibility in training and vocational education* (pp. 249–289). Utrecht, Netherlands: Lemma.

Reetz, L. (1984). *Wirtschaftsdidaktik* [Didactics of business and economic education]. Bad Heilbrunn, Germany: Klinkhardt.

Siemon, J. (2001). *Modellunternehmen Arnold & Stolzenberg GmbH* [Virtual enterprise Arnold & Stolzenberg GmbH] [CD-ROM]. Bad Homburg v.d.H., Germany: Gehlen.

Tramm, T. (1997). *Lernprozesse in der Übungsfirma* [Learning processes in training firms]. Habilitation thesis, Faculty of Economy and Business Studies. Göttingen, Germany.

Wigand, R., Picot, A., & Reichwald, R. (1998). *Information, organization and management—Expanding markets and corporate boundaries.* Chichester, England: Wiley.

Chapter 9

Curriculum Work and Instructional Design as Different Perspectives on Teaching

Hermann Josef Abs
German Institute for International Educational Research

This chapter raises the question of what instructional design (ID) and curriculum as different guidelines for teachers mean to professional teaching. First, one type of curriculum is explained. Second, the political context of a recent curriculum evaluation is described. Third, results of this curriculum evaluation are reported. Starting from these results, some basic differences between curriculum work and the approach of instructional design to teaching and learning are analyzed. As a last step, some consequences are suggested.

CURRICULUM

The *Oxford English Dictionary* defines *curriculum* as "a regular course of study or training"; and as Jackson (1996, p. 5) continues in the *Handbook of Research on Curriculum*, the first English usage quoted by the *Oxford English Dictionary* is included in a report on German universities from 1824. There one may find the following quotation: "When the German student has finished his curriculum . . ." So in its original meaning, curriculum is the name for the set of courses one has to pass to obtain a degree or certificate at a certain educational institution.

Today English and German still seem to have a similar understanding of the word *curriculum.* But taking a closer look one can find fundamental differences. According to Jackson (1996), the word *curriculum* has a two-

211

fold meaning. In a broader sense, curriculum is everything children and youth must do in order to become fully accepted members of society. In this ethnographical sense, curriculum operates both inside and outside of school. In a more narrow sense, curriculum signifies a "series of consciously directed training experiences that the schools use" to unfold the abilities of the individual (Bobbitt, 1972, p. 43; Jackson, 1996). However, the German language does not share any of these meanings. Curriculum is neither the experience outside of schools nor the experience inside of schools. In modern German the word *curriculum* is a foreign word that can be used as a synonym for the German word *Lehrplan,* and the German word *Lehrplan* could be translated as syllabus of teaching contents or of teaching objectives.

Thus, looking more closely at the different meanings of the word *curriculum* one can recognize different teaching traditions. Curriculum as a preestablished experience of the students is the American tradition, in which a teacher has to put a well-defined program into action. Curriculum as a plan of teaching contents is the German-speaking tradition, in which the teacher has to transform a plan and develop major parts of the program by him- or herself.

This may be called a simplification but it helps to make things clear. Of course, American curricula leave a certain amount of freedom to the teacher and modern German curricula are more than pure tables of content. For example, some German school curricula may follow the so-called T-form; for an example, see Table 9.1.

TABLE 9.1
Example of a German Curriculum Following the T-form:
Eighth-Grade Catholic Religious Education at Grammar Schools

Teaching unit 3.4: Islam—Allah the only God
Students identify Islam as the religion in which Allah is worshipped as the one and only God. They know that belief in Allah leaves its mark on private and public life.

Muslims in Germany	Experience of assimilation and separation
Mohammed and the Quran	Direct revelation, mediated by Gabriel,
Self-image of Muslims:	no historical approach
completion of Abraham's belief and of	Mohammed's meetings with Christians and
the history of revelation	Jews, exclusion
Belief in Allah as the one and only God	The five pillars
Intertwining of public and religious life	Law of the Quran as law of the state
	Men and women in Islam
	→ History, teaching units 3 and 4
	→ Protestant Religious Education, teaching unit 8
	→ Ethics, teaching unit 2

Note. From Ministerium für Kultus und Sport Baden-Württemberg (1994, p. 244).

At the top of the T are the title of a teaching unit and the teaching objectives, on the left side below are the binding contents, and on the right side are further hints. These further hints are not obligatory and mostly consist of more specific contents. Moreover, in some cases these further hints include links or connections to other teaching units of the same or a different subject, methodical references, and even further information on media. As a supplement to each grade, general remarks on developmental psychology may be given. But even this kind of elaborated school curriculum is not a screenplay or script for the teacher, and quite a few teachers in Germany would protest if a new curriculum tried to dictate in detail how they should teach. A central term of their professional code of conduct is "pedagogical freedom," which should be the opposite of pure contingency. Pedagogical freedom is expected to be balanced in that it should reflect the educational value of the contents and the significance they could have for a certain group of students. It is the teacher's responsibility to choose the sequence of teaching units during the school year, to specify contents, to pick suitable media and methods. In short, it is the profession of the teacher to plan the learning environment. He or she is responsible for the series of consciously directed training experiences that in the American tradition form the curriculum.

CURRICULUM WORK AND ITS POLITICAL CONTEXT

This section gives a report about a current effort to evaluate school curricula in Germany. As Germany is a federal republic, the state functions are shared by the federal government and the 16 states. Especially in the field of cultural and educational policy, each state enjoys considerable leeway for political decision making. Each state has its own school curriculum, and thus it is not possible to talk about Germany as a whole in this respect. Rather, one has to take a closer look at the individual states. For this reason, this chapter concentrates on the State of Baden-Württemberg, which has a population of 10 million, compared to the total German population of 80 million. The inquiry further is restricted to the curriculum for grammar schools. Relevant curricula in this case date from 1994 and are currently in a process of replacement. The curricula for the last 2 years of grammar school, which are the 12th and the 13th grade in Baden-Württemberg as in most other German states, were already presented in 2001 by curriculum commissions. Every curriculum commission consists of four teachers and a member of the State Institute for Education and Teaching. As in most cases of curriculum construction, the work of the commissions was restricted by guidelines from the political authorities, in this case the Ministry of Cultural Affairs and Sports. These guidelines include substantial modifications in the class schedules and the request to give more attention to new time-consuming learning methods and to the acquisition of core skills. An antecedent curriculum evaluation did not take place.

While the commissions were still at work, the idea of curriculum evaluation spread and even reached the State Institute for Education and Teaching, where a great curriculum evaluation was planned during the summer of 2000. But when political authorities realized that a scientific evaluation of the curriculum would take at least 1 year, the plans were changed and the ministry did its own opinion poll (Ministerium für Kultus und Sport Baden-Württemberg, 2001). The organization of school teaching was supposed to change so fundamentally and so rapidly that it seemed senseless for political authorities to take a closer look at how the old curriculum worked. First, in March 2001 it was decided to shorten grammar school from 9 to 8 years: Pupils who start their grammar school career from the year 2004 onwards will take their university entrance exams as 12th graders and not, as most German students nowadays, during the 13th year in school. The already finished curricula for the 12th and 13th school years will—without further considerations to the psychological development of students—be used as curricula for 11th and 12th graders. Second, in October 2001 it was announced that there would be no statewide curricula at all in the school of the future. Instead, schools will have to formulate their own curricula and will be controlled by the formulation of standards, which students have to meet by taking central exams to pass every second grade, beginning with the 6th grade. This meets a more general policy tendency to change from input steering to output steering.

These facts should serve as examples for the political embeddedness of curriculum work. Nearly any curriculum work can be the target of political decision making, regardless of whether pedagogical reasoning or research is taken into account. This doesn't necessarily mean that it is a bad decision to shorten grammar school by 1 year. Actually, it is a decision that is not a result of pedagogical or psychological discourse but rather of political and economic discourse. The main argument in this discourse is the comparatively high age of German academics when they apply for their first job on the European labor market.

SOME RESULTS OF A RECENT CURRICULUM EVALUATION

What is to be done if political authorities have canceled scientific evaluation? In this situation, research profits from a characteristic of German constitutional law. There is one subject in German schools that is not the object of exclusive supervision by the government and that therefore can have its own evaluation without the necessity of governmental decisions. This is religious education. According to Article 7 of the German Constitution, religious education is a regular subject at schools, being both under the supervision of the government and the supervision of the churches. So the churches can decide to have a curriculum evaluation even if state authorities fail.

In the current case, there is a joint venture by the Protestant Church and the Catholic Church to evaluate the curricula of Protestant Religious Education and Catholic Religious Education (Abs, 2002; Michalke-Leicht & Stäbler, 2002); both churches together cover over 80% of the population of Baden-Württemberg. Two questionnaires were developed—one for teachers and one for students. These questionnaires were sent to selected classes and selected teachers all over the state in order to represent the different rural and urban areas. Between 60% and 70% of the questionnaires were returned. A database of 461 students' questionnaires (220 Protestant and 241 Catholic) and 162 teachers' questionnaires (80 Protestant and 82 Catholic) was compiled. In this chapter, only the teacher side is considered.

The questionnaire covered both open and closed questions about different aspects of the curriculum. The questions can be organized into the following categories:

1. Personal background of the teacher: In this category the questions dealt with the professional experience of a teacher, his or her status, sex, and further subjects at school.

2. Formal aspects: This category includes questions concerning the workability of the curriculum. Here it was asked if the structure was clear and if the terminology was comprehensible. Furthermore, teachers were asked to evaluate the amount of lessons suggested for each curriculum unit and whether compulsory and voluntary curriculum units were balanced in the right proportion.

3. Subject matter aspects: This category focuses on the selection of contents. Teachers were asked about essential contents from their perspective and about the balance of different contents. Further questions in this category concerned the sufficient consideration of gender issues and whether contents were chosen according to the students' interests.

4. Use of the curriculum: Teachers were supposed to answer how often and for what purpose they use the curriculum. Questions concerning work together across different fields of studies were also asked in this category. (Hints for working together across different fields of studies—literally they are called "subjects-connected-teaching"—were presented for the first time in the current curriculum.)

5. Educational psychology aspects: Only a few questions dealt with educational psychology. For example, teachers were asked for units they

would assign to a higher or lower level class. Then there was a question about the methodological hints of the curriculum, and finally teachers were asked to hand in suggestions on how to increase the lasting effect of their teaching.

The results from the last two categories promise to be of general interest. First, the question of usage is presented, for which the evaluation sheet had the form shown in Table 9.2. What can be learned from these results? The results can be viewed as a confirmation of similar findings by Künzli and Santini-Amgarten (1999), who compared curriculum use by German and Swiss teachers. The curriculum has a strong influence on the selection of contents and on time planning during the academic year. But curricula generally do little to verify whether a certain content has been taught successfully. Only 8.0% of the teachers state that the curriculum has an influence on their assessment. In this one can see the rather low attention German teachers pay to diagnostic questions in the year 2000. The second result described in this chapter also reflects this finding. Meanwhile, in light of Germany's bad PISA (Programme for International Student Assessment) outcome (Baumert et al., 2001), and the discussion on the development of national educational standards (Klieme et al., 2003), things may have started to change. Instead, the curriculum is used for the information of pupils and parents. In this usage another function of curricula is visible, namely, the legitimization of learning content. Overall, it is obvious that curricula exert only little control on the microprocesses of teaching.

These results were discussed with different groups of teachers and teacher students. Thus, it was possible to formulate a list of quality demands for well-designed curricula from a teacher's perspective (Table 9.3). Quality dimensions and criteria—and this may be true not only for curriculum

TABLE 9.2
Use of Curricula by Teachers

For what purpose do you use the curriculum?	
(You are allowed to mark more than one possibility)	
for planning the academic year	77.0%
for planning teaching units	94.0%
for the preparation of individual lessons	24.1%
for inspiration for the contents	65.0%
for information about educational psychology	8.0%
for the information of pupils	50.6%
for the information of parents	44.4%
for the preparation of examinations	8.0%
for	6.0%
[free records: looking for connections with different subjects	2.4%]
[preparation for the university entrance examination	1.2%]

TABLE 9.3
Quality Demands on Curricula by Teachers

Quality Dimension	Criteria
Legitimization	Clear normative guidelines (educational task)
	Reasons why certain content should be learned
Coherence	Connection of content within a subject
	Connection of content between subjects
Intelligibility	Precision of learning objectives
	Adequacy of objectives and learning content
Time	Well-balanced calculation of time
	No more time for compulsory content than necessary
Psychological	Developmental appropriateness
	Affiliation with the experience of pupils

work—are based on a certain usage. If one wants to extend the functions of curricula, one has to get rid of the socially shared use of curricula. Another field of reflection—for example, the field of instructional design—shows the possibilities of extending the uses and functions of curricula more clearly. Additional dimensions of curricula may be considered if one takes the possibilities of instructional design into account (Table 9.3a).

By comparing these lists of dimensions, one can see how the main focus of curriculum work in the German-speaking tradition is different from that of instructional design. But at the moment, it's not quite clear whether one should, and how one could, integrate the ID-specific quality dimensions into curriculum work. A special difficulty in this context is that curriculum work in Germany is done by teachers without the participation of instructional designers. And this difficulty will intensify when, in the future, schools themselves have to take responsibility for their curriculum work. In contrast to these findings, it is interesting to note that 69% of the respondents in the aforementioned curriculum evaluation would like their curricula to contain more methodical hints. So, it seems that a majority of teachers want curricula that take ID considerations into account.

TABLE 9.3a
Further Quality Demands on Curricula From
the Perspective of Instructional Design

Quality Dimension	Criteria
Psychological	Congruity with considerations derived from learning psychology and psychology of motivation
Methodical	Congruity with principles of instructional design and with instructional models
Medial	Appropriate use of different technical resources and media

A second result of general interest consists of suggestions on how to increase the lasting effect of learning. In the answers given to these questions, one can see many of the teachers' beliefs about learning psychology. There was an open question about this topic in the evaluation form, and 80% of the teachers made one or even several suggestions. The answers have been categorized and are arranged according to their frequencies in Table 9.4.

How should these results be valued from the viewpoint of the German understanding of curriculum as a pure plan of teaching contents or teaching objectives? We have seen that learning psychology or instructional prescriptions are not a traditional part of German curricula. Nevertheless, teachers did not shrink from giving their suggestions on learning psychology in the context of a curriculum evaluation. Only two teachers referred to this context and noted that the question about the lasting effect of learning is a question of subject matter didactics and not of the curriculum and that this question asks too much of a curriculum. But in spite of this criticism, one can see that most teachers, whether they were aware of it or not, accepted the shift in the evaluation form from questions that focus on aspects traditionally belonging to the field of curriculum to questions naturally belonging to the field of learning psychology. The results thus indicate that curriculum work may be used as an instrument to improve teaching in accordance with the teachers. One remaining issue is, What kind of support is needed, if in future curriculum work is the task of every single school?

A different question is how to work with the answers regarding their content. Of course, it is possible to integrate the different suggestions into a model of learning, and some readers will recognize elements of different models of learning in the categories used in Table 9.4. This could be interesting for curriculum work that is done by experts. In this case, one will also take into account suggestions that did not turn up at all. For example, none of the teachers called for a stronger modularization of content. This is a remarkable fact at a time when modularization is a popular slogan in educational debates at German universities, and a fact that reflects the current trend in school learning to emphasize class as a community of sustained learning. Overall, individual suggestions could be interpreted meaningfully. But what remains a problem is the great variety of suggestions: There are teachers who talk about teaching as setting standards of achievement, others as working on a good school climate. Some teachers want to professionalize instruction, others emphasize students' experiences outside of school. Some believe in the power of good character, and others concentrate on the selection of the right content. How can the diversity of suggestions be integrated into curriculum work and instructional design? In the following, it is argued that teaching diversity can be integrated into curriculum work more easily than into instructional design.

TABLE 9.4
Teachers' Suggestions on How to Increase the Lasting Effect of Teaching

1. Elaborative learning	39
more learner activity (activity is the central term in this category),	
don't read only short quotations but rather whole texts,	
extend the scope and reduce the number of topics,	
use holistic methods, role playing,	
integrate significant experiences into learning,	
creative methods, creative writing—painting	
2. Organization of content	29
better coordination and interaction of different topics,	
a concept of teaching contents which covers all grades is needed,	
look at one topic from different perspectives,	
no voluntary units and intensify compulsory units,	
gradual increase in complexity	
3. Memorization learning	24
Repetition, pupils have to learn certain texts by heart	
4. Reductive learning	18
learn slogans,	
mark basic knowledge,	
concentrate on elementary content,	
summaries and comments as supplement to the class book,	
write minutes every lesson	
5. Teacher(s)	18
authenticity, tolerance, spirituality, open-mindedness,	
unity of teaching and living,	
more and better teacher-training,	
counseling-groups for teachers,	
personality of the teacher is the crucial point	
6. Students (and their social context)	17
take students' experience seriously,	
talk with parents, integrate their families,	
consider the students' interests	
7. School (mainly: open the school to the world outside)	16
excursions, internships,	
interviews with people of other professions during school lessons,	
more recognition from the head teacher	
8. Connect subjects	14
subjects should complement each other,	
working on projects [which integrate different subjects],	
working together on different fields of studies	
9. Content	8
doubt and faith should get more importance,	
Bible and theology should be dealt with to a larger extent,	
more information than missionary work	
10. Examinations	4
more control of students' homework and lower grades,	
higher demands on students	
11. Concentrate on biographies	4
units focusing on Christian personalities,	
draw from the biographies of students,	
single persons as models of everyday life	

DIFFERENCES BETWEEN INSTRUCTIONAL DESIGN AND CURRICULUM WORK

The last 10 years show great efforts of ID to individualize learning. Some of the projects presented in this volume are major examples of the individualization of learning through electronically based learning environments. ID tries to cope with the individual by using technological progress. This requires an expert culture on the instructional side, a culture that is characterized by a knowledge of procedures and specialized skills in evaluating the products of these procedures. As a result, the teaching process is undergoing a process of anti-individualization, a process to which ID owes its great success. In contrast, the German curriculum tradition is characterized by the protection of the individuality of the teacher. This means on the one hand that curriculum work, which does not support the individualization of teaching, will hardly find acceptance in Germany, and on the other hand that one has to ask whether the individualization of teaching is useful for instructional purposes.

Considering the role of the teacher in educational settings, one can see that the topic of this chapter is aligned with more general controversies, not only in Germany but also in the whole of Europe. Transformation processes in Europe starting in the economic sector also reached the educational system in the last decade. One example, among others, that reflects the changing role of teachers is the current controversial debate in Russia about replacing the teacher-centered "maturity certificate" with standardized procedures of assessment for the entry to higher education (Mitter, 2003). This general topic of standardized educational assessments would be worth considering by ways of particular comparative analysis (Klieme et al., 2003). But in the context of this volume, this chapter concentrates on the influence of curricula versus instructional design on the processes of teaching rather than on possible outputs like students' achievements.

Most educational scientists today are in favor of individualized learning. But there is no research that tries to measure the effects of teaching as an activity teachers feel responsible for. Perhaps the fruitful individualization of instruction or teaching is a greater challenge for instructional design than the individualization of learning. But what does the fruitful individualization of teaching mean? German teachers who work under the condition of curriculum, which means essentially a plan of teaching contents, aren't necessarily aware that their pedagogical freedom leads to individualized teaching. Indeed, a curriculum is often experienced as the absence of regulations for the process of teaching, but the sense of this absence is rarely talked about. Perhaps the reason for this silence lies in the uncertainty as to whether the concept of individualized teaching pays off for the learner. This is reason enough to list some psychological reasons for the presumption that individualized teaching will increase the effect of learning activities.

1. One might stress the individualization of teaching as a prerequisite for the authenticity of the teacher. Teachers can help their students more easily to develop those skills that they themselves have fully developed. In this sense, authenticity will be accepted as a component for the lasting effect of interaction between pupil and teacher.

2. Individualization can be regarded as a chance for the teacher to put into practice those skills he or she is willing to practice. Only in this way will he or she be able to give examples of adequate practice as well as intrinsic motivation, and only this will produce effective learners.

3. The individualization of teaching can be considered as a means to strengthen a feeling of responsibility for the outcome of the teaching. Teachers who reflect on their work and see themselves as more than willing executors of learning programs will be more likely to accept responsibility for the quality of school learning.

4. The individualization of teaching is a prerequisite for the adjustment of learning contents to special groups of students and situations.

Yet one shouldn't be too enthusiastic about the concept of individualized teaching. The pitfalls are obvious: How should teachers who aren't able to use their freedom in a sensible way be dealt with? Nevertheless, there is no alternative to recognizing teaching in school settings as a widely individualized business until today. Both instructional design and curriculum have to cope with individualized teaching if they want to be successful in the context of schools.

As already stated, it seems even more difficult to integrate the teacher's individuality than the individuality of learners. ID, based on specialized knowledge, the division of labor and technique, is different from a teacher's approach to the complexity of instruction. A teacher's approach is mainly based on personal experience, and until now there has been little mediation between the idiosyncratic construction of teaching and effective learning environments by teachers on the one hand, and ID and its mostly electronic learning environments on the other. Mediation has neither been achieved when teachers are able to help their students in the handling of electronic learning environments nor when they are able to lead their students to the construction of multimodal statements (Snyder, 2001). In the background of new information and communication technologies as a means of instruction appears a deeper challenge for teachers standing in competition with the new hypermedia (Loveless, DeVoogd, & Bohlin,

2001): In former days, teachers mediated all information in class, so that the teacher could be looked at as the only hypermedium. Nowadays, teachers are confronted with other very powerful hypermedia inside and outside the classroom. This has consequences for their role that have not yet been completely dealt with. In the hypermedia competition between teachers and e-learning environments, teachers may see themselves "targeted as consumers of technology within the educational market place" (Buckingham, Scanlon, & Sefton-Green, 2001, p. 27), which means that they are no longer the leading hypermedium but rather teaching assistants in a preplanned environment. In this situation one can observe some retaliatory measures, for example, when educational theory tries to extend the educational task of teachers (Loveless et al., 2001): By giving the teaching profession seemingly new and higher tasks, one may protect its self-esteem. For example, Snyder (2001) formulated a demand to scaffold the student's way from using media to the reflection of the different processes of mediation. This alters the focus, but the original problem of integrating teaching as an individualized practice with concepts of ID or instructional psychology in general is not solved by these means.

Oser and Baeriswyl (2001) stated that, "from the point of view of the empirically based theories, learning cannot be left to discretion of teachers in the name of professional freedom" (p. 1042). With their choreographies of teaching and learning, they develop an approach that integrates professional freedom and instructional psychology. According to Oser and Baeriswyl, the fundamental restriction to pedagogical freedom is the psychological structure of the learning process. This structure differs with regard to types of learning goals as concept building, conflict resolution, or automation. With regard to a certain type of learning goal, the psychological structure—the so-called basis model of learning—is compelling. Only inasmuch as teachers are aware of the psychological structure of the learning process are they free to choose methods and social forms—the so-called visible structure—in order to enhance motivation and consider personal characteristics of the learner or situational circumstances. The distinction between a compelling psychological structure of learning that can be realized in different ways of teaching according to different students and situational contexts can be looked on as a core distinction of the teaching profession. The sense of individualized teaching consists in working with this distinction. Whereas in individualized ID learning environments students themselves have to choose which way of learning may fit their needs, alternatively this decision is taken by the teacher. In both cases, someone has to decide, and this decision should be based on high abilities in diagnosing learning needs.

Before conclusions are drawn, Table 9.5 sums up the various first principles that account for the difficulties in connecting German curriculum work with the instructional design approach to learning.

TABLE 9.5
A Comparison of First Principles in ID and Curriculum Work

Instructional Design	Curriculum Work
What is the leading orientation?	
Psychological control of learning	Normative selection of contents
Who are the agents?	
Experts	Teachers
How do they work?	
Systematic procedures that follow fixed models	Politically bounded discourse
What are the products used for?	
Used to organize the work of learners	Used to legitimate and organize the work of teachers
What do they want to support?	
Individualized learning (electronic learning environments as hypermedia)	Individualized teaching (teachers as hypermedia)
Who decides about ways of learning?	
Students	Teachers

CONCLUSIONS

What are the conclusions from the empirical results and reflections on curriculum and instructional design? In the following, possible consequences are suggested. For this purpose, the current model of curriculum work is presented (Table 9.6) and supplemented (Table 9.6a). Hopmann and Künzli (1998) developed fields of decision making in curriculum work, distinguishing between a political level where governmental decisions take

TABLE 9.6
Fields of Decision Making in Curriculum Work

Fields of Decision Making in Curriculum Work	Considering the Past	Interposition in the Present	Considering the Future
Political level	What is the significance of our cultural heritage?	What is the educational task?	What are the qualifications needed?
Programmatic level	What are the limitations by external constraints?	How can we balance these different aspects?	What is the ideal scheduling of education?
Level of practice	What seems suitable in the realm of a certain discipline?	What is the function of a content in a course of study?	What seems suitable in a certain everyday culture?

Note. According to Hopmann and Künzli (1998).

TABLE 9.6A
Complements to the Fields of Decision Making in Curriculum Work
From an ID Perspective

Level of learning	What are the developmental limitations?	What is the compelling basis model of learning?	What is the psychological type of the learning goal?

place, a programmatic level concerning the work of curriculum commissions, and a level of practice concerning the inner constraints of schooling. On each level, they defined topics that are open to discussion in the construction of a curriculum. More concretely, this means that curriculum work has to consider constraining factors on every level—what was valid in past times and what should happen in the future. In addition, curriculum work always has to mediate the past and the image of the future. Hopmann and Künzli's model should cover all fields that are relevant in the construction of a new curriculum. It is a descriptive, not normative, model of curriculum work. This enables one to formulate the various fields of decision making as open questions.

Going beyond this model by Hopmann and Künzli (1998), what changes may occur as a result of a discussion on the pretensions of ID and instructional psychology? If the model is still supposed to cover all levels of decision making in curriculum work, one level of consideration has to be completed, namely, the level at which learning comes into question (Table 9.6a). It seems necessary to add this level in order to keep the pedagogical freedom of teachers from reaching a level of pure contingency. In the section Some Results of a Recent Curriculum Evaluation, it was shown that teachers themselves are in favor of curricula that support their professional work on a learning psychology basis. In the section that followed and here, the use of the Oser and Baeriswyl (2001) basis models of learning during teaching and curriculum work is shown. This approach helps to link the demands of empirically based learning psychology and teaching as an individualized practice. One advanced consequence is that the construction of new curricula will require teamwork in which both teachers and experts of educational psychology participate. The basis-models approach will also be useful when teachers want to combine preplanned instructional design materials with their own planning of certain learning environments. Further on instructional designers have to take into account the function of teachers as coordinators of instruction and to take them seriously as intended users of ID products. For this reason, products have to offer choices for individual decision making, not only for the learner but also for the teacher. In order to qualify teacher decisions, ID products should offer hints for how to diagnose whether certain material is really suitable for certain students.

REFERENCES

Abs, H. J. (2002). Zur Evaluationsmethodologie [On evaluation methodology]. In W. Michalke-Leicht & W. Stäbler (Eds.), *Gezählt, gewogen und befunden. Eine Evaluation zum Lehrplan für den Religionsunterricht am Gymnasium in Baden-Württemberg (2000–2001)* [Numbered, weighed, and divided. An evaluation of the religious education curriculum for grammar schools in Baden-Württemberg (2000–2001)] (pp. 32–38). Münster, Germany: Lit.

Baumert, J., Klieme, E., Neubrand, M., Prenzel, M., Schiefele, U., Schneider, W., Stanat, P., Tillmann, K. J., & Weiß, M. (Eds.). (2001). *PISA 2000. Basiskompetenzen von Schülerinnen und Schülern im internationalen Vergleich* [PISA 2000. Basic competencies of students in international comparison]. Opladen, Germany: Leske & Budrich.

Bobbitt, J. F. (1972). *The curriculum.* New York: Arno Press.

Buckingham, D., Scanlon, M., & Sefton-Green, J. (2001). Selling the digital dream. Marketing educational technology to teachers and parents. In A. Loveless & V. Ellis (Eds.), *ICT, pedagogy and the curriculum. Subject to change* (pp. 20–40). New York: Routledge/Falmer.

Hopmann, S., & Künzli, R. (1998). Entscheidungsfelder der Lehrplanung [Fields of decision making in curriculum work]. In R. Künzli & S. Hopmann (Eds.), *Lehrpläne: Wie sie entwickelt werden und was von ihnen erwartet wird. Forschungsstand, Zugänge und Ergebnisse aus der Schweiz und der Bundesrepublik Deutschland* [Curricula: How they are developed and what is expected from them. State of research, approaches, and results from Switzerland and the Federal Republic of Germany] (pp. 17–34). Zürich, Switzerland: Rüegger.

Jackson, P. W. (1996). Conceptions of curriculum and curriculum specialists. In P. W. Jackson (Ed.), *Handbook of research on curriculum. A project of the American Educational Research Association* (pp. 3–40). New York: Simon & Schuster Macmillan.

Klieme, E., Avenarius, H., Blum, W., Döbrich, P., Gruber, H., Prenzel, M., Reiss, K., Riquarts, K., Rost, J., Tenorth, H. E., & Vollmer, H. J. (2003). *The development of national educational standards in Germany.* Berlin, Germany: Federal Ministry of Education and Research (BMBF).

Künzli, R., & Santini-Amgarten, B. (1999). Wie Lehrpläne umgesetzt und verwendet werden [How curricula are realized and used]. In R. Künzli, K. Bähr, A. V. Fries, G. Ghisla, M. Rosenmund, & G. Seliner-Müller (Eds.), *Lehrplanarbeit. Über den Nutzen von Lehrplänen für die Schule und ihre Entwicklung* [Curriculum work. On the use of curricula for schools and school development] (pp. 144–167). Zürich, Switzerland: Rüegger.

Loveless, A., DeVoogd, G. L., & Bohlin, R. M. (2001). Something old, something new. Is pedagogy affected by ICT? In A. Loveless & V. Ellis (Eds.), *ICT, pedagogy and the curriculum. Subject to change* (pp. 63–83). New York: Routledge/Falmer.

Michalke-Leicht, W., & Stäbler, W. (Eds.). (2002). *Gezählt, gewogen und befunden. Eine Evaluation zum Lehrplan für den Religionsunterricht am Gymnasium in Baden-Württemberg (2000–2001)* [Numbered, weighed, and divided. An evaluation of the religious education curriculum for grammar schools in Baden-Württemberg (2000–2001)]. Münster, Germany: Lit.

Ministerium für Kultus und Sport Baden-Württemberg [Ministry of cultural affairs and sports Baden-Württemberg]. (1994). *Bildungsplan für das Gymnasium der Normalform vom 4. Februar 1994* [Curriculum for grammar schools from Feb. 4th, 1994]. Villingen-Schwenningen, Germany: Neckar-Verlag.

Ministerium für Kultus und Sport Baden-Württemberg [Ministry of cultural affairs and sports Baden-Württemberg]. (2001). *Allgemeinbildendes Gymnasium: Evaluation der Bildungspläne von 1994. Ergebnisse der Auswertung* [Evaluation of the curriculum for grammar schools from 1994. Results from interpretation]. www.leu.bw.schule.de/allg/lehrplan/gymnasium/eval.pdf

Mitter, W. (2003). A decade of transformation: Educational policies in central and eastern Europe. *International Review of Education, 49*(1–2), 75–96.

Oser, F. K., & Baeriswyl, F. J. (2001). Choreographies of teaching: Bridging instruction to learning. In V. Richardson (Ed.), *Handbook of research on teaching* (4th ed., pp. 1031–1065). Washington, DC: American Educational Research Association.

Snyder, I. (2001). "Hybrid Vigor." Reconciling the verbal and the visual in electronic communication. In A. Loveless & V. Ellis (Eds.), *ICT, pedagogy and the curriculum. Subject to change* (pp. 41–59). New York: Routledge/Falmer.

Chapter 10

Information and Communication Technology Transforming the Teaching Profession

Bernard Cornu
IUFM of Grenoble and Ministry of Education, France

SOCIETY IS CHANGING

Nowadays, society is changing very quickly. School and education are deeply involved in these changes. There are two major changes:

1. The change due to the democratization of education and the massification of schools: Fortunately, more and more children can access school. But they are then more and more diverse, and schools are heterogeneous. This changes the contents and the methods of education. Schools do not exist apart from society: Social and economic problems penetrate schools, and, especially in large urban areas, violence is increasing, and teaching in difficult conditions is sometimes a serious problem for some teachers. The social context of school changes the teaching profession.

2. Information and Communication Technology (ICT): Information technology (computer science) deals with the processing of digital information—the processing of zeros and ones. Communication technology deals with the transport of digital information. The two have merged, leading to ICT. This is what is making technology more powerful, more efficient, and cheaper. After a phase when ICT was emerging in education, there was a phase when ICT was applied to education. Now, we have entered two more phases: the integration of ICT into education and the transforming of education by ICT (Khvilon, Anderson, & van Weert, 2002).

KNOWLEDGE IS CHANGING

Digitized knowledge is now accessible everywhere. It is superabundant, dynamic, interactive; printed knowledge was stable, it did not evolve quickly. Digital knowledge can be considered to be a new kind of knowledge, and there is an increase of new knowledge and faster access to knowledge. But there may be a risk of confusing digital information and digital knowledge. Spender (1996) described some characteristics and aspects of digital knowledge:

> It is an Information Revolution we are currently experiencing . . . and it is the new technologies that are launching education. . . . [I]t is not even possible to make the old distinction between teacher and learner. . . . As we move from book culture to digital culture, we are on the brink of being able to rethink the entire process of teaching and learning. . . . As we move from a print culture to a digitized culture, we move from stable information to moving information. . . . Stable information: a body of knowledge which can be acquired, taught, passed on, memorised and tested. . . . Suddenly it is not the oldest information, the longest lasting information that is the most reliable and useful. It is the very latest information that we now put the most faith in and which we will pay the most for. . . . When information was stable, teachers could spend their time studying the sources, . . . could become the experts, do their training and get their qualifications then enter the classrooms and pass on the information to the students. . . . [T]he cycle could continue. . . . Information is becoming interactive.

Knowledge is no longer organized in a chain form (the one who knows teaches the one who does not know, who then can know and teach, etc.). It is now a network process, and everyone, the teacher as well as the learner, is equally involved in the network. This change in the organization of knowledge will have consequences for the hierarchy of educational systems: Up to now they were organized according to the chain of knowledge, they now have to take into account the network organization of knowledge.

There is a risk of our mixing knowledge and information. The two are different. In order to become knowledge, information needs some transformation in which persons are involved and that is linked with problems to be solved and with larger fields of knowledge. ICT deals with information, education deals with knowledge. Technology cannot replace science, computer tools cannot replace knowledge.

ICT enhances collective intelligence. Collective intelligence is not only the juxtaposition, the sum of individual intelligences. There is a kind of "added value" due to the collective dimension. The Internet and ICT are tools for developing collective intelligence. Lévy (2000) explained how ICT and the Internet enhance collective intelligence:

> Internet is mainly a tool, the more recent we found for perfecting our intelligence through cooperation and exchange. . . . The true revolution of Internet is not at all a revolution of machines, but of communication between human beings. . . . Internet enhances our capacity for collective learning and intelligence. . . . Each community realises that it is one of the dimensions of the production of human sense. . . . Internet forces us to experiment new ways of being together. . . . The ethic of collective intelligence, consisting in interlacing different points of view. (author's translation)

DISCIPLINES ARE CHANGING

Each discipline is changing under the influence of ICT. For example, mathematics is changing. Mathematical activity now involves trying, experimenting, visualizing, simulating, modeling. ICT has developed an experimental approach of mathematics. New concepts, new methods have appeared. We now have an algorithmic approach to mathematics. ICT provides tools for problem solving. Mathematics has become more experimental, more numerical, more algorithmic. Similar comments could be made about any discipline, and we could describe the changes in experimental sciences, in human sciences, in literature, and so on.

ICT does not appear as one more discipline. It is mostly a tool to be integrated into each discipline. But what is more, it is no longer possible to split the knowledge into traditional disciplines, and education needs to address the complexity of knowledge. The questions pupils now face, the understanding of the world, require new proficiencies and new knowledge that is not included when new disciplines are merely added to the traditional ones. Morin (2001) suggested a possible organization of knowledge in a more global curriculum:

1. Teach the weaknesses of knowledge: what is human knowledge? Teach its errors, its illusions; Teach to know what to know is!
2. Teach the principles of relevant knowledge. One must be able to take into account global and fundamental problems, in which partial and local knowledge will then be used. The knowledge cannot be split into disciplines. One must be able to consider the objects of knowledge in their context, in their complexity, in their whole.
3. Teach the human condition. Teach the unity and the complexity of human nature. This needs input from biology, from human sciences, from literature, from philosophy. Teach the relationship between the unity and the diversity of what is human.

4. Teach the world identity. Teach knowledge at a worldwide level. Teach the history of the planetary era, teach the solidarity between all the parts of the world.

5. Teach how to face the uncertainties. Sciences have established a lot of certainties, but they also have revealed many uncertainties. Teach the uncertainties in physics, in biology, in history.

6. Teach understanding. Understanding in all its meanings, mutual understanding between human beings. And teach what misunderstanding is. It is a crucial basis for peace education.

7. Teach the ethics of humanity preparing citizens of the world. Teach how democracy relates to the mutual control between society and individuals.

ICT has not only to be applied to traditional disciplines: It changes disciplines themselves, and it changes the organization of knowledge.

ACCESS TO KNOWLEDGE IS CHANGING

Knowledge is now accessible in very diverse ways, at any time, from any place. It is no longer only in the teacher's head or in libraries! There are more and more resources available: Web resources and educational portals, CD-ROMs, virtual environments, and so on. One can access knowledge not only at school, but at home or anyplace.

This changes pedagogy and instruction. The traditional method, based on the chain model and on the delivery of knowledge by teachers, is not very well adapted to the new tools. The marketplace model, in which one can access knowledge in different orders according to one's choices and decisions is made possible for all. "Real questions" appear in classrooms: questions for which the answer is not already in the classroom, as was the case traditionally; therefore the rule is not to find "the answer which the teacher knows and which he/she wants me to find," but to ask questions such as: Does this question have an answer? Is there someone who knows the answer? How can I contact someone who knows the answer? Is there some resource where can I find the answer?

ICT helps pedagogical methods based on projects and favors team working. ICT is not only a new tool to be used for traditional methods. It helps to renew the method profoundly. Do not just put the old methods in the new technologies or the new technologies in the old methods, but think how ICT changes pedagogy! Also, self-learning and distance learning are developing with ICT.

All these remarks lead to the question of the specificity of school. Some main characteristics of school as the only place where knowledge is available and distributed are no longer valid; school is changing, and one must ask the question as to the new role of the school.

TEACHING IS CHANGING

The traditional classroom was designed as an economical and social system: having a group of pupils and a teacher at the same place at the same time. But ICT makes new types of "classrooms" possible: classroom activities at the same place at different times, at different places at the same time, or at different places at different times.

The "new classroom" should not replace presence by distance, but combine distance and presence. One must use the diversity and the complementarity of possible strategies, tools, and resources. The new classroom is "communicant" rather than "distance."

ICT brings new concepts to the school, such as Multimedia, Hypertext, Virtuality, Interactivity. Here are the elements of a new culture. ICT in education is not only a technological topic; it is a matter of pedagogy and culture.

The main component of teaching remains unchanged. The teacher is the mediator between the pupil and the knowledge. The teacher has to make pupils acquire knowledge and control the outline of the curriculum; he or she also has to guide the children's personality development and prepare the citizen of tomorrow. But being the mediator and the guide is much more complicated in the ICT society. Knowledge is available anywhere, but in an uncontrolled form, and the teacher has to help the pupil to distinguish accurate and valid knowledge, to sort out, organize, hierarchize the knowledge. The teacher also has to design the instruction, using the new tools and resources available through ICT. ICT can be integrated into the whole set of activities of the teaching profession: designing lessons and performing teaching, as well as in the administrative tasks and as a new way of communicating and cooperating with others.

THE ROLE OF THE TEACHER

The teacher cannot ignore all the changes in the knowledge, in the access to knowledge, in the pedagogy, and in the school. The role of the teacher is changing profoundly. Many studies and reports have been published about the role of the teacher, and it is useful to be aware of some of them.

In 1966, UNESCO published very interesting "Recommendations on the Condition of Teaching Personnel," adopted by the Special Intergovernmental Conference on the Status of Teachers in October 1966. These recommendations define the place and role of teachers in society, state some educational objectives and policies, insist on preparation for the profession and on further education for teachers, and state the rights and responsibilities of teachers and some principles for their employment and career, salaries, and social security; they also give conditions for effective teaching and learning. Every teacher should read these recommendations, which are still very accurate!

In 1996, the International Commission for Education in the 21st Century, chaired by Jacques Delors, published its report to UNESCO, *Learning: The Treasure Within*. In this report appear the famous "four pillars of education"—learning to know, learning to do, learning to live together, and learning to be—as well as the main tensions that make education more and more difficult: the tensions between local and global, between tradition and modernity, between short term and long term, between spiritual and material values, between technology and human beings. Following this work, in 2001 the French National Commission for UNESCO published the report of a working group, *Winds of Change in the Teaching Profession* (Cornu, 2001). In this report, it is shown that the expectations of society have changed, in a context of democratization of school, increasing complexity of society, and globalization of the world. There are two major roles for teachers today: prepare citizens in a changing world, and make pupils acquire knowledge and skills. Teachers are expected to teach their pupils to live together, to transmit the fundamental values of society and the universal values of humanity, and to actually live these values at school.

The evolutions of society, the new expectations toward teachers, and the changes that ICT brings lead to a huge quantity of new proficiencies for teachers. For instance, according to different studies, teachers must now be able to

> Master the Knowledge; Help accessing the Knowledge, sorting it, hierarchising it, organizing it; Master the processes of teaching and learning; Transmit the knowledge; Teach conceptualizing, theorizing, modeling, abstracting; Transmit the taste for knowledge; Arise curiosity; Make pupils be successful at their exams; Be a guide, a tutor, a mediator; Be an advisor, an organizer, a leader, an evaluator; Contribute to producing Knowledge and Teaching; Use and question research; Be a technician, an engineer; Put in action an educational policy; Guarantee equity; Transmit the fundamental values of society; Prepare the citizens of tomorrow; etc. . . .

Clearly, this is not possible. The competency of teachers can no longer be considered individually. It is more and more collective competency (a team profession) and evolutionary competency (in the context of lifelong training). Also, teachers cannot be in charge of all the new tasks that are necessary in school. The teaching profession is changing, leading to a new Teaching Profession, but there are also new Teaching Professions appearing (pedagogical technicians, assistants, tutors, software specialists, etc.).

ICT and computers will not replace teachers! They have a more and more complex and difficult role, and the human and social dimension of education is essential. Pupils are not self-learners; there is a role for school, a role for the teacher. The virtual school is not without teachers! But in the knowledge society, in the information and communication society, there is a need for an extension of the concepts School and Teacher.

TEACHER TRAINING

The changes in the role of school and of teachers have an impact on teacher training and must be integrated into teacher training. Two major principles must be taken into account:

Generalization: ICT is not only for the most enthusiastic teachers and volunteer teachers. It is now a necessity for all teachers, and there is a need for generalization of ICT in teacher education.

Integration: ICT must not be considered to be one more discipline beside the others. ICT influences all disciplines and changes education in all of its dimensions (in the classroom, in personal work, at home, in libraries, in the administration of schools, etc.). It has to be integrated into education in general and therefore into teacher education, not only as a new content but as a resource and a tool in all dimensions of teacher education.

Some principles should be taken into account for ICT in teacher education:

One cannot provide future teachers with all the knowledge and proficiencies they will need for their career because things will change a lot, in unpredictable ways. We must make teachers capable of evolving and adapting permanently.

Rather than talking about ICT in education, one should actually use ICT in teacher education.

Teachers usually teach not the way they were told, but reproduce, more or less consciously, the way they were taught. Therefore, in teacher education, methods are as important as content because they affect the way teachers will behave.

In teacher education, every future teacher should personally experiment with "something new," something they can do or understand better thanks to ICT.

Teaching is a profession, teachers are professionals; in the field of ICT, teachers need professional tools.

Teacher training should help future teachers and teachers to get over the different stages of ICT in education: ICT first emerges as something external. Then one tries to apply ICT to education without changing the traditional methods and tools but by improving them by the addition of an ICT dimension. The third step is the one of integration, where ICT becomes part of education, not as an added subject, but integrated into each subject and each component of education. Moving further, we are now at a time when ICT starts transforming education.

Teacher training curricula should include different components: learning how to use the basic equipment and resources; integrating ICT as a tool for learning and teaching each subject; communication (e-mail, etc.) and distance activities in education; new cooperative ways of learning and teaching; ethical aspects.

THE ETHICAL DIMENSION

ICT brings new questions and demands new reflection. Teachers should be able to take part in the discussions about ICT; it is not clear that ICT is automatically something good and useful, and there are many arguments against ICT in education:

Movies, radio, and TV were supposed to change teaching and learning . . . but they did not bring major changes.

The same amount of money could be used in more efficient ways; for example, for recruiting more teachers.

Pupils are more motivated with ICT, but what do they actually learn? Do they really learn better?

Teachers have to run from one machine to the next and solve a lot of technical problems, find the key to the computer room, make sure that all computers work, install appropriate software, etc., and this is a waste of time.

Is it sensible to use sophisticated machines . . . just for learning typing?

ICT induces a nonsequential way of thinking and this may be an obstacle to learning.

With the use of ICT, we prepare consumers rather than citizens.

Our aim is not to give a definite answer to such questions. But it is at least necessary to address such questions in teacher education so that future teachers can reflect on it and form their own opinion.

From an ethical point of view, ICT brings up several types of questions. The major ones are:

1. Does ICT increase or reduce the digital divide?
2. With the use of ICT, do we prepare mainly citizens or consumers?

The question of globalization is a crucial one. ICT can make cultures uniform, but also better known and spread, shared around the world. Are we heading toward a global culture? Or does ICT allow a development of local cultures? According to Michel Serres, a French philosopher, "A new universal humanism is appearing. Humanism is becoming technically possible!" The digital divide is not only a matter of developed or developing countries. The divide occurs in each country, at each school, in each classroom: At each level, ICT can introduce new gaps, new divides. Such a question must be addressed in teacher education.

The question of merchandization and the commercialization of knowledge and teaching is a new one for teachers and educators. Education appears to be a profitable domain, and many private companies try to make profit from it. The role of schools and teachers is to be aware that knowledge is a public good, that education is a public service. But one cannot ignore the role of private companies, and new types of cooperation can be developed.

A NEED FOR POLICIES

The development of ICT and the need for integrating ICT into education make necessary strong policies, at different levels: at the national level, of course, but also at the very local level (the level of a school, of a classroom) and, on the opposite end of the spectrum, at the world level.

At the world level, strong political recommendations have been made. For example, the Dakar Framework for Action (adopted during the World Education Forum in Dakar, Senegal, April 2000) stated that "we hereby collectively commit ourselves to the attainment of the following goals: . . . ensuring that by 2015 all children, particularly girls, children in difficult circumstances and those belonging to ethnic minorities, have access to and complete free and compulsory primary education of good quality."

The framework (UNESCO, 2000) also gave some hints for strategies:

Harness new information and communication technologies to help achieve Education For All goals:

1. ICT must be harnessed to support EFA goals at an affordable cost. These technologies have great potential for knowledge dissemination, effective learning and the development of more efficient education services. This potential will not be realised unless the new technologies serve rather than drive the implementation of education strategies. To be effective, espe-

cially in developing countries, ICTs should be combined with more traditional technologies such as books and radios, and be more extensively applied to the training of teachers.

2. The swiftness of ICT developments, their increasing spread and availability, the nature of their content and their declining prices are having major implications for learning. They may tend to increase disparities, weaken social bonds and threaten cultural cohesion. Governments will therefore need to establish clearer policies in regard to science and technology, and undertake critical assessments of ICT experiences and options. These should include their resource implications in relation to the provision of basic education, emphasising choices that bridge the "digital divide," increase access and quality, and reduce inequity.

3. There is a need to tap the potential of ICT to enhance data collection and analysis, and to strengthen management systems, from central ministries through sub-national levels to school; to improve access to education by remote and disadvantaged communities; to support initial and continuing professional development of teachers; and to provide opportunities to communicate across classrooms and cultures.

4. News media should also be engaged to create and strengthen partnerships with education systems, through the promotion of local newspapers, informed coverage of education issues and continuing education programmes via public service broadcasting.

The meeting of the OECD Education Ministers (Paris, April 2001) produced recommendations about "Investing in Proficiencies for All":

We have noted that, while the use of ICT in education and training is expanding rapidly in most of our countries, much remains to be done. The development of teachers' own ICT skills is one need, the development of ICT infrastructure and support of more effective uses of ICT as an aid to learning are others. We see the potential benefits and are determined to put in place policies which help all students and teachers reap them. . . . We recognise the increased demand for a wide range of competencies . . . to participate in the knowledge economy. . . . We are determined to work further on this, taking a broad view to include the needs of a knowledge society and not just those of a knowledge economy.

Regarding ICT in the education systems in Europe, Eurydice (European Commission, February 2000) stated the main aspects to be addressed by policies for integrating ICT into education and makes some remarks:

1. National policy and official documents on the use of ICT
2. National or official bodies responsible for supervising the national policy
3. National projects for the introduction of technology are on the increase

4. Schedule for implementing the projects
5. Sharing responsibility for the purchase and maintenance of hardware
6. Expenditure on equipment predominates in specific budgets
7. Projects with a variety of aims (equipment, distribution of software, teachers' skills, pupils' skills, development of software, use of the Internet . . .)
8. Many countries include ICT in the primary-level curriculum
9. The most common approach to ICT in primary education is to use it as a tool
10. ICT is in almost all curricula at lower secondary level
11. A variety of approaches to ICT coexist in lower secondary education (separate subject, tool for other subjects . . .)
12. ICT in most curricula at general upper secondary level
13. ICT is usually taught as a separate subject in general upper secondary education
14. Specialist ICT teachers are mostly found at secondary level
15. In-service training: often available, rarely compulsory

Finally, considering how rapidly things change with ICT, and considering how it changes education, though we do not know very much about the real effects of it, there is of course a major need for research, development, and evaluation.

As we have seen, there are more questions than answers about the role of the teacher in the 21st century. Things are evolving very rapidly, we do not know what schools will be like in 10 or 20 years, but we have to anticipate, to prepare teachers for the next century. This is a great challenge for educational systems and for teacher training institutions: Train today the teacher of tomorrow!

REFERENCES

Cornu, B. (2001). *Winds of change in the teaching profession.* Paris: French National Commission for UNESCO.

Delors, J. (1996). *Learning: The treasure within.* Paris: UNESCO Publishing.

Information Network on Education in Europe (European Commission). (2000, February). *Information and communication technology in the education systems in Europe: National education policies, curricula, teacher training.* Extract of the report "Key data on Education in Europe" (4th ed.). Available online at http://www.eurydice.org/Publication_List/En/FrameSet. htm

Khvilon, E. (Coordinator), Anderson, J., & van Weert, T. (Eds.). (2002). *Information and communication technology in education: A curriculum for schools and programme of teacher development.* Paris: UNESCO.

Lévy, P. (2000, November 29). L'intelligence collective [The collective intelligence]. *Le Monde.*

Morin, E. (2001). *Seven complex lessons in education for the future.* Paris: UNESCO Publishing.

OECD Education Ministers. (2001, April). *Investing in proficiencies for all.* Final communiqué of the meeting of Ministers of Education, Paris. Available online at www.oecd.org/dataoecd/40/8/1924078.pdf

Spender, D. (1996, September). *Creativity and the computer education industry.* Plenary lecture at the International Federation for Information Processing Congress, Canberra, Australia. Available online at http://www.acs.org.au/ifip96/dales.html

UNESCO. (1966). *Recommendation concerning the status of teachers.* Paris: Author.

UNESCO. (2000, April). *Dakar Framework for Action.* Adopted during the World Education Forum in Dakar, Senegal. Available online at http://www.unesco.org/education/efa/ed_for_all/dakfram_eng.shtml

Linking ICT, Knowledge Domains, and Learning Support for the Design of Learning Environments

Joost Lowyck
Jan Elen
Catholic University of Leuven, Belgium

Instructional design (ID) efforts often start from the assumption that precise knowledge about goals and target-group characteristics is sufficient to build effective and efficient learning environments. Discrepancy between goals and actual situation is, then, dissolved with the help of methods, tools, procedures, and activities. This approach has proven to be valuable in numerous cases (e.g., industrial training settings). However, in regular educational settings, ID is hardly used.

This contribution deals with the issue of ID in research-based universities. First, evolutions with respect to information and communication technology (ICT), knowledge domains, and learning support are discussed. The second section presents a case study at the Catholic University of Leuven (Belgium). Both sections document the increasing importance of ID in university settings, including consensus about the following features of learning processes:

Learning is *active*. Activity by the learner rests upon the perspective that it is primarily "mental" or "cognitive" (Shuell, 1988). The active nature of learning suggests that knowledge, skills, and attitudes result from a mentally effortful process the learner has to engage in (Bereiter & Scardamalia, 1989).

Learning is *constructive* (De Corte, 1990; Glaser, 1991; Osborne & Wittrock, 1983; Resnick, 1989; Shuell, 1986, 1988). The acquisition of knowledge requires a constructive activity of the learner who attributes meaning to incoming information. As Rumelhart and Ortony (1977) contend: "Normal people are not tape recorders, or video recorders; rather they seem to process and reprocess information, imposing on it and producing from it knowledge which has structure" (p. 99).

Learning is *cumulative* (Resnick, 1989; Shuell, 1986, 1988; Voss, 1987). In learning new material, successful learners not only attribute meaning to incoming information, they integrate it into their prior knowledge (e.g., Glaser, 1984). This cumulative nature of learning highlights the critical role of prior knowledge in learning.

Learning is *self-regulated* (Brookfield, 1985; Corno, 1986; Simons, 1989). This aspect focuses on the learner's role in managing and controlling the learning process. Among others, Simons and colleagues (e.g., De Jong & Simons, 1990; Simons, 1989) revealed that self-regulation not only involves appropriate organizational and cognitive activities of the learner, but equally monitoring and evaluation of learning processes and outcomes.

Learning is *goal-oriented*. Bereiter and Scardamalia (1989) mentioned that for meaningful learning to occur, the learner needs the intention to do so. Salomon and Globerson (1987) called this the "mindfulness" of the learning process.

Learning is *contextualized*. Recent studies have clearly demonstrated that knowledge is contextualized. It is affected by the circumstances in which it is developed. The context is both physical and sociocultural.

THREE MAJOR CHALLENGES

Though many components of a learning environment or learning community can be described, we limit the scope of our quest to ICT, knowledge domains, and learner support. It may be expected that they in a synergic way will contribute to the quality of university education and learning.

ICT

"Traditional" universities have existed since the Middle Ages. Their education approach has been gradually refined to be better adapted to the core tasks. However, fast knowledge development and technological evolutions challenged that adaptation. Since computers became more powerful and multifunctional, they can be used as textbook, writing tool, calculator, video recorder, audio recorder, and so on. Information is multimedial (different symbol systems are used together) and alinear to ease access. Moreover, multitasking allows doing all this concurrently. However, a computer is not exclusively a personal device for individual information processing, but a powerful tool for synchronous (e.g., chatting) or asynchronous (e.g., e-mail) communication. As a consequence, the integration of functionalities, symbol systems, processing capabilities, communication facilities, and various information structures into one machine makes discussions about media selection obsolete.

Although universities are aware of the necessity to convert usual approaches to education into new forms of flexible learning, the conditions for an intruding innovation are not yet clearly met. Rapid and complex evolutions often bring about less rational decisions. Moreover, prospection of the potential of ICT necessarily depends on past research and experience with "outdated" technological tools. An exclusive focus on specific and isolated technologies is detrimental. More suitable seems an approach in which nontechnological functions of ICT tools are identified. Instructional design research may help to identify functions and contexts in which ICT functionalities can be beneficial.

Nontechnological Functions of ICT Tools

From an instructional and learning point of view, three types of ICT use can be made:

1. The first category relates to the knowledge of computers and computer functionalities (De Corte, Verschaffel, & Lowyck, 1994). For instance, a large number of websites are designed to demonstrate the potential of the Internet for educational purposes. ICT may enlarge the "digital" skills of students by providing specific tools. Students have to learn how to handle these tools and need to acquire relevant ICT skills.

2. A second category of educational use capitalizes on interaction. Laurillard (1993) distinguished between three types. The first is *interactive.* Given a particular input of the student, the system provides a reaction (e.g., simulations, microworlds). Typically, the student decides what happens. The system only reacts based on in-built procedures. In *adaptive* systems, the system guides the learner (e.g., tutorials). Depending on reactions of the learner, the system decides what information to deliver or what task to formulate. Underlying decision-making trees reflect the instructional theory adopted by the designer. Whereas interactive and adaptive systems allow mainly for human–machine interaction, ICT may also mediate human–human interaction when using *discursive* systems (e.g., video- and computer-mediated conferencing). All these systems aim at enabling (often intercultural) collaboration. However, they can only do so if they are part of a hybrid learning environment or a learning community that specifies goals and identifies specific tasks.

3. Finally, ICT can be used as an open tool. In order to accomplish any particular task, a word processor, a statistical program, or a spreadsheet can be used. In a similar vein, particular programs have been elaborated as tools for learning (e.g., learning tool: http://www.sri.com/policy/ctl/html/kozma.htm(soft). Most specific are information-gathering tools. They help students to retrieve, arrange, analyze, and synthesize relevant information.

Confronted with this wide variety of ICT functionalities, it seems inadequate to discuss the use of ICT in general (Dillemans, Lowyck, Van der Perre, Claeys, & Elen, 1998). Rather, it is to be investigated whether a specific function of ICT is appropriate and what this requires from technology. Once this decision is made, more focused choices of technological devices may start.

ICT and Learning

Instructional design aims at identifying guidelines for the design of learning environments. Systematic efforts in ID research help to formulate guidelines with respect to the use of ICT. ID has evolved from clear-cut prescriptions toward more probabilistic, holistic, and pragmatic guidelines (Winn, 1991). Research on the use of technology for learning purposes has rejected the idea of a one-to-one relationship between technology and educational innovation (Kozma, 1991). It revealed that understanding this relationship requires complex if–then relationships. The *if* part consists of the following components: (curricular) context, learning goals, students, learning activities, and ambitions of designers and decision makers. The guidelines specify the functionality of ICT tools as well as the implications and prerequisites related to the use of (specific) ICT tools. The following examples illustrate this point:

- *If* higher order cognitive processes (problem solving, hypothesis testing, decision making) are aimed at, *then* courseware is necessarily highly complex and, consequently, mainly adapted to high-ability students and sophisticated teachers. Therefore, students need to operate on activities that challenge their knowledge and skills in a realistic way. Too easy content is boring and too complex content demotivating.
- *If* higher order thinking is aimed at, *then* the problem of abstraction and decontextualization has to be tackled. It is needless to confront the learner with very exciting visual and auditive stimuli (video clips), because for most educational purposes, a lean mix of symbol systems is sufficient (see Dwyer, 1978). Stimuli in the environment need to be functional for educational purposes.

- *If* coconstruction of knowledge is aimed at, *then* students must be prepared to engage in complex, cooperative problem-solving activities. Often communication is focused on shallow exchange of information, with only a very small percentage of time devoted to the complex cognitive task (see Lowyck, Elen, Proost, & Buena, 1995). Therefore, students as well as tutors need to become skillful in communicating.
- *If* computers are used as information tools, *then* the complexity of distributed information sources comes to the scene. If support is meant to explore open information sources, students need coaching of information searching activities, such as detecting useful information or assessing the value of the information gathered. Moreover, learning to use multiple perspectives is necessary in open information landscapes (Spiro, Feltovich, Jacobson, & Coulson, 1991).
- *If* computers are used as communication tools, *then* the quality of the group (network) is of utmost importance in terms of prior knowledge, motivation, cognitive skills, and communication skills. Consequently, students need support in acquiring all necessary task-oriented communication skills by modeling their activities and using on-line tutoring of their activities and processes.
- *If* open, distributed, and multifaceted environments are used, *then* the tension between expert and novice is predominant. Open environments are highly suitable for experts in a given domain, but they are equally dangerous for novices (expert–novice paradigm). In order to cope with this dilemma, a guided path from covert and well-structured toward overt and ill-structured information has to be designed.
- *If* computer programs have any effect on students' learning, *then* the intermediate filtering processes (mediating variables) highly determine the effects: how students perceive and interpret the functionality of the program, how they think about computers (task-oriented vs. entertainment), what explicit self-regulating capacities they have, all define the potential of the environment to be transformed into real activities and processes. As a consequence, students need strong support in enhancing their knowledge about the functions of the learning environment ("instructional metacognition"; Elen & Lowyck, 1998).

Knowledge Domains

In numerous research-oriented universities, knowledge domains are the dominant constituents of both curriculum and organization. Academic teaching and learning always aim at supporting students to acquire deep-level understanding and active development of a given discipline or knowledge domain. A sound theoretical base and its concomitant academic skills are assumed to enhance transfer of knowledge in complex domains. Knowledge domains reflect two main evolutions: One is dependent on the relationship between academic disciplines (inner circle), and the other is defined by developments in reality (outer circle).

A Disciplinary View on Knowledge Domains

A main problem in discussing domain knowledge can be understood by the position of academic disciplines in their relationship to the complex and dynamic world in which universities are embedded. Alexander, Schallert, and Hare (1991) referred to three dimensions of knowledge: world knowledge (daily, commonsense knowledge), domain knowledge, and knowledge of a concrete discipline. Universities are mostly organized around (groups of) disciplines that reflect the research domains in a given period of time. Nevertheless, it seems extremely difficult to reach solid consensus about the disciplinary structure of the academic field. Though many classifications have already been elaborated, no definite or satisfying answer has been given (see Donald, 1986; Rukivana & Daneman, 1996). The conviction has prevailed that knowledge domains in different areas were containers of stable, well-validated, and strongly structured information. Consequently, subject matter often gets presented to students as a closed set of interrelated concepts and procedures. Knowing "what," "how," and "when" was simply a matter of activating subsets of information already available in their memory. This conception undoubtedly leads toward conceptual oversimplification and, due to compartmentalization, the inability to transfer knowledge.

More recently, it has been acknowledged that the nature of knowledge domains shifted from well-structured to ill-structured environments. Characteristics of ill-structured domains are: (a) knowledge application requires multiple schemas and perspectives, and (b) depending on a concrete case, different patterns of knowledge are needed, due to the across-case irregularity. One of the main characteristics of functioning within these ill-structured domains is cognitive flexibility and multiple representation of information (Spiro et al., 1991). Consequently, the isolation of monolithic disciplines is questioned by recent evolutions in terms of interdisciplinarity and multidisciplinarity.

From an ID perspective, the focus in university settings on knowledge domains contrasts with the overall neglect of considering domain-specific issues. Indeed, ID tends to use formal content categories and types of learning goals. A typical example is the former Component Display Theory (CDT) of Merrill (1983), who identified two dimensions: (a) formal information categories (e.g., "facts," "rules," "concepts") and (b) behavioral levels. This simplified categorization of information no longer provides an adequate representation. Indeed, the formal representation neglects the subtleties of the domain, the underlying structure, the specific discourse, the lack of stability, the underlying reasoning, and the methodology as well.

Reality View on Knowledge Domains

Constructive approaches to learning heighten the need to reconsider knowledge domains from a more realistic and contextualized perspective. This corresponds to what Piaget (1971) pretends: "To my way of thinking, knowing an object does not mean copying it—it means acting upon it. It means constructing systems of transformations that correspond, more or less adequately, to reality" (p. 15). The Cognition and Technology Group at Vanderbilt (1993) referred to so-called macrocontexts that provide a common ground for experts in various areas, as well as for teachers and students from diverse backgrounds, to communicate in ways that build collective understanding: "Macrocontexts are semantically rich environments that can be used to integrate concepts across the curriculum and in which meaningful, authentic problems can be posed" (p. 9). In this approach, disciplines as formal structures of knowledge are no longer central in building knowledge. Scardamalia and Bereiter (1996) also rejected a formal approach and point to its ineffectivity. Possible reasons for that shortage of effectivity are due to the following characteristics of education: product orientation, unintelligibility, lack of opportunity for reflection, emphasis on reproduction of information, overload, remoteness from experienced reality, busywork, powerlessness, and low probability of success. This environment needs redesign in order to make understanding adaptive to the world of students.

This new line of thought originated many approaches to bring understanding and knowledge closer to the learner. Examples are coconstruction of knowledge in cooperative settings; use of realistic settings; and project-based, problem-based, and case-based learning (see McKeachie, 1994). Common characteristics of these approaches are use of realistic assignments, cooperation, information gathering and processing, and more natural methods of (process) assessment. It is evidenced that open information landscapes like the Internet strongly underpin this realistic move.

Learning Support

For a long time, universities were ivory towers with access for only the lucky few. With the democratization of access, universities were confronted with a larger and more differentiated student population. Universities gradually became aware of the need to provide learner-directed support in order to foster learning processes and bring about meaningful and valuable learning outcomes. To deliver professional, flexible, and adapted learning support is a challenge for both universities and ID, which relates to a number of issues. A first issue deals with adaptivity. Gradually, instructional design shifted toward student-centeredness. It is a quest for tuning environmental features to students' perceptions and presenting suitable learning tasks. Critical learner variables to be considered are prior knowledge, (meta)cognitive skills, and motivation. To engage in relevant learning becomes easier when a learner has adequate prior knowledge, knows how to process information, and actually wants to learn. Prior knowledge consists of tacit or informal knowledge as well as explicit or intentional "academic knowledge."

A second issue pertains to the provision and use of support devices. At research universities, numerous initiatives are available to students' support, either embedded in course materials or added as specific curriculum features. Especially interesting is the case of first-year students at most European universities, where a substantial number fail despite strong efforts to realize a calibration between students and their learning environment. Students often do not perceive nor adequately use available support. It has therefore been suggested that learners' conceptions about support devices need more systematic consideration. Given their more intense experience with teacher-centered approaches, this is especially the case when learner-centered approaches are introduced.

Through their instructional experiences, learners acquire domain-specific knowledge and skills as well as metacognitive knowledge. This metacognitive knowledge determines how students will behave in a particular learning environment, the kind of decisions they make on learning goals, cognitive activities they execute, and evaluation of learning outcomes they engage in. Metacognitive knowledge, for instance, affects the extent to which students regard themselves as responsible for their learning, and whether they will feel self-responsible or accept external regulation. In a traditional school environment, students are expected not to be self-responsible because knowledge is fixed, exams emphasize reproduction of facts, learning is exclusively individual, technology is fun but not instructionally functional, and learning by heart is highly rewarding.

A third issue directly relates to the intensive use of technological means for support. The technologically mediated nature of students' activities has both first- and second-order implications for studying. Increased flexibility from the students' perspective is an important first-order implication. Indeed, in the absence of direct interactions and the introduction of asynchronous interaction, students can study when they want, whenever it suits them most. Though from an organizational point of view this flexibility liberates learners, it also imposes new requirements. Traditionally, students' lives are regulated by a timetable, specifying when students engage in particular course-related activities. It also indicates when lectures are given, assignments have to be delivered, laboratory exercises are done, and tests can be taken. Such a timetable may help students to plan their study activities. It may also put some pressure on students' activities by acting as a scaffold for extrinsic motivation. However, flexibility with respect to time places the planning burden on the shoulders of the students. For some students (e.g., students with high fear of failure or high levels of procrastination), this can become problematic (Mason, 1996).

It can be expected that the growth of e-learning with increased possibilities to study when and where students want will also generate completely new attitudes and perspectives toward studying. These second-order implications may even be more important to educational systems in general and to students in particular.

Instructional design seems unable to provide a balanced answer to these issues because ID (a) focuses on cognitive issues, (b) specifies formal activities independent of how students transform these activities into "learning" activities, and (c) induces a selective perception of isolated, partial elements of the learning environment. However, students are confronted with a range of formal and informal learning goals. They not only have to adapt to isolated courses but to a complete new environment that lacks stability.

Flexible organization of universities implies brand-new forms of support. In line with the shift from learning environments toward learning communities (Lowyck & Poÿsä, 2001), all actors, like peers, tutors, and experts, play a supportive role more than the fixed environmental components.

INNOVATING UNIVERSITY EDUCATION: CASE STUDY OF THE CATHOLIC UNIVERSITY OF LEUVEN

In the discussion of ICT, knowledge domains and support have been presented as major issues challenging ID at universities. In view of identifying potential contributions of ID to educational innovation, design, and development at universities, a case study is presented. A short description of the evolution of ideas and realizations toward educational innovation at the Catholic University of Leuven (K.U.Leuven) mirrors changes in organizational, didactical, technological, and domain-specific conceptions of teaching and learning at a more general European level. In such a way, evolutions at K.U.Leuven exemplify broader arrangements that are influenced by megatrends in society. We briefly describe some characteristics of the Zeitgeist in order to better understand the actual situation and to be able to suggest necessary innovations.

Background

The 1970s

In the 1970s, the Open, Flexible, and Distance Learning movement challenged higher education institutions in Europe. As was often the case in that decade, the complex phenomenon of innovation was split into a range of separate initiatives. As a result of (a combination of) the drastically changing economic, demographic, and democratic scene, new higher education institutions, including new universities, were built all over the European countries. They had to bring universities—through their spread over the country—close to all citizens as a vehicle to realize the democratization of higher education. Indeed, bridging the gap between haves and have-nots was interpreted in terms of geographical, not psychological or social, measures. No sociocultural or socioeconomic factors might hinder the physical access to higher education because society needs intellectual capital for the new, knowledge-intensive economies after World War II. Along this set of initiatives, open universities were built as well, first to meet the (democratic) needs of people who were hindered in their access to universities or higher education by different, mostly socioeconomic, gender, or sociocultural factors. The open university of the "second chance" was born. When this target group was served, a new phenomenon came to light: the (professional) need of workers of all kinds to update and upgrade their competencies—"the second way." It was the time of the second diploma obtained during the professional career. The allocation and distribution of tasks and responsibilities between higher education institutions was clear. On the one hand, traditional universities with a rather conservative teaching–learning approach served young students with some limited facilities for working students. On the other, open universities with a majority of adult learners were based on a mix of highly attractive educational principles, like open access, flexible routing, and distance learning, and more concretely: (a) individual responsibility in learning what, how, and at what pace; (b) tailored individual study paths; (c) modular structures to adapt to the demands of professions; (d) independent learning with ample support; and (e) absence of formal entry requirements.

In the 1970s, the necessary adaptation of the universities to the needs of society was mainly interpreted as the necessity to build new types of organizations. Consequently, a mere structural answer compatible with the societal reform movement was presented.

The 1980s

Since the split of the unitary and bilingual Catholic University of Louvain in 1968, the new Flemish university of Leuven (K.U.Leuven) invested its main effort in international research endeavors, in order to avoid the danger of shrinking to the level of a mere regional university. This strategy allowed the university to belong among the strongest European universities. However, changes in society, pressure of industry on universities, higher demands for knowledge workers, and new conceptions of learning (the learning organization) challenged K.U.Leuven to invest increasingly in innovative education.

In the 1980s, mainly due to innovations in university teaching methods and technology, traditional universities became interested in new target groups and innovative learning approaches. K.U.Leuven started experimenting with new teaching–learning methods and approaches derived from an open university philosophy. It founded a so-called Open University Unit (1986–1990) with the mission to concentrate on the renewal of ID principles for self-study packages. If and to what degree printed material could be designed to meet the demands of effective and efficient "deep-level" learning was researched.

"Open university" was not interpreted in terms of an organization, but a philosophy. The emphasis was on (a) research of new constructivist methods of learning, (b) development of new approaches to instructional design, and (c) distribution of new design endeavors across faculties and individual teachers. In order to exploit the outcomes generated by the Open University Unit, a task force on innovative university teaching methods was installed. The aim was described as "the search for new ways of teaching at the university, including new information technologies." The report of this working group was used in 1990 as a platform to focus more precisely on innovative use of computers in education. The underlying philosophy of the report was the proclamation of the need for integrating information technology (IT; personal computers, multimedia) in university teaching. The personal computer was expected to support individualization, differentiation, and self-study on the part of the student, while a reduction of routine tasks and time investment for the teacher was equally foreseen. The "image" behind these endeavors is an electronic "teacher," putting usual or traditional didactic principles into computers with emphasis on information delivery, questioning, direct feedback, external regulation of learning activity, and differentiation in terms of pace (linear approach) and, more exceptionally, of content as well (branched approach). Visualization, interactivity, and drill-and-practice were perceived as the most powerful functionalities of IT. The report resulted in investments in new technologies. Therefore, a first series of systematic research and implementation projects was started, sponsored by the University Board and supervised by a Steering Committee. The aim was to use an incremental innovation strategy starting at the very concrete level of interested individual teachers. The call-for-tenders was regulated by a clear procedure, open to all university teachers. Four projects in statistics, computer science, physics, and hematology were granted. Each project lasted 2 years.

The initial focus on stimulating individual professors to implement new technologies into their teaching led toward a ceiling effect. Indeed, technology was used as a mere extension of the didactic approaches already used. Clearly, the needs of traditional university teaching were interpreted in terms of borrowing innovative ideas and approaches from the open universities. The structural approach was replaced by a strategic solution.

The 1990s

Due to the rise of ICT, traditional universities became aware of new target groups, starting with their alumni and broadening their scope to non-traditional students. Consequently, there is a (con)fusion of the task differentiation between traditional and open universities. The boundaries between types of universities (old, new, traditional, open, corporate) and higher education of all kind seem to blur. ICT is used for course delivery, Web learning (e-learning), and student guidance (tutoring, peer discussions, chat boxes, etc.). This orientation toward a mix of tools and measures is dependent on the recent adoption of student-centered learning as the leading educational philosophy. Guided independent learning, collaborative learning, e-learning, and modular approaches are attempts to implement a powerful learning environment. They are incentives for a more hybrid university educational policy, in which networking with other (parts of) universities is implied (Downes, 1998).

The output of the first computer projects at K.U.Leuven showed the following characteristics: (a) mainly supported by an individual teacher or restricted group, (b) focus on add-on to printed course material, (c) aiming at individualization, (d) expecting more comfort for teachers by skipping routine activities, and (e) mainly based on programmed instruction principles. In addition, though the conditions for rewarding a project were clearly meant to document the organizational, didactical, and technological output in order to distribute the outcomes of the project, almost no project realized this altruist objective. In order to remedy this shortage, a consolidation project was launched (DigIT): a Web-based environment that contains relevant information, examples of programs, individual and group support, evaluation of courseware, and others.

In order to support these innovations in a more continuous way, a new line of innovative projects was launched. They cover three important aims: educational research, development of instruments and methods, and implementation of innovations. The projects are related to the specific university educational policy "guided independent learning"; are embedded in the university quality assurance strategies; follow a systematic procedure for proposal, acceptance, and evaluation; and are supervised by the Educational Council. All these characteristics aim at a systemic and systematic approach, enabling the university to develop an intensive and coordinated innovation strategy, compatible with its general educational philosophy.

It is expected that putting a higher weight on projects that are adopted by the departments and faculties will enable more encompassing and lasting outputs. By doing so, there is a gradual change from externally controlled teaching, information delivery, individualization, and evaluation of knowledge as a product toward student-controlled learning, knowledge development, collaborative learning, and process evaluation.

It can be observed that due to the complexity of the necessary innovations at the university level, there is an explicit choice for a mix of organizational, didactical, curricular, and technological measures. These decisions bring about a hybrid innovative approach.

State of the Art: ICT at K.U.Leuven

Along with the innovation projects, which focus on a broad range of educational issues, the specific ICT innovation is guided by an "ICTO group" (ICT and Education), a multidisciplinary expert group on the use of ICT in education. This group is responsible for preparing the measures to be taken at the university level to cope with the drastic and hectic evolutions in technology. Telecommunications, computer sciences, media (multimedia), Web-based learning, infrastructure, Internet access, and electronic (learning) platforms all are part of the concern. Ensuring wide access, the selection of a learning management system, and reuse of instructional materials are some of the major issues addressed.

Because the university develops an educational policy that stimulates the use of computers at all levels of its organization, there is a need for a continuous investment in infrastructure, organization, finances, and manpower. Surveys concerning the use of computers by higher education students report 80% of the students to be able to use computers for their study. There is, moreover, an increasing use of computers in curriculum, student guidance, and organization of activities, due to the communication facilities. Students at K.U.Leuven have access to computers at KotNet (computers available at the university student houses), can lease computers, have access to PC rooms at different locations, and so on. This has become especially important since the universitywide adoption of a specific learning management system (Toledo) as the major vehicle for course-related information delivery, communication, and evaluation.

However, the focus on technological issues is not the ultimate goal of the educational policy. There is a clear tendency to elaborate "all-in" innovations with the following characteristics: (a) strengthen the link between educational and ICT innovations, (b) stimulate the ownership of innovations at the decentralized level of departments and faculties, and (c) realize synergy between didactical, technological, organizational, and media-related issues. It is clear that a mere technology-driven approach nowadays is out of the picture.

The innovation of university teaching–learning refers to new design endeavors with respect to teaching and learning, embedded in a hybrid knowledge space in which instructional agents (teachers, tutors, peers, software) and students codesign their learning environment. Moreover, due to communication technologies, not only learning environments but, equally, learning communities are built. All this implies the necessary skills of both professors and students to interactively design the optimal environments and communities. Consequently, not only the teachers have to be (re)trained, but the students as well, from a perspective of interactively building the necessary knowledge space.

CONCLUSION

The analysis presented here reveals that educational development at research-based universities and ID are confronted with similar issues. Moreover, solutions are looked for in a similar direction. It is clear that ID may offer a number of general, though beneficial, principles to the development of education at universities. Acting in line with these principles may help to avoid major problems. The following are some examples of such principles:

1. Be specific about the reason why ICT is used and ensure that the technology fully enables the intended use. Use technology as a tool for providing domain-related information, as an interactive device, or as a regular tool.

2. Make sure that students perceive the benefit of using technology. ICT does not automatically generate learning. It is mainly a tool to be used in a broader learning environment.

3. The kind of activities learners engage in is of major importance, because activities determine the final result. Allow learners to be active. The learner has to be challenged and be encouraged to ask questions and look for possible answers.

4. Ensure compatibility between (a) support provided, (b) learner characteristics, and (c) goals put forward. Research has evidenced that support is inadequate if not directed to the instructional goals. Moreover, insufficient or even too much support can be detrimental to the learning process.

Too much support hinders the learners in their crucial task to be (mentally) active.

5. Take care learners have a full understanding of (a) the goals and (b) the functionality of the different components of their learning environment. If these requirements are not fulfilled, learners get no opportunity to be self-regulated and to adapt their learning activities to the instructional goals.

6. Ensure consistency between goals and information provided. Learning is mindful, goal oriented, and effortful. Hence, it is obvious that these efforts are to be directed toward the goal. This implies that relevant, adequate, and realistic information is presented to the students.

7. Realize compatibility between goals and tests. If the learning goal is to acquire problem-solving skills, confronting the students with prototypical problems in an assessment center, rather than a reproductive multiple-choice test, is indicated.

The generality of these principles highlights the need for a further operationalization in a university context. Moreover, it seems that certain issues are not addressed by instructional design. A learning environment, for instance, encompasses far more than the (electronic) distribution of course materials. It requires the design of a full learning environment or even a learning community with integrated goals, actors, support, and content.

More fundamentally, it seems that the design and development of education at a university must depart from a radically different conception of reality. Instructional design takes a "design and development from scratch" approach. Educational development at universities cannot but take an "alter what is available in view of optimization" approach. The reality is that "a training," "a course," "an application" in most cases is already available.

The analysis can also be regarded as an attempt to formulate a research agenda with two major categories. The first category refers to reality-monitoring research that studies the context for universities. The availability and use of technological tools, the organizational structure, the demographic characteristics of users as well as their preferences are investigated. This type of research is crucial to make adequate decisions at both the macro- and mesolevels. Considering new opportunities, the second category seems even more fundamental. For universities, the central research question reads as follows: How can the use of multiple information resources and computer-mediated collaboration by a multicultural student population be supported to foster the acquisition of meaningful learning?

The following is an illustrative list of more precise research questions:

1. How do students from different cultural backgrounds perceive the relationship between (multicultural) collaboration and meaningful learning; what is the impact of different perceptions in this respect on learning activities engaged in by students; how can such perceptions be changed if they are counterproductive?

2. What is the role of the language used in multicultural collaboration settings; to what extent do language skills affect learning outcomes in multicultural collaborative contexts that are highly text-based?

3. What different types of collaboration can be identified and how do these different types interact with different types of students and/or different types of (meaningful) learning outcomes?

4. What tasks and tutoring activities may support ICT-embedded collaborative learning activities; how can this support be built into the technological environment and/or delivered through computer-mediated interaction?

5. How can active participation and the acquisition of information searching, processing, and evaluation be promoted?

6. What is the difference between synchronous and asynchronous collaboration with respect to the cognitive and metacognitive activities engaged in by students; what is the impact of varying cognitive and metacognitive activity profiles on learning results?

7. Does studying in a virtual university setting changes learners' metacognitive knowledge and how do these changes affect the learning process; what variables or mechanisms affect learning directly and what variables mediate learning in virtual universities?

To investigate these questions requires a varied and complex methodology. Laboratory studies focusing on the (theoretical) impact as well as design experiments in real contexts are needed. Qualitative and quantitative data are helpful to gain complementary insights. Finally, in order to bring about learning-related innovation, a huge investment in training of policymakers, teachers, and students is needed. These training efforts may take different formats, including virtual ones, and will be multidisciplinary: Teachers will have to know how to handle technology, how to combine symbol systems in multimedia environments, how to use it for educational purposes, how to analyze learning needs, and how to support computer-based, multicultural collaborative learning. The actual and widespread implementation of powerful learning environments in virtual universities is clearly a challenge for universities as organizations as well as for managers of education, teachers, and students. In conclusion, a systematic and systemic approach to innovative design and development is clearly needed.

REFERENCES

Alexander, P. A., Schallert, D. L., & Hare, V. C. (1991). Coming to terms: How researchers in learning and literacy talk about knowledge. *Review of Educational Research, 61*(3), 315–343.

Bereiter, C., & Scardamalia, M. (1989). Intentional learning as a goal of instruction. In L. B. Resnick (Ed.), *Knowing, learning, and instruction: Essays in honor of Robert Glaser* (pp. 361–392). Hillsdale, NJ: Lawrence Erlbaum Associates.

Brookfield, S. (1985). Self-directed learning: A conceptual and methodological exploration. *Studies in the Education of Adults, 17*(1), 19–32.

Cognition and Technology Group at Vanderbilt. (1993). Designing learning environments that support thinking: The Jasper series as a case study. In T. M. Duffy, J. Lowyck, & D. H. Jonassen (Eds.), *Designing environments for constructive learning* (pp. 9–36). Heidelberg, Germany: Springer-Verlag.

Corno, L. (1986). The metacognitive control components of self-regulated learning. *Contemporary Educational Psychology, 11*(4), 333–346.

De Corte, E. (1990). Acquiring and teaching cognitive skills: A state-of-the-art of theory and research. In P. J. D. Drenth, J. A. Sergeant, & R. J. Takens (Eds.), *European perspectives in psychology* (Vol. 1, pp. 237–263). London: Wiley.

De Corte, E., Verschaffel, L., & Lowyck, J. (1994). Computers and learning. In T. Husén & T. N. Postlethwaite (Eds.), *The international encyclopedia of education* (2nd ed., pp. 1002–1007). New York: Pergamon.

De Jong, F., & Simons, P. (1990). Cognitive and metacognitive processes of self-regulated learning. In J. M. Pieters, P. R. J. Simons, & L. De Leeuw (Eds.), *Research on computer-based instruction* (pp. 81–100). Lisse, Switzerland: Swets & Zeitlinger.

Dillemans, R., Lowyck, J., Van der Perre, G., Claeys, C., & Elen, J. (1998). *New technologies for learning: Contribution of ICT to innovation in education.* Leuven, Belgium: Leuven University Press.

Donald, J. G. (1986). Knowledge and the university curriculum. *Higher Education, 15,* 267–282.

Downes, S. (1998). *The future of online learning.* Manitoba, Canada: Brandon. Available: http://www.assiniboinec.mb.ca/user/downes/future

Dwyer, F. M. (1978). *Strategies for improving visual learning: A handbook for effective selection, design, and use of visualized materials.* State College, PA: Learning Services.

Elen, J., & Lowyck, J. (1998). Students' view on efficiency of instruction: An exploratory survey-study on instructional metacognitive knowledge of university freshmen. *Higher Education, 36*(2), 231–252.

Glaser, R. (1984). Education and thinking. The role of knowledge. *American Psychologist, 39*(2), 93–104.

Glaser, R. (1991). The maturing of the relationship between the science of learning and cognition and educational practice. *Learning and Instruction, 1,* 129–144.

Kozma, R. B. (1991). Learning with media. *Review of Educational Research, 61*(2), 179–211.

Laurillard, D. (1993). *Rethinking university teaching.* London: Routledge.

Lowyck, J., Elen, J., Proost, K., & Buena, G. (1995). *Telematics in open and distance learning: Research methodology handbook.* Leuven, Belgium: Catholic University of Leuven, Center for Instructional Psychology and Technology.

Lowyck, J., & Poÿsä, J. (2001). Design of collaborative learning environments. *Computers in Human Behavior, 17*, 507–516.

Mason, R. (1996). *Anatomy of the virtual university.* Available: http://edfac.unimelb.edu.au/virtu/info/robin.html

McKeachie, W. J. (1994). *Teaching tips: Strategies, research, and theory for college and university teachers* (9th ed.). Lexington, MA: Heath.

Merrill, M. D. (1983). The component display theory. In C. M. Reigeluth (Ed.), *Instructional-design theories and models: An overview of their current status* (pp. 279–334). Hillsdale, NJ: Lawrence Erlbaum Associates.

Osborne, R. J., & Wittrock, M. C. (1983). Learning science: A generative process. *Science Education, 67*(4), 489–508.

Piaget, J. (1971). *Genetic epistemology.* New York: Norton.

Resnick, L. B. (1987). *Education and learning to think.* Washington, DC: National Academy Press.

Resnick, L. B. (1989). Introduction. In L. B. Resnick (Ed.), *Knowing, learning and instruction: Essays in honor of Robert Glaser* (pp. 1–24). Hillsdale, NJ: Lawrence Erlbaum Associates.

Rukivana, I., & Daneman, M. (1996). Integration and its effect on acquiring knowledge about competing scientific theories from text. *Journal of Educational Psychology, 88*, 272–287.

Rumelhart, D., & Ortony, A. (1977). The representation of knowledge in memory. In R. C. Anderson, R. J. Spiro, & W. E. Montague (Eds.), *Schooling and the acquisition of knowledge* (pp. 99–135). Hillsdale, NJ: Lawrence Erlbaum Associates.

Salomon, G., & Globerson, T. (1987). Skill may not be enough: The role of mindfulness in learning. *International Journal of Educational Research, 11*(6), 623–637.

Scardamalia, M., & Bereiter, C. (1996). Adaptation and understanding: A case for new cultures of schooling. In S. Vosniadou, E. De Corte, R. Glaser, & H. Mandl (Eds.), *International perspectives on the design of technology-supported learning environments* (pp. 149–163). Mahwah, NJ: Lawrence Erlbaum Associates.

Shuell, T. J. (1986). Cognitive conceptions of learning. *Review of Educational Research, 56*(4), 411–436.

Shuell, T. J. (1988). The role of the student in learning from instruction. *Contemporary Educational Psychology, 13*, 276–295.

Simons, P. R. J. (1989). Learning to learn. In P. Span, E. De Corte, & B. Van Hout-Wolters (Eds.), *Onderwijsleerprocessen: Strategieën voor de verwerking van informatie* (pp. 15–25). Lisse, Switzerland: Swets & Zeitlinger.

Spiro, R. J., Feltovich, P. J., Jacobson, M. J., & Coulson, R. L. (1991). Knowledge representation, content specification and the development of skill in situation-specific knowledge assembly: Some constructivist issues as they relate to cognitive flexibility theory. *Educational Technology, 31*(9), 22–25.

Voss, J. F. (1987). Learning and transfer in subject-matter learning: A problem-solving model. *International Journal of Educational Research, 11*, 607–622.

Winn, W. D. (1991). The assumptions of constructivism and instructional design. *Educational Technology, 31*, 38–40.

Part III

DELIVERY SYSTEMS, INFORMATION AND COMMUNICATION TECHNOLOGY, AND MEDIA IN EDUCATION

Norbert M. Seel
Albert-Ludwigs-University of Freiburg, Germany

Sanne Dijkstra
University of Twente, The Netherlands

In recent years the fields of instructional design (ID) and curriculum development have continued to evolve, assimilating and advancing theories of teaching, learning, and information and communication technology (ICT). Especially with regard to ICT, we can state that in the past decades, emerging—and rapidly evolving—information and communication technologies have pervaded all sectors of the industrial and everyday world, and they have driven changes in industrial production and almost all business practices. Parallel with this development, we can observe that ICT has always had a central influence on debates about necessary reforms of educational objectives and the practice of instruction. This observation can be traced back to the time when textbooks were introduced into teaching, and the same holds true with regard to computers when they were introduced into teaching in the early 1960s. With all technical innovations, it was supposed that their use in instruction would improve what teachers had been doing all along. Accordingly, the telephone, radio, television, the overhead projector, the video, and the computer were all heralded as technologies that would substantially change education and instruction (Dijkstra, 1997).

INSTRUCTIONAL DESIGN AND MEDIA SELECTION

When we reconsider the origin and development of ID as both a discipline and technology, we can say—in a slightly exaggerated manner—that information technology has continuously been the motor propelling instructional design. The high esteem for "information technology" (sometimes it may be more appropriate to speak of technical equipment) in the field of ID—but not necessarily also of curriculum development—can be traced back to the time when Pressey (1926) pleaded for the introduction of teaching machines in instructional settings. Some decades later, Skinner (1958) and others adapted this view and combined it with the model of operant conditioning that led to teaching machines and programmed instruction. With its roots in behaviorism, ID has actually centered around information technology and media for a long time (see, e.g., Gagné, 1987), and today media and information technology are still often considered the decisive factor for the further development of ID.

Effective teaching with media has been at the core of instructional research and practice for more than five decades, and actually there is not any medium or feature of a medium that has not been extensively investigated with regard to its effectiveness on learning in various instructional settings (cf. Doerr & Seel, 1997; Levie & Dickie, 1973). As a consequence, we have available a lot of information about the effectiveness of the various instructional media and their features for learning. In summarizing this research on instructional media, Clark (1983, 1994) concluded that media are only vehicles for delivering information and that their effects on learning are always indirect. Only "certain elements of different media, such as animated motion or zooming, might serve as sufficient conditions to facilitate the learning of students who lack the skill being modelled" (Clark, 1983, p. 453). This reserved conclusion evoked a controversial debate in the 1990s concerning the effectiveness of "learning with media." Kozma (1991), for example, contradicted Clark's verdict from a constructivist point of view, and other authors, such as Seel and Winn (1997), focused on the semiotics of learning with media. Altogether, these authors argued (a) that specific media and their attributes can play an important role in learning, and (b) that the use of electronic media change the characteristic features of learning environments (such as cognitive operations on representational formats, interactivity, visualization of semantic structures, feedback).

Moreover, Seel and Winn (1997) concluded from instructional media research that:

1. Media have unique effects in designed instruction.
2. Media affect the perceptual organization of messages in ways that are directly attributable to their unique properties, and in so doing predispose learners to make certain interpretations rather than others.

3. Media affect how learners encode and interpret information because they are directly responsible for the nature of the mental representations that learners construct as a result of interaction with media of communication.
4. The signs and symbols that media use to convey messages can be internalized and used by students as "cognitive" tools for the construction of knowledge.

In the past, most scholars in the fields of didactics and ID agreed that the selection of appropriate media and delivery systems should be considered a most important step in instructional planning. As a consequence, the development of media-selection models was at the core of ID for decades, and even today we can find various models that operate with checklists, matrix formats, and rule-based formats (e.g., Cantor, 1988; Reiser & Gagné, 1983; Reynolds & Anderson, 1992) in order to find the most effective delivery system for a particular case of teaching. These models consider media selection and the determination of the specific delivery of contents to be taught and learned as a rational matter strongly linked to the learners' processing capabilities as well as to goals (how the learner should be able to behave or to think after instruction), strategies, and methods of instruction. However, the emergence of multimedia systems that integrate the various capabilities of electronic media (such as audio records, the digitalization of still and motion pictures, computer animations and simulations, a huge amount of digitalized material on rewritable CDs, toolbars, pop-down menus, and finally Internet protocols and the World Wide Web) into an integrative system raises the question as to whether the issue of media selection is still adequate. Certainly, an instructional designer who wants to develop a learning environment that aims at the mediation of subject matter knowledge about astronomy, especially about the development of stars, has to focus on the question of which mode of delivery will be most effective in order to evoke the learners' curiosity and motivation to learn. Clearly, on the one hand the designer has to choose among different media, such as a text with graphics, a video, a computer animation, or whatever else, that are considered helpful in engaging students in learning activities. But on the other hand, the designer also has to answer the question of the *added value* of a preferred mode of delivery of the contents to be acquired. Twenty years ago, Salomon (1984) demonstrated with regard to the commonplace "TV is easy and print is tough" that the differential investment of mental efforts in learning must be considered a function of the learners' perceptions and attributions. From our point of view, this result corresponds with Clark's (1983) "replacement" argument, according to which the strength of a selected instructional medium depends on the answer to the question as to whether it can be replaced by another medium without any loss of effectiveness on learning and motivation.

We cannot do justice to this argumentation in more detail, but it should be evident that the selection of instructional delivery and media is a complex and multilayered problem that centers around three issues:

1. *Delivery systems are a necessity for the mediation of learning contents to learners.* Accordingly, a central concern of ID has always been to select or develop the most appropriate delivery system for a certain instructional purpose. However, the decisive point is to look carefully for the *added value of a particular delivery system* (e.g., a multimedia system) in comparison with alternative media (e.g., text combined with pictures).

2. *Media play a central role in the development and formation of the individual and collective knowledge of the world.* From the perspective of semiotics, media can expand people's everyday experiences and can contribute to the cognitive organization of these experiences (Seel & Winn, 1997). Furthermore, media can make available particular aspects of the invisible world that otherwise would be incomprehensible. Therefore, with regard to human learning and cognition, we have to attribute central importance to the "mediation" of experiences by specific media (cf. Elliott & Rosenberg, 1987).

3. *Technological literacy or fluency is a prerequisite of both instruction and learning with media.* The use of media in instruction raises the question as to whether the audience is proficient with the technologies applied. If the audience is not proficient with technology, traditional delivery methods should be incorporated; for example, a solution may provide a combination of live classroom events, print, audio, and video materials. Technology-based solutions can be incorporated only if the audience is proficient with technology. Accordingly, proficiency with media is considered a central objective of education, that is, as a learning goal on its own. Therefore, computer or technological *literacy* becomes a central educational goal of the curriculum. Actually, it is commonplace today to list familiarity with computers (including confidence in using emerging technology and the ability to learn new software) as one of society's central "new basic skills" (Murnane & Levy, 1996), including the ability to apply problem-solving skills and manipulate interactive technological applications and tools.

LEARNING AND TEACHING WITH MEDIA

According to Olson and Bruner (1974), we can generally distinguish between *learning through experience* and *learning through media*, which plays a central role in the development and formation of the individual and collective knowledge of the world. A central function of media consists in depicting reality or models of reality. However, the carrier of the depiction together with the conception is also labeled a medium (i.e., the technical meaning of medium). Therefore, Seel and Winn (1997) distinguished the different conceptions of media (the biological conception, the physical conception, the technical conception, the code-related conception, etc.). It is quite simple to classify media in accordance with their mechanical and/ or electronic components, which determine the physical and technical features of media such as television, radio, textbooks, computers, and so on. However, from the view of semiotics and cognition, the technical equipment is a necessary but not a sufficient characteristic of a medium (see Seel & Winn, 1997). The central feature of media is to communicate depictions of the real or imagined world. Any (inter- and intraindividual) communication needs specific means or devices, so-called media, whose functions can only be defined with respect to the context or the behavioral setting in which the media are integrated. The functions of mass media, for example, differ from those of instructional media due to the different contexts in which communication takes place.

From the constructivist perspective, human learning is considered an active process of knowledge construction that is dependent to a large extent on the learner's ability to strategically manage and organize all available information resources. Besides the information already stored in memory, information presented by the external environment is especially relevant. According to Kozma (1991), the learner is sensitive to characteristics of the environment, "such as the availability of specific information at a given moment, the duration of that availability, the way the information is structured" (and presented), "and the ease with which it can be searched" (p. 180). The process of extracting relevant information from the external environment involves the internalization of both the content and the modality of the mediated information (cf. Seel, 1991).

However, media and delivery systems that are considered central parts of the learner's external environment can influence learning on different levels. At first glance, we can distinguish between a macroscopic and a microscopic level. As Kozma (1991) pointed out, in the first case, the entire environment and the way in which media are integrated into it may have the greatest impact on how the students learn and think. Consequently, the larger educational context within which the learner interacts with communicated information is of central interest. At the microscopic level on the other hand, the focus is on fine-grained information processing by means of sign systems. Here, the processing capabilities of an individual as well as the semiotic functions of the individual's interaction with a specific medium are the principal interest (cf. Seel & Winn, 1997).

As with all technical innovations, instructional media and delivery systems were originally used for instruction simply to do a better job at what teachers had been doing all along. As Clark (1994) pointed out, the hope of many scholars was always that the new media could help to achieve higher ordered educational objectives, such as an improvement in the quality of teaching and learning, a reduction of costs, a widening of active participation of students in education, and the development of new curricular components. And even today, the implicit criterion for the success of an instructional technology is often how close it comes to emulating a successful human teacher. Indeed, the possibility of delivering the subject matter and engaging students in acting and learning requires of the instructional designer taking into account not only the contents to be taught but also the various components of delivery systems and ICT. Actually, from the early days of ID until today, new technical devices have motivated instructional designers to continuously improve the representations of the objects of learning and to hypothesize about the possible student actions with these various tools, with the aim of improving knowledge and skills to be acquired in the course of instruction.

Instructional media and delivery systems have evolved to the point where they do have important and unique roles to play in learning. These roles have to do with creating environments, whether simulated or virtual, that students can explore freely or within varying constraints required by guidance in order to construct knowledge and to practice problem-solving methods on their own. The key to the success of this application of media is not so much in how the "message" itself is presented, but in the degree to which students can work out for themselves ways to reduce the dissonance between what the environment presents them with and the knowledge and experience they bring with them when they enter the environment. They relate the represented world to the "genuine" world but simultaneously they presuppose technological literacy or fluency as a prerequisite for learning with media. As we have mentioned before, technology-based solutions for instructional delivery can be incorporated only if the audience is proficient with technology. Scribner and Cole (1981) proposed that literacy is a "set of socially organized practices which make use of a symbol system and a technology for reproducing it. Literacy is not simply knowing how to read and write a particular script but applying this knowledge for specific purposes in specific contexts of use" (p. 236). It follows that if being literate means being able to communicate using accepted symbol systems, then the ability to understand and use new technologies must be a form of literacy. Technological literacy or fluency is not only the ability to read and write. That means that it is not enough to be able to access, for example, a website or to create one's own; it is also the ability to broadcast a message so that it can be noticed or easily found by others. Accordingly, modern conceptions of technological literacy are often connected with two general educational goals: development of skills in problem solving and development of information-managing skills (cf. Seel & Casey, 2003).

This leads to the next important point, namely, considering the possible impact of new information technology on learning and instruction. Nowadays, the use of ICT is mainly considered to serve as a problem-solving tool that provides effective ways of teaching problem-solving skills (Ziegler & Terry, 1992). Extended use of the computer as a tool to expedite the processes of problem solving may help shift the focus from the end product and from the acquisition of facts to their manipulation and understanding; it encourages curiosity and creativity. Various features of ICT may help students become better problem solvers: (a) The new technologies are interactive systems; (b) the locus of control is shifted to the learner; (c) the computer can simulate experiments and model real situations; (d) immediate feedback is given to student responses; and (e) in several cases, the computer can perform operations (e.g., simulations) that are impossible or impractical on alternative media. Indeed, the status of computer technology today makes nearly all other media in the technical sense of the word obsolete and useless. Moreover, the technology is able to produce all the forms of representation on which students can operate.

DELIVERY MODELS

Within the last two decades, new information technologies have emerged, and more and more institutions are using or are planning to use these new technologies to meet specific educational objectives. The new technologies allow one to apply computer-assisted instruction, interactive videodisc instruction, integrated multimedia workstations, computer and video conferencing, and so on. Therefore, we can easily find conceptions of "computer-based learning," "technology-enhanced learning environments," "virtual environments," and "hybrid learning environments," all of which are dominated by ICT. This can be demonstrated with the example of "blended learning," which refers to learning that combines multiple delivery methods throughout the entire learning process. The central argument is that more methods of delivering information are available than ever before, and that successful blended learning maximizes the use of all possible delivery methods to reach the goal of the curriculum (cf. Valdez, 2001).

On the assumption that each delivery system can be characterized by different instructional criteria or components, such as the intended actions of learners, the type of presented material, or the means of communication, Paquette and Rosca (2003) have introduced a classification of delivery models in correspondence with the well-known intentions of ID. Table III.1 gives an overview of the popular delivery systems we are concerned with in current models of ID, and we can also use this matrix as a framework for the chapters of Part III of this volume. The central idea of Paquette and Rosca

TABLE III.1

Categories of Delivery Models

Main Components	Types of Delivery Models				
	Distributed Classroom	*Self-Training on the Web*	*Online Training*	*Communities of Practice*	*Performance Support System*
Learners' actions	Receive input, ask questions, complete exercises	Autonomous learning, access information	Ask questions, cooperation, telediscussions	Cooperation, telediscussions, information exchange	Exercises, case studies, simulations
Facilitators	Presenter	Training manager	Trainer, presenter	Group animator	Support manager
Main type of material	Presentations, videos, information websites	Internet and multimedia training	Productions, informative websites	Productions, informative websites	Activity guide, contextualized help files
Model-specific tools	Videoconferencing system, browser, presentation tools	Browser, search engine, multimedia support	Forum, e-mail, multimedia documents	Forum, e-mail, multimedia documents	Computer systems and organizations' databases
Means of communication	Synchronous telecom	Asynchronous telecom	Asynchronous telecom	Asynchronous telecom	Asynchronous telecom
Required services	Technical support	Communication support	Communication support	Communication support	Systems technical support
Delivery locations	Classroom, multimedia room	Residence, workplace	Residence, workplace	Residence, workplace	Workplace

Note. From Paquette and Rosca (2003).

is that a basic collection of five delivery models can be used as a starting point for instructional planning and adapted to the needs, objectives, contexts, and constraints of a new learning system. Actually, this concept of a library of delivery models can provide adaptable and combinable functions to construct expertise for the engineering, use, and analysis of delivery models. It is interesting that these authors and others (e.g., Spector & Ohrazda, 2003) define instructional design as an engineering discipline in which the development of instructional systems is somewhat similar to software engineering systems. The general trend is to control the learning process through the development of increasingly better technology—including the development of both "soft" and "hard" technology.

However, when we take into consideration current conceptions of teaching with new media, such as blended learning, we can say that the availability of tremendous amounts of electronic media in our daily lives has conditioned us to not investigate the associated processes of communication in instructional settings. We take them for granted, and often choose not to examine the characteristics of media and their effects on learning. But in choosing to turn away from such an examination, we lose the ability to fully understand the instructional potentials of new media. Do we know what is actually learned? Which knowledge and skills are acquired? For example, until we understand what multimedia are and what they can do, it will be difficult to understand their potential impact on learning. In particular, the capability of interfacing new information technologies for hybrid forms of audiovisual communication requires an investigation of the effects of these communicative techniques on the learner. Altogether, we have to postulate a new generation of research on instructional media that takes into account their involvement in current delivery models as depicted in Table III.1. We are strongly convinced that this research has to go beyond the traditional research on instructional media, because the new electronic media are not only devices for supporting instruction. Rather, they have substantially changed the characteristic features of learning environments and instructional settings.

"Because good science consists of asking interesting questions that give hope of being answered, good methodology is essential to good science" (Simon & Kaplan, 1989, p. 20). In accordance with this verdict, the postulated new generation of media research in the field of ID presupposes an effective methodology of evaluation. However, new media and their attributes do not produce the same results in all situations due to the learners' subjective dispositions and existing knowledge structures. Therefore, media research must emphasize the interactions between media attributes, learner characteristics, and situation variables. Salomon (1979) already introduced such a research program in the late 1970s, based on the assumption "that specific media attributes, when used as carriers of the critical information to be learned, call on different sets of mental skills and, by so doing, cater to different learners" (p. 9). This means that media research must focus on aptitude–treatment interactions, aiming at an optimal match between knowledge structures and learning tasks. And only in this very differentiated view can media play their significant instructional role. However, the individual knowledge structures are givens, and, although they are dynamic, they can be influenced in the short run only a little, even under favorable conditions. One solution for this problem may be in the development of adaptive learning environments, whose principles are described by Leutner (chap. 13, this volume). This leads to the next section of this introduction.

THE CONTENT OF THE CHAPTERS

Only recently have we begun to conceive the educational uses of media that go beyond typical classroom teaching. For this reason, most instructional applications of media have been didactic. That is to say, the ID procedures and prescriptive theories guiding the selection of instructional strategies have been used exclusively in light of what has to be taught and who has to learn it.

The highlights of the chapters of Part III center around (a) the integration of ICT in education, (b) the evaluation of technology-enhanced learning environments, and (c) the improvement of the adaptability of those learning environments.

Spector (chap. 12) starts with considerations of multiple uses of ICT in education. He starts with a special focus on the automatization of ID with the help of computers. Spector argues persuasively that ID is an engineering discipline, and that the development of instructional systems and support tools for instructional designers and developers is somewhat similar to software engineering systems and support tools for software engineers. Consequently, automation in software engineering will serve as the basis for this discussion of automation in instructional design. In the last 20 years there have been a number of attempts to automate some of the processes involved in planning and implementing instructional systems and learning environments. These efforts are briefly reviewed as a way of indicating the range of potential applications of ICT in education at a meta level. Although the applications discussed primarily involve the use of technology to support various instructional planning and design activities, the implications for use in other teaching–learning activities are suggested. The lessons learned from previous attempts to integrate technology into teaching and learning are important to consider in order to avoid wasting scarce resources and promising exaggerated outcomes, and so that systematic and systemic improvements in living and learning can be sustained through the intelligent use of new technologies.

Leutner's chapter (chap. 13) on instructional principles for adaptive learning environments focuses on self-regulation abilities and instructional support of students' learning in open learning environments. This support, as it is outlined in the chapter, should be "adaptive," meaning that there should be a dynamic fit between the amount of support a learner needs for effective learning and the amount of support the learning environment provides to the learner. Ten principles for designing adaptive learning environments are presented in the chapter. Four of these instructional design principles deal with adapting the amount, the sequence, the content, and the presentation format of instruction. Others deal with adapting the difficulty of practice tasks, adapting the way in which new concepts are defined in tutorial programs, adapting the delay time the learning environment needs to respond to a learner's input, adapting the kind and the amount of advice a learner receives in exploratory learning with computer simulations, adapting the menu structure of computer software in a software training program, and—last but not least—with basic questions of system control versus learner control and self-regulation in learning. Common to all presented principles is that they are based on cognitive psychological theory and that they have proved to be effective in published experimental studies.

Aiming at connecting curriculum, instruction, and assessment, Savenye's chapter (chap. 14) is concerned with the important issue of evaluating Web-based learning. She argues that institutions worldwide are turning to distance learning methods to reach new students, to extend to their current students more flexible courses, to curb rising educational costs, and to remain competitive in the information age. Currently many of these institutions are exploring the use of online and Web-based technologies to deliver courses and services. Distance education courses typically are developed using a systematic process of instructional design. Evaluation is employed as part of developmental testing of courses and systems. Although almost routinely called for, formative evaluation engenders particular problems and issues, and is not, in fact, always conducted. In this chapter, Savenye explores issues related to the conducting of evaluations of Web-based learning systems and software. She begins by discussing types of open and distance learning systems and courses. She then presents levels of evaluation and what may be evaluated at those levels, and finally she discusses methods for conducting evaluations, along with how to analyze and use the resulting data and findings.

Olkinuora, Mikkilä-Erdmann, and Nurmi (chap. 15) describe an approach for evaluating the pedagogical value of multimedia learning material. The target of this chapter is, first, to present a theoretical framework for investigating learning material and, second, to demonstrate by way of an empirical study the problems of creating effective multimedia learning environments in the domain of science. The emphasis in the empirical study is on comparing the effects of working with multimedia- and textbook-based materials and especially on describing the actual learning and working processes with multimedia. In this chapter, multimedia and hypermedia are seen as almost synonymous because both of them make use of many digital media formats (text, pictures, videos, animations, etc.) and often have a nonlinear structure and various interactive elements that enable users to engage with the material.

In the final chapter of Part III, Weber (chap. 16) describes a project on case-based learning and problem solving in an adaptive Web-based learning system. Most previous learning systems and electronic textbooks accessible via the Web lack the capabilities of individualized help and adaptive learning support that are the emergent features of on-site intelligent tutoring systems. This chapter introduces ELM-ART, an intelligent interactive educational system to support the learning of programming and problem solving in LISP. ELM-ART demonstrates how interactivity and adaptability can be implemented in Web-based tutoring systems. The knowledge-based component of the system uses a combination of an overlay model and a case-based learning model. With these different types of user models, ELM-ART supports both adaptive navigation and individualized help on problem-solving tasks. Adaptive navigation support is achieved by the annotation of links and by individual curriculum sequencing. Problem-solving support is provided by a cognitive diagnosis of solutions to programming tasks based on a case-based episodic learner model and by examples individually selected from the user's learning history.

REFERENCES

Cantor, J. A. (1988). Research and development into a comprehensive media selection model. *Journal of Instructional Psychology, 15*(3), 118–131.

Clark, R. E. (1983). Reconsidering research on learning from media. *Review of Educational Research, 53*, 445–459.

Clark, R. E. (1994). Media will never influence learning. *Educational Technology Research and Development, 42*(2), 21–29.

Dijkstra, S. (1997). Educational technology and media. In S. Dijkstra, N. M. Seel, F. Schott, & R. Tennyson (Eds.), *Instructional design: International perspectives: Vol. 2. Solving instructional design problems* (pp. 137–144). Mahwah, NJ: Lawrence Erlbaum Associates.

Doerr, G., & Seel, N. M. (1997). Instructional delivery systems and multimedia environments. In S. Dijkstra, N. M. Seel, F. Schott, & R. D. Tennyson (Eds.), *Instructional design: International perspectives: Vol. 2. Solving instructional design problems* (pp. 145–182). Mahwah, NJ: Lawrence Erlbaum Associates.

Elliott, W. R., & Rosenberg, W. L. (1987). Media exposure and beliefs about science and technology. *Communication Research, 14*, 164–188.

Gagné, R. M. (Ed.). (1987). *Instructional technology: Foundations.* Hillsdale, NJ: Lawrence Erlbaum Associates.

Kozma, R. B. (1991). Learning with media. *Review of Educational Research, 61*(2), 179–211.

Levie, W. H., & Dickie, K. E. (1973). The analysis and application of media. In R. M. W. Travers (Ed.), *Second handbook of research on teaching* (pp. 858–882). Chicago: Rand McNally.

Murnane, R. J., & Levy, F. (1996). *Teaching the new basic skills: Principles for educating children to thrive in a changing economy.* New York: Martin Kessler Books/The Free Press.

Olson, D. R., & Bruner, J. S. (1974). Learning through experience and learning through media. In D. R. Olson (Ed.), *Media and symbols: The forms of expressions, communication, and education* (pp. 125–150). Chicago: National Society for the Study of Evaluation.

Paquette, G., & Rosca, I. (2003). Modeling the delivery physiology of distributed learning systems. *Technology, Instruction, Cognition, and Learning, 1*(2).

Pressey, S. L. (1926, March 20). A simple apparatus which gives tests and scores—and teaches. *School and Society, 23.*

Reiser, R. A., & Gagné, R. M. (1983). *Selecting media for instruction.* Englewood Cliffs, NJ: Educational Technology Publications.

Reynolds, A., & Anderson, R. H. (1992). *Selecting and developing media for instruction* (3rd ed.). New York: Van Nostrand Reinhold.

Salomon, G. (1979). *Interaction of media, cognition and learning.* San Francisco: Jossey-Bass.

Salomon, G. (1984). Television is "easy" and print is "tough." The differential investment of mental effort in learning as a function of perceptions and attributions. *Journal of Educational Psychology, 76*(4), 647–658.

Scribner, S., & Cole, M. (1981). *The psychology of literacy.* Cambridge, MA: Harvard University Press.

Seel, N. M. (1991). *Weltwissen und mentale Modelle* [World knowledge and mental models]. Göttingen, Germany: Hogrefe.

Seel, N. M., & Casey, N. C. (2003). Changing conceptions of technological literacy. In P. Attewell & N. M. Seel (Eds.), *Disadvantaged teens and computer technologies* (pp. 35–55). Münster, Germany: Waxmann.

Seel, N. M., & Winn, W. D. (1997). Research on media and learning: Distributed cognition and semiotics. In R. D. Tennyson, F. Schott, S. Dijkstra, & N. M. Seel (Eds.), *Instructional design: International perspectives: Vol. 1. Theories and models of instructional design* (pp. 293–326). Mahwah, NJ: Lawrence Erlbaum Associates.

Simon, H. A., & Kaplan, C. A. (1989). Foundations of cognitive science. In M. I. Posner (Ed.), *Foundations of cognitive science* (pp. 1–47). Cambridge, MA: MIT Press.

Skinner, B. F. (1958, October 24). Teaching machines. *Science, 128,* 969–977.

Spector, J. M., & Ohrazda, C. (2003). Automating instructional design: Approaches and limitations. In D. H. Jonassen (Ed.), *Handbook of research in educational communications and technology* (2nd ed., pp. 685–699). Bloomington, IN: Association for Educational Communications and Technology.

Valdez, R. J. (2001). *Blended learning: Maximizing the impact of an integrated solution.* Bellevue, WA: Click2Learn.

Ziegler, E. W., & Terry, M. S. (1992). Instructional methodology, computer literacy, and problem solving among gifted and talented students. *International Journal of Instructional Media, 19*(1), 45–51.

Chapter 12

Multiple Uses of Information and Communication Technology in Education

J. Michael Spector
Syracuse University

In the course of applying various information and communication technologies (ICT) to instructional design (ID), many important lessons have been learned. These lessons are discussed and reviewed in this chapter so as to suggest implications for other aspects of learning and instruction. The efforts reviewed primarily involve research and development associated with the planning and implementation of large-scale instructional systems.

The territory to be covered introduces (a) the use of advising systems in instructional planning, (b) systems that generate instruction from rich content sources, (c) decision support and knowledge management systems in education, (d) collaborative design of instructional systems and learning environments, and (e) the use of system dynamics to support learning in complex domains. One key lesson learned from these efforts is that weaker systems, which aim to extend and empower human problem solving and decision making, are generally more successful than stronger systems, which aim to replace the roles and activities of human designers. Such lessons are discussed in the context of a set of principles that may be applied to many instructional and learning situations.

Educational and instructional research has changed considerably in the last 20 years. Broadly stated, situated cognition provides the foundation for the current learning perspective that informs instructional planning processes. A naturalistic and pragmatic view of knowledge, and consequently of learning, informs recent learning research (Dijkstra, 2000; Goodyear, 2000; Jonassen, Hernandez-Serrano, & Choi, 2000). The implications of these perspectives for ID have not received as much attention, but they form an essential part of the conceptual framework for intelligent performance support systems (IPSS) for ID (Spector, 1999).

Technology has been steadily advancing and making possible entirely new kinds of instructional systems and learning environments. ICT now provides a powerful, network-based setting for the creation of knowledge management systems for many challenging and complex planning and decision-making contexts (Spector & Davidsen, 2000). As yet, there have been limited applications of these network-based, distributed technologies to the design of instructional systems and learning environments. A key component of the conceptual framework for an IPSS for ID will be explicit support for distributed design and development based on support from an underlying knowledge management system designed specifically for instructional planners (Spector, 1999). This chapter includes an examination of projects that involve networks along with distributed and collaborative design and development made possible through underlying knowledge management technologies. The chapter concludes with reflections about lessons learned, the principles involved, and the potential for future research and development.

INSTRUCTIONAL PRINCIPLES

In the course of efforts to provide automated support for various instructional design activities and processes, a number of important distinctions have been developed in association with lessons learned and principles to consider for future efforts (Dijkstra, Seel, Schott, & Tennyson, 1997; Spector, 1994, 1995; Spector, Polson, & Muraida, 1993; Tennyson, Schott, Seel, & Dijkstra, 1997). There are at least five principles that are fundamental to planning and implementing instructional systems and learning environments (Spector, 2001). These principles are summarized in Table 12.1. Merrill (2001) presented a somewhat different set of first principles that comprise a problem-centered view of instruction, emphasizing such things

TABLE 12.1
Five Principles Fundamental to Learning and Instruction

Principle	Elaboration
Learning	Learning is fundamentally about change.
Experience	Experience is the starting point for understanding.
Context	Context determines meaning.
Integration	Relevant learning contexts are often broad and multifaceted.
Uncertainty	People generally know less than they are inclined to believe.

as activating prior knowledge, demonstrating new principles and procedures, applying new knowledge to solve problems, and integrating new
knowledge to broaden understanding of a problem domain.

The Learning Principle orients thinking about the nature of learning
and desired learning outcomes. The notion that learning involves change is
certainly not new and can be found in classical theorists (e.g., Piaget, 1929;
Vygotsky, 1978) as well as in current research (e.g., Lave & Wenger, 1990;
Sfard, 1998). Although both individual and social processes are involved in
learning (Bruner, 1985; Collins, 1991; Leont'ev, 1978; Nardi, 1996; Salomon, 1993), nearly everyone accepts the notion that in order to show that
learning has occurred in an individual, group, or organization, one must be
able to cite evidence of change in such things as behavior, beliefs, capabilities, knowledge, mental models, patterns of activity, skills, and so on. This
principle is not a defense of any particular learning theory. Rather, it is intended to represent what most learning researchers acknowledge either implicitly or explicitly. Making this principle explicit has two advantages. First,
the notion of observing and analyzing changes over time and through various instructional interventions and learning activities is emphasized as a
fundamental part of learning research. Second, change processes are given
a central role in learning (Ellsworth, 2000).

The Experience Principle maintains that understanding is based on and
in experience. This notion is central to situated learning (Lave, 1988; Lave
& Wenger, 1990) and is embedded in many prominent ID models, including cognitive apprenticeship (Collins, 1991; Collins, Brown, & Newman,
1989) and problem-based learning (Barrows, 1985). Experience as the
starting point for understanding implies that learning should be situated in
meaningful activities and that new learning should be related to earlier
learning activities. People generally learn what they do—they learn from
their overt activities as well as from their reflections on those activities. Instruction is generally aimed at expanding the range, quality, and depth of
what people can do. This principle is not a defense of individual learning.
Rather, language (e.g., communication with peers and experts) plays an
ongoing and central role in experience. Moreover, the things that people
do and can learn to do involve experiences and interactions with others.

The Context Principle is closely related to the Experience Principle. Activities occur in a context and often that context involves artifacts, assumptions, coordinated activities, communication with others, and so on (e.g.,
Lave & Wenger, 1990; Leont'ev, 1978; Malone & Crowston, 1993; Sfard,
1998). Knowledge of the context of previous learning experiences is crucial
for the design of new learning activities. Realizing the context in which
later experiences are likely to occur can also help instructional planners develop meaningful learning contexts (Barrows, 1985; Reigeluth & Stein,
1983; Silberman, 1998; Tennyson et al., 1997). Accepting the Context Prin-

ciple goes beyond merely emphasizing the centrality of meaningful and authentic learning activities. When the Context Principle is understood alongside the other principles, the significance of cognitive flexibility becomes evident (Spiro, Coulson, Feltovich, & Anderson, 1988; Spiro, Feltovich, Jacobson, & Coulson, 1992; Spiro et al., 1987). Providing support for multiple representations of problems and situations and helping learners develop their ability to confront new situations and promote higher level understanding in complex and challenging situations are legitimate learning outcomes.

The Integration Principle builds directly on the other principles. As learners gain knowledge, skill, and understanding in a domain, the multidimensional aspect of problems and situations can and should be taken into account in an explicit manner. All too often a curriculum or educational program focuses on a narrow view of problem situations. Real-world problems do not come neatly compartmentalized in a way that corresponds to subject domains or disciplines within an academic setting (Dörner, 1996; Forrester, 1992; Sterman, 1994). The challenge for genuine integration is evident in school and college settings, in which a compartmentalization of available information and methods into subject domains makes the organization and delivery of content possible while providing identification of and occasionally access to domain experts. However, when this compartmentalization into subject disciplines becomes entrenched, and artificial barriers between disciplines are created, integrating this knowledge in the context of solving complex problems becomes nearly impossible (see Dijkstra, chap. 6, this volume). For example, it is possible to create models of how a predator and prey population interact in a particular ecology. However, in order to effect meaningful change in such settings, understanding economics, organizational behavior, politics, and psychology may all play central roles. The same kind of multifaceted considerations apply to the use of technology to support learning and instruction (e.g., Driscoll, 1998; Spector, 1994, 1995, 2001; Spector & Anderson, 2000).

The Uncertainty Principle suggests that it is all too easy to exaggerate what is known, well founded, or widely recognized. All too often, more certainty and confidence is attached to particular claims than is warranted. The consequence of ignoring this principle is that exaggerated promises might be made with regard to adopting particular instructional approaches or making particular educational reforms. Exaggerated promises can result in unreasonable expectations and less support for promising innovations than would otherwise have been the case. This principle is not an endorsement of positivism. Rather, the Uncertainty Principle is a reminder that a scientific attitude is conducive to progress. A scientific attitude involves doubt, questioning, and discomfort at not having ultimate answers and final solutions. A scientific attitude involves a willingness to experiment and revise beliefs based on outcomes. Having questions is much different than having answers. With regard to complex domains, which are addressed later in this chapter, the Uncertainty Principle becomes a central requirement for improving understanding (Davidsen, 1993, 1994, 1996; Dörner, 1996; Spector & Anderson, 2000; Sterman, 1994).

Together, these five principles (see Table 12.1) provide a framework for examining the instantiation of current learning perspectives in various settings and for considering how ICT can best be used to support the creation of instructional systems and learning environments. The next several sections explore specific ICT technologies in various educational settings and introduce a number of lessons learned or not yet learned.

INSTRUCTIONAL DESIGN AND INSTRUCTIONAL GENERATION

There are terminological issues to resolve prior to treating automated support for ID. In some contexts, ID refers to the full range of planning, implementation, evaluation, and management activities. In other contexts, ID is treated more narrowly and only includes the analysis and planning activities associated with the development of instructional systems and learning environments. ID on either interpretation occurs at different levels and, depending on the level, involves different kinds of activities (see Table 12.2).

At the activity level, it is important to distinguish the nature of desired outcomes and link those outcomes to appropriate learning activities (Richey, Fields, & Foxon, 2001). Some outcomes require mastery of a specific procedure that must be performed automatically and in a consistent manner regardless of the specific situation (e.g., safety checks, assembly of a device, etc.). Other outcomes require an understanding of variables in the situation

TABLE 12.2
Instructional Design Levels and Associated Activities

Level	Sample Activity
Enterprise/organization	Clarify the organization's mission statement and strategic goals.
Program/curriculum	Establish desired competencies for those completing the program.
Course/module	Identify course requirements and prerequisite knowledge and skill.
Lesson/unit of instruction	Determine resources required to support indicated sequences.
Learning activity/ learner interaction	Specify roles and responsibilities for indicated activities.

that require significant adjustment on the part of those involved (e.g., inter-acting with clients). Habituating activities are appropriate in some circumstances, whereas reflective activities are appropriate in others.

It is possible to distinguish ill-defined from well-defined problem situations at some level of granularity (Davidsen, 1996; van Merriënboer, 1997). When the problem situation is well defined, certain kinds of activities are generally appropriate and known to work. Much less is known about how best to support learning in ill-defined domains, although system dynamics appears to be one promising technology for such situations (see the subsequent discussion). A problem situation can be ill defined in terms of assumptions and relevant inputs, in terms of methods and processes to attain desired outcomes, or in terms of desired goals and outcomes. In some cases, it is possible to transform apparently ill-defined aspects into more well-defined aspects or to make simplifying assumptions in order to make progress.

The automatic generation of instruction has worked only for well-defined domains. Examples of systems that automatically generate instruction include Electronic Trainer, GTE (Generic Tutoring Environment), and XAIDA (Experimental Advanced Instructional Design Advisor) (Spector, 1999). These systems were all designed to extract content information from an expert source, prompt the developer for a desired learning outcome, and then produce at least a prototype lesson based on that input. The expert source was typically a human subject-matter expert, although XAIDA was successfully linked to a digital content source (Spector, Arnold, & Wilson, 1996).

The big lesson learned from these various efforts is that strong support (replacing an activity previously performed by human experts with a computer agent) for ID is more appropriate for well-defined activities in well-defined learning domains. GTE and XAIDA both involved some aspects of strong support, and both were successful within those constraints. As it happens, the more interesting problems often occur in ill-defined settings. Since it is reasonably well known how ICT can be used to support learning in well-defined problem situations, most of the remainder of this chapter is devoted to the use of ICT to support less well-defined domains and activities, including much of ID.

Lessons not learned through these and related efforts to automate instructional processes include (a) specific activities and interventions that optimally support specific learning outcomes in complex domains; and (b) how to assess progress of learning in complex domains. To set the stage for a discussion of how these unresolved issues might be addressed, two technologies now being used to successfully support some ill-defined aspects of learning and instruction—decision support and knowledge management systems—are discussed.

DECISION SUPPORT AND KNOWLEDGE MANAGEMENT IN EDUCATION

It is possible to represent the development of information systems as a progression from simple to complex systems. The relevant dimensions of complexity (see Fig. 12.1) include the number of users (one person, one type of user, many types of users, etc.) as well as the intended uses (one purpose, one set of related uses, multiple uses that are loosely related, etc.).

The progress that has occurred with regard to the development of ICT to support increasingly complex situations in business and industry is beginning to be seen in educational settings as well. Historically, ICT advances have been developed for industry or government for specific purposes and then found their way into other settings. An example of this can be found with regard to meta-data tagging. SGML (Standard Generalized Markup Language) was developed for the publishing industry with predecessor versions dating back to the 1960s. Only recently has the notion of developing tags for knowledge objects that might be reused and repurposed for a variety of learning purposes become a recognized and supported area of investigation. Ironically, instructional tags were suggested more than 5 years ago but remain unexplored (Spector et al., 1996).

Decision Support Systems for ID

As noted earlier, weak systems are those that are intended to extend the capabilities of humans and are generally well suited for supporting activities in complex and ill-defined domains. Some decision support systems have

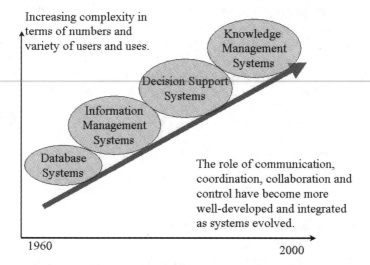

FIG. 12.1. Increasing complexity of information systems.

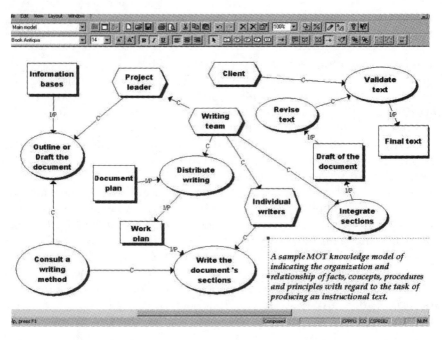

FIG. 12.2.   MOT—a knowledge-modeling tool for instructional planning.

been developed with stunning success for relatively well-defined domains. Indeed, expert systems and electronic performance support systems in general have met with much success in well-defined domains.

Notably, progress in applying these technologies to the domain of instructional planning (not especially well structured) has also met with success. In general, the "upstream" support of ID (analysis of needs, strategic and tactical lesson/course/curriculum planning, and instructional project management) is not as well supported as "downstream" activities such as the delivery of instruction and creation of microworlds and other kinds of learning environments. Powerful decision support tools for ID have been developed over a 10-year period at LICEF—the Center for Research at Télé-Université (the distance learning university for the University of Quebec; see http://www.licef.teluq.uquebec.ca/anglais/index.html). An example of such a decision support planning tool for ID is the knowledge-modeling tool called MOT (*modélisation par objets types*; see Fig. 12.2).

Knowledge Management Systems for ID

Knowledge management systems represent an extension of a previous generation of ICT tools that integrates many aspects of computer-supported collaborative work (CSCW) environments. Key characteristics of knowledge management systems include (see Fig. 12.1):

1. Communications among various users for a variety of purposes (e.g., integrated support for e-mail, discussion forums, and chat sessions).
2. Coordination of activities of various users for different purposes (e.g., the ability to share calendars, schedule resources, etc.).
3. Collaboration among user groups on the creation, modification, and dissemination of a variety of artifacts (e.g., shared workspaces and the ability to share documents so that team members can edit, annotate, lock/unlock, and distribute documents).
4. Control of processes to ensure progress and integrity of projects (e.g., controlled access to relevant resources, automated version control, integrated audit trails, etc.).

Powerful CSCW tools and systems have already had an impact in business, industry, and government and have made their way into various downstream instructional implementations. Such knowledge management systems are now beginning to be used to support upstream instructional planning and development processes. As a consequence, what instructional designers do and how instructional design team members interact is changing.

Two examples involving the use of knowledge management systems in the less well-defined aspects of upstream instructional planning include a European Fifth Framework Project called Adapt[IT] (Spector, Eseryel, & Schuver-van Blanken, 2001; see also http://www.7m.com/aspire/case/cs_adaptit_01.htm) and efforts at Syracuse University to integrate the Xerox Docushare system into ID (Ganesan, Edmonds, & Spector, 2001). Figure 12.3 depicts a knowledge management system in use to support education planning and implementation.

There are as yet insufficient data to draw conclusions and make inferences with regard to these changes. However, there are sufficient data to support formulation of a conceptual framework and initial hypotheses concerning how best to integrate knowledge management into the design of instruction (Spector & Edmonds, 2002).

The system depicted in Fig. 12.3 is based on Xerox Docushare, a system developed in the United States for sharing, exchanging, and managing documents. As it happens, this system supports all four critical functions of a knowledge management system: communication, coordination, collaboration, and control, as does the SevenMountains Integrate/Aspire system and several others (e.g., Lotus Notes).

These applications of knowledge management to ID suggest that instructional practice will continue to be transformed by technology and that ill-

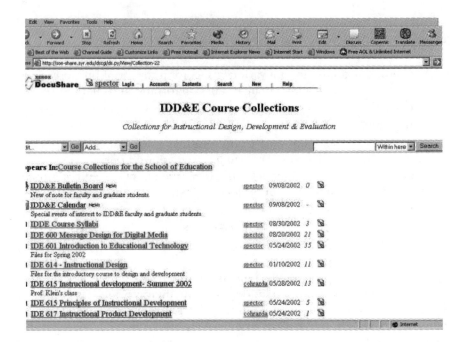

FIG. 12.3. A knowledge management system used to support education.

defined domains can indeed be better supported by ICT than is now possible. This last topic is pursued briefly in the next section.

COMPLEX DOMAINS AND SYSTEM DYNAMICS

Complex systems emerged as a separate field of study in the latter half of the 20th century (Forrester, 1961). According to the pattern cited earlier, this technology was first developed to solve a military problem for the government of the United States. Subsequent applications in business and industry soon followed (Forrester, 1985, 1992; Senge, 1990). Since then, a number of persons in the system dynamics community have developed strong interests in applying system dynamics to educational settings (Davidsen, 1993, 1994, 1996; Spector & Davidsen, 1997, 1998, 2000; Sterman, 1994). Characteristics of complex domains include:

1. Numerous, interrelated components.
2. Nonlinear relationships among system components.
3. Delays in effects within the system.
4. Changes in internal system structure (e.g., changes in dominant influencing factors or how components are related).

5. Dynamic behaviors and results specific to the current state of a system.

6. Uncertainty and fuzziness.

Two particular aspects of system dynamics and systems thinking in general are especially relevant to this discussion and the principles developed at the beginning of this chapter. First, system dynamics and its close cousin, systems thinking, provide the technology to support multiple representations of complex and ill-structured domains. Causal influence diagrams most often associated with systems thinking can help learners acquire a holistic perspective to a problem situation that is especially relevant when attempting to integrate multiple dimensions and aspects of a problem. Stock and flow diagrams, most often associated with system dynamics, provide a visual representation of causal relationships that can be used to generate interactive simulations to support decision making, experimentation, hypothesis, and policy formulation. All of these activities are important for the support of deep understanding in complex and ill-structured domains.

Second, these two types of representation are quite different and can be used individually to support different learning outcomes. They can also be used together to support a particular approach to learning in complex domains called *model-facilitated learning* (Spector & Davidsen, 2000; see Fig. 12.4). Model-facilitated learning is built around the notions of graduated

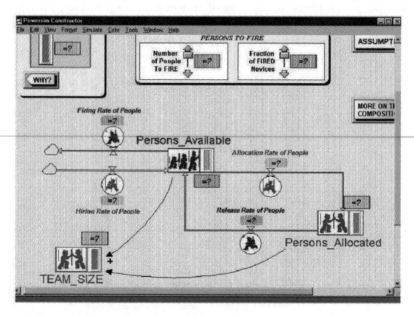

FIG. 12.4. Transparency and graduated complexity in model-facilitated learning.

complexity (gradually increasing the complexity of problem situations in which learners are immersed) and transparency (providing learners with access to underlying models used to generate output data and behavior in simulations). The two arrows labeled with the plus sign in Fig. 12.4 are derived from a causal loop representation that can be shown separately for the entire system. Figure 12.4 shows that as more persons become available, the size of project teams tends to increase. How many people are available for team assignments depends on several flow rates; hiring and firing rates influence the available pool of available project personnel, as do the rates at which people are assigned to and released from projects. Such a representation can promote a systemic view of a complex system. The flows into and out of rectangular-shaped containers represent a visualization of the underlying mathematical function that can be explored in more detail (e.g., a specific formula associated with a component). In addition, multiple levels of elaboration are available, and interaction typically occurs in small groups after a period of interaction with the computer-based simulation, consistent with the principles of experience, context, and integration.

What is not well established is whether, when, and how model-facilitated learning or some other approach promotes understanding for various learners with regard to a variety of problems and scenarios in complex domains. One possible explanation for the knowledge deficit in this area is the lack of a reliable and well-established procedure for assessing progress of learning. As it happens, the use of annotated causal influence diagrams may prove to be a reliable method to assess learning in complex domains (Christensen, Spector, Sioutine, & McCormick, 2000; Seel, Al-Diban, & Blumschein, 2000; see Fig. 12.5). The basic assumption behind this meth-

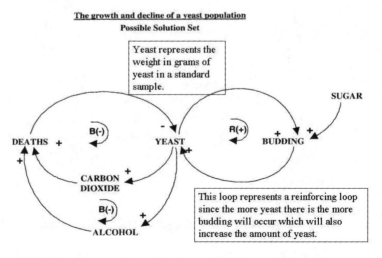

FIG. 12.5. Annotated causal influence diagrams used to assess learning.

odology is that experts in a domain exhibit recognizable patterns of causal representations for various problem situations. Beginning learners in a complex domain exhibit relatively chaotic causal representations that are recognizably different from those of experts. As learning progresses, those causal representations gradually begin to resemble those of experts. The notion is not that there is a single correct causal representation. Rather, since these annotated representations lend themselves to multiple levels of analysis (comparing major influence factors, analyzing descriptions of factors, noting differences and similarities in delays and directions of influence, etc.), the notion is that they provide a way to operationalize the degree to which a novice practitioner has become a recognized member of a community of practice.

There are insufficient data to determine how successful this assessment mechanism will be. However, the efforts reported thus far indicate much promise (Christensen et al., 2000; Seel et al., 2000).

CONCLUDING REMARKS

With regard to progress in the specific area of automated support for instructional design, it is possible to conclude that strong support only works for those activities and processes that are well defined, which are relatively few in ID. The same principle extends to instructional delivery as exhibited in such systems as GTE. When the subject domain and outcomes are very well defined, instructional support can be much more prescriptive than when the subject and outcomes are less well defined. This is not surprising nor is it inconsistent with a learner-centered approach that encourages learner construction of knowledge objects and artifacts. What would be inconsistent with a learner-centered approach would be to argue that all learning activities should be open-ended and nonprescriptive, regardless of purpose, nature of the task, or characteristics of individual learners. This last remark represents a position consistent with the Uncertainty Principle introduced at the beginning of this chapter.

With regard to trends in ICT in education, it seems reasonable to conclude that new opportunities to support learning as well as the planning and creation of meaningful learning environments and successful instructional systems will continue to emerge. How new technologies will affect the way that instructional designers work will be interesting to observe. Whether changed patterns of interaction result in improved learning will be especially interesting to determine. Both areas are rich in terms of potential research contribution to learning and instruction.

Although meta-data tagging schemes and the notion of knowledge objects promise the potential to reduce the cost of producing learning environments and instructional systems while promoting quality and improving learning, there is very little evidence that this is occurring. Lest the ID community become overly optimistic, it is worth observing that the introduction of object-oriented programming in software engineering did not make it easier for nonprogrammers to create programs nor did it accelerate the process of acquiring competence and expertise as a software engineer. Similar promises have been made with regard to knowledge objects and new information and communication technologies. Some have even argued that teachers and instructional designers will become obsolete as knowledge objects proliferate and access technologies become more powerful (Schank & Cleary, 1995). It is much more likely that what teachers, instructional designers, and students do will change gradually on account of ICT.

Whether such changes will contribute to improved learning outcomes and deeper insights into especially problematic and challenging areas remains largely unknown. As Dijkstra (2001) argued, instruction involves communications in which both the student and the teacher can take the initiative. The purpose of the communication is to facilitate learning. Technology can support both teachers and learners, but technology cannot replace the communication. Finally, though it may be true that we know less than we are inclined to believe, it is also quite likely that ICT can help us to learn things that we thought were beyond our grasp.

ACKNOWLEDGMENTS

The author would like to thank the editors of this volume for their assistance in improving the manuscript. This chapter is based on a presentation made at the international conference "Addressing the Challenges of Learning Through Technology and Curriculum" held at the University of Freiburg, May 2–5, 2001, organized by Professor Norbert Seel and his many able colleagues and graduate students. Thanks to all of the participants for their comments and reactions to that earlier version.

REFERENCES

Barrows, H. S. (1985). *How to design a problem-based curriculum for the preclinical years.* New York: Springer-Verlag.

Bruner, J. S. (1985). Models of the learner. *Educational Researcher, 14*(6), 5–8.

Christensen, D. L., Spector, J. M., Sioutine, A., & McCormack, D. (2000, August). *Evaluating the impact of system dynamics based learning environments: Preliminary study.* Paper presented at the 18th International Conference of the System Dynamics Society, Bergen, Norway.

Collins, A. (1991). Cognitive apprenticeship and instructional technology. In L. Idol & B. F. Jones (Eds.), *Educational values and cognitive instruction: Implications for reform* (pp. 121–138). Hillsdale, NJ: Lawrence Erlbaum Associates.

Collins, A., Brown, J. S., & Newman, S. E. (1989). Cognitive apprenticeship: Teaching the crafts of reading, writing, and mathematics. In L. B. Resnick (Ed.), *Knowing, learning, and instruction: Essays in honor of Robert Glaser* (pp. 453–494). Hillsdale, NJ: Lawrence Erlbaum Associates.

Davidsen, P. I. (1993). System dynamics as a platform for educational software production. In B. Z. Barta, J. Eccleston, & R. Hambusch (Eds.), *Computer mediated education of information technology professionals and advanced end-users* (pp. 27–40). Amsterdam: North-Holland.

Davidsen, P. I. (1994). The systems dynamics approach to computer-based management learning environments: Implications and their implementations in Powersim. In J. D. W. Morecroft & J. D. Sterman (Eds.), *Modeling for learning organizations* (pp. 301–316). Portland, OR: Productivity Press.

Davidsen, P. I. (1996). Educational features of the system dynamics approach to modelling and simulation. *Journal of Structured Learning, 12*(4), 269–290.

Dijkstra, S. (2000). Epistemology, psychology of learning and instructional design. In J. M. Spector & T. M. Anderson (Eds.), *Integrated and holistic perspectives on learning, instruction and technology: Understanding complexity* (pp. 213–232). Dordrecht, Netherlands: Kluwer.

Dijkstra, S. (2001). Principles of design for multimedia-based training. *Journal of Structural Learning and Intelligent Systems, 14*(4), 467–482.

Dijkstra, S., Seel, N., Schott, F., & Tennyson, R. D. (Eds.). (1997). *Instructional design: International perspectives: Vol. 2. Solving instructional design problems.* Mahwah, NJ: Lawrence Erlbaum Associates.

Dörner, D. (1996). *The logic of failure: Why things go wrong and what we can do to make them right* (R. Kimber & R. Kimber, Trans.). New York: Holt.

Driscoll, M. (1998). *Web-based training: Using technology to design learning experiences.* San Francisco: Jossey-Bass.

Ellsworth, J. B. (2000). *Surviving change: A survey of educational change models.* Syracuse, NY: ERIC Clearinghouse on Information and Technology.

Forrester, J. W. (1961). *Industrial dynamics.* Cambridge, MA: MIT Press.

Forrester, J. W. (1985). 'The' model versus a modeling 'process'. *System Dynamics Review, 1*(1), 133–134.

Forrester, J. W. (1992). Policies, decision, and information sources for modeling. *European Journal of Operational Research, 59*(1), 42–63.

Ganesan, R., Edmonds, G. S., & Spector, J. M. (2001). The changing nature of instructional design for networked learning. In C. Jones & C. Steeples (Eds.), *Networked learning in higher education* (pp. 93–109). Berlin: Springer-Verlag.

Goodyear, P. (2000). Environments for lifelong learning: Ergonomics, architecture and educational design. In J. M. Spector & T. M. Anderson (Eds.), *Integrated and holistic perspectives on learning, instruction and technology: Understanding complexity* (pp. 1–18). Dordrecht, Netherlands: Kluwer.

Jonassen, D. H., Hernandez-Serrano, J., & Choi, I. (2000). Integrating constructivism and learning technologies. In J. M. Spector & T. M. Anderson (Eds.), *Integrated and holistic perspectives on learning, instruction and technology: Understanding complexity* (pp. 103–128). Dordrecht, Netherlands: Kluwer.

Lave, J. (1988). *Cognition in practice: Mind, mathematics and culture in everyday life.* Cambridge, England: Cambridge University Press.

Lave, J., & Wenger, E. (1990). *Situated learning: Legitimate peripheral participation.* Cambridge, England: Cambridge University Press.

Leont'ev, A. N. (1978). *Activity, consciousness, personality.* Englewood Cliffs, NJ: Prentice-Hall.

Malone, T., & Crowston, K. (1993). The interdisciplinary study of coordination. *Computing Surveys, 26*(1), 87–119.

Merrill, M. D. (2001). First principles of instruction. *Journal of Structural Learning and Intelligent Systems, 14*(4), 459–466.

Nardi, B. (Ed.). (1996). *Context and consciousness: Activity theory and human–computer interaction.* Cambridge, MA: MIT Press.

Piaget, J. (1929). *The child's conception of the world.* New York: Harcourt, Brace, Jovanovich.

Reigeluth, C. M., & Stein, F. (1983). The elaboration theory of instruction. In C. M. Reigeluth (Ed.), *Instructional-design theories and models: An overview of their current status* (pp. 335–381). Hillsdale, NJ: Lawrence Erlbaum Associates.

Richey, R., Fields, D. C., & Foxon, M. (with Roberts, R. C., Spannaus, T., & Spector, J. M.). (2001). *Instructional design competencies: The standards* (3rd ed.). Syracuse, NY: ERIC Clearinghouse on Information and Technology and the International Board of Standards for Training, Performance and Instruction.

Salomon, G. (Ed.). (1993). *Distributed cognitions: Psychological and educational considerations.* New York: Cambridge University Press.

Schank, R., & Cleary, C. (1995). *Engines for education.* Hillsdale, NJ: Lawrence Erlbaum Associates.

Seel, N. M., Al-Diban, S., & Blumschein, P. (2000). Mental models & instructional planning. In J. M. Spector & T. M. Anderson (Eds.), *Integrated and holistic perspectives on learning, instruction and technology: Understanding complexity* (pp. 129–158). Dordrecht, Netherlands: Kluwer.

Senge, P. (1990). *The fifth discipline: The art and practice of the learning organization.* New York: Doubleday.

Sfard, A. (1998). On two metaphors for learning and the dangers of choosing just one. *Educational Research, 27*(2), 4–12.

Silberman, M. (1998). *Active training: A handbook of techniques, designs, case examples, and tips.* San Francisco: Jossey-Bass.

Spector, J. M. (1994). Integrating instructional science, learning theory, and technology. In R. D. Tennyson (Ed.), *Automating instructional design, development, and delivery* (pp. 243–259). Berlin: Springer-Verlag.

Spector, J. M. (1995). Integrating and humanizing the process of automating instructional design. In R. D. Tennyson & A. E. Barron (Eds.), *Automating instructional design: Computer-based development and delivery tools* (pp. 523–546). Berlin: Springer-Verlag.

Spector, J. M. (1999). Intelligent support for instructional development: Approaches and limits. In J. V. D. Akker, R. M. Branch, K. Gustafson, N. Nieveen, & T. Plomb (Eds.), *Design approaches and tools in education and training* (pp. 279–290). Dordrecht, Netherlands: Kluwer.

Spector, J. M. (2001). An overview of progress and problems in educational technology. *Interactive Educational Multimedia, 3,* 27–37.

Spector, J. M., & Anderson, T. M. (Eds.). (2000). *Integrated and holistic perspectives on learning, instruction and technology: Understanding complexity.* Dordrecht, Netherlands: Kluwer.

Spector, J. M., Arnold, E. M., & Wilson, A. S. (1996). A Turing test for automatically generated instruction. *Journal of Structural Learning, 12*(4), 310–313.

Spector, J. M., & Davidsen, P. I. (1997). Creating engaging courseware using system dynamics. *Computers in Human Behavior, 13*(2), 127–155.

Spector, J. M., & Davidsen, P. I. (1998). Constructing learning environments using system dynamics. *Journal of Courseware Engineering, 1,* 5–12.

Spector, J. M., & Davidsen, P. I. (2000). Designing technology-enhanced learning environments. In B. Abbey (Ed.), *Instructional and cognitive impacts of Web-based education* (pp. 241–261). Hershey, PA: The Idea Group.

Spector, J. M., & Edmonds, G. S. (2002). Knowledge management in instructional design. *ERIC-IT Digest.* Syracuse: The ERIC Clearinghouse on Information and Technology.

Spector, J. M., Eseryel, D., & Schuver-van Blanken, M. J. (2001, June). *Current practice in designing training for complex skills: Implications for design and evaluation of Adapt[IT].* Paper presented at ED-Media 2001, Tampere, Finland.

Spector, J. M., Polson, M. C., & Muraida, D. J. (Eds.). (1993). *Automating instructional design: Concepts and issues.* Englewood Cliffs, NJ: Educational Technology Publications.

Spiro, R. J., Coulson, R. L., Feltovich, P. J., & Anderson, D. (1988). Cognitive flexibility theory: Advanced knowledge acquisition in ill-structured domains. In V. Patel (Ed.), *Proceedings of the 10th Annual Conference of the Cognitive Science Society* (pp. 433–439). Hillsdale, NJ: Lawrence Erlbaum Associates.

Spiro, R. J., Feltovich, P. J., Jacobson, M. J., & Coulson, R. L. (1992). Cognitive flexibility, constructivism and hypertext: Random access instruction for advanced knowledge acquisition in ill-structured domains. In T. Duffy & D. Jonassen (Eds.), *Constructivism and the technology of instruction* (pp. 57–75). Hillsdale, NJ: Lawrence Erlbaum Associates.

Spiro, R. J., Vispoel, W., Schmitz, J., Samarapungavan, A., & Boerger, A. (1987). Knowledge acquisition for application: Cognitive flexibility and transfer in complex content domains. In B. C. Britton (Ed.), *Executive control processes* (pp. 177–200). Hillsdale, NJ: Lawrence Erlbaum Associates.

Sterman, J. D. (1994). Learning in and about complex systems. *System Dynamics Review, 10*(2–3), 291–330.

Tennyson, R. D., Schott, F., Seel, N., & Dijkstra, S. (Eds.). (1997). *Instructional design: International perspectives: Vol. 1. Theory, research, and models.* Mahwah, NJ: Lawrence Erlbaum Associates.

van Merriënboer, J. J. G. (1997). *Training complex cognitive skills: A four-component instructional design model for technical training.* Englewood Cliffs, NJ: Educational Technology Publications.

Vygotsky, L. S. (1978). *Mind in society: The development of higher psychological processes* (M. Cole, V. John-Steiner, S. Scribner, & E. Souberman, Eds. and Trans.). Cambridge, MA: Harvard University Press.

Chapter 13

Instructional Design Principles for Adaptivity in Open Learning Environments

Detlev Leutner
Duisburg-Essen University, Germany

In an open learning environment, the learner him- or herself decides when, where, what, and why to learn. Thus, learning in an open environment is a special case of self-regulated or self-directed learning (see Boekaerts, Pintrich, & Zeidner, 2000). The problem, however, is that the ability to regulate one's learning itself has to be learned ("learning to learn"), and the learner needs adaptive support when the learning environment is changed from a traditional closed to a new open format. Adaptivity is present in a learning environment when there is an optimal dynamic fit between the amount of support a learner needs for learning and the amount of support the learning environment provides. Responsibility for such an optimal fit between learner and learning environment is the teacher's, an "art of teaching" that was almost described by Skinner (1954). This chapter, however, deals with the questions of how an individual learner's need for instructional support can be met within a computer-based open learning environment and what kind of principles can be thought of to adaptively improve the fit between the learner and the computer-based learning environment (Leutner, 1992a, 1995, 1998a, 1999).

The chapter is organized into three parts: In the first part, in order to be able to answer questions like "What kind of support should be provided?" and "Which should be adapted to what?," a few basic concepts of learning, teaching, and instruction are treated. In the second part, 10 adaptation principles are presented that proved to be effective in a series of published experimental studies with computer-based instructional systems. Finally, in the third part, the application of these 10 principles to open learning environments is discussed.

SOME BASIC CONCEPTS FROM INSTRUCTIONAL PSYCHOLOGY

Learning can be defined from two different points of view (Leutner, 1998a). According to the first view, learning is an automatic process of the acquisition of knowledge, which is a genuine cognitive psychology point of view. According to the second view, learning is a goal-directed process of the acquisition of knowledge in the sense of "studying," "training," and so on, which is a genuine educational point of view. Within this view, learning means "teaching oneself" or "being one's own teacher," teaching being itself a goal-directed process that aims at the control of learning processes. Thus, *self-regulated learning* deals with the self-control of learning processes, and this raises the question of whether the learning process can be decomposed into smaller components. An answer to this question can be found in Klauer's (1985) "framework for a theory of teaching," in which the concept of "teaching function" is proposed.

Following Klauer (1985), teaching and learning (i.e., learning according to the educational view) can be described as controlling the application of *teaching functions*. Teaching functions are functions that have to be fulfilled so that learning (in the sense of knowledge acquisition) can take place. Based on cognitive psychological theories of the human memory, the following teaching functions can be postulated:

1. The learner must be motivated (teaching function "motivation").
2. The learner has to have access to that information which is to be learned (teaching function "information").
3. The learner has to process the information (teaching function "information processing").
4. The learner has to store the information in memory and must be able to retrieve the newly acquired knowledge (teaching function "storage and retrieval").
5. The learner must be able to apply the knowledge and to transfer it to new contexts of application (teaching function "application and transfer").
6. Last but not least, the learner has to control and regulate the application of all these teaching functions in such a way that the goals at which the functions are aiming will be reached (teaching function "regulation and control").

From everyday experience as well as from studies in learning and instruction (e.g., Leopold & Leutner, 2002; Leutner & Leopold, 2003a, 2003b), we know that there are large individual differences in the ability to control the application of teaching functions for oneself, that is, to be a self-regulated learner: For example, some learners tend to stop their learning activities too late or too early, which leads to insufficient learning results on the one hand or to unnecessary learning effort on the other (Leutner, 1992c, 1993a; Tennyson & Rothen, 1977; Vos, 1995). As another example, we know from many studies that scores on learning strategy inventories do not usually correlate with test and exam scores: Students often report themselves to be controlled, strategic learners but they are obviously not able to control and regulate the application of learning strategies in such a way that their learning results are improved (Leopold & Leutner, 2002; Leutner, Barthel, & Schreiber, 2001).

Adaptive learning and instruction means to distribute the responsibility for the control and the regulation of teaching functions dynamically between the learner and the learning environment: If the learner him- or herself is able to control and regulate the application of teaching functions, then there is no need for instructional support. However, if the learner is not able, then some agents within the learning environment should be responsible for offering exactly that amount of support the learner needs (Fig. 13.1). This can be achieved by either eliminating or compensating for specific deficits of the learner or by taking advantage of specific abilities (Salomon, 1972).

Adaptive learning environments can be designed according to two different adaptation procedures: The first procedure, macroadaptation, is to implement some kind of offline adaptation, which means to have an open-

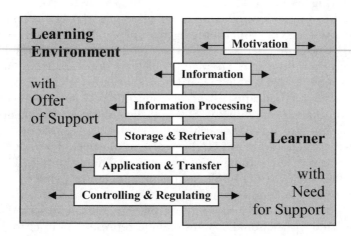

FIG. 13.1.   Teaching functions in an adaptive learning environment.

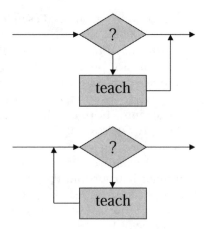

FIG. 13.2. Macroadaptation (upper figure) and microadaptation (lower figure).

loop, feedforward control of the learning process (upper part of Fig. 13.2); this is to externally adapt the way of teaching to some features of the learner that are assumed to be quite constant over time. The second procedure, microadaptation, is to implement some kind of online adaptation, which means to have a closed-loop, feedback control of the learning process (lower part of Fig. 13.2); this is to internally adapt the way of teaching to some features of the learner that change moment-by-moment. Learning environments with offline adaptation may be called adaptable, those with online adaptation may be called adaptive (Leutner, 1998a).

Focusing on computer-assisted instructional systems, so-called Intelligent Tutoring Systems (ITS; e.g., Wenger, 1987) seem to represent a rather high road of implementing adaptation principles. An ITS is constructed based on principles of artificial intelligence and can be characterized by having three basic components: (a) an expert module that is able to solve problems in a specific domain of knowledge which are not preprogrammed, (b) a diagnosis module that is able to learn from the learner and, for example, to simulate his or her conceptions and misconceptions of the domain of knowledge, and (c) a tutor module that is able to generate instructional principles which—again—are not necessarily preprogrammed. Up to now, however, only a very limited number of ITS have successfully been developed for very specific and restricted domains of knowledge. Thus, although ITS represent a rather high road of implementing adaptation principles, it seems to be a high but very bumpy road.

As opposed to Intelligent Tutoring Systems, so-called Adaptive Computer-Assisted Instructional Systems seem to represent a rather low road of implementing adaptation principles. However, without having to apply principles of artificial intelligence, adaptation principles can be predesigned and programmed in a rather simple way. Thus, Adaptive Computer-Assisted Instructional Systems represent a low but rather smooth way of implementing adaptation principles.

In the following section, 10 examples of adaptation principles are presented. All of them have been implemented in computer-assisted instructional systems with traditional programming or authoring tools and without using artificial intelligence software. And all of them are based on cognitive-psychological theory and related empirical research: They have been empirically investigated by conducting experimental studies (most of them following a control-group design), and they have been proven to be effective in increasing the learning outcomes of students. Having presented the principles and the related research, I will discuss how the principles can be applied to open learning environments.

TEN ADAPTATION PRINCIPLES FOR COMPUTER-ASSISTED INSTRUCTIONAL SYSTEMS

The following principles are presented according to the same schema: First, the instructional problem to be addressed and then the way in which to diagnose the problem are outlined. Second, the type of adaptation is noted, and the adaptation approach is described. Third, the empirical evidence for the effectiveness of the approach and further reading are referenced.

Principle 1: Adapting the Amount of Instruction

One of the most important instructional problems is to decide how much learning and instruction is necessary in order to reach a given goal. Especially in situations of self-regulated learning, we know that many students overestimate their level of academic achievement. As a consequence, these students stop learning too early, before they have really reached the goal of learning. As a result, they are not able to pass exams successfully. On the other hand, we know that a reasonable amount of students underestimate their level of academic achievement. As a consequence, these students stop learning too late, when they have overlearned a given subject to a large and unnecessary degree. As a result, they will receive excellent grades in exams but they will have wasted learning time and effort that could have been used for learning other materials and subjects. Obviously, this is a problem in self-regulated learning. However, it is also a problem in situations in which students are instructed and in which external agents in the learning environment try to control and regulate students' learning processes.

Assuming that it is not a very easy educational task to get students to be self-regulated learners, there is a quite simple way of compensating for students' inability to assess their level of goal attainment by applying a very simple principle of microadaptation. The adaptation approach has been called the "moving test window" (Leutner, 1992c). The rationale is as follows: Given that the specific goal of learning and instruction to be addressed can be represented by a universe of items, the learner has to work through a series of randomly chosen practice items (receiving informative feedback following each response) as long as he or she has five correct item responses in direct sequence (see Fig. 13.3 for an example): The nominal binomial probability of observing five correct responses in a test of five items implies that the learner has reached a competence level of 75% or higher. However, the assumptions underlying the binomial test model (Klauer, 1987) are obviously not fulfilled when practice items are used as test items, because the ability parameter, which has to be assumed to be constant over the time of testing, will increase, due to the fact that learners receive informative feedback following each item response. Thus, learning will take place, what is indeed intended during practice. Experimental research was conducted (Leutner, 1993a) to solve the test-length dilemma of requiring as many test items as possible (for getting the most highly *reliable* test scores) and, at the same time, requiring as few test items as possible (for getting the most highly *valid* estimates of the current level of increasing ability). Participants in the two experiments were university students, and the subject matter was concept learning in the field of mathematics (geometry) and writing (punctuation rules). The results, contrasting this very simple decision principle with other, more sophisticated decision principles (e.g., Tennyson & Rothen, 1977; see also Vos, 1995), indicate that the "moving test window" with a window width of five practice items is very robust against violations of the binomial assumption of a constant ability parameter: This decision rule for adapting the amount of instruction during practice can reasonably well guarantee that students do not stop learning too early or too late, thereby being able to reach the intended goal of learning and/or instruction.

At first glance, the moving-test-window approach seems to be applicable only in very simple-structured drill-and-practice situations in which no

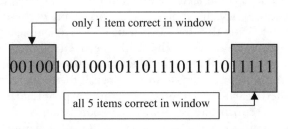

FIG. 13.3.   Moving test window with five practice items.

more than one goal is addressed. However, the rule can also be applied to more complex situations with more than one goal. In such a case, it is only necessary to present a random sequence of practice items across goals, while keeping a record of the number of test windows and goals involved (see Leutner, 1992c).

Principle 2: Adapting the Sequence of Instructional Units

Some students are not able to realistically estimate their level of comprehension when reading some instructional material, which can be diagnosed by letting students solve comprehension items at the end of an instructional unit. A simple way to compensate for this inability and to eliminate miscomprehension and misunderstandings is to apply classical principles of programmed instruction, following the old and well-known ideas of nonlinear programmed instruction (Crowder, 1959; see Leutner, 1998a). These ideas are simply implemented by having the student solve a comprehension item and—if the answer is not correct—by forwarding (branching) him or her back to the instructional unit read before (Fig. 13.4) or to some other remedial instructional units. One question concerning this approach is where to place the comprehension items; for example, following each screen page of a computer-based training (CBT) program or as an item bundle at the end of a large chapter of a CBT program. Experimental research, with university students learning from a science text, shows that it is more effective to have item bundles at the end of a chapter (Nussbaum & Leutner, 1986a).

Principle 3: Adapting the Content of Information

For hypertext learning environments it is well known that many students "get lost in hyperspace." A comparable problem is present when searching a large database, such as PsycLit or the SSCI (Social Sciences Citation In-

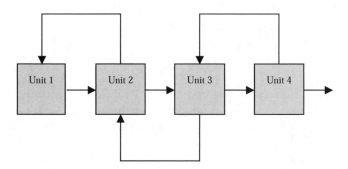

FIG. 13.4. Traditional programmed instruction with branching between instructional units.

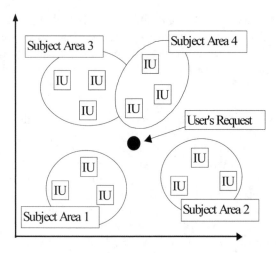

FIG. 13.5.   User's request and lexical similarity of information units (IU).

dex): Here one often gets too many references—sometimes several thousands—for a given inquiry. In both cases, hypertext and information retrieval, learners have problems finding some specific information they are looking for. A way to compensate for a learner's deficits is to offer him or her, given a specific request, *lexically similar* information units. Such units can be found by analyzing the so-called tri-gram structure of a user's request and comparing this structure with the tri-gram structures of all other information units given in the database or hypertext (Bruenken, 1998). Given this analysis, it is quite simple to rank all units according to their calculated similarity to the request and to offer the most similar units to the user (Fig. 13.5). Research studies (Bruenken, 1998; Bruenken, Schreiber, & Leutner, 1998) on designing a user interface for a medical hypertext reveal that this procedure generates information offers that are assessed to be useful by professional medical doctors. For further research on adaptive hypertexts, see Brusilovsky, Kobsa, and Vassileva (1998).

Principle 4: Adapting the Presentation Format of Information

Information can be presented to a learner in different representation formats, especially pictorially and textually. Furthermore, learners may differ concerning their preference for learning with pictorial or with textual learning material. Based on this cognitive-style distinction of visualizers and verbalizers, one can expect that visualizers will be impeded when they do not have access to their preferred pictorial material during learning. A simple way to help compensate for the learning deficit of visualizers is to pro-

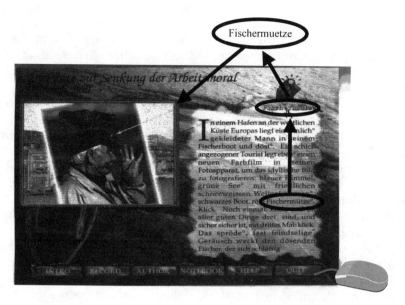

FIG. 13.6.   Short story with choice options for explaining unknown words.

vide them with pictures on demand by choosing a macroadaptation approach. This was evaluated in a multimedia learning environment (Plass, Chun, Mayer, & Leutner, 1998). Students had to read a literary text in a foreign language. The text, a short story, was presented on a PC, and unknown words could be looked up either by requesting a text translation of the word or by requesting a picture that represented the meaning of the word (Fig. 13.6). Some words had only text explanations available, other words had both. The visualizer–verbalizer learning style was measured by direct observation of students' preferential choice behavior when they had to choose between a picture and a text explanation (Leutner & Plass, 1998). The results showed that the choice option especially helped visualizers in comprehending the story: They had great problems remembering those propositions that had unknown words explained only by text translations; however, they had no problems remembering those propositions that had unknown words explained by both pictorial and textual material (for related research, see Mayer, 1997, 2001; Schnotz & Kulhavy, 1994; Weidenmann, 1994).

Principle 5: Adapting Task Difficulty

Many learners have problems in choosing a suitable level of difficulty when they have the choice between different tasks or problems during learning. Sometimes they choose tasks that are too easy, sometimes they choose tasks that are too hard. Moreover, some learners tend to choose too hard a task in general, and some learners tend to choose too easy a task in general. Whatever is chosen, when the choice does not fit the learner's ability level, learning effectiveness and efficiency will be lowered. But there are ways to compensate for a learner's choice deficits by advising him or her online what kind of problem to choose. One of these ways follows a study of Nussbaum and Leutner (1986b) on discovery learning. In that study, university students worked on a large number of practice problems. The problems had been constructed like figural-matrix-like intelligence-test items, and a small number of rules were sufficient for solving them all. The students' task was to discover those rules. All the problems corresponded to the test model of Rasch (1960; see also Rost, 1988) and, thus, for each level of student ability there were a number of problems with a level of difficulty that corresponded to the level of their ability (Fig. 13.7). By running the experiment, Nussbaum and Leutner (1986b) demonstrated that students learned best when they worked on a set of problems that were individually allocated in such a way that they were quite easy in relation to a given student's individual level of ability measured before he or she started discovery learning. Following an idea of Litchfield, Driscoll, and Dempsey (1990), Weinberg, Hornke, and Leutner (1994) implemented the Nussbaum–Leutner macroadaptation approach as a microadaptation approach on a PC. The computer was programmed to choose the best fitting problem online in such a way that when a student's level of ability increases, the difficulty of the best fitting problem also increases. By running an experiment with university students, Weinberg et al. demonstrated that students' level of ability increased remarkably from pretest to posttest when they received informative feedback on the correct problem solution during discovery learning.

p(correct solution)

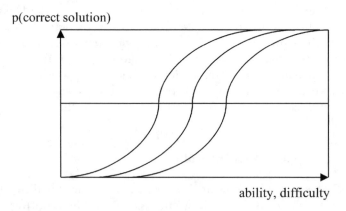

ability, difficulty

FIG. 13.7.   Item-characteristic curves following the Rasch model.

Principle 6: Adapting Concept Definitions

In concept acquisition, many students have problems storing and retrieving the meaning of recently learned new concepts, which results in wrong definitions and erroneous classifications of objects that belong or do not belong to the concept in question. Such a deficit of knowledge can be reduced by implementing a microadaptation approach during concept learning. The basic idea is to introduce the definition of a new concept in terms of other concepts that have been learned just before. Thus, the geometry concept "rectangle" in Fig. 13.8 is not introduced in terms of the distant superordinate concept "four-sided figure" (being a four-sided figure with four angles of 90 degrees). Instead, and given that the concept "parallelogram" has recently been learned, the rectangle is introduced in terms of the concept "parallelogram" (being a parallelogram with four angles of 90 degrees). This approach corresponds to Norman's (1973) idea of web learning (see also Treinies & Einsiedler, 1993), and by running two experiments, one with secondary school students and the other with university students (Leutner, 1992a, 1992b), it could be demonstrated that students' learning of geometry concepts is indeed improved when the approach is implemented in a CBT program.

Principle 7: Adapting System Response Time

In beginning to develop a specific cognitive skill, students should avoid practicing false routines that are based on insufficient knowledge (see An-

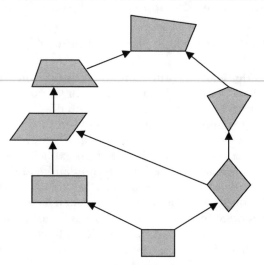

FIG. 13.8.   Abstraction hierarchy of four-sided geometrical figures.

derson, 1983, 1993, and his well-established theory on procedural learning). When a student works on practice problems, insufficient knowledge can be assumed when the student thinks about solving the problem a long time, but the proposed solution is wrong. Thus, wrong problem solutions with long response times might be indicative of low knowledge. Following ideas of Tennyson and Park (1984), this diagnostic indicator can be used to implement a highly effective microadaptation approach for eliminating knowledge deficits while practicing for skill acquisition. The basic idea is to prevent the learner from finding and, thus, practicing a wrong problem solution by explaining to him or her how to find the correct solution. This can be achieved by adaptively controlling the system response or delay time when a problem is presented to the learner. The online adaptation rule is the following: When the learner displays a wrong solution, the system response time for the next problem will be reduced, and the learner will receive the explanation of the correct solution before he or she will have generated a wrong solution. The expectation is that the explanation leads to further skill development, and the learner will then, it is hoped, be able to generate the correct solution for the next problem him- or herself within the limits of the given system response time. Then, when the learner displays the correct solution, which is indicative of skill improvement, the system response time before explaining the solution of the next problem will be increased, giving the learner more opportunities for practicing the skill. However, when there is again a false solution, the system response time is again reduced, and so on, until a prespecified level of skilled behavior is reached. In two experiments with high school and with university students learning German punctuation rules in writing, Leutner and Schumacher (1990) demonstrated that this approach works very well indeed.

Principle 8: Adapting Advice in Exploratory Learning

In the past decade, learning with computer simulations has become increasingly popular (DeJong & VanJoolingen, 1998), and often a discovery learning setting is used: The learner is confronted with a runnable simulation of a complex dynamical system, and his or her task is to figure out how the system works. Thus, the learner has to acquire knowledge in a domain in which the relevant information is not given explicitly: To the contrary, the information is implicit, hidden in the simulation, and has to be made explicit by some skillful exploration behavior. Many learners, however, have great problems in successfully exploring such a computer simulation. As a result, they tend to miss important information and, when they have to make decisions, the decisions are false or less effective. Obviously, these learners have deficits in their exploration behavior (see Kroener, 2001; Suess, 1996), and a microadaptation approach can be designed to compensate for these deficits by automatically advising the learners when they re-

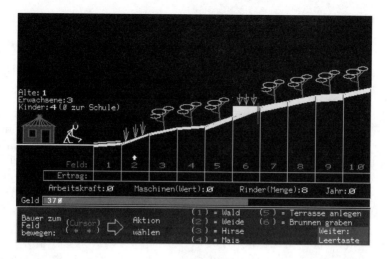

FIG. 13.9. User interface of the computer simulation game "Hunger in the Sahel."

peatedly show false decisions. Such an approach was implemented and evaluated for the computer simulation game "Hunger in the Sahel" (Leutner & Schrettenbrunner, 1989; see also Leutner, 1993b, 2002), displayed in Fig. 13.9. "Hunger in the Sahel" is an instructional computer simulation game that is being used in many geography classes in Europe. The task of the learner is to play the game in the role of a farmer in North Africa: Apart from general decisions (family planning, education, mechanical modernization, etc.), the farmer has to determine the use of 10 lots of land that differ in steepness. The decisions, the climate, and other ecological factors determine the agricultural profit and thus the family's ability to survive. The instructional goal is not to play the game most effectively but to acquire knowledge about how to live and how to survive as a farmer in the geographic area of the Sahel in North Africa. To help the learner reach this goal, adaptive advice was implemented in the game. For example, the learner receives—whenever necessary—warnings (e.g., "If you dig too many water holes, the ground water level may collapse."), corrections (e.g., "There are too many goats on your pasture. Do you want to send them to distant pastures?"), and elaborate comments on events (e.g., "Drought! Not enough water for the plants. Harvest will be poor without irrigation."). Furthermore, the learner is dynamically made aware of using a help-screen page with background information.

A series of three experimental studies with secondary school students and with university students demonstrated that having advice available in a situation where it is obviously helpful and needed helps learners to acquire knowledge about the simulated domain (Leutner, 1992a, 1993b).

**Principle 9: Adapting the Menu Structure of Computer
Software in Software Training Programs**

Learning to use complex computer software most efficiently is a very slow
process of knowledge and cognitive skill acquisition, and, in the early stages
of this process, learners are often lost in the complex "menu space" of the
software: choosing, for example, a menu without choosing any functions
within the menu; repeatedly using, when available, the undo function; and
so on. In order to compensate for a learner's orientation problems and to
successively eliminate knowledge and skill deficits, and following ideas of
Leutner and Vogt (1989), a specific macroadaptive approach to software
training was developed and evaluated. According to this "Double-Fading
Support" approach, which is based on Carroll's (1990; Carroll & Carrithers,
1984) training-wheels idea and on cognitive theories of skill acquisition
(Anderson, 1983, 1993), two types of user support when learning to use a
complex software system—locking the software's functionality and detailed
guidance when working on problems—are gradually faded out during the
training course, in such a way that the learners are able to use the complex
software with minimal instructional support at the end of the course. Two
30-hour training experiments on two different computer-aided design software systems and with technical university students as participants demonstrated the effectiveness of the approach, especially for software with a
deeply structured menu system (Leutner, 2000; Weinberg, 1998).

**Principle 10: Adapting System Control
Versus Learner Control**

Many learners have great problems in self-regulating their learning process,
specifically in self-regulating the application of learning strategies. Often,
although sufficient general cognitive abilities may be available, this inability
results in low achievement or "underachievement." Based on ideas of
Schreiber (1998), a macroadaptation approach was developed and evaluated in order to reduce students' deficits in controlling and regulating the
application of learning strategies. The approach can be implemented as a
pretraining program, and the basic idea is that—besides teaching single
learning strategies—it is useful to instruct students to apply the learning
strategies in such a way that the goals of the specific strategies will be
reached. In a series of four experiments, with university students and with
participants in a vocational retraining program, and measuring how much
knowledge students were able to acquire from reading an instructional text
after having completed the training, it could be demonstrated that the
training program works: The students who received the combined regula-
tion-and-strategy training program outperformed those who received the

strategy training and no training, and the students who received the strategy training also outperformed those without any training (Leutner, Barthel, & Schreiber, 2001; Leutner & Leopold, 2003b; Schreiber, 1998).

DISCUSSION: APPLYING ADAPTATION PRINCIPLES IN OPEN LEARNING ENVIRONMENTS

At the outset of this chapter, an open learning environment was characterized as a learning environment in which the learner him- or herself decides when, where, what, and why to learn. Thus, learning in an open learning environment is nothing but a special case of self-regulated learning, and many learners, due to their low learning ability, have to be expected to need help in such a learning environment. As a solution to this problem, the suggestion was to design adaptive learning environments by augmenting a given learning environment with teaching functions that can be adapted or that adapt themselves to the specific needs of a specific learner: If a learner is able to fulfill all teaching functions for him- or herself, then there is no need for instructional support (see Fig. 13.1); however, if the learner is not able to fulfill all teaching functions, then there is a strong need for support.

Most of the adaptation principles proposed in this chapter were implemented as a kind of "virtual learning assistant" in a given computer-based instructional system. Some of these systems are tutorials for teaching and explaining new materials; others are drill-and-practice programs, computer simulations, hypertexts, or database systems. Some of the adaptation principles are intended to *directly* control a student's learning process: The virtual learning assistant directly realizes those teaching functions that are not realized by the student without asking the student whether he or she is willing to follow. Another way would be to design the virtual learning assistant as an agent who monitors the learner concerning his or her effectiveness in realizing teaching functions by him- or herself and who adaptively *advises* the learner what to do when the observed effectiveness is low. Further research is needed to explore the pros and cons of such an advisement approach. However, in case of doubt, a reasonable "meta"-adaptation principle would be to flexibly switch between a control and an advisement strategy, and smoothly fade out external control whenever and as soon as possible. Thus, implementing external control of learning processes into a learning environment does not really contradict the idea of self-regulated learning or the idea of learning in an open learning environment, because many if not most of the learners indeed need—at least in the beginning—external monitoring and adaptive external control when they try to learn in open learning environments. The fading-out of instructional support gives the opportunity to the learner to take over the responsibility for his or her own learning step by step and, thus, to develop self-regulated learning abilities.

Of course, it is rather pure fiction to expect that all teaching functions and all necessary adaptation principles can be realized by implementing virtual learning assistants in computer-based open learning environments. Without relying on artificial-intelligence approaches, the adaptation principles proposed in this chapter focus on traditional approaches to the design of computer-based learning environments. As a consequence, all those adaptive learning aids that cannot be defined and preprogrammed based on a clear rule system have to be supplied by real-human instead of virtual-computer learning assistants (Astleitner & Leutner, 1994).

ACKNOWLEDGMENT

This work was partly supported by grants from the German Science Foundation (DFG Le 645/3-1, Le 645/4-1, Le 645/6-1 and -2).

REFERENCES

Anderson, J. R. (1983). *The architecture of cognition.* Cambridge, MA: Harvard University Press.

Anderson, J. R. (1993). *Rules of the mind.* Hillsdale, NJ: Lawrence Erlbaum Associates.

Astleitner, H., & Leutner, D. (1994). Computer in Unterricht und Ausbildung [Computers in school and vocational education]. *Zeitschrift für Pädagogik, 40,* 647–664.

Boekaerts, M., Pintrich, P. R., & Zeidner, M. (Eds.). (2000). *Handbook of self-regulated learning.* San Diego, CA: Academic Press.

Bruenken, R. (1998). *Automatische Rekonstruktion von Inhaltsbeziehungen zwischen Dokumenten* [Automatically reconstructing the content-related similarity of text documents]. Aachen, Germany: Shaker.

Bruenken, R., Schreiber, B., & Leutner, D. (1998). Benutzeradaptives Information-Retrieval in Informations- und Lehrsystemen: Modell und experimentelle Validierung [User-adaptive information retrieval in information and learning systems]. In W. Hacker (Ed.), *Computergestuetzter Abstract-Band zum 41. Kongreß der Deutschen Gesellschaft für Psychologie* (p. 15.14). Dresden, Germany: Technische Universität.

Brusilovsky, P., Kobsa, A., & Vassileva, J. (Eds.). (1998). *Adaptive hypertext and hypermedia.* Dordrecht, Netherlands: Kluwer.

Carroll, J. M. (1990). *The Nürnberg funnel: Designing minimalist instruction for practical computer skill.* Cambridge, MA: MIT Press.

Carroll, J. M., & Carrithers, C. (1984). Blocking learner error states in a training-wheels system. *Human Factors, 26,* 377–389.

Crowder, N. A. (1959). Automating tutoring by means of intrinsic programming. In E. Galanter (Ed.), *Automatic teaching: The state of the art* (pp. 109–116). New York: Wiley.

DeJong, T., & VanJoolingen, W. R. (1998). Scientific discovery learning with computer simulations of conceptual domains. *Review of Educational Research, 68,* 179–201.

Klauer, K. J. (1985). Framework for a theory of teaching. *Teaching and Teacher Education, 1,* 5–17.

Klauer, K. J. (1987). *Kriteriumsorientierte Tests* [Criterion-referenced tests]. Göttingen, Germany: Hogrefe.

Kroener, S. (2001). *Intelligenzdiagnostik per Computersimulation* [Assessing intelligence using computer simulations]. Münster, Germany: Waxmann.

Leopold, C., & Leutner, D. (2002). Der Einsatz von Lernstrategien in einer konkreten Lernsituation bei Schülern unterschiedlicher Jahrgangsstufen [The use of learning strategies in a concrete learning situation by students of different ages]. *Beiheft der Zeitschrift für Pädagogik, 45,* 240–258.

Leutner, D. (1992a). *Adaptive Lehrsysteme* [Adaptive instructional systems]. Weinheim, Germany: Psychologie Verlags Union.

Leutner, D. (1992b). Erwerb von Wissen über eine Hierarchie geometrischer Begriffe bei Kindern im Schulalter: Kognitive Ökonomie und vernetztes Lernen durch adaptive Definition neuer Begriffe [The acquisition of knowledge about a hierarchy of geometry concepts by children at school: Cognitive ergonomics and web learning by adaptively defining new concepts]. *Zeitschrift für Entwicklungspsychologie und Pädagogische Psychologie, 24,* 232–248.

Leutner, D. (1992c). Das Testlängendilemma in der lernprozeßbegleitenden Wissensdiagnostik [The test-length dilemma in assessing knowledge during learning]. *Zeitschrift für Pädagogische Psychologie, 6,* 233–238.

Leutner, D. (1993a). Das gleitende Testfenster als Lösung des Testlängendilemmas: Eine Robustheitsstudie [The moving test window as a solution to the test-length dilemma: A robustness study]. *Zeitschrift für Pädagogische Psychologie, 7,* 33–45.

Leutner, D. (1993b). Guided discovery learning with computer-based simulation games: Effects of adaptive and non-adaptive instructional support. *Learning and Instruction, 3,* 113–132.

Leutner, D. (1995). Adaptivität und Adaptierbarkeit multimedialer Lehr- und Informationssysteme [Adaptivity and adaptability of multimedia learning systems]. In L. J. Issing & P. Klimsa (Eds.), *Information und Lernen mit Multimedia* (pp. 139–147). Weinheim, Germany: Psychologie Verlags Union.

Leutner, D. (1998a). Instruktionspsychologie [Instructional psychology]. In D. H. Rost (Ed.), *Handwörterbuch Pädagogische Psychologie* (pp. 198–205). Weinheim, Germany: Psychologie Verlags Union.

Leutner, D. (1998b). Programmierter und computerunterstützter Unterricht [Programmed and computer-based instruction]. In D. H. Rost (Ed.), *Handwörterbuch Pädagogische Psychologie* (pp. 404–409). Weinheim, Germany: Psychologie Verlags Union.

Leutner, D. (1999). Adaptivität in offenen Lernumgebungen [Adaptivity in open learning environments]. In H. Astleitner & A. Sindler (Eds.), *Pädagogische Grundlagen virtueller Ausbildung* (pp. 57–78). Vienna: WUV-Universitätsverlag.

Leutner, D. (2000). Double-fading support—A training approach to complex software systems: Theory, instructional model, and two training experiments. *Journal of Computer-Assisted Learning, 16,* 347–357.

Leutner, D. (2002). The fuzzy relationship of intelligence and problem solving in computer simulations. *Computers in Human Behavior, 18,* 685–697.

Leutner, D., Barthel, A., & Schreiber, B. (2001). Studierende können lernen, sich selbst zum Lernen zu motivieren. Ein Trainingsexperiment [University students are able to learn to motivate themselves for learning: A training experiment]. *Zeitschrift für Pädagogische Psychologie, 15,* 155–167.

Leutner, D., & Leopold, C. (2003a). Lehr-lernpsychologische Grundlagen selbstregulierten Lernens [Instructional psychological foundations of self-regulated learning]. In U. Witthaus, W. Wittwer, & C. Espe (Eds.), *Selbstgesteuertes Lernen—Theoretische und praktische Zugänge* (pp. 43–67). Bielefeld, Germany: Bertelsmann.

Leutner, D., & Leopold, C. (2003b). Selbstreguliertes Lernen als Selbstregulation von Lernstrategien. Ein Trainingsexperiment mit Berufstätigen zum Lernen mit Sachtexten [Self-regulated learning as self-regulation of learning strategies. A training experiment on learning from text]. *Unterrichtswissenschaft, 31*, 38–56.

Leutner, D., & Plass, J. L. (1998). Measuring learning styles with questionnaires versus direct observation of preferential choice behavior: Development of the Visualizer/Verbalizer Behavior Observation Scale (VV-BOS). *Computers in Human Behavior, 14*, 543–557.

Leutner, D., & Schrettenbrunner, H. (1989). Entdeckendes Lernen in komplexen Realitätsbereichen: Evaluation des Computer-Simulationsspiels "Hunger in Nordafrika" [Discovery learning in complex domains: Evaluation of the computer simulation game "Hunger in the Sahel"]. *Unterrichtswissenschaft, 17*, 327–341.

Leutner, D., & Schumacher, G. (1990). The effects of different on-line adaptive response time limits on speed and amount of learning in computer-assisted instruction and intelligent tutoring. *Computers in Human Behavior, 6*, 17–29.

Leutner, D., & Vogt, A. (1989). Didaktisch begründete Anforderungen an schulgeeignete CAD-Systeme [Educational requirements for CAD software which is suitable for schools]. In Landesinstitut für Schule und Weiterbildung (Ed.), *CAD-Technik in berufsbildenden Schulen und Kollegschulen 1988* (pp. 30–46). Soest, Germany: Soester Verlagskontor.

Litchfield, B. C., Driscoll, M. P., & Dempsey, J. V. (1990). Presentation sequence and example difficulty: Their effect on concept and rule learning in computer-based instruction. *Journal of Computer-Based Instruction, 17*, 35–40.

Mayer, R. E. (1997). Multimedia learning: Are we asking the right questions? *Educational Psychologist, 32*, 1–19.

Mayer, R. E. (2001). *Multimedia learning.* Cambridge, England: Cambridge University Press.

Norman, D. (1973). Memory, knowledge and the answering of questions. In R. L. Solso (Ed.), *Contemporary issues in cognitive psychology* (pp. 135–165). New York: Wiley.

Nussbaum, A., & Leutner, D. (1986a). Die Auswirkung der Schwierigkeit textbegleitender Fragen auf die Lernleistung [The effect of the difficulty of text-related questions on learning achievement]. *Zeitschrift für Entwicklungspsychologie und Pädagogische Psychologie, 18*, 230–244.

Nussbaum, A., & Leutner, D. (1986b). Entdeckendes Lernen von Aufgabenlösungsregeln unter verschiedenen Anforderungsbedingungen [Discovery learning of problem-solving rules under varying levels of problem difficulty]. *Zeitschrift für Entwicklungspsychologie und Pädagogische Psychologie, 18*, 153–164.

Plass, J. L., Chun, D., Mayer, R. E., & Leutner, D. (1998). Supporting visualizer and verbalizer learning preferences in a second language multimedia learning environment. *Journal of Educational Psychology, 90*, 25–36.

Rasch, G. (1960). *Probabilistic models for some intelligence and attainment tests.* Copenhagen, Denmark: Nielsen & Lydicke.

Rost, J. (1988). *Quantitative und qualitative probabilistische Testtheorie* [Quantitative and qualitative probabilistic test theory]. Bern, Switzerland: Huber.

Salomon, G. (1972). Heuristic models for the generation of aptitude-treatment interaction hypotheses. *Review of Educational Research, 42*, 237–343.

Schnotz, W., & Kulhavy, R. (Eds.). (1994). *Comprehension of graphics.* Oxford, England: Pergamon.

Schreiber, B. (1998). *Selbstreguliertes Lernen* [Self-regulated learning]. Münster, Germany: Waxmann.

Skinner, B. F. (1954). The science of learning and the art of teaching. *Harvard Educational Review, 24*, 86–97.

Suess, H.-M. (1996). *Intelligenz, Wissen und Problemlösen. Kognitive Voraussetzungen für erfolgreiches Handeln bei computersimulierten Problemen* [Intelligence, knowledge, and problem solving]. Göttingen, Germany: Hogrefe.

Tennyson, R. D., & Park, S. I. (1984). Process learning time as an adaptive design variable in concept learning using computer-based instruction. *Journal of Educational Psychology, 76,* 452–465.

Tennyson, R. D., & Rothen, W. (1977). Pre-task and on-task adaptive design strategies for selecting number of instances in concept acquisition. *Journal of Educational Psychology, 69,* 586–592.

Treinies, G., & Einsiedler, W. (1993). Hierarchische und bedeutungsnetzartige Lehrstoffdarstellungen als Lernhilfen beim Wissenserwerb im Sachunterricht der Grundschule [Hierarchical and net-based presentations of subject matter as learning aids in science knowledge acquisition at primary school level]. *Psychologie in Erziehung und Unterricht, 40,* 263–277.

Vos, H. J. (1995). Application of Bayesian decision theory to intelligent tutoring systems. *Computers in Human Behavior, 11,* 149–162.

Weidenmann, B. (1994). *Wissenserwerb mit Bildern* [Acquiring knowledge with pictures]. Bern, Switzerland: Huber.

Weinberg, I. (1998). *Probleme von Softwaretrainings und Lösungsansaetze: Instruktionspsychologische Entwicklung eines Double-Fading-Support-Konzepts für komplexe Softwaresysteme* [Solving problems of software training: Developing a double-fading support approach for complex software systems]. Aachen, Germany: Shaker.

Weinberg, I., Hornke, L. F., & Leutner, D. (1994). Adaptives Testen und Lernen—Effekte von Rückmeldungen unterschiedlichen Informationsgehaltes [Adaptive testing and learning—Effects of varying informative feedback]. In K. Pawlik (Ed.), *39. Kongreß der Deutschen Gesellschaft für Psychologie* (Abstracts, Vol. 2, p. 780). Hamburg, Germany: Psychologisches Institut I der Universität.

Wenger, E. (1987). *Artificial intelligence and tutoring systems.* Los Altos, CA: Morgan Kaufmann.

Chapter 14

Evaluating Web-Based Learning Systems and Software

Wilhelmina Savenye
Arizona State University

Educational organizations worldwide are increasingly delivering courses and programs via distance education technologies. Moore and Kearsley (1996) in their classic book *Distance Education: A Systems View,* as well as Simonson, Smaldino, Albright, and Zvacek (2003) in their book on distance education, discussed the many technologies that have been used for distance education, including print, audio and videocassettes, radio and television, and teleconferencing. Although all of these technologies are still used, the Internet is becoming the tool of choice for distance delivery. The World Wide Web, in particular, offers us many means for delivering learning materials, as well as providing Internet-based telecommunications tools.

One trend is that courses delivered on the Web may or may not be part of distance courses. In fact, courses we design for distance students may attract more students who live nearby, but who want the flexibility such courses offer. In this chapter, I discuss Web-based software as part of distance education courses and systems, as well as such software used on its own as part of "flexible" or "distributed" courses, not necessarily as part of distance education.

Although my focus in this chapter is primarily on Web-based learning materials, it must be recognized that technologies, too, are converging. When we teach a Web-based course, for instance, we can incorporate print materials, Web databases of information, graphic and photographic illustrations, animations, and other multimedia in the form of audio and video lectures and demonstrations, as well as asynchronous and synchronous communications, teleconferencing, and e-mail. It can be expected that this trend will continue. There are some who challenge the utility of instructional design methodologies for solving learning problems in high-technology environments (Gordon & Zemke, 2000). However, I contend that converging and emerging technologies call for adapting instructional design methodologies.

It is interesting that in the United States some see distance education as, in fact, pushing developments in higher education in general. For instance, Charles M. Cook, the director of the New England Association of Schools and Colleges' Commission on Institutions in Higher Education, described this push in a recent issue of the *Chronicle of Higher Education*: "It's [distance education is] in a better position to assess student learning than a traditional establishment." He added, "It's the future of both traditional and nontraditional education" (Carnavale, 2001, p. A44). With this increased focus on evaluation and assessment in both distance learning and traditional instruction, I believe instructional design is poised to make even stronger contributions to education.

OPEN LEARNING, DISTANCE LEARNING, AND WEB-BASED LEARNING

Perspectives on Web-based distance learning worldwide indicate that software, courseware, and systems are converging in most educational environments. Definitions, too, converge. Let's begin our review by examining definitions of open, distance, and Web-based learning.

What Is Open Learning?

Some authors suggest that distance learning is a category of open learning. Thorpe (1988), for instance, considered open learning an umbrella term, and that distance learning is a subset or particular example of one type of open learning. Thorpe used the terms interchangeably in the title of her book, *Evaluating Open and Distance Learning*, and suggested that there is confusion about the definition of these terms. It should be noted that most of Thorpe's examples come from the British Open University, a pioneer in the open learning approach, and which uses distance learning. She herself suggested that, at least in the 1980s, outside the British Kingdom the term *distance learning* predominated.

In contrast, Marland (1997) argued that open learning is a concept or trend within distance education. He, too, however, called open learning an approach rather than a technique, one that emphasizes learner needs and learner control.

Race (1994), in *The Open Learning Handbook,* argued that the term *flexible learning* would be more useful, but agreed that the terms open learning, distance learning, and flexible learning are often interchanged. He noted that open learning often connotes that anyone can join, and often at any time. However, he added that truer hallmarks of open learning include learner choice over pace, place, time, and/or processes. Race argued that, by his definition, well-designed open learning may be "indistinguishable in itself from any other effective sort of learning . . ." (p. 29).

Others argue that open learning and distance learning do not overlap. Rumble (1997) provided what may be the most useful view. He contended the terms are not synonymous. Rumble defined open learning as "an imprecise phrase describing any form of educational provision in which the restrictions placed on students are minimized, and in which decisions about learning are taken by the learners themselves" (p. 4). He concluded by suggesting that open learning is a *philosophy* of education, whereas distance education is a *method* of education.

Approaches to Distance Learning

Rumble (1997) defined distance learning as "a process of teaching-learning in which the learner is physically separated from the teacher" (p. 3). He added that typically in distance education students study using materials, so some forms are called "resource-based learning" or "self-study" and that "independent learning" approaches allow these types of learning to occur. He contrasted this methodology with what might be called traditional, conventional, or contiguous education, in which the learners and teachers are in the same place, a classroom. In the United States, this is often called f:f or face-to-face education, or sometimes "brick-and-mortar" classrooms, as opposed to more virtual, distance classrooms.

Moore and Kearsley's (1996) definition of distance education provides details to engage us in our discussion of systematic instructional design and evaluation of Web-based learning materials:

> Distance education is planned learning that normally occurs in a different place from teaching and as a result requires special techniques of course design, special instructional techniques, special methods of communication by electronic and other technology, as well as special organizational and administrative arrangements. (p. 2)

Calvert (1989) opened up the definition of distance education to include learning that occurs not just at a distance, but as "formal instruction delivered mainly to remote locations and/or asynchronously" (p. 93). Often, students who enroll in distance courses do so not because they live far from campus, but because they prefer this asynchronous feature. It allows them to work on coursework anytime, day or night, without coming to campus, thus offering them the flexible learning mentioned by many distance education theorists and practitioners.

Toward a Convergence

Calvert brings us to a convergence of one sort that will lead us into Web-based learning of many sorts. Calvert (1989), in her discussion of instructional design strategies for distance learning, noted that the strategies vary depending on whether a course is seen as an extension of the classroom on campus or a correspondence-type course. She argued that these two types of approaches rooted in the history of distance education lead to different design strategies, and she added that one leads to more radical change in education than the other. She contended that when instructors simply extend their classrooms asynchronously or at a distance, they tend not to make great instructional changes. However, correspondence courses historically, at the British Open University and now at many such institutions worldwide, were developed by a team including instructional designers. They rely on the self-study materials discussed earlier. Therefore, courses that are based on this model are developed using systematic processes of instructional design, are radically different from classroom courses, and, she argued, represent a transformation of education.

I would agree and extend her argument to say that courses developed this way—using instructional design, and when using the sophisticated multimedia and communications capabilities the Web offers—represent such transformative change in education. Palloff and Pratt (1999), in fact, contend that "cyber" distance technologies allow us to build learning communities that enhance "transformative learning," that is, learning based on self-reflection and the interpretation of what the student learns (p. 129).

Open universities tend to follow the model developed by the British Open University, which is the transformative/correspondence one; that is, with subject-matter faculty working in teams with instructional designers to develop courses which are then delivered by many other tutors, often other faculty. In the United States this model is newer; however, it is being used by publishers who offer courses, and by several private and for-profit institutions. The more prevalent model in the United States currently is the extension-of-the-classroom model, in which faculty, often alone or with few resources, develop new versions of their courses to be offered at a distance, increasingly using the technology of the Web.

I suggest that the philosophy and approach taken in developing Web-based systems, courses, and software, whether they foster open, flexible, or distance learning, are influenced by the learning purpose. These philosophies and approaches will in turn influence the design and evaluation strategies used.

Types of Web-Based Distance Learning Systems, Courses, and Software

As can be inferred from the earlier discussion, Web-based learning materials may form part of an open learning system or a distance learning system. They also may form part of a classroom-based educational or training degree program or course, or even a stand-alone learning system. McGreal (2000), in fact, has developed a 13-level taxonomy of courses that vary in their degree of distance capability and mediation. Courses and degree programs, and to a lesser extent stand-alone software, can only be evaluated as part of the systems to which they belong. In this section, I look at the ways Web-based learning software and materials are used to form all or part of courses or learning programs, because here, too, we have convergences that will influence what is evaluated and how evaluation is done.

Fully Web-Based Courses.   Many courses are increasingly being delivered fully via the Web in a flexible or distant manner. Such courses do not require students to come to campus or training centers to meet in classes at all; all work is done independently, using Web-based and other resources. Typically a Web-based course system includes not only print and multimedia materials, but communications systems, including asynchronous threaded discussions, synchronous or "live" chat, and e-mail. This type of course is also increasingly being offered in training settings in business, in which travel and work time costs may thus be saved.

Hybrid Courses.   Many Web-supported courses feature some required on-campus class meetings. For instance, students may be required to come to meet on campus once or twice at the beginning to help them start the course and learn how to use the hardware and software systems involved in course delivery. Often, a few campus sessions at the end of the course are required in which students may make live presentations. In hybrid courses, students often meet on-campus on several additional occasions throughout the course. In some content areas, hybrid courses are becoming the norm. Hybrid courses may also be employed in industry; however, they are not as common.

Traditional Courses With Web Supplements.   On many campuses, and in some training settings, instructors are encouraged to develop Web-based learning materials to supplement even their campus-based courses. At a minimum, instructors upload their syllabi, handouts, and some readings.

Many would argue, however, that this is simply another form of print delivery, one that does not truly use the power of the Web. A more appropriate use of the Web is in classroom-based courses that either are supplemented with, for instance, multimedia tutorials, Web-based research assignments, or Web-quests. Additionally, many campus-based courses use discussion and chat systems, or at least e-mail systems, to increase the level of interactive student participation in a course.

Stand-Alone Web-Based Software and Materials for Learning. Finally, Web-based software and programs may serve as stand-alone learning materials; they are not necessarily developed as part of particular courses or training programs, although they may be accessed by learners in those courses or programs, either on their own or as required assignments.

In the upcoming sections of this chapter, I first focus on evaluating Web-based materials that form all or part of learning systems or of courses or training programs. Then I discuss methods for evaluating stand-alone Web-based learning software.

PERSPECTIVES ON EVALUATION OF WEB-BASED LEARNING

What Is Evaluation?

Educational Evaluation. Evaluation is many things to many people, and can be used powerfully to do many things. Popham (1993), in his book on educational evaluation, pointed out that long ago evaluation meant simply measuring student learning. He noted that now, "Systematic educational evaluation consists of a formal appraisal of the quality of educational phenomena" (p. 7). Thorpe (1988), in her book on evaluating open and distance learning, provided a similar and very thorough definition: "Evaluation is the collection, analysis and interpretation of information about any aspect of a programme of education and training, as part of a recognized process of judging its effectiveness, its efficiency and any other outcomes it may have" (p. 5). Evaluation as described in these definitions usually provides a comparison of the value of two or more programs, often for purposes of selecting programs, or deciding on their continuance.

Formative and Summative Evaluation. Evaluation is also a standard phase within most instructional design models (cf. Gagne, 1985; Gagne, Briggs, & Wager, 1992; Gustafson & Branch, 1997; Smith & Ragan, 1999; Sullivan &

Higgins, 1983). What is done in instructional design is not precisely the same as described in these earlier definitions. Dick, Carey, and Carey (2001), for instance, described two types of evaluation, formative and summative. Formative evaluation involves collecting data during development to provide information to be used in improving an instructional product or program. Although many use the term *formative evaluation*, other terms may be used, such as the term *monitoring*, used by Freeman (1997), or what Driscoll (1998) called rapid-prototype or alpha and beta evaluation.

In contrast, summative evaluation involves collecting data once a program has been produced to determine its final effectiveness. Many of the same methods are used; however, the data help make a sort of "go/no-go" decision rather than being used to revise the product while it is being developed.

Distance educators and Web-based developers are typically not as interested in summative evaluation as formative, because they are developing rapidly changing systems and software and need to use formative evaluation data to revise and improve them.

Instructional Software Evaluation.   Another category of evaluation is considered to be product or software evaluation. Typically, software evaluation uses many of the same methods used for formative evaluation; however, the decisions involved may make it more like summative, that is, a program is being selected or not.

In this review, I focus primarily on formative evaluation, or what is sometimes called developmental testing, or even developmental research. As noted, formative evaluation can provide the most value for instructional designers in improving their Web-based and distance learning systems, programs, courses, and software.

Levels of Evaluation

Evaluation can be conducted at any level in a Web-based flexible or distance learning system. These levels can include society, system or institution, degree or specialty program, course, module, or a set of Web pages. Freeman (1997), in his book *Managing Open Systems*, suggested that ongoing formative evaluations be conducted as part of "quality assurance systems" (p. 133). Before discussing how to conduct formative evaluations, let's first look at these levels.

Mega Evaluation.   Kaufman (2000), in what he termed *mega planning*, advocated working not only at the macro level of the organization itself, but at the level of society and external clients, the mega level. He called this "strategic planning-plus." Kaufman added that mega planning includes implementation and continuous evaluation processes, using outcomes-based benchmarks to measure and ensure improved performance. At this broad level, Kaufman advocated calibrating programs with an ideal vision as part of quality management. In a similar vein, Knott (1994) suggested conducting evaluations by collaborating with many members of the affected constituents. Mega evaluation, like mega planning, is not too frequently used, in part due to limitations of resources.

System- or Institutionwide Evaluation. More commonly, evaluation is conducted at a system- or institutionwide level. A system might include several campuses in a regional educational system, or a consortium of institutions, or several units across a business organization. A system may also comprise one institution alone that may conduct overall evaluations. My university, for instance, collects course evaluation data from all students enrolled in all courses offered or cross-listed by the Distance Learning area of the College of Extended Education. Currently this includes over 5,000 students enrolled in 70 fully or partially Web-based courses (of over 50,000 students overall enrolled at the university). Evaluations are also conducted on the university's correspondence and televised courses.

Degree, Certificate, or Specialty Programs. Evaluations are also commonly conducted to evaluate the success of, or improve during implementation and development, degree programs. Hiltz (1990) described such an evaluation conducted on a project in the United States called "Tools for the Enhancement and Evaluation of a Virtual Classroom." She evaluated a series of many fully and partially online courses in such areas as computer science, mathematics, management, and statistics, all of which used the online tools on which the project was based.

The British Open University, like other open universities, has a long history of conducting evaluations of its offerings in various subject matter areas (cf. Rumble, 1992, 1997; Thorpe, 1988).

Individual Courses. Although not conducted as often as one would hope, instructors and staff often conduct formative evaluations of individual courses or learning modules. Freeman (1997) suggested that there are several levels of evaluation here, too, that include the human factor; that is, course or program level, individual tutor or instructor level, and the individual learner level.

Web-Based Software, Modules, Websites, or Web Pages. The effectiveness of software such as small tutorials or learning modules, as well as websites that consist of sets of Web pages, may also be evaluated. I discuss this type of evaluation as Web-based software evaluation.

CONDUCTING FORMATIVE EVALUATIONS
OF WEB-BASED LEARNING SYSTEMS

Excellent resources exist to aid evaluators in planning larger scale evaluations of Web-based learning systems, which may include whole institutions, consortia, or degree or certificate programs. Let's review a few of these resources and summarize key areas evaluators may consider in planning their evaluations.

Success Factors

Rumble of the British Open University in 1992 developed his guide to *The Management of Distance Learning Systems.* In his view, the success of a distance learning system or program can be judged by using four main categories of criteria:

- providing opportunities for access to education and training,
- completion and drop-out rates (completion, persistence, and graduation rates),
- the quality of output,
- cost-efficiency and cost-effectiveness. (p. 86)

Rumble stressed that the opportunities for learners to participate be flexible. He cautioned that the Open University's experience has shown that determining completion rates in an open system is not easy. For instance, students in the Open University system may purchase course materials but not enroll in the course. Some may enroll but not start studying for the course. Some institutions, among them the British Open University, do not register students, therefore, until they have studied for a period of time. Comparing data across institutions may therefore be difficult. Persistence rates, however, can be measured, as can completion rates.

Of note are Rumble's (1992) suggestions that dropout rates may be reduced using various methods. He suggested providing good study materials, providing proper advice to students as they begin their studies as well as during the course of their programs, and creating a positive and supportive climate for students to seek help as they pursue their studies. Thorpe (1988) suggested also evaluating the quality and guidance provided by an organization's personnel to students.

Student Learning

The quality of output of a learning system refers to the overall quality of student learning. Grades and course completion can be reviewed, but Rumble (1992) suggested developmental testing, external assessment, and external validation, as well. He further recommended considering such measures as the extent to which students' degrees transfer to higher level degree institutions, perceptions of the value of the degree, and the value employers place on their new employees' distance training.

Freeman (1997) recommended that baseline data should be collected that can be used to measure performance improvement. These data might include performance data from other similar programs, from past offerings of the programs, or with various types of absolute standards. In addition, baseline data for competitive programs might include current market share, demographic information, numbers enrolled, current inputs, such as costs, and current outputs, including graduation rates and employment rates.

Cost-Efficiency, Cost-Effectiveness, and Performance Indicators

In another work, Rumble (1997) covered costs and economics of open and distance learning in more detail. He gave suggestions for measuring cost-efficiency, that is, the ratio of output to input. He noted that organizations might be effective but not efficient.

Cost-effectiveness concerns the quality of outputs. One way in which evaluators, planners, and managers may measure effectiveness is against an absolute standard, such as graduation rates or standardized scores. Other means include comparing scores and grades from the distance system with those of comparable different systems. Much as Kaufman (2000) did, Rumble (1997) recommended "value-added performance indicators" (p. 163), such as the difference in performance between entry and exit tests, or the difference between pretest and posttest scores in some courses in the program.

In an innovative example that extends this value-added performance approach to the transformation of education in the United States, the Western Governor's University now uses entry tests keyed to program competencies to determine, in concert with a mentor professor, what courses or methods of study a student should follow. A student must past competency-based exit tests as the primary means to earn a degree, rather than simply showing completion of courses (Carnavale, 2001). The University of Phoenix also combines course completion with performance on competency-based tests to determine success in many of their distance programs (S. Brewer, personal communication, October 20, 2000).

CONDUCTING FORMATIVE EVALUATIONS
OF WEB-BASED LEARNING COURSES

In investigating how to evaluate Web-based courses, several general categories of questions and data categories emerge. The first is the quality of the instructional design of the course and materials. The other questions make up three main categories of information, namely: implementation, attitudes, and student learning outcomes. I review these areas in detail in this section. The final category of information, review of stand-alone Web-based learning software, is discussed in the next section.

Reviews of Courses and Course Materials

The American Council on Education's (1996) *Distance Learning Evaluation Guide* presents a set of guidelines in a sort of checklist for use by their College Credit Recommendation Service reviewers. The approach is primarily one that Dick, Carey, and Carey (2001) would call "instructional design review," in which the evaluators would not necessarily collect survey or test data, but would review all course materials. Reviewers use the checklist statements and evaluate learning materials in the areas of learning design, objectives and outcomes, materials, technology, learner support, organizational commitment, and subject.

Similarly, a list of factors to consider when reviewing Web-based courses was developed by Khan and Vega (1997) through a survey of educators. The factors are many and include criteria in such areas as clarity, interactivity, content, accessibility, navigation, learning styles served, and use of technology.

Simonson (1997) and others (Freeman, 1997; Harrison, 1999; Race, 1994; Thorpe, 1988), in contrast, describe data that evaluators and developers can use in improving distance learning courses. Most of the data apply as well to Web-based distance courses, and fall into categories described later.

Implementation

Information is gathered to answer questions regarding how well the Web-based course is working for learners, instructors, and other participants. Data are typically collected through questionnaires, interviews, and observations. For instance, students may be asked their perceptions of the quality of multimedia resources, such as PowerPoint lectures or audio or video clips. A critical concern is how easily students may access resources from their computers. Most Web-based course management systems collect data regarding how frequently, and for how long, students access the course and its components.

If the impact of marketing efforts is of interest, students could be asked how they learned about the course, and what they expected it to be. They might be questioned about other educational or training options they had and why they chose this one.

Institutional issues mentioned earlier apply at the course level as well. In our distance courses we are concerned that students both at our university and elsewhere find it easy to register for the course and, if necessary, to apply to our university as a degree-seeking or nondegree student.

Many institutions now offer various support services to distance students. Even when evaluating one course, students may be queried regarding the quality and accessibility of library materials and services, counseling and advising, textbooks and other reading materials, and even social or entertainment options of the institution.

Also related to implementation are issues dealing with the specific usability, quality, and technical accessibility of our Web materials. These are presented in more detail later, when I discuss evaluating Web-based learning software.

Attitudes

The attitudes of all participants and constituents in Web-based courses are important. No matter how good the quality of a course, if learners find it unappealing, boring, or irrelevant, the course will not help them or other students to learn. This is particularly true in that such courses require more independent learning initiative on the part of students.

Learner attitudes are usually measured at the end of courses using questionnaires, and often also by interviewing a sample of students in more depth. My colleagues and I have also used periodic informal discussions during the course to monitor student satisfaction, though those are not anonymous, and so serve a different function from anonymous surveys. For instance, in our formative evaluation of a fully Web-based distance learning course on teaching with technology, we measured students' attitudes using the standard university course evaluation instrument, a more focused survey developed specifically for this course, and an informal online discussion (Savenye, 2000b). (The reader may also refer to Savenye & Robinson's, 2004, review of qualitative research methods in educational technology for a discussion of other methods for assessing and observing learner attitudes.)

Learners are usually asked to rate their degree of satisfaction with aspects of the Web-based course. At a broad level, we typically ask students to rate the quality of the course overall and compared with other campus-based courses, as well as whether they would enroll in another such course. Students are usually also asked their perceptions of the pace, value, and appeal of the course, as well as about technical aspects. In addition, as computer-mediated communication is critical to the success of a Web-based course (cf. Bull, Bull, & Sigmon, 1997; Lewis, Whitaker, & Julian, 1995), it is productive to ask students their opinions about the discussion, chat, and e-mail systems. In a systemwide use for such student attitude and perception data, Palloff and Pratt (1999) described a survey used by one community college in the United States to help students assess whether they have the skills, learning strategies, and discipline that distance learning courses often require.

In courses that are part of larger Web-based programs or systems or when courses have been developed by teams, it is also important to determine instructor attitudes toward teaching the course and using the Web-based materials. Other constituents, such as training managers, staff members, and those who hire graduates of a program, may also be queried. I have often found, in fact, that such inquiries engender a positive attitude in all involved, as they are often impressed by the "quality assurance" tone of the formative evaluations.

Student Learning

Most would agree that student learning is paramount in Web-based courses. Student learning can be measured in a multitude of ways. How this is done depends on the course goals, content area, instructors, institutional goals, setting, and learners. It is recommended in Web-based courses, especially those that are fully Web-based and/or at a distance, that multiple measures and types of measures of learning be used. Students need regular feedback and need to monitor their own progress. Students all study differently and are better at different types of tasks. Especially when they must work regularly on their own, different types of performance measures, if possible, make more of the measurements fairer to all (Dabbagh, 2000; Ko & Rossen, 2001).

Security is another reason to use multiple measurements of performance, cautioned Ko and Rossen (2001). It is easier for an instructor to compare different samples of student performance across several assessments.

Again, it is often important to collect baseline data regarding what learners know at the beginning of a course, or in comparable situations. Pretests may be used, as may precourse data from past students. If it is not certain that they know anything about the topic, small surveys might be used, though these do not allow for strict pre–post comparisons of performance.

Various types of assessments that can be employed both in measuring student progress and in evaluating the effectiveness of Web-based courses are discussed next.

Exams and Quizzes.   Many courses, subjects, and settings lend themselves to quizzes and exams. These are especially useful for assessing background knowledge and verbal information and concepts, but may also be employed to measure intellectual skills. Freeman (1997) suggested developing assessment systems. Whether instructor- or computer-scored, the format of the assessments may include closed-book or open-book exams. For reasons of test security, though exams may be taken online, some instructors and organizations, such as in many open universities, have regional centers to which students travel to take proctored exams. In the United States, many university testing centers are collaborating so that students enrolled in distance courses may complete proctored exams at a university center nearby. It could even be arranged that someone proctor an exam in a trainee's work setting.

Many good resources exist for test-question design. Dick, Carey, and Carey (2001), for instance, provided guidelines for types of test items that can be used with various types of behavior stated in objectives, such as "identify," "discuss," "solve," "develop," and "generate." Harrison's (1999) book on designing self-directed learning provides suggestions for how to write multiple-choice, true/false, and free-form questions.

Discussions.   Online discussions may be used simply to enhance participation in a course, or for both practice and assessment. Discussions may be moderated by the instructor, by students, by invited experts, or using a combination of these moderators. Typically, moderators post study and discussion questions a few days before a discussion, respond to students as it proceeds, and then post a summary of the key points discussed after its conclusion. Most online course-delivery systems include asynchronous discussion software, but some instructors also hold video, audio, or telephone conferences.

Papers and Projects.   In many Web courses, students write research papers and essays as they do in campus-based courses. They typically submit papers either via e-mail or an electronic drop box. It is important to aid students' learning by sending them feedback in a timely manner. Students' papers may also be posted for other students to review. Clear directions and guidelines should be developed to aid students in writing their papers.

In many courses, students are required to develop projects that are not strictly papers. For instance, in our courses, students write lesson plans, conduct software evaluations, develop instructional software, and build multimedia presentations as part of their graded work. Checklists help students to know how they will be evaluated on such projects. Again, it is often worthwhile for students to share these projects, either formally or informally, with each other, using the course website.

In all of our Web-based courses, we support and require that students develop some projects as members of groups. Not only does this enhance the social aspects of the course and make it more enjoyable (usually) for students, but they may learn from each other as much as from the instructor in this type of setting. DeNigris and Witchel (2000) provided an evaluation form that students can use to rate the performance of their group and of group members.

Other means of assessing student learning include portfolios and student-negotiated assessments (Freeman, 1997).

After reviewing the many ways we can assess student learning outcomes in Web courses, let's turn our attention to how to evaluate Web-based learning software, whether used in systems, courses, or stand-alone.

CONDUCTING EVALUATIONS OF WEB-BASED LEARNING SOFTWARE

Stand-alone Web-based learning software may, as Dick, Carey, and Carey (2001) suggested, be subjected to evaluation with real students and instructors, using methods described earlier. It is either implemented and pilot tested in Web-based courses, or at least used by a range of learners who represent the target audience.

Frequently, however, Web-based learning software is evaluated by subjecting it to review processes. An evaluation form that is easy for many instructors to adapt for Web-based software was developed by Heinich, Molenda, Russell, and Smaldino (1999) for evaluating computer multimedia materials. They suggested that educators rate such aspects of the software as: its match with the curriculum, accuracy, clarity of language, freedom from bias, and learner participation.

Instructional Design

Some authors recommend reviewing software with a broad instructional design question in mind, such as, "Is the course designed in such a way that users actually learn?" (Hall, 1997). In contrast, Hooper, Hokanson, and Bernhardt (2000) developed a detailed set of criteria that are used to judge the Learning Software Design Competition. Instructional design features are judged under educational effectiveness. Reviewers rate such aspects as how the software promotes learning, higher order thinking, and understanding. Reviewers also determine the extent to which the software teaches transferable skills, is challenging, is suited to the audience, and provides opportunities to explore.

In an instrument I developed to aid faculty and staff in evaluating software for instruction, I suggest reviewing the degree to which the software represents a complete and sound lesson, including opportunities for learner performance of, and feedback on, the skills and knowledge to be learned (Savenye, 2000a).

Technical Quality

Once the learning value of the software has been established through the instructional design review, it is time to determine if the software is acceptable in aspects of its technical quality. Hall (1997), for instance, suggested that the ease with which learners can navigate through the software is important. There should be clear directions, a course map, and easy options for exiting and reentering the software.

Hannafin and Peck (1988), in their advice for designers of computer software for learning, recommended, too, that learning efficiency be considered; that is, that the activities provide sufficient learning for the time involved.

Hooper, Hokanson, and Bernhardt (2000) called this category *project application*. In addition to the features already noted, they added that learners should clearly be able to note their progress, that users are not frustrated, that the use of media is integral to the learning goal, that installation is easy, and that cuing or help systems are available.

Website and Web Page Design

For Web-based learning software, there are many guidelines for Web page design, which have evolved in part from screen design guidelines, but which address the unique capabilities of the Web. Porter (1997), in her book on virtual classrooms, provided extensive criteria for evaluating educational websites. Among her suggestions are that reviewers ensure visitors will understand the purpose of the site, will want to visit it, and will receive the information they need when they need it.

As with software considerations, the design of the page is important. Porter (1997) also suggested reviewing the overall tone of pages, how much information is presented on a screen at once. Is it a typed handout or a well-designed page, for instance? Reviewers may need to be aware that many users, too, do not scroll down pages for more information. How information is "chunked" across a site and pages is important for learning, as is provision of visual and textual cues, such as bolding, headings, color, arrows, charts, white space, and organization.

For more information about Web usability, the work of Jakob Nielsen is invaluable. Nielsen (2000), in his book *Designing Web Usability*, provided many examples of how designers can enhance the appeal, clarity, navigation features, accessibility, and global value of their Web pages and sites. Evaluators have adapted many of his guidelines for use in rapid prototyping and formative evaluations.

CONCLUSION AND IMPLICATIONS

Those who analyze trends in educational technology stress the importance of instructional design principles and evaluation in developing Web-based learning products, the pervasiveness of computers and telecommunications systems, the increasing impact of distance learning, and the changing role of the teacher (Ely, Foley, Freeman, & Scheel, 1995). Sullivan, Igoe, Klein, Jones, and Savenye (1993), in their survey of the perspectives of instructional design professionals, faculty, and students, found that most believe that future innovations in technology will continue to impact our field.

Looking ahead, I anticipate that fostering and assessing learning in Web-based environments will become even more complex. As did Foshay (2001), I call upon instructional designers to meet the challenge of the Web.

The Web can yield enhanced interaction and interactivity, both critical for successful distance learning (Gunawardena & McIsaac, 2004). Tiffin and Rajasingham (1995) took the view that education is communications. They described what they call the virtual class, in which students are supported in becoming autonomous learners through new and not-yet-invented types of cybertools, again fostered by the Web. The Web allows instructors to develop powerful multimedia presentations, including animations, video, and sound.

The Web also allows us to build learning communities online (Bull, Bull, & Sigmon, 1997), but we will need to learn more about supporting such communities. Supporting students in becoming autonomous, open learners in these communities will continue to be a challenge. Several of the university instructional design and learning research projects of my colleagues and me may contribute to this effort (cf. Savenye, Olina, & Niemczyk, 2001).

Instructors, too, need considerably more support than many of our organizations have been able to provide. Instructors are the key to making instruction meaningful, engaging, and even life-enhancing, in many Web-based environments. Beaudoin (1990), Gunawardena (1992), Hannafin and Savenye (1993), and others have noted the expanding roles and responsibilities of instructors in highly technological and distance environments. Faculty will need the training, resources, support, and reward systems that will enable them to best use, and to design, Web-based learning software and courses.

It is critical that we provide scaffolding for self-directed learners in these more open Web-based environments. The development of materials that include cognitive apprenticeships, problem-based learning, and case-based learning holds promise for self-directed Web courses as well (cf. Achtenhagen, 2000; Dijkstra, 2000; Jonassen, Hernandez-Serrano, & Choi, 2000; Seel, Al-Diban, & Blumschein, 2000). Greene and Land (2000) have provided an example of research we may consider conducting on types and utility of scaffolding to provide learners in Web-based environments. Goodyear (2000) also helps us focus on the changing learners in these environments, and he noted that we must continue to anticipate these changes and to design user-centered environments. Race (1994) provided strong arguments for ways to adapt instructional design principles for open learning. We can also look to the work of Hannafin and his colleagues (cf. Hannafin, Hannafin, Land, & Oliver, 1997; Hannafin & Land, 1997; Hill & Hannafin, 1997) for research and design considerations for open-ended learning environments. In these environments, motivation is also a strong factor and more work is needed in this area (cf. Miltiadou & Savenye, 2000). Sullivan, Ice, and Niedermeyer (2000) reminded us that instructional design efforts are often short-term and provided suggestions for implementing and sustaining long-term learning and change programs.

My colleagues and I hope to continue our investigations of ways to engage in evaluation activities that improve learning in complex technology-based environments, in higher education (cf. Savenye, 1998; Savenye & Smith, 1997) and in schools (cf. Savenye et al., 2003). We will also continue to learn lessons from applying evaluation tools to aid learning in even more open environments, including museums, botanical gardens (Savenye, Socolofsky, Greenhouse, & Copeman, 1997), and zoos (Savenye, Schnackenberg, & Jones, 1997).

As Spector (2000) noted, holistic and integrative approaches are necessary for fostering complex learning. Building strong learners and quality learning materials in Web-based learning will call upon all our resourcefulness in integrating instructional design in creative and open ways.

I perceive many challenges before all of us as we attempt to use and keep up with the capabilities of the Web and its succeeding generations of technologies for education globally. Our goal is always to help our students and trainees learn. I believe evaluation, particularly formative evaluation as part of systematic instructional design, is one of the most powerful tools available to us in improving education via our Web-based learning programs.

REFERENCES

Achtenhagen, F. (2000). Reality, models and complex teaching–learning environments. In J. M. Spector & T. M. Anderson (Eds.), *Integrated and holistic perspectives on learning, instruction and technology: Understanding complexity* (pp. 159–174). Dordrecht, Netherlands: Kluwer.

American Council on Education. (1996). *Distance learning evaluation guide.* Washington, DC: Author.

Beaudoin, M. (1990). The instructor's changing role in distance education. *American Journal of Distance Education, 4*(2), 21–29.

Bull, G., Bull, G., & Sigmon, T. (1997, September). Common protocols for shared communities. *Learning and Leading with Technology, 25*(1), 50–53.

Calvert, J. (1989). Instructional design for distance learning. In K. A. Johnson & L. J. Foa (Eds.), *Instructional design: New alternatives for effective education and training* (pp. 92–105). New York: National University Continuing Education Association, American Council on Education, Macmillan.

Carnavale, D. (2001, April 13). Assessment takes center stage in online learning. *Chronicle of Higher Education,* pp. A43–A45.

Dabbagh, N. (2000). Multiple assessment in an online graduate course: An effectiveness evaluation. In B. L. Mann (Ed.), *Perspectives in Web course management* (pp. 179–197). Toronto: Canadian Scholars Press.

DeNigris, J., & Witchel, A. (2000). *How to teach and train online: Teaching the learning organization with tomorrow's tools today.* Needham Heights, MA: Pearson Custom.

Dick, W., Carey, L., & Carey, J. (2001). *The systematic design of instruction* (5th ed.). New York: Longman.

Dijkstra, S. (2000). Epistemology, psychology of learning and instructional design. In J. M. Spector & T. M. Anderson (Eds.), *Integrated and holistic perspectives on learning, instruction and technology: Understanding complexity* (pp. 213–232). Dordrecht, Netherlands: Kluwer.

Driscoll, M. (1998). *Web-based training: Using technology to design adult learning experiences.* San Francisco: Jossey-Bass Pfeiffer.

Ely, D. P., Foley, A., Freeman, W., & Scheel, N. (1995). Trends in educational technology 1991. In *Instructional technology: Past, present and future* (2nd ed., pp. 34–60). Englewood, CO: Libraries Unlimited.

Foshay, W. R. (2001). Can instructional design deliver on the promise of the Web? *Quarterly Review of Distance Education, 2*(1), 19–34.

Freeman, R. (1997). *Managing open systems.* London: Kogan Page.

Gagne, R. M. (1985). *The conditions of learning and theory of instruction* (5th ed.). Fort Worth, TX: Holt, Rinehart & Winston.

Gagne, R. M., Briggs, L. J., & Wager, W. W. (1992). *Principles of instructional design* (4th ed.). Fort Worth, TX: Harcourt, Brace.

Goodyear, P. (2000). Environments for lifelong learning: Ergonomics, architecture and educational design. In J. M. Spector & T. M. Anderson (Eds.), *Integrated and holistic perspectives on learning, instruction and technology: Understanding complexity* (pp. 1–18). Dordrecht, Netherlands: Kluwer.

Gordon, J., & Zemke, R. (2000, April). The attack on ISD. *Training,* pp. 43–53.

Greene, B. A., & Land, S. M. (2000). A qualitative analysis of scaffolding use in a resource-based learning environment involving the World Wide Web. *Journal of Educational Computing Research, 23*(2), 151–179.

Gunawardena, C. N. (1992). Changing faculty roles for audiographics and online teaching. *American Journal of Distance Education, 6*(3), 58–71.

Gunawardena, C. N., & McIsaac, M. S. (2004). Distance education. In D. H. Jonassen (Ed.), *Handbook of research for educational communications and technology* (2nd ed., pp. 355–395). New York: Simon & Schuster Macmillan.

Gustafson, K. L., & Branch, R. M. (1997, May). *Survey of instructional development models* (3rd ed.). Syracuse, NY: ERIC Clearinghouse on Information & Technology, Syracuse University.

Hall, B. (1997). *Web-based training cookbook.* New York: Wiley.

Hannafin, M. J., Hannafin, K. M., Land, S. M., & Oliver, K. (1997). Grounded practice and the design of constructivist learning environments. *Educational Technology Research and Development, 45*(3), 101–117.

Hannafin, M. J., & Land, S. M. (1997). The foundations and assumptions of technology-enhanced student-centered learning environments. *Instructional Science, 25,* 167–202.

Hannafin, M. J., & Peck, K. L. (1988). *The design, development and evaluation of instructional software.* New York: Macmillan.

Hannafin, R. D., & Savenye, W. C. (1993, June). Technology in the classroom: The teacher's new role and resistance to it. *Educational Technology,* pp. 26–31.

Harrison, N. (1999). *How to design self-directed learning programs: A guide for creators of Web-based training, computer-based training, and self-study materials.* Boston: McGraw-Hill.

Heinich, R., Molenda, M., Russell, J. D., & Smaldino, S. E. (1999). *Instructional media and technologies for learning.* Upper Saddle River, NJ: Merrill.

Hill, J. R., & Hannafin, M. J. (1997). Cognitive strategies and learning from the World Wide Web. *Educational Technology Research and Development, 45*(4), 37–64.

Hiltz, S. R. (1990). Evaluating the virtual classroom. In L. M. Harasim (Ed.), *Online education: Perspectives on a new environment* (pp. 133–169). New York: Praeger.

Hooper, S., Hokanson, B., & Bernhardt, P. (2000). A competition to promote the design of educational software. *TechTrends, 45*(2), 3–4.

Jonassen, D. H., Hernandez-Serrano, J., & Choi, I. (2000). Integrating constructivism and learning technologies. In J. M. Spector & T. M. Anderson (Eds.), *Integrated and holistic perspectives on learning, instruction and technology: Understanding complexity* (pp. 103–128). Dordrecht, Netherlands: Kluwer.

Kaufman, R. (2000). *Mega planning: Practical tools for organizational success.* Thousand Oaks, CA: Sage.

Khan, B. H., & Vega, R. (1997). Factors to consider when evaluating a Web-based instruction course: A survey. In B. H. Khan (Ed.), *Web-based instruction* (pp. 375–378). Englewood Cliffs, NJ: Educational Technology Publications.

Knott, T. (1994). *Designing & evaluating distance education: A guide to collaboration.* Memphis, TN: Diasphera Publications, Publishers for American Academy for Distance Learning and Training.

Ko, S., & Rossen, S. (2001). *Teaching online: A practical guide.* Boston: Houghton Mifflin.

Lewis, J., Whitaker, J., & Julian, J. (1995). Distance education for the 21st century: The future of national and international telecomputing networks in distance education. In Z. Berge & M. Collins (Eds.), *Computer mediated communication and the online classroom* (Vol. 3, pp. 13–30). Cresskill, NJ: Hampton Press.

Marland, P. (1997). *Towards more effective open and distance teaching.* London: Kogan Page.

McGreal, R. (2000). The tele-campus online course directory. In B. L. Mann (Ed.), *Perspectives in Web course management* (pp. 103–115). Toronto: Canadian Scholars Press.

Miltiadou, M., & Savenye, W. (2000). Applying social cognitive constructs of motivation to enhance student success in online distance education. In M. R. Simonson & K. Sparks (Eds.), *The 22nd Annual Proceedings of Selected Research and Development Presentations at the October, 2000 National Convention of the Association for Educational Communications and Technology, Sponsored by the Research and Theory Division, Long Beach, CA, February, 2000* (pp. 211–226). Columbus, OH: AECT.

Moore, M. G., & Kearsley, G. (1996). *Distance education: A systems view.* Belmont, CA: Wadsworth.

Nielsen, J. (2000). *Designing Web usability.* Indianapolis, IN: New Riders.

Palloff, R. M., & Pratt, K. (1999). *Building learning communities in cyberspace: Effective strategies for the online classroom.* San Francisco: Jossey-Bass.

Popham, W. J. (1993). *Educational evaluation* (3rd ed.). Boston: Allyn & Bacon.

Porter, L. A. (1997). *Creating the virtual classroom—Distance learning with the Internet.* New York: Wiley.

Race, P. (1994). *The open learning handbook: Promoting quality in designing and delivering flexible learning* (2nd ed.). London: Kogan Page.

Rumble, G. (1992). *The management of distance learning systems.* Paris: UNESCO, International Institute for Educational Planning.

Rumble, G. (1997). *The costs and economics of open and distance learning.* London: Kogan Page.

Savenye, W. (1998, June). *Evaluating the impact of video and Web-based distance learning courses.* Paper presented at the annual meeting of EDMEDIA/TELECOM, Freiburg, Germany.

Savenye, W. (2000a). *Evaluation of Computer-Instructional Software form.* Unpublished instrument, Arizona State University, Tempe.

Savenye, W. C. (2000b). Reflections on developing a Web-based *Teaching with Technology* course. In J. M. Spector & T. M. Anderson (Eds.), *Integrated and holistic perspectives on learning, instruction and technology: Understanding complexity* (pp. 35–60). Dordrecht, Netherlands: Kluwer.

Savenye, W., Dwyer, H., Niemczyk, M., Olina, Z., Kim, A., Nicolaou, A., & Kopp, H. (2003). Development of the digital high school project: A school–university partnership. *Computers in the Schools, 20*(1), 3–14.

Savenye, W. C., Olina, Z., & Niemczyk, M. (2001). So you are going to be an online writing instructor: Issues in designing, developing and delivering an online course. *Computers and Composition, 18,* 371–385.

Savenye, W. C., & Robinson, R. S. (2004). Qualitative research issues and methods: An introduction for educational technologists. In D. H. Jonassen (Ed.), *Handbook of research for educational communications and technology* (2nd ed., pp. 1045–1071). New York: Simon & Schuster Macmillan.

Savenye, W., Schnackenberg, H., & Jones, H. (1997, March). *Measuring learning and attitudes in a "really open" learning environment: Visitor evaluation at the Phoenix Zoo.* Paper presented at the annual meeting of the American Educational Research Association, Chicago.

Savenye, W., & Smith, K. (1997, February). *Enhancing interaction in an outcomes-based distance learning environment.* Paper presented at the annual meeting of the Association for Communications and Technology, Albuquerque, NM.

Savenye, W., Socolofsky, K., Greenhouse, R., & Copeman, R. (1997, November). *A visit to the desert: Summative evaluation of the comprehensive desert exhibit.* Paper presented at the annual meeting of the American Evaluation Association, San Diego, CA.

Seel, N. M., Al-Diban, S., & Blumschein, P. (2000). Mental models and instructional planning. In J. M. Spector & T. M. Anderson (Eds.), *Integrated and holistic perspectives on learning, instruction and technology: Understanding complexity* (pp. 129–158). Dordrecht, Netherlands: Kluwer.

Simonson, M. R. (1997). Evaluating teaching and learning at a distance. In T. E. Cyrs (Ed.), *Teaching and learning at a distance: What it takes to effectively design, deliver and evaluate programs*

(New Directions for Teaching and Learning, No. 71, pp. 87–94). San Francisco: Jossey-Bass.

Simonson, M., Smaldino, S., Albright, M., & Zvacek, S. (2003). *Teaching and learning at a distance: Foundations of distance education* (2nd ed.). Upper Saddle River, NJ: Merrill.

Smith, P. J., & Ragan, T. J. (1999). *Instructional design* (2nd ed.). Upper Saddle River, NJ: Merrill.

Spector, J. M. (2000). Building theory into practice in learning and instruction. In J. M. Spector & T. M. Anderson (Eds.), *Integrated and holistic perspectives on learning, instruction and technology: Understanding complexity* (pp. 79–90). Dordrecht, Netherlands: Kluwer.

Sullivan, H. J., & Higgins, N. (1983). *Teaching for competence.* New York: Teachers College Press.

Sullivan, H., Ice, K., & Niedermeyer, R. (2000). Long-term instructional development: A 20-year ID and implementation project. *Educational Technology Research and Development, 48*(4), 87–99.

Sullivan, H. J., Igoe, A. R., Klein, J. D., Jones, E. E., & Savenye, W. C. (1993). Perspectives on the future of educational technology. *Educational Technology Research and Development, 41*(2), 97–110.

Thorpe, M. (1988). *Evaluating open and distance learning.* Harlow, Essex, England: Longman Open Learning.

Tiffin, J., & Rajasingham, L. (1995). *In search of the virtual class: Education in an information society.* London & New York: Routledge.

Chapter 15

Evaluating the Pedagogical Value of Multimedia Learning Material: An Experimental Study in Primary School

Erkki Olkinuora
Mirjamaija Mikkilä-Erdmann
Sami Nurmi
University of Turku, Finland

The aim of this chapter is, first, to present our theoretical framework for investigating learning material and, second, through an empirical study, to demonstrate the problems of creating effective multimedia learning environments in the domain of science. The emphasis in the empirical study is on comparing the effects of working with multimedia and with textbook-based materials, as well as on describing the actual learning and working processes with multimedia. In this chapter, multimedia and hypermedia are seen as almost synonymous, because both make use of many digital media formats (text, pictures, videos, animations, etc.) and often have a non-linear structure and different interactive elements that enable users to engage with the material.

During the 1980s and 1990s, there was a rapid increase in commercially produced multimedia learning materials. At the same time, there was both optimism and skepticism about the pedagogical quality of the multimedia material available (cf. Chen & Zhang, 2000; Lehtinen, 2000; Nurmi & Jaakkola, 2002). Digital multimedia materials have been said to hold many promises, but among these new possibilities there can also be found many challenges and difficulties for teachers and students alike. However, many of these promises have no clear unequivocal evidence from scientific research.

1. These quite new learning materials are found to be very motivating for students to work with (e.g., Ayersman, 1996). To some extent, the moti-

vation effect can be explained by the novelty of these computer-based materials. This motivational effect is nevertheless self-evident, but in some students (e.g., those who have computer anxiety) the effects can be adverse (cf. Åkerlind & Trevitt, 1999; Brosnan, 1998).

2. Multimedia materials are said to be very engaging and hold the student's attention (Jonassen & Reeves, 1996). This means that when working with multimedia materials, students are concentrating on learning assignments and contents, and their task orientation is preserved. The other side of the coin is superficial engagement and surface-level processing if students are just focusing on the "entertaining" features of multimedia (e.g., sounds and visual effects).

3. The nonlinear structure of multimedia resources offers possibilities to roam through the information space according to the needs and interests of the student at his or her own pace. In that way, the control of learning can be thought of as given to the student him- or herself, as the control in more linear (e.g., traditional textbook) materials lies in the material itself or is teacher-governed (e.g., Lawless & Brown, 1997). This open information structure can be both very useful and challenging for advanced students, whose metacognitive abilities to monitor and guide their own learning are developed. Yet multimedia requires that students continuously construct a coherent understanding of the content as a whole (Rouet & Levonen, 1996). On the other hand, this openness of material can exceed the capabilities of certain students, and the effect of nonlinearity hinders effective learning. Open structure underlines the importance of navigation through multimedia, and often students are lost or just drift through material if they do not have clear objectives for their work.

4. One of the most important features of multimedia materials is the possibility to embed various cognitive tools within them (Harper, Hedberg, Corderoy, & Wright, 2000). Cognitive tools may include interactive elements that allow students to explore, manipulate, and observe the effects of their inputs, so that they can engage with the given content more deeply. Hence, interactive tools extend the affordances of multimedia far beyond the mere representation of content with different media formats. Thus, students need more guidance and scaffolding when using these tools to get the full advantage of them.

5. Although learning with multimedia material has been found in many studies (e.g., Ayersman, 1996; Liao, 1998) to be superior or at least equal when compared to different, more traditional forms of instruction, the reliability of those media comparison studies can be questioned. For example, often in these studies the overwhelming amount of investment and effort by teachers and researchers was not taken into account. Furthermore, there is also the greater probability of "null hypothesis" studies, which are not as

likely to be published compared to studies in which significant effects are found, which has to be taken into account.

When considering the effects of multimedia in learning, we must bear in mind that almost always all the other factors of the teaching–learning context are at least as important as the features and quality of the multimedia material used in a given situation (cf. Lehtinen, 2000). The factors that have an effect on emerging learning and working processes and outcomes include variables like the nature of tasks given to students; the characteristics, abilities, intentions, skills, and previous knowledge of teacher(s) and learners; the physical settings; the social and psychological climate of the activity environment; and the properties of the learning material used (Tergan, 1997). Also, the interpretations, perceptions, and meanings students make when faced with the actual learning environment have a strong impact on the quality of their learning as well as on the personal experiences they build up (Järvelä, Lehtinen, & Salonen, 2000; Olkinuora & Salonen, 1992).

This indicates the importance of considering the whole learning environment and the actual learning and working processes with multimedia when trying to evaluate the pedagogical value of multimedia learning material. Therefore, the focus in multimedia learning research should be moved toward a more process-oriented case research instead of media comparison and effectiveness research, which has dominated research in previous decades (Kozma, 1994; Jonassen, Campbell, & Davidson, 1994; Mayer, 1997; Reeves, 1998). Based on this refocusing issue, in the empirical part of our work we emphasize the process analysis of working with multimedia rather than just comparing the effects of multimedia and text material, although for getting an overall comprehension of the effectiveness of multimedia, comparison results are also presented.

In our opinion, the more fruitful issue in possible learning outcomes with multimedia materials is the question of the quality or level of learning. Multimedia can be assumed to produce deeper understanding and robust mental construction about given content being learned, but it is not as suitable for the learning and reproduction of factual knowledge (e.g., Olkinuora, Mikkilä-Erdmann, Nurmi, & Ottosson, 2001).

A FRAMEWORK FOR THEORETICALLY AND EMPIRICALLY ANALYZING THE ROLE OF LEARNING MATERIALS

We have developed a common framework that emphasizes the interactional nature of instructional processes, in which learning materials (textbooks, multimedia, etc.) can be seen as an important factor influencing the

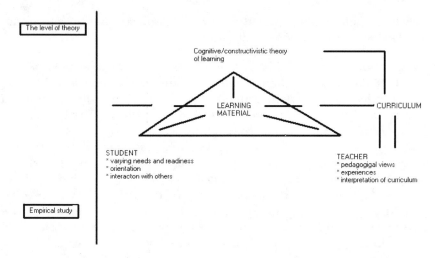

FIG. 15.1.   Conceptual framework for research on learning material.

quality of the learning process (the framework is presented in a slightly modified form in Fig. 15.1; cf. Mikkilä & Olkinuora, 1994, p. 152).

As symbolized by its central position in Fig. 15.1, the learning material has a significant role in the teaching–learning process because of its systemic relations to all the other important components influencing that process. The teacher can use multimedia material as a teaching tool and hence it can influence the suggested activities of learners through the learning assignments, guidance, and assessment included in it. With the emergence of the constructive conception of learning, the focus in the analysis of learning materials has moved from regarding them as teachers' teaching tools to seeing them as students' learning tools. When analyzing the pedagogical value of a certain multimedia material, for instance, we should take into account the specific functions aimed at in the pedagogical context. We can briefly mention the following as possible examples of these: (a) illustrating, animating, simulating, and demonstrating target phenomena; (b) bringing experiential, emotional, or phenomenological elements into material in order to increase students' motivational interest in certain contents; (c) fostering problem-based learning by presenting, with different media formats and representations, typical problems and complex solving situations from a given field; and (d) arousing cognitive conflicts by presenting conceptions and examples that differ from students' own ideas in order to foster conceptual change (cf. Dillon & Gabbard, 1998).

It is important to note that each of the interacting agents—the teacher, the learning material, the learners themselves, and also, to some extent, the other students in the classroom—exert some control over the cognitive and social interactions in the situation and, via these, over the quality of learning and its outcomes. It is also worth noting that the control of each interaction partner may be positive or negative (fostering or hindering learning), weak or excessive, and direct or indirect. Thus, from the point of view of successful teaching arrangements, the systemic balance between controls exerted by the subsystems is very important.

ELABORATION OF THEORETICAL EXPECTATIONS CONCERNING THE BENEFITS OR RESTRICTIONS OF UTILIZING MULTIMEDIA MATERIAL BY DIFFERENT GROUPS OF STUDENTS

New types of computer-based learning materials, such as multimedia, have been regarded as deviating essentially from more traditional learning materials particularly in allowing a much greater degree of freedom in the search for information and, thus, more self-directed interaction with the material at hand. Possible reasons for failures, especially concerning certain students, are also linked to the question of student control in the situation. It is not enough to offer opportunities for student control and regulation of the process if their prior knowledge concerning the knowledge contents to be learned is weak, if students' self-regulation skills in learning or technical skills in searching for information and using interfaces are poorly developed, and if their orientation influencing the interpretation of the situation (and hence the types of goals and motives arising in the situation) is inadequate or biased. In the literature on the subject, the analysis of match or mismatch between the degrees of freedom for students and their readiness for utilizing them properly has often remained at an unspecified level. We think that the following theoretical perspectives may be helpful for a more profound analysis of the role and quality of multimedia material in learning processes.

The first perspective concentrates on the relations between the degree of teacher regulation of learning and that of student regulation in teaching situations or arrangements (Vermunt, 1998; Vermunt & Verloop, 1999). The central idea of this theoretical view can be presented in a schematic and surmised form as in Table 15.1 (Vermunt & Verloop, 1999): If the external control (strong regulation by a teacher or by the learning material utilized) in instructional conditions is strong, but students possess a high level of self-regulation skills or are used to instruction that presupposes it, a destructive friction may arise with harmful consequences for high-quality learning. On the other hand, if the degree of teacher regulation (or of material-based regulation) of learning is low and the readiness of students for self-regulation is high, they are in congruence with each other and the process of learning is probably effective. However, from the point of view of

TABLE 15.1
Interplays Between Three Levels of Teacher Regulation
and Three Levels of Student Regulation of Learning Processes

Degree of Student Regulation of Learning	Degree of Teacher Regulation of Learning		
	Strong	Shared	Loose
High	Destructive friction	Destructive friction	Congruence
Intermediate	Destructive friction	Congruence	Constructive friction
Low	Congruence	Constructive friction	Destructive friction

Note.   According to Vermunt and Verloop (1999).

long-term objectives, it may be even more appropriate that the demands for self-regulation in learning situations be slightly (but not much) higher than the present inclination of students in order to produce constructive friction. This kind of pedagogical principle coincides well with the conception of expertise outlined by Bereiter and Scardamalia (1993). According to them, teaching accompanied by progressive problem solving, in which problems become gradually more and more demanding, surpassing the present level of solving skills, produces a dynamic and continuously developing expertise.

When we apply this theory to a learning situation in which students study certain contents with the help of multimedia material and solve problems or assignments, we can present the following assumptions: Provided that the content to be learned is relatively demanding and complex for the age level in question (i.e., includes many types of information, abstract concepts, and target phenomena that have not been taught previously or are not familiar to students otherwise) and one doesn't receive scaffolding from the teacher, those students having low self-regulatory capability may feel cognitive overload and destructive friction despite being generally motivated by the appealing-looking multimedia material. They may approach the contents eagerly in the beginning, but when they don't understand the contents well, cannot discern the most relevant information from the point of view of task solving, and cannot seek further information in a goal-directed way, they may lose their task orientation, start to browse the material without any particular intention in mind (cf. nonmindful drifting; e.g., Jacobson & Archodidou, 2000; Tergan, 1997), and end up with poor learning outcomes. Conversely, students having better self-regulatory capabilities and who experience the contents and the problems to be solved as properly challenging usually proceed in a more goal-directed and appropriate way when seeking further information by utilizing the cognitive tools provided by the multimedia material. Because of the accumulation of successful experiences in corresponding situations, they can feel constructive friction, which may maintain and even strengthen their intrinsic motivation during the process. Thus, relevant, task-focused motivation keeps up the seeking of appropriate information, increases the probability of achieving high-level learning outcomes, and increases those students' perceptions of the value of multimedia-type study materials' allowing much control of the process by the students themselves.

However, the capacity for acting in a self-regulated way is not always a sufficient condition for its actual application in the learning situation. Therefore, the second theoretical perspective we want to raise is the viewpoint of situational, motivational orientations. For actual application, one also needs to be properly motivated, that is, interested in the contents and motivated by the challenge of demanding tasks. Of course, the lack of self-regulation skills in the situation may lead to frustration and reduced motivation. On the other hand, accumulated experiences (especially failures) within a student's educational and learning history may produce a certain kind of inclination or vulnerability in learning situations to interpret the situation in a certain way in a given domain of knowledge or school subject, which in turn triggers certain motives and goals. Many studies concerning situational, sociomotivational orientations have shown their effects on the ways pupils approach learning tasks, and of the progressive or regressive development of learning readiness (Lehtinen, Vauras, Salonen, Olkinuora, & Kinnunen, 1995).

We have classified these situational orientations into four categories: *task orientation, socially dependent orientation, ego-defensive orientation,* and *noncommitment orientation.* Task orientation is usually linked with a deep approach, progressive development, and the motivation to be positively challenged with demanding tasks, whereas the other orientations are often connected to learning difficulties and to ineffective action from the point of view of achieving higher order learning goals (Olkinuora & Salonen, 1992). For instance, if a student is prone to social dependency in a situation where he or she is not very willing to make self-directed and independent efforts, he or she easily becomes helpless and seeks hints and tips from others right from the beginning of the process (Salonen, Lehtinen, & Olkinuora, 1998). Students typically oriented in this way are happier in a learning situation with strong teacher-regulated teaching because they feel more secure and are "overconsumers" of external support and guidance. Skillful and gradually fading scaffolding is needed for them to strengthen their self-reliance and self-regulation skills. Ego-defensive orientation easily leads to avoidance behavior in demanding situations. Due to expectation of failure, the student feels threatened in these situations and does not, therefore, concentrate intensively on the task at hand or the problems to be solved. He or she may instead try to find some compensatory tactics in order not to lose face. When we combine the views of both the theoretical perspectives described here, we can understand more clearly why studying, even with the help of high-quality multimedia material, does not always lead to a successful process and good learning outcomes, not to mention situations in which poorly designed multimedia material is utilized.

Our studies on the individual and group levels have indicated that those students who approach learning contents and assignments in a task-oriented way usually learn more than students oriented in the other ways previously described. Task-oriented interpretations of study situations seem to promote learning goals (cf. Boekaerts, 1995) and foster progressive development in the long run (Lehtinen et al., 1995). This kind of accumulation of successful experiences strengthens self-reliance in future learning situations and helps the student to concentrate deeply on the tasks at hand without anxiety or feelings of helplessness (cf. the concept of domain-specific self-efficacy in Bandura, 1997). One can assume that the typical affordances and cognitive tools provided by the best multimedia materials serve the interests of task-oriented students who can utilize them in an independent, self-regulated way particularly well. However, when multimedia materials are utilized as learning tools in a collaborative way, the models and peer coaching offered by more advanced students may help less advanced students to be more task-oriented, and also help them to good learning outcomes.

All of this depends, however, on the special features and quality of design of the multimedia material at hand. The specific qualities of the multimedia material applied in this study are described in the empirical section.

EMPIRICAL STUDY

Research Objectives and Problems

The main aim of the research was to build a learning environment in which the students engaged in collaborative and exploratory learning using interactive multimedia. This particular environment tries to engage students in meaningful and mindful learning, as well as to increase the amount of task-oriented work. The learning tasks the students were dealing with were so complex and cognitively challenging that success would require collaboration with peer learners. In addition, multimedia with its strong power of visualization and other interactive features would, in principle, provide support for students' deeper understanding of the content being learned (see, e.g., Kozma, Russell, Jones, Marx, & Davis, 1996; Jacobson & Archodidou, 2000). The main goal was that students would construct their knowledge by exploring the multimedia and solving different types of tasks in pairs, which was in line with the principle of "learning with technology" (adopted from Jonassen, Peck, & Wilson, 1999). Thus, the multimedia material was not

TABLE 15.2
Experimental Design

	Before	Working Phase 1	Immediately After Working	Working Phase 2	Immediately After Working	2 Weeks After
Experimental Group 1	Pretest	Working with text	Posttest 1	Working with multimedia	Posttest 2	Delayed posttest
Experimental Group 2	Pretest	Working with multimedia	Posttest 1	Working with text	Posttest 2	Delayed posttest

taking the place of a teacher, was not directly teaching the students (no transmission of knowledge; not "learning from technology"). On the other hand, in order to get a more extensive view of the effects of multimedia on learning processes and outcomes, learner pairs were also given textbook material dealing with the same topic. In this way, it was possible to compare the work between multimedia and linear text material.

The research problems set for the study were the following:

1. What are the learning/working processes and the nature of social interaction of the observed student pairs in the multimedia condition?
2. Do the achieved learning outcomes differ between the two comparison groups working in multimedia and text material conditions and in two experimental situations (see Table 15.2 for details)?
3. Do the differences between the comparison groups vary according to the type of tasks (in factual, generative, and problem-solving tasks)?

Experimental Design and Methods

Participants were 36 students from an urban Finnish comprehensive school. Students were 11 years old. The students were randomized into 18 pairs, and were then divided into two experimental groups, each consisting of 9 pairs. In the first phase, one group (Group 2) worked with multimedia and the other (Group 1) with text material. After this phase, they swapped so that Group 1 worked with multimedia and Group 2 with text material (see Table 15.2). Each of these working phases lasted 2 hours, and both of them were conducted during 1 week.

Before the working phases, students were pretested with respect to their prior knowledge of the subject matter, as well as to computer skills and attitudes toward computers. After each working phase, posttests were carried out measuring student pairs' learning outcomes based on the two types of learning materials. Two weeks after the project, delayed posttests were administered to find out the longer term learning effects. The posttests were identical in each of the phases. All assignments and tests consisted of three types of questions: factual, generative, and problem solving. By comparing the learning outcomes concerning different types of materials and between the different working phases, we can find out how the types of material affect the learning outcomes, and whether the learning impact is long-lasting (see Table 15.2 for details about the experimental design).

During the multimedia working phases, the work of four student pairs with multimedia (two from each group) was videotaped. The observed pairs were selected from randomized pairs so that two of them (Pairs 1 and 2) consisted of more advanced students whose self-regulation skills were good and common working habits resemble task orientation, and the other two pairs (Pairs 3 and 4) included less advanced students. These students' classifications were based on their pretest scores, previous grades, and the teacher's personal descriptions of them. This allowed us to compare the working processes and outcomes of different student pairs.

The student pairs' working and learning processes were analyzed using a system that concentrates on verbal interaction, social interaction, and cognitive processing (for more details, see Kumpulainen & Mutanen, 1999). Students' ways of seeking information and utilizing multimedia material were also analyzed. These process analyses, in addition to comparison of quantitative group-level results, provide valuable information about the nature of the influence of the multimedia material. By these observations we can describe students' ways of working with multimedia, which helps to clarify how this kind of material triggers task-related interaction and collaborative learning within each of the observed pairs of students. The observed pairs were also interviewed in order to reconstruct how they experienced the two experimental conditions from a motivational point of view. Only the pairs working in the multimedia condition were observed, because we were particularly interested in the actual processes that evolved around the computer when working with multimedia. Information about the ways and experiences when working with the linear text material was more indirect, based on the interviews mentioned before.

Learning Materials

The subject matter to be studied dealt with the brain, the (mal)functioning of the central nervous system, and the neurological basis of epilepsy. These contents can be regarded as complex and demanding for students of the age participating in this field experiment. During the working phases, student pairs solved problems and assignments that required them to explore different parts of the learning material. These assignments directed students' working with the materials. Both digital learning material and textbook material included the same basic contents, and both working phases were carried out by students working in pairs without any teacher guidance. The text material was constructed based on the contents of the multimedia as well as on relevant textbook material. The text material was 17 pages long and was enriched with a few pictures taken from certain books and from the multimedia material utilized in this project.

The title of the multimedia material used in this research is *Aivohakkeri* ("Brain Hacker"; Federation of Epilepsy, 1997), which focuses on epilepsy and its neurobiological basis. We regarded this multimedia as very appropriate for our purposes. *Aivohakkeri* can be considered to be of high quality, because its design has followed the design principles of pedagogical multimedia material proposed by Jacobson and Archodidou (2000) quite well. First, *Aivohakkeri* takes advantage of the powerful representational opportunities of multimedia because its content is presented in the form of a variety of media formats and tools for self-regulated exploration. Second, the content being learned is contextualized; that is, the content is connected to real-life situations and surroundings. One can take as an example of this contextualization the inclusion of a teenage boy suffering from epilepsy as a demonstration case. In this way, even more abstract and theoretical content is anchored to everyday-life contexts. Third, the presented theoretical knowledge is made more concrete by providing different cognitive tools within multimedia in order to facilitate thought-provoking interaction between the learner and the content. By utilizing them, students can, for instance, explore the effects on visual field of different types of damage to the optic nerve (see Fig. 15.2). Fourth, concrete examples of different issues concerning epilepsy and abstract concepts applicable to those cases are

FIG. 15.2. An example of one cognitive tool used inside the multimedia material. With this interactive tool, students can explore, manipulate, and observe the effects of different types of damage to the optic nerves.

linked together in a way that would help a student to integrate these levels with each other.

In our opinion, however, this multimedia material also included some deficiencies of design. The user interface of the multimedia was a bit clumsy and occasionally difficult to use. The linking between different content areas, and between concrete examples and their theoretical explanations, could also be more numerous and clearer. Potentially the most crucial drawback of this multimedia is the lack of overall indexing of contents. The structure of multimedia offers hardly any guidance for proceeding and browsing through the vast amount of information included in it. There is, however, one "wizard" that mainly provides advice on how to use the multimedia on a procedural level, but guidance on content and cognitive levels is missing (i.e., there are no recommendations on which content to start the browsing from, where to go next, etc.). Therefore, the design of this multimedia relies heavily on students' self-regulation abilities, their motivation to learn, and their interest to explore the material.

Hypothesis of Working With These Learning Materials

Based on the preceding description of the selected multimedia material, its use can be assumed to be motivating for students and cognitively engaging, producing thought-provoking interaction between students and contents. In general, the multimedia material can be expected to be more motivating for students than the linear text material. Therefore, we assume that deeper levels of understanding and, thus, improved learning outcomes, especially in more applied tasks, can be achieved with multimedia. However, this assumption may not hold at the level of every student. As mentioned before, we think that applying multimedia and facing complex content and demanding tasks may produce difficulties for some students. Students not capable of effective self-regulation and vulnerable to other than task-centered orientation in particular will face problems. This is thought to diminish the motivating effects of multimedia. These problems of non-task-oriented students apply to the context of studying with the help of linear text material, but to a lesser extent. They are more familiar with working with that kind of material, and perhaps they don't feel confusing or cognitive overload when most central information is presented in only one "channel" or mode. The lack of relevant guidance by a teacher may also be harmful for students with poor self-regulatory skills. They may experience the destructive friction described by Vermunt and Verloop (1999) more easily. Students possessing good self-regulatory skills and those who feel that the tasks are positively challenging may benefit more from the multifaceted opportunities of multimedia materials. Nevertheless, less advanced students with lower self-regulation skills and non-task-orientation might also reach meaningful and deeper learning and good outcomes when working in pairs. Collaboration and interaction between partners may include, in successful cases, efficient peer coaching and scaffolding (cf. Vygotsky, 1978), provided that the other partner is a more advanced student.

Results

The Nature of the Working and Learning Processes of Observed Student Pairs

According to the analyses of student pairs' working processes, the applied multimedia material seems to elicit and maintain pupils' task orientation quite well. Three of the observed four pairs were, most of the time, aiming at achieving the learning objectives and carrying out the assigned tasks. This was also the case concerning the less well achieving pupils. This is a result worth noting, because the subject matter was not easy to learn and is perhaps not very interesting for pupils of that age. Although concentration on tasks was generally good, the level of cognitive processing clearly varied among different pairs. While two of the observed pairs (more advanced students; Pairs 1 and 2) were capable of deeper and exploratory learning (i.e., meaningful learning), the other two pairs worked more at a procedural/surface level (Pair 4) or spent more time on off-task processing (Pair 3). On average, the time spent on task-oriented working was usually distributed rather evenly between exploratory (i.e., reflective and deeper level learning) and procedural (i.e., surface-level) processing, and the amount of off-task behavior was quite low, except in the case of Pair 3 (see Fig. 15.3).

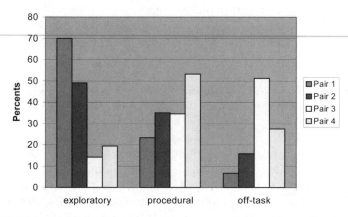

FIG. 15.3.   The distribution of cognitive processing among observed student pairs during working with multimedia material.

TABLE 15.3
Results From Two Pupil Pairs Contrasted With Each Other

	Prior Knowledge		Working Phase 1		Working Phase 2		Delayed Posttest
	Assignments	Pretest	Assignments	Posttest	Assignments	Posttest	Posttest
Pair 1	19	6	30	5	**34**	**8**	8
Pair 3	12	1	**18**	**3**	22	4	3

Note. Scores of the multimedia context are marked in **bold**.

The observed cognitive processing was also connected to the test scores achieved by these pairs: The pair that worked in the most exploratory way (Pair 1) achieved the highest scores, and the pair with the lowest level of cognitive processing (Pair 3) achieved the lowest scores. In Table 15.3, the scores of the best and the poorest observed pairs in each phase of the experiment are presented. These scores are also in line with our starting premises that more advanced and task-oriented student pairs (e.g., Pair 1) are more successful than less advanced pairs (e.g., Pair 3) irrespective of the learning material used. *Assignments* refer to the tasks given by the researchers to direct the working of the pairs concerning both types of learning materials (theoretical range of sum scores = 0–41). Posttests refer to the five tasks that measured learning outcomes (theoretical range of sum scores = 0–10). When performing the posttests, pupil pairs did not have the learning materials at their disposal.

Pair 1 seems to have achieved a goal-oriented, collaborative, and cognitively meaningful search for information with the multimedia material. Their way of working fits well with the outcome scores they achieved, especially in the phase of studying contents by utilizing multimedia. These findings are also confirmed in the interview of this pair, in which they regarded their working with multimedia as enjoyable, inspiring, and very task-oriented. The other pair (Pair 3), on which we concentrate for the purposes of contrast in this example, did not reach a consensus concerning the objectives, and the quality of their collaboration remained poor. This can also be seen in their interview, where they admitted that there had been many social conflicts and a lack of mutual understanding. These problems were not due to the features of the multimedia used, but more to a weak personal relationship between these students. The members of this pair also had a very different opinion about multimedia and its usefulness. The pair's scores on indicators describing the relevance of their cognitive processing, social interaction, and linguistic expressions, classified according to the analysis system developed by Kumpulainen and Mutanen (1999), indicate a less effective way of working with learning materials than that of the aforementioned pair of students. Thus, it is not surprising that their scores on work tasks and tasks measuring learning outcomes also remained considerably lower than those of the other observed pair. It also worth noting that, from the point of view of our specified hypotheses, they performed better in the context of the linear text material.

Most of the verbal interaction between pupils within pairs involved negotiating ways of using the multimedia, as well as the external features of the multimedia. In addition to the high amount of procedural and surface-level verbal interaction, the proportion of exploratory talk (reflecting deeper knowledge construction) was still moderate when compared to working with the schoolbook-type learning material. The percentage of exploratory talk clearly differed between the observed student pairs (see Fig. 15.4). Episodes of argumentation and articulation were few within Pair 3. Although two of the four pairs conducted quite a lot of exploratory talk, in only one of the pairs did argumentation take place frequently (Pair 1).

In terms of social interaction, the student pairs worked quite collaboratively. All the pairs collaborated for more than half of the working time, and three out of four spent over 70% of the time doing so (see Fig. 15.5). Thus, multimedia material seemed to serve as a good basis for collaborative activities and learning. It may be that multimedia material could maintain the focus of all learners on contents, that is, on the information presented on the screen, and so foster a shared understanding and task-related interaction. Multimedia material can be regarded as a shared frame of reference that students can utilize during collaboration.

Altogether, half of the observed student pairs achieved a high quality in their working and deeper levels of processing (Pairs 1 and 2). Thus, their learning fulfilled the requirements of meaningful constructive learning (as presented by Jonassen et al., 1999), whereas the other two student pairs

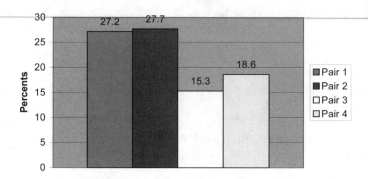

FIG. 15.4.   The amount of exploratory talk among observed pairs during multimedia working.

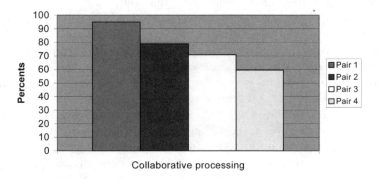

FIG. 15.5. The amount of collaborative processing among observed pairs
during multimedia working.

(Pairs 3 and 4) did not reach this level. The learning and information processing of these latter pairs occurred at a surface level, without reflective and deeper reasoning. They tended to concentrate more on the external and visible features of the multimedia than on the contents and subject matter.

Multimedia material seems to support some pairs, but not all, to achieve meaningful learning. Multimedia, with its opportunities to facilitate deeper cognitive processing in students, could be considered to fully reveal itself only to more advanced students. The open and interactive tools of multimedia might be too challenging or require too much self-regulation for less advanced students (e.g., Pair 3, in our case), and only more advanced students (e.g., Pairs 1 and 2) are ready for these new challenges. Although multimedia materials can be regarded as motivating tools for students to use and work with, these motivating effects might be hindered by the raised requirements for self-regulative work that multimedia demands. According to our assumptions, the more advanced and self-regulated students succeeded better with multimedia material than the less advanced students. However, the differences between them could be narrowed if multimedia material is able to motivate weaker students toward a relatively task-oriented way of working and if it provides enough guidance even for less advanced students as well.

The Overall Effects of Multimedia Versus Text Material on Learning

When we compared the quantitative effects of multimedia and text materials, our main interest focused on the posttest scores of the first working phase, when both experimental groups faced the same tasks for the first

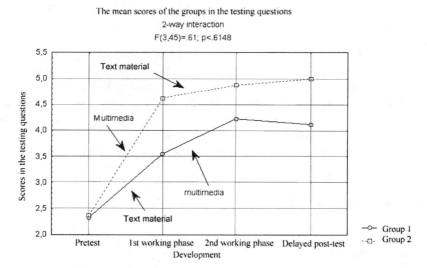

FIG. 15.6.   Mean posttest scores of experimental groups.

time after working with different types of materials. According to the results, the work with multimedia material consistently produced slightly better results than work with linear text (see Fig. 15.6). At posttest 1, Experimental Group 1 achieved a mean score of 3.6 with text material, and Experimental Group 2 working with multimedia had a mean score of 4.6. However, the score differences were not statistically significant, $t(15) = -1.26$, $p = .23$, but this may be partly due to the small number of student pairs. However, based on these scores we can state that, on the whole, multimedia material was at least as effective as text material when it comes to quantitative learning outcomes.

Did the Effects of Learning Materials Vary as a Function of Different Task Types?

The posttests consisted of three different types of tasks, namely, factual, generative, and problem-solving. When examining the effects of type of material on performances in different kinds of tasks at posttest 1, multimedia material seemed to produce significantly better scores, $t(15) = -2.58$, $p = .02$, than text material in tasks that required problem solving and knowledge application (see Table 15.4). This might be due to the abilities of multimedia to present the information from many perspectives and illuminate the relations between different concepts more effectively. On factual and generative questions, there were no statistically significant differences in the posttest scores between the experimental groups after the first working phase, $t(15) = -0.37$, $p = .72$; $t(15) = -0.83$, $p = .42$. However, when comparing the effect sizes between pre- and posttests with different learning materials (see Table 15.4; changes in percents), it can be concluded that multimedia material was superior in factual and problem-solving tasks, and text material was more effective in generative tasks. The fact that the multimedia material was fostering better results in factual tasks whereas text material produced higher scores in generative tasks is against our expectations and points to the need for developing specific aspects of theory further, provided that the same kind of findings will be repeatedly found. Table 15.4 presents the scores from the pretest and posttest 1 after the first working phase.

Conclusions Concerning Learning With Multimedia

It is difficult, perhaps even impossible, to accurately separate the effects of multimedia material on learning results and processes from the effects of other variables affecting the learning environment. Therefore, when studying the educational value of multimedia, it is important to take into account all the variables in the learning environment (i.e., teacher, student, context, task, material, test variables). Merely the use of multimedia material does not guarantee or cause high-quality learning, because learning— in an ideal case—requires individual cognitive efforts, collaborative knowledge building, and situated interaction with context (cf. Nurmi & Jaakkola, 2002). In fact, there is only an indirect link between media and learning. At least as important for learning as the features of multimedia is a way of implementing multimedia material pedagogically by a teacher, and the nature and structure of the social learning environment in its entirety.

On the basis of this study, we can conclude that multimedia material is not some sort of magic trick that can be used to get all student pairs to work and learn in a collaborative and reflective way. Some pairs reached the level of meaningful, constructive, high-quality learning, whereas others did not. However, multimedia material can engage most students in task-oriented processing and foster exploratory working. Moreover, multimedia material seems to support collaborative working, and therefore its utilization can be recommended in collaborative learning environments. In interviews, the students considered multimedia material to be very motivating to work with, which may in part be due to novelty attraction. We assume that educational multimedia materials can be most valuable when they are used as authentic information sources and as materials for exploratory and problem-based learning in collaborative learning environments. However, the quality of the pedagogical design of such materials and ways of implementing them in instruction are the most important factors, not the technology applied in the multimedia materials as such.

TABLE 15.4
Mean Scores Between Experimental Groups in Pretest and Posttest 1 on Different Task Types

	Experimental Group 1			Experimental Group 2			t Test	
	Scores	SD	Change in Percents	Scores	SD	Change in Percents	t Value	p Value
Pretest								
Factual	1.0	1.22	—	0.4	1.01	—	1.048	.310
Generative	0.7	1.19	—	1.2	1.09	—	-1.066	.302
Problem solving	0.7	0.50	—	0.6	0.53	—	.459	.653
Posttest 1								
Factual	1.6	1.24	+60	**1.8**	**0.89**	**+350**	-.368	.718
Generative	1.4	1.01	+100	**1.9**	**1.13**	**+58.30**	-.830	.416
Problem solving	0.6	0.53	-14.3	**1.1**	**0.35**	**+83.3**	-2.579	.021*

Note. Working with multimedia marked in **bold**.

*$p < .05$.

349

Only by doing relevant process-oriented research in varied contexts and domains of knowledge will we become capable of assessing, at a more elaborated level, the pedagogical value and functions of utilizing multimedia materials. We also need more profound and further specified theoretical models to interpret what actually happens in these processes, and how the interaction of multiple factors linked to the self-regulative skills of learners, the features of multimedia materials, and the teaching arrangements of teachers produces certain learning outcomes. It seems that theories such as that of Vermunt and Verloop (1999), concerning the degree of match between readiness of students for self-regulation and the level of self-regulation demanded by instructional arrangements, and that of situational orientations (Lehtinen et al., 1995) are useful for developing more elaborated theoretical models of this required type.

REFERENCES

Åkerlind, G., & Trevitt, A. (1999). Enhancing self-directed learning through educational technology: When students resist the change. *Innovations in Education and Training International, 36*(2), 96–105.

Ayersman, D. (1996). Reviewing the research on hypermedia-based learning. *Journal of Research in Computing in Education, 28*(4), 500–526.

Bandura, A. (1997). *Self-efficacy: The exercise of control.* New York: Freeman.

Bereiter, C., & Scardamalia, M. (1993). *Surpassing ourselves: An inquiry into the nature and implications of expertise.* Chicago: Open Court.

Boekaerts, M. (1995). Self-regulated learning: Bridging the gap between metacognitive and metamotivation theories. *Educational Psychologist, 30*(4), 195–200.

Brosnan, M. (1998). *Technophobia: The psychological impact of information technology.* London: Routledge.

Chen, Q., & Zhang, J. (2000). Using ICT to support constructive learning. In D. Watson & T. Downes (Eds.), *Communications and networking in education: Learning in a networked society* (pp. 231–241). London: Kluwer.

Dillon, A., & Gabbard, R. (1998). Hypermedia as an educational technology: A review of the quantitative research literature on learner comprehension, control and style. *Review of Educational Research, 68*(3), 322–349.

Federation of Epilepsy. (1997). *Aivohakkeri* [Brain hacker] [CD-ROM]. Helsinki, Finland: Author.

Harper, B., Hedberg, J., Corderoy, B., & Wright, R. (2000). Employing cognitive tools within interactive multimedia applications. In S. Lajoie (Ed.), *Computers as cognitive tools: Vol. 2. No more walls* (pp. 227–246). Mahwah, NJ: Lawrence Erlbaum Associates.

Jacobson, M. J., & Archodidou, A. (2000). The design of hypermedia tools for learning: Fostering conceptual change and transfer of complex scientific knowledge. *Journal of the Learning Sciences, 9*(2), 149–199.

Järvelä, S., Lehtinen, E., & Salonen, P. (2000). Socio-emotional orientations as a mediating variable in teaching learning interaction: Implications for instructional design. *Scandinavian Journal of Educational Research, 44*(3), 293–306.

Jonassen, D., Campbell, J., & Davidson, M. (1994). Learning with media: Restructuring the debate. *Educational Technology Research & Development, 42*(2), 31–39.

Jonassen, D., Peck, K., & Wilson, B. (1999). *Learning with technology: A constructivist perspective.* Upper Saddle River, NJ: Prentice-Hall.

Jonassen, D., & Reeves, T. (1996). Learning with technology: Using computers as cognitive tools. In D. Jonassen (Ed.), *Handbook of research for educational communications and technology* (pp. 693–719). New York: Macmillan.

Kozma, R. (1994). A reply: Media and methods. *Educational Technology Research & Development, 42*(3), 11–14.

Kozma, R., Russell, J., Jones, J., Marx, N., & Davis, J. (1996). The use of multiple, linked representations to facilitate science understanding. In S. Vosniadou, E. De Corte, R. Glaser, & H. Mandl (Eds.), *International perspectives on the design of technology-supported learning environments* (pp. 41–60). Mahwah, NJ: Lawrence Erlbaum Associates.

Kumpulainen, K., & Mutanen, M. (1999). The situated dynamics of peer group interaction: An introduction to an analytic framework. *Learning and Instruction, 9,* 449–473.

Lawless, K., & Brown, S. (1997). Multimedia learning environments: Issues of learner control and navigation. *Instructional Science, 25,* 117–131.

Lehtinen, E. (2000). Information and communication technology in education: Desires, promises, and obstacles. In D. Watson & T. Downes (Eds.), *Communications and networking in education: Learning in a networked society* (pp. 311–328). London: Kluwer.

Lehtinen, E., Vauras, M., Salonen, P., Olkinuora, E., & Kinnunen, R. (1995). Long-term development of learning activity: Motivational, cognitive and social interaction. *Educational Psychologist, 30*(1), 21–35.

Liao, Y. (1998). Effects of hypermedia versus traditional instruction on students' achievements: A meta-analysis. *Journal of Research on Computing in Education, 30*(4), 341–360.

Mayer, R. (1997). Multimedia learning: Are we asking the right questions? *Educational Psychologist, 32*(1), 1–19.

Mikkilä, M., & Olkinuora, E. (1994). Problems of current textbooks and workbooks: Do they promote high-quality learning? In M. De Jong & B. Van Hout-Wolters (Eds.), *Process-oriented instruction and learning from text* (pp. 151–164). Amsterdam: VU University Press.

Nurmi, S., & Jaakkola, T. (2002). Teknologiset oppimisympäristöt ja oppiminen [Technology-supported learning environments and learning]. In E. Lehtinen & T. Hiltunen (Eds.), *Opettajuus ja oppiminen* (pp. 114–129). Turku, Finland: Painosalama.

Olkinuora, E., Mikkilä-Erdmann, M., Nurmi, S., & Ottosson, M. (2001). *Multimediaoppimateriaalin tutkimuspohjaista arviointia ja suunnittelun suuntaviivoja* [Research-based assessment of multimedia learning material and main lines of planning] (Finnish Educational Research Association, Research in Educational Sciences 3). Turku, Finland: Painosalama.

Olkinuora, E., & Salonen, P. (1992). Adaptation, motivational orientation, and cognition in a subnormally performing child: A systemic perspective for training. In B. Y. L. Wong (Ed.), *Contemporary intervention research in learning disabilities: An international perspective* (pp. 190–213). New York: Springer.

Reeves, T. (1998). *The impact of media and technology in schools. A research report prepared for The Bertelsmann Foundation* [On-line]. Available: http://www.athensacademy.org/instruct/media_tech/reeves0.html

Rouet, J., & Levonen, J. (1996). Studying and learning with hypertext: Empirical studies and their implications. In J. Rouet, J. Levonen, A. Dillon, & R. Spiro (Eds.), *Hypertext and cognition* (pp. 9–24). Mahwah, NJ: Lawrence Erlbaum Associates.

Salonen, P., Lehtinen, E., & Olkinuora, E. (1998). Expectations and beyond: The development of motivation and learning in a classroom context. In J. Brophy (Ed.), *Ad-*

vances in research on teaching: Vol. 7. Expectations in the classroom (pp. 111–150). Greenwich, CT: JAI.

Tergan, S. (1997). Multiple views, contexts, and symbol systems in learning with hypertext/ hypermedia: A critical review of research. *Educational Technology, 37*(4), 5–18.

Vermunt, J. D. (1998). The regulation of constructive learning processes. *British Journal of Educational Psychology, 68*, 149–171.

Vermunt, J. D., & Verloop, N. (1999). Congruence and friction between learning and teaching. *Learning and Instruction, 9*, 257–280.

Vygotsky, L. (1978). *Mind in society.* Cambridge, MA: Harvard University Press.

Chapter 16

Case-Based Learning and Problem Solving in an Adaptive Web-Based Learning System

Gerhard Weber
University of Education Freiburg, Germany

Learning via the Internet is one of the fastest growing areas in the World Wide Web. Not only universities are using the Internet for delivering complete courses or providing materials for classes, but also companies more and more are using the Internet for online training courses in further education. Catchwords like "learning on the job" and "learning on demand" show the demand for learning and training that is offered around the clock and can be accessed from home or from anyplace in the world. However, most existing Web-based learning systems only provide static hypertext pages that offer not much more than printed texts or slides of presentations. In many cases, streaming videos, animated pictures, and interactive animations enhance Internet-based learning with features that cannot be found in traditional printed texts. But most of these learning systems are far away from the capabilities that on-site learning programs can offer to support the learning process. Especially in the case of the acquisition of problem-solving skills, intelligent tutoring systems (ITS) have shown advantages over simple textbooks and even over learning in traditional classes (Anderson, Corbett, Koedinger, & Pelletier, 1995).

There is one fundamental problem with online learning systems. The assistance that a colleague or a teacher typically provides in a normal classroom situation is not available. Therefore, some kind of adaptation of the learning system to the single learner may be helpful to improve the learning process. Adaptive learning systems are especially useful in acquiring knowledge and skills in a new domain. The first steps of learning especially can be supported successfully with an intelligent tutoring system.

The question remains whether it is possible to deliver functionality similar to on-site intelligent tutoring systems via the Internet. Or, is the Internet generally limited to different types of presentation and not as suitable for direct interaction? In this chapter, we want to show that an intelligent tutoring system that supports case-based learning and problem solving can be delivered as an online learning system on the Internet. As mentioned before, some kind of adaptivity is needed to effectively support learning with a computer program. In the following, we describe different types of adaptation that can be found in on-site and online learning systems. Then we will show how ELM-ART, an intelligent tutoring system for learning programming with the programming language LISP, uses some of these adaptation mechanisms for improving the learning process.

ADAPTATION IN COMPUTER-BASED LEARNING SYSTEMS

Existing learning systems (on-site intelligent tutoring systems and adaptive hypermedia systems as well as online learning systems) use different types of adaptation techniques (Brusilovsky, 1996). These include curriculum sequencing, adaptive presentation and adaptive navigation support, intelligent analysis of students' solutions, interactive problem-solving support, and example-based problem-solving support.

The goal of *curriculum sequencing* (also referred to as instructional planning technology) is to provide the student with the most suitable, individually planned sequence of knowledge units to learn and sequence of learning tasks (examples, questions, problems, etc.) to work with. Curriculum sequencing helps the student to find an "optimal path" through the learning material. A classic example from the domain of teaching programming is the BIP system (Barr, Beard, & Atkinson, 1976). More recent examples include ITEM-IP (Brusilovsky, 1992) and SCENT-3 (Brecht, McCalla, & Greer, 1989). Two kinds of curriculum sequencing techniques can be distinguished. High-level sequencing, or knowledge sequencing, determines the next concepts or topics to be taught. Low-level sequencing, or task sequencing, determines the next learning task (problem, example, test) within the current topic (Brusilovsky, 1992). In the context of Web-based education, curriculum sequencing technology becomes very important to guide the student through the hyperspace of available information. Curriculum sequencing was implemented in different forms in some adaptive educational systems, for example, ELM-ART (Weber & Specht, 1997), CALAT (Nakabayashi et al., 1997), InterBook (Brusilovsky & Schwarz, 1997), AST (Specht, Weber, Heitmeyer, & Schöch, 1997), MANIC (Stern, Woolf, & Kuroso, 1997), and DCG (Vassileva, 1997).

The goal of *adaptive presentation* is to adapt the content of a hypermedia page to the user's goals, knowledge, and other information stored in the user model. In a system with adaptive presentation, the pages are not static but adaptively generated or assembled from different pieces for each user. For example, with several adaptive presentation techniques, expert users may receive more detailed and deep information, while novices receive additional explanations. Adaptive presentation is very important in the Web context where the same "page" has to suit very different students. Only two Web-based learning systems implement full-fledged adaptive presentation: C-Book (Kay & Kummerfeld, 1994) and De Bra's adaptive course on hypertext (Calvi & De Bra, 1998). Both these systems apply the conditional text technique. A special form of adaptive presentation—adaptive insertable warnings about the learning state of the page—is used in ELM-ART (Weber & Specht, 1997), AST (Specht et al., 1997), and InterBook (Brusilovsky & Schwarz, 1997).

The goal of *adaptive navigation support* is to support the student in hyperspace orientation and navigation by changing the appearance of visible links. In particular, the system can adaptively sort, annotate, or partly hide the links of the current page to simplify the choice of the next link. Adaptive navigation support can be considered as an extension of curriculum sequencing technology into a hypermedia context. It shares the same goal: to help students to find an "optimal path" through the learning material. At the same time, adaptive navigation support is less direct than traditional sequencing: It guides students implicitly and leaves them with the choice of the next knowledge item to be learned and the next problem to be solved. In an Internet-based context where hypermedia is a basic organizational paradigm, adaptive navigation support can be used very naturally and efficiently. The most popular form of adaptive navigation support on the Web is annotation. It is implemented in ELM-ART (Weber & Specht, 1997), InterBook (Brusilovsky & Schwarz, 1997), WEST-KBNS (Brusilovsky, Eklund, & Schwarz, 1997), and AST (Specht et al., 1997). InterBook also applies adaptive navigation support by sorting. Hiding is used in De Bra's adaptive course on hypertext (Calvi & De Bra, 1998).

Intelligent analysis of student solutions deals with students' final answers to educational problems (which can range from a simple question to a complex programming problem) no matter how these answers were obtained. Unlike nonintelligent checkers that can tell no more than whether the solution is correct, intelligent analyzers can tell exactly what is wrong or incomplete and which missing or incorrect piece of knowledge may be responsible for the error. Intelligent analyzers can provide the student with extensive error feedback and update the student model. A classic example from the domain of teaching programming is PROUST (Johnson, 1986); more recent examples are CAMUS-II (Vanneste, 1994) and ELM-PE

(Weber & Möllenberg, 1995). The intelligent analysis of problem solutions is a very suitable technology in the context of slow networks. It needs only one interaction between browser and server for a complete solution. It can provide intelligent feedback and perform student modeling when more interactive techniques would be less useful. Currently, there are at least two adaptive learning systems on the Web that implement some type of intelligent analysis of student solutions: ELM-ART, an ITS for programming in LISP (Weber & Specht, 1997), and WITS, an ITS for differential calculations (Okazaki, Watanabe, & Kondo, 1997).

The goal of *interactive problem-solving support* is to provide the student with intelligent help on each step of problem solving—from giving a hint to executing the next step for the student. The systems that implement this technology can watch the actions of the student, understand them, and use this understanding to provide help and to update the student model. A classic example from the domain of teaching programming is the LISP-TUTOR (Anderson & Reiser, 1985). Interactive problem-solving support is not as popular in Web-based systems as in on-site systems because, up to now, server-based Web applications are not "interactive" enough to support watching the student actions and providing help on each step. Each interaction between browser and server may take a visible amount of time and the requirement to perform it on each step may ruin the problem-solving process. The situation will probably change when the Java technology becomes more mature. However, three systems demonstrate that interactive problem-solving support technology can work on the Web: PAT-Online (Ritter, 1997) uses a server-based approach and lets the student submit several problem-solving steps that are checked in one transaction (i.e., it is a combination of interactive problem-solving support and intelligent analysis of student solutions); Belvedere (Suthers & Jones, 1997) and ADIS (Warendorf & Tan, 1997) use the Java technology to support real interactivity.

In an *example-based problem solving* context, students solve new problems by taking advantage of examples from their earlier experience. In this context, an ITS helps students by suggesting the most relevant cases (examples explained to them or problems solved by them earlier). An example from the domain of teaching programming is ELM-PE (Weber, 1996b). Example-based problem solving does not require extensive client–server interaction and, therefore, can be used easily in adaptive learning systems on the Web. The only system that uses this technology online is ELM-ART (Weber & Specht, 1997).

All these adaptation techniques require at least a rudimentary type of user modeling. Whereas presentation adaptation and simple types of curriculum sequencing can be based on (typically rough) stereotype user models, adaptive navigation support and dynamic types of curriculum sequencing require at least overlay user models. The most sophisticated adaptation techniques (intelligent analysis of student solutions, interactive problem-solving support, and example-based problem solving) require more advanced artificial intelligence techniques than typically are used in intelligent tutoring systems (e.g., rule-based or case-based reasoning). In the future, adaptive collaboration support, specially designed for the context of Web-based education, may complete this collection of adaptation techniques.

USER MODELING AND ADAPTATION IN ELM-ART

The introductory LISP course ELM-ART (ELM Adaptive Remote Tutor) is an example of a substantial adaptive Web learning system that uses different types of adaptivity. It consists of an electronic textbook enhanced with significant interactive features (e.g., tests and quizzes, interactive programming support and program evaluation, and interaction with tutors or other learners via a chat room). This section explains how adaptivity works in ELM-ART and describes the different types of knowledge representation and the underlying student modeling.

ELM-ART distinguishes two different types of knowledge representation. On the one hand, the electronic textbook with all the lessons, sections, and units is based mainly on domain knowledge and deals with acquiring this knowledge. On the other hand, the episodic learner model, ELM, deals with the procedural knowledge necessary to solve programming problems.

The Multilayered Overlay Model

The declarative domain model is represented in terms of a conceptual network that consists of units to be learned from the electronic textbook. The units are organized hierarchically into lessons, sections, subsections, and terminal (unit) pages. Terminal pages can introduce new concepts, present lists of test items to be worked at, or offer problems to be solved. Each unit is an object containing slots for the text unit to be presented with the corresponding page and for information that can be used to relate units and concepts to each other. Slots store information on prerequisite concepts, related concepts, and outcomes of the unit (the concepts that the system assumes to be known if the user worked through that unit successfully). Additionally, each unit can have a list of test items or a programming problem to be solved by the learner.

The user model related to this declarative conceptual domain knowledge is represented as a multilayered overlay model. The first layer describes whether the user has already visited a page corresponding to a concept. This information is updated whenever the learner enters a page. The second layer contains information on which exercises or test items related to this particular concept the user has worked at and whether he or she successfully worked at the test items up to a criterion or solved the programming problem. The third layer describes whether a concept could be inferred as known via inference links from more advanced concepts the user already worked at successfully. Whenever a unit has been recognized as learned, this information will be updated in all inferred units (via inference links). This is a recursive process that stops whenever a unit already has been marked as learned or inferred. Finally, the fourth layer describes whether a user has marked a concept as already known. Information in the different layers is updated independently. So, information from each different source does not override others.

The multilayered overlay model supports both the adaptive annotation of links and individual curriculum sequencing. Links that are shown in an overview on each page or in the table of contents are visually annotated according to five learning states of the corresponding concepts:

1. A concept is annotated as "already learned" if enough exercises or test items belonging to that concept or the programming problem have been solved successfully.
2. The concept is annotated as "inferred" where the concept is not "already learned" and it was inferred as learned from other concepts (third layer).
3. The concept is annotated as "stated as known by the user" in case the user marked this concept as already known and there is no information that the concept is "already learned" or "inferred."
4. A concept is annotated as "ready and suggested to be visited" where it is not assigned to one of the first three learning states and all prerequisites to this concept are assigned to one of the first three learning states.
5. A concept is annotated as "not ready to be visited" if none of the other four learning states hold.

Link annotation is used as a hint only. That is, a learner can visit each page even if it is not recommended to be visited. Figure 16.1 shows an example of link annotation in ELM-ART.

In ELM-ART, individual curriculum sequencing means that the system's suggestion of the next page to visit is computed dynamically according to the general learning goal and the learning state of the concepts as previously described. The next suggested concept to be learned is the one that is not assigned to one of the first three learning states and that is the next one

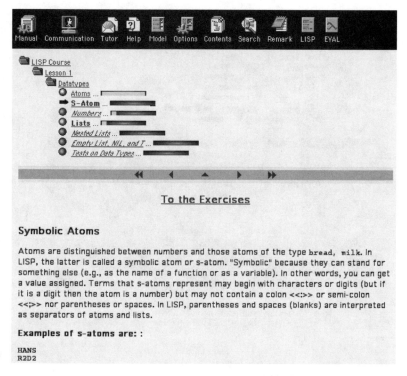

FIG. 16.1. Annotation in ELM-ART.

ready to be learned. Figure 16.2 shows an example of how ELM-ART guides the learner to the next best concept to be learned.

As mentioned before, the multilayered overlay model gets the most confident information from the results of users' attempts to solve test items. In ELM-ART, three principally different types of test items are supported: forced-choice, multiple-choice, and free-form. In forced-choice test items, users have to answer a question by selecting one of the alternative answers (see Fig. 16.3 for example); in multiple-choice test items, users have to answer a question by selecting all correct answers provided by the system; and in free-form test items, users can freely type an answer to the question asked.

In the LISP course, tests play a twofold role. On the one hand, tests are used to check whether the user possesses the correct declarative knowledge. This is especially useful in the beginning of the course when a lot of new concepts (data types and function definitions) are introduced. On the other hand, tests can be used in evaluation tasks to check whether users are able to evaluate LISP expressions correctly. Skills used in evaluation are the inverse of the skills used to generate function calls and function definitions.

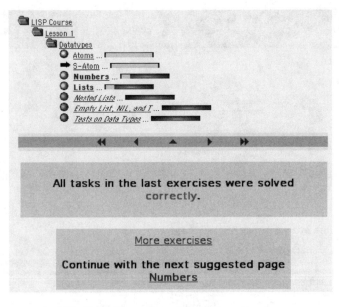

FIG. 16.2.   Suggestion of a next learning step.

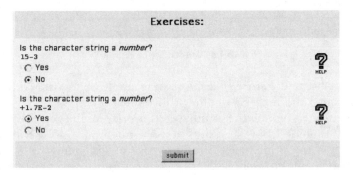

FIG. 16.3.   Forced-choice test.

Evaluation skills are needed to decide whether programs work correctly and to find errors in programming code. Program creation skills are practiced in special tasks. They are supported by the episodic learner model approach described in the next section.

The Case-Based Learning Model

Whereas learning of the declarative domain knowledge (i.e., programming concepts) is supported by the multilayered overlay model, procedural learning (i.e., learning of programming and general problem-solving skills) is supported by a case-based learning approach. In ELM-ART, case-based learning is realized by an episodic user model. This episodic learner model is built up by the system while observing the user's progress in solving programming problems. That is, the model learns by observing the learner similarly to a human tutor. In the following, a short description of how an episodic user model works is given. A more detailed description of the episodic learner model approach can be found in Weber (1996a).

The representation of the domain knowledge used in episodic modeling consists of a heterarchy of concepts and rules (Weber, 1996a). Concepts comprise knowledge about the programming language LISP (concrete LISP procedures as well as superordinate semantic concepts) and schemas of common algorithmic and problem-solving knowledge (e.g., recursion schemata). The concept frames contain information about rules describing different ways to solve the goal stated by this concept. Additionally, there are bug rules describing errors observed by other students or buggy derivations of LISP concepts, which, for example, may result from confusion between semantically similar concepts.

The individual learner model consists of a collection of episodes that are descriptions of how problems have been solved by a particular student. These descriptions are explanation structures (in the sense of explanation-based generalization; Mitchell, Keller, & Kedar-Cabelli, 1986) of how a programming task has been solved by the student. That is, stored episodes contain all the information about which concepts and rules were needed to produce the program code the students offered as solutions to programming tasks. Episodes are not stored as a whole. They are distributed into snippets (Kolodner, 1993), with each snippet describing a concept and a rule that was used to solve a plan or subplan of the programming task. These snippets are stored as episodic instances with respect to the concepts of the domain knowledge. In this way, the individual episodic learner model is interrelated with the common domain knowledge.

The episodic learner model plays the role of an expert who tries to explain how a solution to a programming task may have been produced by a programmer. During diagnosis of program code, information from the individual episodic learner model is used to shorten the diagnostic process and to adapt to the user. The episodic learner model is updated with information from the diagnostic process. To construct the learner model, the code produced by a learner is analyzed in terms of the domain knowledge on the one hand and a task description on the other. This cognitive diagnosis results in a derivation tree of concepts and rules the learner might have used to solve the problem. These concepts and rules are instantiations of units from the knowledge base. The episodic learner model is made up of these instantiations. In ELM, only examples from the course materials are preanalyzed, and the resulting explanation structures are stored in the individual case-based learner model. Elements from the explanation structures

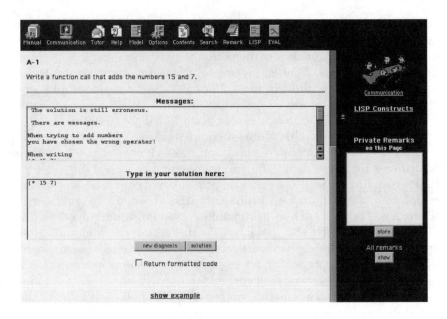

FIG. 16.4.   Problem-solving feedback.

are stored with respect to their corresponding concepts from the domain knowledge base, so cases are distributed in terms of instances of concepts.

These individual cases—or parts of them—are used in ELM-ART for two different adaptation purposes. First, episodic instances can be used during further analyses as shortcuts if the actual code and plan match corresponding patterns in episodic instances. The ELM model and the diagnosis of program code is described in more detail in Weber (1996a). Figure 16.4 shows an example of a feedback message from the diagnosis of a wrong user solution to a simple coding problem.

Second, an advantage of episodic modeling is its potential to predict code the programmers will produce as solutions to new programming tasks. These predictions can be used to search for examples and remindings that are useful for solving the new task. This analogue component is described in Weber (1996b). Figure 16.5 shows an example of how in ELM-ART a reminding to a previous solution is presented in the example window.

EVALUATION OF LEARNING WITH ELM-ART

ELM-ART directly stems from the on-site learning environment ELM-PE (Weber & Möllenberg, 1995). So, comparing results of learning with ELM-ART to results from learning with ELM-PE will give an idea of how well one can learn with a Web-based learning system. In ELM-PE, students used the

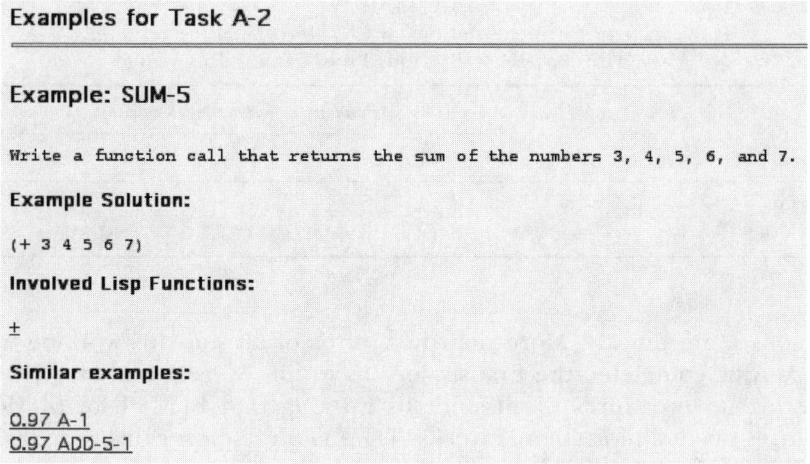

Examples for Task A-2

Example: SUM-5

Write a function call that returns the sum of the numbers 3, 4, 5, 6, and 7.

Example Solution:

(+ 3 4 5 6 7)

Involved Lisp Functions:

±

Similar examples:

0.97 A-1
0.97 ADD-5-1

FIG. 16.5.   Presentation of a programming example.

system to solve programming tasks in parallel to the traditional classroom course. ELM-PE offered automatic diagnosis of problem solutions and the individual presentation of example solutions based on the episodic learner model. In ELM-ART, presentation of the texts and all explanations were given by the system in addition to all adaptive features previously mentioned. Crucial to a learning situation is how successful and how fast learners complete the course. Results from the final programming tasks (three tasks on recursive programming) show that students learning with ELM-ART were more often successful in solving the third, most difficult, programming problem (see Table 16.1).

It is interesting that this effect not only holds for learners with previous programming knowledge but also for the very beginners (Table 16.2). This may be interpreted as a hint that adaptive techniques in combination with interactive feedback and knowledge-based problem-solving support may result in a more successful learning situation.

There is one more finding that supports the success of ELM-ART. Students participating in our introductory LISP course completed the first six

TABLE 16.1
Percentage of Correct Solutions of the Three Final Programming
Problems After Lesson 6 in ELM-PE and ELM-ART

Courses	Problem 1 (A-List-Test)	Problem 2 (Count-Item)	Problem 3 (List-up-to-Atom)
ELM-PE ($N = 28$)	100%	93%	54%
ELM-ART ($N = 23$)	96%	96%	87%

TABLE 16.2
Percentage of Correct Solutions of the Third Final Programming
Task With Respect to Previous Programming Knowledge

	Previous Programming Knowledge	
Courses	With	Without
ELM-PE	64.4% (n = 14)	42.9% (n = 14)
ELM-ART	91.7% (n = 12)	81.8% (n = 11)

lessons more quickly. More than two thirds of all students working with ELM-ART completed the first six lessons within 6 weeks or less, whereas more than two thirds of all students working with ELM-PE in previous courses needed more than 7 weeks. The main reason for this remarkable difference is the availability of computers. The on-site learning environment ELM-PE was available only on specially equipped computers in the department. These computers were reserved 2 hours a week for each student. Conversely, ELM-ART could be accessed from most computers in the university (and even from home). We observed students starting work in the morning before classes started, continuing during the lunch hour, and proceeding in the evening. Therefore, a lot of students finished the course within a very short period of time. This may be one reason for the very good results in the final programming tasks. Students were able to concentrate on learning LISP much more than with the more occasional learning and practice sessions required by ELM-PE.

CONCLUSION

ELM-ART is an example of how an ITS can be implemented on the Web. It integrates the features of electronic textbooks, learning environments, and intelligent tutoring systems. User modeling techniques like overlay models or more elaborated episodic learner models are well suited for adaptive guidance and individualized help and problem-solving support in Web-based learning systems.

The main result of the evaluation studies already done with ELM-ART and reported in this chapter is the finding that Web-based educational systems can be as effective as traditional elaborated ITSs. The main reason is that a Web-based educational system can be highly interactive, adaptive, and adaptable, at least with a fully programmable Web server like ELM-ART (based on CL-HTTP). These features are based on two user modeling techniques (overlay models and episodic learner models) that represent declarative domain knowledge and procedural reasoning knowledge and interact within the course. Perhaps the Web can help ITS to move from laboratories (where most of these "intelligent" systems are used, due to the enormous requirements in computing power and capacity) to classrooms and to permanent availability in distance learning.

In spite of these specific results regarding ELM-ART, the scope and the importance of intelligent tutoring systems in instruction has to be discussed more generally. Often, it is argued that ITSs are not capable of simulating the learning process of a learner and the process of understanding of a human tutor in all its facets. Certainly, these processes can be simulated only approximately, up to now. And the communication between the learner and a computer tutor is very limited, too. However, in a pedagogical, especially instructional, situation, the reasonableness of the modeling process is not as important as the practical effectiveness of such a learning tool. Even with a human tutor, we don't ask whether he or she has a correct model of the student's learning process, we look at the effects of tutoring. Results of assessing the effectiveness of ITSs with respect to the two-sigma problem (Bloom, 1984) show that machine tutors already exist that are at least as effective as human tutors in one-to-one human tutoring (Corbett, 2001). This is especially true for learning situations in traditional classrooms where teachers cannot support all learners as effectively as in one-to-one tutoring. As most of these results stem from studies with tutoring systems in more formalized domains (e.g., mathematics, sciences, and programming), further development and investigations are necessary to show whether ITSs can be as effective in less formalized domains, too.

ELM-ART is implemented with the programmable Web server CL-HTTP (URL: http://www.ai.mit.edu/projects/iiip/doc/cl-http/home-page. html). Some implementation details can be found in Brusilovsky, Schwarz, and Weber (1996). ELM-ART can be accessed via the following URL: http:// cogpsy.uni-trier.de:8000/TLServ-e.html.

REFERENCES

Anderson, J. R., Corbett, A. T., Koedinger, K. R., & Pelletier, R. (1995). Cognitive tutors: Lessons learned. *Journal of the Learning Sciences, 4*, 167–207.

Anderson, J. R., & Reiser, B. (1985). The LISP tutor. *Byte, 10*, 159–175.

Barr, A., Beard, M., & Atkinson, R. C. (1976). The computer as tutorial laboratory: The Stanford BIP project. *International Journal on Man–Machine Studies, 8*, 567–596.

Bloom, B. S. (1984). The 2 Sigma problem: The search for methods of group instruction as effective as one-to-one tutoring. *Educational Researcher, 13*, 3–15.

Brecht, B. J., McCalla, G. I., & Greer, J. E. (1989). Planning the content of instruction. In D. Bierman, J. Breuker, & J. Sandberg (Eds.), *Proceedings of 4th International Conference on AI and Education* (pp. 32–41). Amsterdam: IOS Press.

Brusilovsky, P. (1992). A framework for intelligent knowledge sequencing and task sequencing. In C. Frasson, G. Gauthier, & G. I. McCalla (Eds.), *Second International Conference on Intelligent Tutoring Systems, IST'92* (pp. 499–506). Berlin: Springer-Verlag.

Brusilovsky, P. (1996). Methods and techniques of adaptive hypermedia. *User Modeling and User-Adapted Interaction, 6*, 87–129.

Brusilovsky, P., Eklund, J., & Schwarz, E. (1997). Adaptive navigation support in educational hypermedia on the World Wide Web. In S. Howard, J. Hammond, & G. Lindgaard (Eds.), *INTERACT97, The 6th IFIP World Conference on Human–Computer Interaction* (pp. 278–285). New York: Chapman & Hall.

Brusilovsky, P., & Schwarz, E. (1997). User as student: Towards an adaptive interface for advanced Web-based applications. In A. Jameson, C. Paris, & C. Tasso (Eds.), *6th International Conference on User Modeling* (pp. 177–188). Vienna: Springer-Verlag.

Brusilovsky, P., Schwarz, E., & Weber, G. (1996). ELM-ART: An intelligent tutoring system on World Wide Web. In C. Frasson, G. Gauthier, & A. Lesgold (Eds.), *Third International Conference on Intelligent Tutoring Systems, ITS-96* (Vol. 1086, pp. 261–269). Berlin: Springer-Verlag.

Calvi, L., & De Bra, P. (1998). A flexible hypertext courseware on the Web based on a dynamic link structure, interacting with computers. *Interdisciplinary Journal of Human–Computer Interaction, 10*, 143–154.

Corbett, A. (2001). Cognitive computer tutors: Solving the two-sigma problem. In M. Bauer, P. J. Gmytrasiewicz, & J. Vassileva (Eds.), *User Modeling 2001: Proceedings of the Eighth International Conference, UM2001* (pp. 137–147). Berlin: Springer-Verlag.

Johnson, W. L. (1986). *Intention-based diagnosis of novice programming errors.* London: Pitman.

Kay, J., & Kummerfeld, R. J. (1994). An individualized course for the C programming language. In *Proceedings of Second International WWW Conference.* Chicago: Elsevier.

Kolodner, J. L. (1993). *Case-based reasoning.* San Mateo, CA: Morgan Kaufmann.

Mitchell, T. M., Keller, R. M., & Kedar-Cabelli, S. T. (1986). Explanation-based generalization: A unifying view. *Machine Learning, 1*, 47–80.

Nakabayashi, K., Maruyama, M., Kato, Y., Touhei, H., & Fukuhara, Y. (1997). Architecture of an intelligent tutoring system on the WWW. In B. d. Boulay & R. Mizoguchi (Eds.), *AI-ED'97, World Conference on Artificial Intelligence in Education* (pp. 39–46). Amsterdam: IOS Press.

Okazaki, Y., Watanabe, K., & Kondo, H. (1997). An implementation of the WWW based ITS for guiding differential calculations. In P. Brusilovsky, K. Nakabayashi, & S. Ritter (Eds.), *Proceedings of Workshop "Intelligent Educational Systems on the World Wide Web" at AI-ED'97, 8th World Conference on Artificial Intelligence in Education* (pp. 18–25). Kobe, Japan.

Ritter, S. (1997). Pat Online: A model-tracing tutor on the World Wide Web. In P. Brusilovsky, K. Nakabayashi, & S. Ritter (Eds.), *Proceedings of Workshop "Intelligent Educational Systems on the World Wide Web" at AI-ED'97, 8th World Conference on Artificial Intelligence in Education* (pp. 11–17). Kobe, Japan.

Specht, M., Weber, G., Heitmeyer, S., & Schöch, V. (1997). AST: Adaptive WWW-courseware for statistics. In P. Brusilovsky, J. Fink, & J. Kay (Eds.), *Proceedings of Workshop "Adaptive Systems and User Modeling on the World Wide Web" at 6th International Conference on User Modeling, UM97* (pp. 91–95). Chia Laguna, Sardinia, Italy: Carnegie Mellon Online.

Stern, M., Woolf, B. P., & Kuroso, J. (1997). Intelligence on the Web? In B. d. Boulay & R. Mizoguchi (Eds.), *AI-ED'97, 8th World Conference on Artificial Intelligence in Education* (pp. 490–497). Amsterdam: IOS Press.

Suthers, D., & Jones, D. (1997). An architecture for intelligent collaborative educational systems. In B. d. Boulay & R. Mizoguchi (Eds.), *AI-ED'97, 8th World Conference on Artificial Intelligence in Education* (pp. 55–62). Amsterdam: IOS Press.

Vanneste, P. (1994). *The use of reverse engineering in novice program analysis.* Unpublished doctoral thesis, Katholieke Universiteit Leuven, Belgium.

Vassileva, J. (1997). Dynamic course generation on the WWW. In B. d. Boulay & R. Mizoguchi (Eds.), *AI-ED'97, 8th World Conference on Artificial Intelligence in Education* (pp. 498–505). Amsterdam: IOS Press.

Warendorf, K., & Tan, C. (1997). ADIS—An animated data structure intelligent tutoring system or Putting an interactive tutor on the WWW. In P. Brusilovsky, K. Nakabayashi, & S. Ritter (Eds.), *Proceedings of Workshop "Intelligent Educational Systems on the World Wide Web" at AI-ED'97, 8th World Conference on Artificial Intelligence in Education* (pp. 54–60). Kobe, Japan.

Weber, G. (1996a). Episodic learner modeling. *Cognitive Science, 20,* 195–236.

Weber, G. (1996b). Individual selection of examples in an intelligent programming environment. *Journal of Artificial Intelligence in Education, 7,* 3–31.

Weber, G., & Möllenberg, A. (1995). ELM programming environment: A tutoring system for LISP beginners. In K. F. Wender, F. Schmalhofer, & H.-D. Böcker (Eds.), *Cognition and computer programming* (pp. 373–408). Norwood, NJ: Ablex.

Weber, G., & Specht, M. (1997). User modeling and adaptive navigation support in WWW-based tutoring systems. In A. Jameson, C. Paris, & C. Tasso (Eds.), *User Modeling: Proceedings of the Sixth International Conference, UM97* (pp. 289–300). New York: Springer.

Author Index

Subject Index

379

C

Case(s), 31, 34, 38, 76, 85, 86, 90–92, 127, 137, 176, 190, 213, 222, 239, 253, 263, 276, 296, 341, 343, 353, 356, 362

Case-based learning, 245, 268, 326, 353–355, 357, 359–361, 363, 365, 367

Case-based reasoning (CBR), 22, 76, 89, 90–96, 99, 100, 101, 103, 107, 112–114, 357, 366

Causal diagram(s), 8, 64, 65

CDT Component Display Theory, 244, 256

Clients, 86, 134, 276, 315

Coaching, 9, 21, 38, 47, 60, 61, 73, 84, 151, 157, 243, 338, 343

Cognitive apprenticeship (CA), 45, 51, 60, 61, 68, 70, 113, 129, 273, 284, 285

Cognitive flexibility, 85, 88, 244, 256, 274, 287

Cognitive flexibility theory, 256, 287

Cognitive psychology, 10, 20, 24, 51, 70, 88, 290, 306

Cognitive science, 44, 45, 47, 64, 71, 95, 107, 112, 114, 169, 269, 287, 367

Collaboration, 35, 40, 41, 90, 93, 97, 104, 107–109, 111, 113, 119, 241, 253, 254, 279, 328, 338, 343–345, 357

Collaborative learning, 62, 114, 250, 251, 254, 256, 340, 348

Collective intelligence, 228, 229, 237

Communication, 3, 6, 8–10, 18, 19, 34, 41, 44, 53, 56, 67, 71, 97, 139, 142, 147, 153, 157, 158, 164, 175, 190, 194, 221, 226, 227, 229, 233–235, 237, 239, 241, 243, 251, 252, 257, 259, 261, 263–265, 268, 269, 271, 273, 279, 284, 311, 318, 321, 328, 351, 365

Communication technologies, 3, 10, 34, 139, 194, 221, 235, 252, 257, 271, 284

Component Display Theory, 244, 256

Computer assisted instruction, 19, 263, 306

Computer simulation, 64, 88, 300, 301, 306

Computer technologies, 143, 269

Computer-Assisted Instructional System(s), 292, 293
  adaptive, 292, 293

Computer-based instruction, 46, 255, 305–307

Concept, 18, 22, 30, 31, 40, 48, 50, 85, 99, 100, 109, 152, 191, 197, 219–222,
265, 290, 294, 299, 306, 307, 310, 338, 358, 359, 361

Constraints (administrative), 8, 41, 100, 107, 135, 136, 138, 162, 173, 223, 224, 262, 265, 276

Constructivism, 9, 10, 14, 87, 256, 285, 287, 328

Constructivist(s), 10, 13, 14, 19, 21, 22, 71, 75–78, 82–88, 249, 256, 258, 261, 328, 351

Context(s), 1, 44, 47, 52, 57, 60, 72, 75, 79, 80, 86, 106, 113, 166, 195, 222, 241, 254, 261, 262, 265, 272, 273, 275, 290, 341, 350, 352

Conversation, 15, 30, 32, 62, 175

Cooperation, 151, 208, 209, 229, 235, 245, 264

Course design, 169, 311

Course evaluation, 316, 332

Courses, 149, 211, 247, 267, 309, 311–323, 326, 329, 353, 363, 364

Culture, 2, 3, 47, 48, 116, 129, 146, 148, 151, 152, 168, 220, 223, 228, 231, 235, 285

Curricular goal(s), 141, 193, 194, 196, 199, 205

Curriculum design, 138, 139, 140, 145, 148, 149, 151, 192

Curriculum development, 1, 2, 11, 13, 47, 131, 132, 133, 134, 135, 136, 137, 138, 139, 140, 142, 143, 169, 193, 257, 258

Curriculum evaluation, 141, 211, 214, 215, 217, 218, 224

Curriculum goals/objectives, 202, 204

Curriculum problem, 139, 141, 145, 148, 193, 195

Curriculum research, 132, 140, 142

Curriculum work, 141, 211, 213–215, 217, 218, 220–225

D

Data, 23, 27, 32–34, 38, 39, 42, 44, 52, 57, 63, 64, 67, 94, 98, 102, 106, 107, 109–112, 128, 135, 141, 148, 166, 168, 172–180, 182, 184, 185, 198, 205, 236, 237, 254, 267, 277, 279, 282, 283, 315–321, 359, 367